CONTESTED ANTIQUITY

NEW ANTHROPOLOGIES OF EUROPE

Michael Herzfeld, Melissa L. Caldwell, and Deborah Reed-Danahay, *editors*

CONTESTED ANTIQUITY

Archaeological Heritage and Social Conflict in Modern Greece and Cyprus

Edited by Esther Solomon

Indiana University Press

This book is a publication of

Indiana University Press
Office of Scholarly Publishing
Herman B Wells Library 350
1320 East 10th Street
Bloomington, Indiana 47405 USA

iupress.org

 The paper used in this publication meets the minimum requirements of the American National Standard for Information Sciences—Permanence of Paper for Printed Library Materials, ANSI Z39.48-1992.

Manufactured in the United States of America

Cataloging information is available from the Library of Congress.

ISBN 978-0-253-05596-5 (cl)
ISBN 978-0-253-05597-2 (pb)
ISBN 978-0-253-05598-9 (ebook)

1 2 3 4 5 26 25 24 23 22 21

tu m'abysses
tu m'oasis
[. . .]

Matsi Hatzilazarou
"Dédicace à rebours"
("Dedication in Reverse")
1985

To my husband, Yannis Kaloyannis

Contents

Acknowledgments

This book is based on several years of research on and interest in issues of contested archaeological heritage and the significance of material culture in people's lives. Along the way, I have benefited from conversations with many heritage scholars, archaeologists, museologists, and social anthropologists, both in Greece and the UK. Among them, I want to single out my dearest colleagues Styliana Galiniki, Areti Adamopoulou, Eleana Yalouri, Rea Kakampoura, and the late anthropologist Sotiris Dimitriou, whose mentoring was an endless source of inspiration.

I owe a very great debt to Professor Michael Herzfeld for his trust and invaluable support, both at the beginning and the end of this journey; without him, this book would not have been possible.

Professor Christopher Tilley, who in the 2000s supervised my PhD dissertation on the social significance of Minoan archaeological heritage on the island of Crete, read an earlier draft of this book. I am deeply grateful for his comments, love, and advice.

I would also like to extend my thanks to the Department of Fine Arts and Art Sciences of the University of Ioannina for providing me with some of the necessary time to complete my research; to Kathleen Hart, Robert Chatel, and Matina Dedikousi for their help in several stages of my work; to the photographer Dimitris Giovis for his evocative cover photo; and to Indiana University Press for honoring me by publishing this book.

Many ideas analyzed in this volume form the core of interests of a new collectivity in Greece, called *Dialogues in Archaeology*. Since 2015, the members of this active group have organized an annual, broadly interdisciplinary conference on issues related to the role of antiquities and archaeological practice in society. Our first gathering in 2015 was a surprise when hundreds of archaeologists, heritage practitioners, academics, students, artists, art historians, museologists, architects, and many others creatively debated their views on theoretical and practical aspects of the subject. Some of the contributions to this volume were first presented in the session "Archaeology and Memory Wars" that I chaired in those first Dialogues—a topic that triggered a great deal of interest and valuable feedback. To all the participants, those on the panel, the audience, and the organizing committee go many thanks—also because they revealed a different, self-critical, and socially engaged view of archaeological practices in Greece and Cyprus.

My warmest thanks go to the contributors to this book. With them, I share not only similar interests in Greek heritage discourses but also common project work and bonds of friendship. I wish to thank them all for their cooperation, their trust, and the patience they have shown in having to tolerate me for years. Among them, Katerina Konstantinou, an MA student whom I supervised at the University of Ioannina, is the youngest (and bravest); I wish her good luck in the next steps of her career.

Tolerance and patience are also the virtues of my family, especially Ellie and Makis Solomon; Efi and Victor Batis; Victor, Eva and Anna Solomon; my husband, Yannis Kaloyannis; and, last but not least Ellie Kaloyannis, my daughter. For their endless love and support, I am deeply grateful.

CONTESTED ANTIQUITY

Introduction

Contested Antiquity in Greece and Cyprus

Esther Solomon

THIS BOOK WAS prepared between 2015 and 2018. The writing of its introduction coincided with everyday images and news stories about thousands of Syrian and other refugees drowned in the Aegean Sea during their attempts to escape war and danger and reach Lesvos and other Greek islands. Orange lifejackets and thermal blankets abandoned on beaches soon became material symbols of an immense human tragedy and indifference to human life that my (deeply questioned) identity as a European citizen has found hard to accept.

Greece's response to this unprecedented phenomenon has been intense and mixed. Despite the recent rise of Far Right rhetoric and the widespread hardship associated with the debt and Eurozone crisis that have buffeted the country since 2010, people of different ages and class backgrounds have rushed to join NGOs committed to providing relief for refugees. Acts of altruism have marked everyday social life, especially in reception areas, as have xenophobic narratives and exploitation of desperate newcomers, partly understood within the same political-economic context of austerity and its depredations.

During this same period, the murder of the Syrian archaeologist Khaled al-Asaad while trying to protect the World Heritage Site of Palmyra sparked international outcry.

The footage of the destruction of the site's monuments by IS militants was ceaselessly reproduced on the web, the news, and social media. It was condemned as a crime against humanity and was used by some as an anti-Muslim argument.[1] Yet it was loosely, if at all, associated with the myriad deaths occurring every day along the sea borders of the EU.

Then, an incident went rather unnoticed. In Za'atari, a refugee camp in Jordan, Syrian artists used kebab skewers, clay, and discarded materials to "reconstruct" in miniature Palmyra and other heritage sites of their homeland. "This is a way for them [i.e., the Za'atari residents] not to forget. As artists, we have an important role to play," Mahmoud Hariri, a former art teacher and resident of the camp, told the United Nations Refugee Agency.[2] This was an act of resistance, perhaps of secondary importance when compared to his living conditions, yet one that reminds us of James Scott's "weapons of the weak" (1985), weapons that trigger reflection on heritage values in times of conflict and the role of material culture of the past in people's hopes for a better future.

In the months that followed, apart from solidarity, compassion, and material aid, collectivities in Greece have also advocated making cultural bonds with the asylum seekers, many thousands of whom remained entrapped in hotspots around the country or forcefully shipped back to Turkey as part of a deal between Greece and the EU. References to the immense flow of Greek refugees from Turkey, known as "the Asia Minor Catastrophe," who arrived in Greece in the 1920s, most of them at the same island ports, became frequent: a peculiar memory work was here at stake. The Archaeological Museum of Thessaloniki, a city also known as the "mother of refugees" due to the great number of expelled Greeks it received after the Greek-Turkish War in 1922–23, put on an exhibition of the classical sculptures brought to Thessaloniki by the refugees of Rhaedestus, in modern Turkey.[3] The museum curators inevitably connected their exhibition to current Syrian flows, thus causing an extensive and emotional debate on the materiality of refugees' memory within the current discursive framework on heritage, affect, and emotions (Smith and Campbell 2015; Tolia-Kelly, Waterton, and Watson 2017). Moreover, artists, cultural organizations, schools, and museums got actively involved in this new memory discourse, which called for political activism and humanitarianism.[4] The story of the Syrian refugees became a trendy and at the same time politically charged issue bound up with recent Greek traumatic history and, more important, with reflection on the management of cultural difference in multicultural but increasingly intolerant European societies.

The stories around the Greek and Syrian antiquities, the refugees' pain, and their spatial trajectories make us think that heritage is related not only to cultural memory and social identity (local, national, gender, religious, ethnic or other), as many scholars have shown in the last decades (Fairclough et al. 2008; Graham and Howard 2008; Harvey 2008; Smith, Messenger, and Soderland 2010; Benton and Cecil 2010; Harrison 2010, 2013; Macdonald 2013; Waterton and Watson 2015a; Logan, Nic Craith, and Kockel 2015) but also inevitably to conflict. Heritage is ultimately at the heart of this matter: it causes opposition, ambiguity, contestation, memory wars, or even physical destruction, whereas at the same time, it may serve as a platform for resistance, healing, reconciliation, and peacebuilding. In the turbulent social, political, and financial conditions people often experience, the material remains of the past do become a "dissonant" (Tunbridge and Ashworth 1996), "difficult" (Macdonald 2009; Logan and Reeves 2009b), "dark" (Roberts and Stone 2014), and variously contested heritage that deserves our attention and critical analysis.

The active use of the past in the present is what transforms objects and material remains into practiced heritage—heritage that, in one way or another, is implicated in cultural processes of everyday life (Smith 2006, 44; Harvey 2008; Waterton and Watson 2015b, 2) and becomes meaningful for different social groups despite (or rather, because of) its oppositional meanings, values, interpretations, and deployment.

Contested Antiquity tries to make sense of such practiced archaeological heritage in Greece and, to a lesser extent, in Cyprus. Contributors to the volume seek to problematize oppositional and conflicting views and uses of archaeological sites, monuments, landscapes, objects, and practices. They deal with concepts of emplaced memory and contested identity by focusing on those uses of Greek antiquities, long invoked in the name of Western values, that are not identified with the official constructions of the Greek past.

My intention through editing this volume was to focus on not only ideological conflicts derived by or within hegemonic politics of the past but also bottom-up negotiations of dominant narratives regarding the meaning and the management of Greek antiquity. Thus, the book deals with various forms of contestation of significant ancient material culture and, through them, social practices and relations that describe social reality in the two countries from the late nineteenth century to nowadays.

Contributions lie at the cross point of intellectual history, archaeology, anthropology, cultural geography, museum and cultural studies. They bring together under one roof scholars with different methodological approaches. Yet all of them are interested in the "social life" of antiquities, to use Appadurai's well-known term (1986), as well as in a critical history of archaeological practice in Greece and Cyprus, where they were born, raised, and (for most of them) trained and work as archaeologists, museologists, or anthropologists. As people collaborating with one another on various occasions—friends and colleagues in museums and academia—they have shaped a new approach to Greek archaeological heritage analysis informed by recent advances in social theory. And most important, through their work on the Greek ancient past and its remains, they make meaningful and thought-provoking statements in and about its present.

Archaeology and the Heritage Debate

Among the different categories of heritage, archaeological monuments and objects constitute a significant group due to the emphasis given to materiality and their different, remote temporalities, which impact on the present. Archaeology concretizes heritage and place: it makes them both visible, sensed, memorable, and widely accessible.

Within the prevailing Western tradition of memory as recollection (largely based on Aristotelian thought) and the linear conception of time, archaeological monuments have been analogically associated with memory, constituting its durable "solid metaphors" (Tilley 1999) that can be "made and unmade" (Küchler 1999; Yalouri 2010; cf. Nelson and Olin 2003; Young 1993).[5] Their destruction in modernity is often considered as tantamount to oblivion and identity loss, whereas heritage conservation is seen as enhancing people's generalized need to secure their vanishing relationship with the past.

As a by-product of Enlightenment thinking, archaeology has constituted a distinct set of principles regarding the acquisition of knowledge about the distant past (Trigger 1989, 55–61; Jenkins 2003). Since the nineteenth century, served by national educational systems and powerful memory institutions such as national museums, archaeology has been an important agent in the thread that united modernity with nation-building, colonialism, and territorial establishment (Meskell 1998; Boswell and Evans 1999; Sloan 2003; Dyson 2006). Often implicated in the uneasy relationship between different communities as well as between communities and authorities, scholars and the public (all of whom make use of emblematic ancient objects, landscapes, and sites, whether "musealized" or not), archaeology has also connected or alienated the national and the local as well as the local and the global (Hodder 1998, Appadurai 2008; cf. Harvey 2015), and it has significantly contributed to the production of the changing faces of places and localities.

In the last decades of the twentieth century, the postcolonial paradigm and the development of postprocessual theory have led to a growing scholarly interest in the social, political, and ideological implications of archaeology (Shanks and Tilley 1992; Shanks 2008; Abu Khafajah and Badran 2015), and the heritage of the neglected groups, especially that of minorities and indigenous people. Archaeological theory has been employed in current research on people's "multiple pasts" and the "pre-modern" material culture of First Nations in America, Aboriginals in Australia, and other indigenous groups (Smith 2004),[6] who are often identified with more than one place and form their plural identities according to evolving motives.

Behind such pursuits for a democratization of heritage research, one can feel the engagement of archaeologists, museum professionals, and anthropologists with the disenfranchised, their tendency to empower communities through social programs, and their will to enable the educational potential of heritage. Within a framework of globalized action and communication, archaeological practice is also presently perceived and promoted as a kind of activism, a commitment to fight against social injustice while assuming ethical responsibilities toward the public (Crooke 2008; Sandell 2002; Breglia 2006; Herzfeld 2012; and Stefanou and Antoniadou, this volume).[7]

Archaeologists' interest in local knowledge is also the result of the encounter between archaeology and anthropology fostered in the last decades and the development of material culture studies as a hospitable interdisciplinary field

(Tilley 2001; Tilley et al. 2006; Shankland 2012) that accommodates perspectives and research themes from the different disciplines that inform heritage. Thus, the emphasis put on not only the dynamic role of objects in society but also the sensorial aspects of their materiality and their perceived agency in shaping social relations and human values has brought archaeology closer to the social sciences than ever before.

Part of this disciplinary rapprochement is also the popularity of archaeological ethnography (Shankland 1996, Edgeworth 2006; Castaneda and Matthews 2008; Hamilakis and Anagnostopoulos 2009a), which informs the research of many contributors to this volume (Anagnostopoulos; Konstantinou; Stefanou and Antoniadou). In an influential introduction to a special issue of *Public Archaeology* on the subject, Hamilakis and Anagnostopoulos envisioned archaeological ethnography as a "trans-disciplinary and trans-cultural space that enables researchers and diverse publics to engage in various conversations, exchanges and interventions" in relation to material traces from various times (2009b, 65), whereas Bender, Hamilton, and Tilley (2007) have highlighted the need for an ethnography of both the excavation and the excavators.

As all contributions to this volume reveal, the same idea of practiced heritage discussed earlier serves as a powerful link between archaeology and anthropology. Moving from the material remains of the past to what people feel, think about, and do with these remains in the present is the contact point between the two disciplines, their temporalities and their concerns about social relations then and now.

Heritage Contestation: What, When, Why

Two directions have characterized recent approaches to archaeological heritage. The first, politically and ideologically aware, has focused mainly on top-down analyses, producing representational critiques and emphasizing the role of heritage in the construction of the nation-state, the production of "otherness," and the consolidation of elite power—what Smith has termed "authorized heritage discourse" (2006, 29) or, in Walter Benjamin's words, the construction of history as a "homogeneous and empty time" (Arendt 1968, 261). The overall academic debate has been largely based on the employment of a Foucauldian archaeology of knowledge (in this case, of the archaeological knowledge itself) and the rapprochement between the ends of hitherto binary oppositions: memory and history, nature and culture, people and things, objectivity and subjectivity, individual and social action, private and public domain.

The second approach, coined as "memorial" (Butler 2006, 471), has benefited a great deal from applied social research and bottom-up analyses, and in a way, it has "anthropologized" the heritage debate. It is interested in symbolic, communal, and broadly social meanings of material culture; multiple counternarratives and countermemories; subaltern voices; and all categories of personal and local heritage—what David Harvey has called "small heritages" (2008, 20).

Both approaches are employed by the contributors to this book.

Yet is heritage inevitably related to conflict, dispute, and contestation? As Tunbridge and Ashworth suggest, all forms and manifestations of heritage can create dissonance, as long as they are selected and named as "heritage" (1996; cf. Smith and Waterton 2009, chapter 3). What is (i.e., decided as) someone's heritage is not (i.e., it is decided that it is not) someone else's. This fact is reinforced because behind each such selection lies a structure of power that makes relevant decisions, or, as Benjamin has put it, in the cultural arena of a past charged with the time of now "the ruling class gives the commands" (Arendt 1968, 261).

Although political and intellectual elites in nation-states have long paved the way for the unified perception of a common past that mitigates tensions and uneasiness, different interpretations of and attitudes toward cultural heritage arise amid the ruptures formed at the transition from modernity to postmodernity, from nationalism to the acceptance of a country's multiple "pasts," from archaeology to a postmodern archaeology (or rather, archaeologies) and the opening up of a complex discussion on communities, heritage, and its stakeholders. Social tensions, conflict, and traumatic memories are reflected in fragmentary versions of a group's identity and history, as well as in confrontational approaches to a national or colonial time and its associated power regimes.

As people's engagements with the past transcend the familiar and trivial patterns of the authorized heritage discourse, we enter into unpredicted, discursive contexts, locations, sites, community life, informal education, oral history, everyday activities, and even sport and other domains in which competition, dispute, and conflict seek justification through specific, useful, and usable versions of the past.

Different reasons can provoke contestation around heritage, depending on the goals, the identity, the history (traumatic or not), the economy, and the political agenda of the social parties involved each time. Such diversity produces not only a variety of meaningful patterns around heritage but also a breeding ground for social research (Silverman 2011a; 2011b; Harrison 2008). Here, we attempt to group some of these interrelated themes that have occupied a great deal of the relevant literature:

- The legal or symbolic ownership of cultural heritage. Issues of objects' repatriation, stories about looted heritage, claimed human remains, and sacred or "sacralized" sites that objectify social identity are entangled in the view of heritage as possession—that is, of objects, landscapes, and monuments that we feel are "rightfully ours" and that, in one way or another, we "localize" (Bender 1998; Hall 2008) and appropriate.

- Related to the first point is the exclusion of social groups from the actual or symbolic use and enjoyment of "their" heritage in order to consolidate authoritative versions of the national past. Issues of social discrimination, monoculturalism, injustice, and violation of human rights are at stake here (Graham, Ashworth, and Tunbridge 2000, 96f). Struggles for social recognition within established social hierarchies are ethnographically explored through acts of heritage contestation, as people and groups claim a different position in their surrounding power structures or try to resist them (Layton 2008).
- Given that the challenging stances of groups and communities to heritage is more rigid when their members constitute part of a represented past—or even more so, when they have experienced it and oppose its dominant meanings or descriptions on pragmatic or moral grounds—a pertinent research category would include several representational critiques of museum displays concerning the validity, accuracy, and morality of exhibited cultures as well as the visualization of indigenous and minority cultures through powerful Western epistemological gazes.[8]
- Preservation and conservation issues: who, how, why, and what (and what not) does a heritage authority decide to preserve for future generations (Tunbridge 2008; Harrison 2008).
- Conflict regarding spatial practices. State authorities collide with local communities concerning urban planning, allowed or impeded community activities, interventions in the landscapes, land uses, the future and aspect of people's settlements and houses, and their "suitable" (or not) aesthetics (Herzfeld 2006, 2009). Given that all of these aspects are often linked to the heritage industry, tourism, property rights, and local economic growth (see Kirshenblatt-Gimblett 1998; Urry 2002; Winter 2014), in such cases claims for community participation in heritage sites management (and thus the preservation of the past seen as an active strategy to create a better future) are generated and variously negotiated.
- Issues of authenticity. Popular cultural representations of heritage for tourist purposes, theme parks, and heritage "simulacra" often clash with the authority of scholarly narratives that contest the use of heritage as a devalued, even "disneyfied" commodity intended for repetitive tourist consumption (Silverman 2015). In some cases, treatment of local populations as tourist commodities in "invented traditions," as Hobsbawm and Ranger have influentially argued,

is also contested on ethical grounds and on its questioned authenticity, whereas performances of local heritage (see Haldrup and Bærenholdt 2015), especially in developing countries, often convey messages of modernity that stand in contrast with the reenacted past (Kirshenblatt-Gimblett 1998, 8).

- Violence and physical erasure of cultural heritage during or after social and ethnic conflict. Acts of intentional heritage destruction as a consequence of armed fights, often accompanied by the tragic loss of human lives, lead to the erasure of a group's rights to land use, self-determination, and commemoration of its suffering (Layton, Stone, and Thomas 2001; Holtorf and Kristensen 2014; Sørensen and Viejo-Rose 2015). Destruction of heritage is a means for the memory cleansing of the defeated even in periods of peace, in the context of enforced gentrification programs that aim to rebrand national and urban identities (Herzfeld 2003, 2006; cf. Demetriou and Erdal Illican 2018 about gentrification efforts and preservation of war heritage in the UN-controlled Buffer Zone of Nicosia that have followed activist attempts to reunite the divided city).
- Should heritage management emphasize cultural differences between nations or ethnic groups? Some scholars maintain that the assertion of cultural differences and their asymmetrical nature is linked to the growth of cultural fundamentalism (Stolcke 1995). It has also been argued that emphasis given to cultural similarities could prove essential in pursuing social harmony through cultural unity. In this spirit, several recent and current EU heritage projects have worked toward constructions of an imagined European cultural identity.[9]
- Ethical approaches to the handling of traumatic heritage and painful memories, "sound" silences, and negative feelings such as shame and guilt (Logan and Reeves 2009a, 2009b; Gegner and Ziino 2012). Concentration camps, sites of torture, atrocities, death, and displacement face embarrassing dilemmas such as having to present history, respect victims, and activate empathy and historical understanding at the same time (Tunbridge and Ashworth 1996; Convery, Corsane, and Davis 2014). Such sites also have a considerable economic and educational potential due to the development of pilgrimage tourism or "thanatourism" (Sather-Wagstaff 2011).
- The "hierarchy of heritage values" (Smith, Messenger, and Soderland 2010) and the role of international institutions. Saving and classifying monuments on a scale according to their universal, national, or local significance may reproduce injustice at the expense of local

groups by eviction, misrepresentation, lack of recognition, or simply by excluding them from day-to-day social interaction with their cultural resources. In this context, the institutionalization of, for example, heritage management of those classified as World Heritage Sites by UNESCO has been criticized as imposing top-down approaches to heritage protection and local populations' rights while obstructing a relational (other than clear-cut and categorical) understanding of heritage (Creighton 2007, cf. Harvey 2015).

From Contestation to Reconciliation and Healing

If heritage is capable of sparking contestation and conflict, wouldn't it also be able to work more positively and contribute to human initiatives that seek to foster dialogue and community cohesion? Can we employ contested heritage as an incentive for achieving multivocality, social coexistence, and mutual understanding across cultural and religious differences?

In the last few years, a great deal has been done in this direction to reinforce the therapeutic and consoling character of heritage (Rowlands 2002, 110–112; Butler 2006; Eyal 2004, 12; Crooke 2005, 2008) and "solutionize heritage rather than problematize it" by including it in peace-building processes (Walters, Laven, and Davis 2017).

As Gil Eyal (2004, 12) has maintained, it is time to shift our conception of public memory as a guarantor of an embattled national identity and use it as a way to overcome trauma and injustice. Acknowledging a difficult, discontinuous, or dark past means coming to terms with suffering and indifference to human rights. Trauma can be undermined within as remembering past crimes, and those who were wronged can play a healing role and provide reconciliation (Eyal 2004; cf. LaFreniere 2012, 40) and civic education.

In postconflict societies, peace-building literature informs us about the need for a sustainable change based on social responsibility, norms of mutual respect, and a bottom-up understanding of neighborliness. Some researchers refer to the capacity of the museums to act as "contact zones" between distinctive cultures (Clifford 1999) or spaces for the challenging of negative preconceptions of the "other" (Solomon and Apostolidou 2018).

Community groups and activists can play an important role in unlocking the potential of memory institutions such as museums and the value that they can add to bottom-up projects between "enemies." Moreover, tourism has been proposed as a space of small-scale but effective dialogue between opposing attitudes to otherness in regions of war and conflict, such as the Palestinian-Israeli contested borderscape (Hammami and Laven 2017), whereas heritage reconstruction programs in former battlefields and zones of war may work as remedies for conflict (Hadzic and Eaton 2017), thus indicating a common ground where both disputed material heritage and social ties can be reconstructed.

Moving to Greece and Cyprus—Remnants of the Ancient Past: Ethnic, National and Global Meanings

The story of the relation of modern Greece to the ancient past and its heritage is a long and complex one that has markedly occupied modern literature.[10]

Antiquarians, adventurers, and collectors as well as political and intellectual elites were immersed in the nostalgia of the West for an ideal Golden Era that fueled the imagination, and these groups had long looked to Greece (under Ottoman rule until 1830) as a landscape worth exploring in their attempt to make sense of themselves as inheritors of the classical legacy (Stoneman 2010). Such an attitude to the past became tantamount to a search for cultural origins in the arts (Greek art was then to be irrevocably identified with ancient Athens, acquiring the connotations of unsurpassed perfection), literature, and political thought (Jenkins 1992; Harloe, Momigliano, and Farnoux 2018). Antiquity functioned as a source of liberal ideas on social progress and reason as well as a source of authority, a justification for expanding the political and economic influence of the Old World over the rest of the world that gradually turned into a "powerful model of utopian dreams" (Jenkins 2003, 168).

Enlightenment as philosophy and nationalism as political ideology gradually permeated the Greek-speaking, Orthodox Christian world of the Ottoman Empire, and the Greek *genos,* an ethnic group formed around mostly religious criteria, was transformed into an *ethnos*, a nation drawn mainly upon political concepts developed during the French Revolution (Stewart 1994; Myrogiannis 2012). An emerging Greek-speaking bourgeoisie that envisaged the gradual Hellenization of Ottoman territories saw the ancient past as a possible path toward the pursuit of ancestral land rights, political growth, and economic wealth as well as the aspired detachment of Greeks from the "backwards" or "uncivilized" Muslims Turks.[11] In a localized version of orientalism, antiquity was a mirror through which the newborn Greek state, and specifically its imagined community, viewed itself, or to paraphrase Gourgouris (1996, 1), antiquity made "the pain of [Greek] society's dreams sensible."

Behind this passionate emphasis on classical heritage, the ideological relation between Greece and Europe, described by Michael Herzfeld as crypto-colonial, looms large. This is the "curious alchemy whereby certain countries, buffer zones between the colonized lands and those as yet untamed, were compelled to acquire their political independence at the expense of massive economic dependence, this relationship being articulated in the iconic guise of aggressive national culture fashioned to suit foreign models. Such countries were and are living paradoxes: they are nominally independent, but that independence comes at the price of a sometimes humiliating form of effective dependence" (2002, 899).

This colonization of Greece in intellectual, economic, and political terms provides us with a broad explanatory framework for the country's political economy to this day as well as its ambivalent position in the global arena. It is therefore of no surprise that archaeology became a tool of governmentalization, a means to exercise power and control heritage (Foucault 2007, 144; cf. Harrison 2008, 177). As one of the most symbolically loaded disciplines in the country, it attempted to "restore" Hellenism, itself a revealing archaeological metaphor dominating public life (and spaces) in Greece. The state educational system also perpetuated a profoundly ahistorical admiration for "the ancestors" and their legacy (Fragoudaki 1997), backed by the intellectual efforts of local folklore studies. These endeavors stressed or even invented cultural continuities from antiquity to modern times, as many researchers have shown (Herzfeld 1982; Danforth 1984; Just 1989; Kakampoura 2006), and tried to differentiate the country from its "oriental" neighbours despite evident cultural similarities.

Moreover, the emphasis placed on classical heritage had obvious repercussions on monuments dating from subsequent periods. Byzantine (and undoubtedly Frankish and Turkish) sites attracted very little attention or were erased altogether in order to enhance classical antiquities, "liberate" them from later additions, and then restore them to their "original purity." In such acts of nationalist, "Hellenic-Orthodox" syncretism (Stewart 1994) encouraging the symbolic and epistemological cleansing of monuments from possible sources of "pollution," the state authorities were to become official agents of heritage destruction.[12]

As the literary theorist Artemis Leontis has shown, the formation of modern Hellenism has greatly relied on the mutual engagement of *logos* and *topos*—that is, of the discursive creation of (an eternal) Greek place (1995). The relationship of the two notions, developed at the intersection of literature and geography, can also be seen in the textual and visual works produced in and about Greece: until the 1930s, ancient heritage indisputably remained the only important part of the nation's history in such discursive creations, whereas with the modernist literary movement of the so-called "Generation of the Thirties," the meaning of Greekness started to be seen as residing not only in antiquity but also in recent traditions, "genuine" works of folk art, demotic songs, and naïve painting. This combined conceptualization of Greekness made use of Western literary tropes (Leontis 1995; cf. Tziovas 1989). In them, an almost metaphysical Greek spirit seemed to cross time periods, artworks, and ageless landscapes; the spirit was not compared to European modernity but liberally absorbed its norms. This was the time of a soul-searching aestheticization of archaeological heritage, with significant implications in poetry (Sakka, this volume), visual arts, and museum exhibitions.[13]

Such a complicated cultural and political enterprise is usually thought of as having been interrupted in 1922 with the end of the so-called Great Idea, the ideology of irredentism and territorial unification of Greek-speaking, Christian populations (Karafoulidou 2018). Whereas until then, archaeology was directly implemented in expansionist strategies, the sorrowful end of the Greek-Turkish War (1919–1922) obliged the country to adopt a different stance: archaeology was no longer used to expand but to consolidate borders, identities, and memories of origins in a homogenized construction of the past. Anything that did not fit in that vision should remain silent.

Not accidentally, antiquity was a recurring theme during all periods of extreme political tensions, such as the dictatorship of Metaxas (1936–1940), with its so-called Third Hellenic Culture and its pompous military reenactments of antiquity (Hamilakis 2007); the Civil War, which used the island of Makronisos, edifyingly called "the New Parthenon," as an exile camp for the ideological "re-education" of the inmates (ibid.); and the junta of the Colonels (1967–1974), which eloquently referred to the country as "Greece of Christian Greeks." Antiquity and specifically the classical heritage represented by the Athenian Acropolis were used to proselytize political beliefs and impose sharp distinctions between a "patriotic" right-wing and an "anti-Hellenic" Communist ideology (cf. Mouliou, this volume).

Archaeology remained an important tool of Greek governmentality in monitoring national conflicts and promoting an all-encompassing patriotism until the early eighties. The generously state-funded excavations conducted in the 1970s by the venerated archaeologist Manolis Andronikos near the village of Vergina in Northern Greece were to form a powerful discourse concerning the "undisputed Greekness of Macedonia" not only in antiquity but also during more recent periods. Thus the neighboring states would never be able to claim any "historically justified" relation to the ancient past of Macedonia and the material exhibited in its museums (Danforth 1995; Kotsakis 1998; Hamilakis 2007, chapter 4). Moreover, the Vergina finds were used to reverse the classicist view of the Hellenistic period as the beginning of the decay of the classical ideal (Voutsaki 2003, 240). Even Thessaloniki, a city founded after the death of the celebrated Alexander the Great that did not flourish until the Roman era, acquired a special, meticulously constructed relationship to Alexander. Local cultural memory was negotiated through a variety of cultural processes strongly alluding to the classical period: public sculptures, public enactments of the ancient past, place-namings, suppression of ethnic heritage (Turkish-Muslim, Jewish, Slavic, etc.), and a widespread "archaeologized" aesthetic (Galiniki 2015; Hastaoglou 2008; Hekimoglou 2012; cf. Galiniki and Solomon 2014). Generous funding for archaeological research and its popularization efficiently counteracted the consideration of Athens as the only legitimate heir of the classical past.

However, in the last two decades of the twentieth century, Greek politics of the past escaped the established canon around the instrumentalization of antiquity and its deployment as a founding national pedigree. The new global demographic and political conditions accompanying the fall of the Berlin Wall, the end of the Cold War, and the arrival of thousands of immigrants in the Greek "consumerist paradise" of the 1990s not only resulted in a first, rather timid, familiarization with the notions of multiculturalism but also brought new and critical insights into the relationship of the country with its past. Material culture theory was introduced in the field mainly by prehistorians (see Kotsakis 1991), who challenged the functionalist and art-historical paradigms in Greek archaeology as well as established archaeological representations in academic writing and museum exhibitions. In 1996, Yannis Hamilakis and Eleana Yalouri published their seminal, oft-cited article "Antiquities as Symbolic Capital in Modern Greek Society," and in 1999 they published "Sacralizing the Past," in which they linked the classical heritage of the country and its related archaeological practices to nationalist uses of sacredness (Hamilakis and Yalouri 1996, 1999). A paradigm shift in Greek archaeology was then advocated to move it away from its supposedly neutral and objective interpretative schemes and toward a socially sensitive and theoretically informed practice.

Structuralist analyses found an exceptional position in archaeological and museological representations of antiquity, and the political connotations of Greek archaeology became more evident than ever (e.g., Damaskos and Plantzos 2008; Voutsaki and Cartledge 2017). Heritage consumption, commoditized tourist experiences, and the pursuit of authenticity through restoration and reconstruction also became the focus of certain studies (Solomon, forthcoming).

It was now time for Greek archaeology's anthropological turn. Ethnographic approaches to archaeological finds and cultural biographies of monuments and sites made a variety of meanings assigned to ancient objects in different historical phases and cultural contexts evident. Thus, in her ethnographic exploration of the Athenian Acropolis, Yalouri (2001) examined the role of the nation's symbolic monument par excellence, within the relationship between the national and the global. Archaeological ethnographies of sites, monuments, historical landscapes, and archaeological excavations (Solomon 2006, 2007; Hamilakis and Anagnostopoulos 2009a; Stroulia and Buck Sutton 2010a; Hamilakis and Ifantidis 2016) explored the role of antiquities in diverse "historicities," subjectivities, and social engagements with the past. The focus on the scholar's ethical and political responsibilities and the interest in public archaeology expressed by heritage practitioners throughout the country have finally given space to a fascinating discourse on local and national cultural memory.

Cyprus

As we move to Cyprus, the implication of archaeology in the political and social life of the country presents significant similarities with Greece but also some considerable differences.

References to the ancient past have been equally appropriated by the Greek-Cypriot community and its intellectual elites in fostering their encounter with the West and, again, their differentiation from the "oriental" Turkish-Cypriots. In addition, in times of nationalist tensions, classical Greek heritage has been used to claim ancestral rights to a land colonized by the Greeks thousands of years before the arrival of the first Turks in the sixteenth century (also see the similar rhetoric in Greece in the 1950s, Mouliou, this volume). In contrast, as a rather small place where conflict is deeply felt, Cyprus highlights colonialism as another aspect of the interrelation between antiquity, nationalism, and social identity.

Nowadays, the Greek Cypriot and Turkish Cypriot communities represent two different ethnicities, languages, and religions (Greek Orthodox and Islam), with constant references to modern Greece and Turkey, respectively. Their conflicting history in the second half of the twentieth century reproduced the difficult relations between the above countries and postcolonial Britain that ruled the island until its independence in 1960, and it was mirrored in demands for union with Greece or annexation to Turkey, respectively. Territorial claims, privileged access of the colonizers to local resources, armed clashes, violence, trauma, and violation of human rights were implicated in the partition of the country after the military coup engineered by the junta in Greece and the invasion of troops from Turkey in 1974.

Moreover, the extensive trade of illicit antiquities has been a basic feature of the colonial regime in Cyprus (Knapp and Antoniadou 1998), which involved members of all communities. European and later American and Australian expeditions and universities played an active role in conducting archaeological research and exporting—aided by locals—massive numbers of finds to museums in Europe and the United States. Politicized uses of antiquities have contributed ever since to the development of a two-sided nationalism, competing senses of place, pillaging and heritage destruction, neglect of the other's monuments, and still polarizing ethnic interpretations of the past (see Bounia and Stylianou-Lambert 2011), explored by Bounia, Stylianou-Lambert, and Nikolaou in the relevant chapter of this book.

Contested Antiquity: Themes and Reflections

In contrast to Cyprus, where heritage disputes have never ceased to characterize local ethnic identity politics, in Greece, the perception of a unified and unifying narrative of the ancient past and its eternal material signifiers appears overwhelming. Yet has it always been so?

In reality, as the relationship of Greece to antiquity has been deeply political, affecting and being affected by the country's relationship to the West and at the same time generating significant tourist income for local economies, archaeological heritage management has been far from uncontested and smoothly run. The identification of Greece with its ancient legacy has not been and still is not without reactions, internal contradictions, open or hidden acts of resistance, and in some cases straightforward conflict.

The contributors to this volume aspire to analyze these contradictory and conflicting engagements with the archaeological heritage in the two countries. Disputed attitudes, identity clashes, and controversial perceptions and uses of Greek antiquity render ancient material culture a source of current meaningful ideas, reminding us that archaeological heritage does matter in the country because discourses around it are deeply entangled in people's lives, identities, and social agency. At the same time, such discourses provide us with the analytical framework for both a critical history and an insightful ethnography of Greek archaeological heritage and its significance from the nineteenth century to today.

Let us now explore the book's main themes.

"Us and Them": Greek Exceptionalism, Mimicry, and Cultural Trauma

A common thread uniting most chapters of this book are the opposing and often conflicting aspects of Greek national identity related to the discursive position of the country in the international scene and particularly in the pantheon of respected and developed states. Perhaps not unsurprisingly in a time that social research acknowledges identity as changeable, dynamic, and relational, discourses on classical heritage give substance to the internal contradictions of modern Greece in relation to the Western others but also in relation to a past that always weighs heavily on the present (Leontis 1995; Gourgouris 1996; Herzfeld 1982, 1987, 1997). Thus, although the present draws its importance (or at least part of it) from the past, it can never confront an open comparison to it.[14]

The constant effort of modern Greece to come to grips with ancestral achievements causes gaps and ruptures, and the Western gaze constantly falls upon these unsolicited discrepancies between past and present, between "them and us." On the other hand, the unequal power relations between Greece and the West that have dominated the former's modern history are often refracted in narratives of victimization and oppression as exercised by the Western powers or, alternatively, of cultural indebtedness to modern Greeks.

Dimitris Plantzos's contribution should be placed within this broad discursive context of Greece's "difficult" relation to the West. The author departs from the idea that not only the classical past of the country but also its present has been colonized, and he examines archaeological spaces as "sites of trauma" in the unfulfilled present of the nation. Drawing from Michael Herzfeld (2002) and Homi Bhabha (1994), he grounds part of his analysis on the concepts of crypto-colonialism and colonial mimicry, respectively, and reflects upon social subjects in Greece in their effort to deal with colonial demands in all fields of public life, internalize the Western lessons on the meaning and the values of the classical legacy, and meet the cultural criteria for a deserved place in modernity.

Plantzos argues that a series of archaeological displays and sites in Athens fulfill a peculiar role: they help the nation revive "the unlived experiences of an imagined past." Nonetheless, these sites—for example, the new Acropolis Museum, the Benaki Museum, the antiquities displayed in the highly-praised (as "efficient and European-style") Athens Metro, and others—present some special characteristics: they are not simply spaces housing or safeguarding Greek antiquities but are special "exhibitionary complexes" (Bennett 1988) that confirm the "Greek exception." Like some respected Western examples of exhibition spaces seeking to "transform that problem [of social order] into one of culture" (ibid., 76), they are positively evaluated as "Western" enough and "modern" enough to display the ancient masterpieces, these unquestioned predecessors of Europeanness. Not accidentally, at these sites, experts follow and sometimes even supersede (unexpectedly?) the standards of Western museums—that is, the colonial display trope par excellence.

Archaeology returns to its etymological history as "discourse about the origins," yet one that seeks to comfort the national subjects. Acclaimed presentations of valued material culture become remedies for cultural trauma, even for the mourning of Greece's unaccomplished modernity and its incomplete acceptance into the Western canon. Antiquities, especially those appropriated and venerated by the colonial gaze, become a discursive means to cope with the country's ever-stigmatized inefficiencies and, having a long time ago acquired the capacity of a nation's possessions, respond to critiques for the marginal role of Greece in the hierarchy of modernized states.

Archaeological Heritage and Political Asymmetries

Among the archaeological activities undertaken in Greece, all of which necessitate the state's bureaucratic authorization and its close supervision, the excavations undertaken by foreign archaeological schools and expeditions—initially by Britain, France, Germany, and the United States—have had a significant impact on the relations of Greece with these countries and the West in general. Since the nineteenth century, foreign scientific activity was dictated by cultural diplomacy, mutual benefits, political agendas, and individual academic motivations.

Relationships between Greek and foreign governments as well as politicians and archaeologists have spanned from in-depth academic collaboration to extreme suspicion and mistrust, the latter pertaining to academic competence, excavation and site management, interpretation, and "use" of finds (Nikolentzos 2003). For Greece, allowing foreign archaeologists to conduct excavations, especially at its legendary sites (e.g., Knossos, Olympia, Delphi, the Athenian Agora), was considered as positively contributing to the prestige and promotion of the country, the protection of monuments, and more important as an asset in all kinds of interstate talks. In contrast, for the countries mentioned earlier, undertaking archaeological activity (and often violating Greek law) was a means for consolidating their cultural, political, and economic influence and, until 1932, for enriching their museum collections (Sakka 2002).

Such crypto-colonial or openly colonial endeavors could advance the scientific and ideological agendas of foreign archaeological schools as well as assert their philanthropy toward Greece in a prestigious cultural field through funding the research and conservation of antiquities and other social work. At the same time, the imposition of their ideological and aesthetic principles on local scholarship and the consolidation of distinctions between them and their Greek colleagues, or within the Western countries involved, perpetuated patronage and subordination grounded on Greece's moral obligations to the Western institutions.

Greek governments often saw the provision of foreign schools with permits to excavate or even export finds to museums abroad (mainly for temporary exhibitions but in some cases permanently) as an asset in their foreign and finance policies (Mouliou 2008). On the contrary, in periods of political transition, such as the early eighties, when the Socialist party PASOK won the national elections in the name of institutional change, blocking or impeding the action of foreign schools, even occasionally, was seen as a weapon for resistance, a sort of "public transcript" (Scott 1985) to the colonialist practices throughout the country.

Crypto-colonialism was also sustained through reciprocal decisions concerning the value of the excavated finds. Until the resolution of the Asine question, explored by Niki Sakka in her chapter, the involved parties agreed that despite the right of Greece to own its excavated heritage as any sovereign nation-state, foreign schools could export as compensation for their work some of their finds, those considered "doubles," "repetitions," or "useless artifacts." After all, foreigners were offering to do what Greece could not due to lack of sufficient financial resources and technical expertise: to adequately dig, safeguard, and conserve bits of an ecumenical heritage. In these negotiations on cultural value, variously supported or contested by Greek politicians and archaeological authorities, Greece's inalienable wealth (i.e., its sanctified heritage) could be exchanged for the "benefit of the country."

Sakka's study is a nuanced account of this complex relationship around the finds of an important Swedish excavation in the interwar period. Understood in the context of Greek and broadly European politics of the time, the excavation in Asine, northeastern Peloponnese, invoked scientific interest in classical antiquity and heritage values commonly shared by the two countries involved, Greece and Sweden. The commercial, industrial, and cultural development Sweden enjoyed in the early twentieth century prompted the country's institutions to participate in excavations, following other European schools in a competitive archaeological game.

The Asine controversy arose when Greece claimed back finds sent to Sweden as a kind of a contentious, temporary loan to be inventoried, conserved, and studied. A continuous back and forth of meetings and fervent negotiations ensued, producing numerous official documents and unofficial, fiery dialogues between ministries, ambassadors, archaeologists, politicians, and journalists.

What was at stake in Asine? The promotion of Swedish scientific interest in Greek heritage? The support of Greece's pursuit of westernization, which entailed the transgression of its own laws? The recognition, in the context of crypto-colonial reciprocity, of Swedish financial sacrifices for the undertaken research? The improvement of the relations between the two countries and the development of collaboration in other, nonarchaeological domains? Or questions of dignity and scientific independence of Greek archaeologists and civil servants?

Whatever the answer might be, what is interesting to note is the multiplicity of responses given to the issue in the early thirties. Members of the Archaeological Council, the Ministry of Foreign Affairs, politicians, and diplomats provided different interpretations of the law and had disagreeing views on the policy that should have been adopted, or even on the value of the finds in question. Compromises regarding the rigidity or flexibility with which Greece should react reveal Greek *disemia* (Herzfeld 1987): the contradicting aspects of modern Greek identity in relation to Western interlocutors; the conflict between the content (or letter) of the law and its employment; and the constructed image of the country in public and its contestation in closer, less official contexts of self-reflection and self-critique.

Greece finally succeeded in getting back the Asine finds. Soon after, it gave Sweden a number of finds considered useless, an unthinkable category by today's legal and ethical standards. This time, no public reaction was aroused. Who could actually know the exact content of all these transported boxes with non-inventoried finds? In any case, in the village of Asine, the bonds between Swedish archaeologists and the locals became those of essential collaboration, mutual trust, and shared emotions for the finds and their value. This is an example, Sakka contends, that on a personal level, national oppositions may be turned into significant "bonding experiences around the excavation field," engaging locals with their heritage and revealing the "disemic" aspects of this complex relationship.

The Cypriot Perspective

The Asine dispute was one among many others that suggests Greek antiquities have been implicated in an ambiguous game of value and exchange of obligations according to local, national, and international political circumstances, gains, and goals, yet it is a game that changes continuously across time and context of social interaction.

Similarly, Alexandra Bounia, Paulina Nikolaou, and Theopisti Stylianou-Lambert analyze the interplay between territorial claims in Cyprus and the performance of ethnic, national, and the colonial interest in the island's antiquities. Drawing from Doreen Massey's work (2005), the authors consider that the spatial scale from local to global or colonial should not be considered a fixed geography but a constructive social process that, linked to various uses of local archaeological heritage, has shaped the "production" of Cyprus as a place and its diverse populations for more than a century.

Thus, in the late nineteenth and early twentieth centuries, conflicting interests and identities, nationalism, and colonialism formed an explosive mixture that still affects the island. A heated power game took different manifestations and involved a vast number of individuals and collectivities: the then British Government, the Greek and Turkish communities, antiquarians, archaeologists, experts and representatives of foreign museums, illicit traders of ancient objects, and local intellectuals. All of them had diverse interests and formed changing alliances in their efforts to exclude other possible stakeholders from the archaeological heritage scene.

The examined period was crucial for the passage of archaeology from antiquarianism to systematic excavation and research. This transition was reflected in contrasting approaches to the unearthed antiquities: antiquarianism wanted them as parts of foreign museum collections of extraordinary objects, whereas some British archaeologists and local elites associated the evolving discipline with their gradual constructions of ethnic and national pasts and wanted the excavated antiquities to be housed in the Museum of Cyprus in Nicosia. Founded in the early years of British administration, the museum initially received support from British classicists and prominent members of both ethnic communities. The authors note it served as a base for negotiating the British involvement in the "sharing" of finds, and later local Greek Cypriot intellectuals used it to support their claim for the annexation of the island to Greece.

The authors focus on not only hegemonic versions of the past but also "small stories" of peasants, workers, and field and dig assistants, either Turks or Greeks, involved in the colonially led enterprise of Cypriot excavations. Their voices, until recently totally unnoticed, reveal their familiarity with the place, their role in the antiquities market, and some small acts through which they confronted the representatives of European museums.

Moreover, in the time of a gradual Hellenization of the island's past and of Cypriot archaeology, the Turkish community and some of its elite members supported the safeguarding of medieval heritage in a museum that still operates in the occupied part of Nicosia. The divide between an ancient Greek and Byzantine heritage on the one hand, and a Frankish-Ottoman Muslim heritage on the other, has persisted through time, and after armed conflict in the 1970s, it has also led to destruction and mutual accusations of disrespectful treatment of what in the meantime has come to clearly and strictly connote "ethnic heritage" in a divided country that creates, invents, commercializes, or omits its links with Greek antiquity accordingly.

Contentious Issues around Archaeological Heritage in Greece after World War II

After World War II and the subsequent Civil War (1946–1949), a period of extreme poverty and destruction of the public infrastructures in Greece, the ancient past acquired new connotations in all fields of social activity. Its significance "in the progress of civilization" served as a symbolic argument during Greek calls for financial aid from the Marshall Plan, aiming to rebuild the Greek economy and prevent the spread of Communism in Western Europe. Marlen Mouliou presents *Greece Calling*, a propaganda document in which US authorities were called to pay tribute to the devastated land of Greece by evoking its remarkable heritage and its heroic struggles. An overall account of the period's discourses on the ancient past and its monuments is critically formed in this chapter by the author, who explores the press from 1948 to the military coup of 1967.

During this harsh period, antiquities were not simply Greece's symbolic capital but part of a considerable investment in its transformation as a tourist destination. Archaeology significantly triggered public interest at that time. New finds; new museum displays; the educational, aesthetic, and cultural values of (a largely unknown) past that the Westerners had long before recognized—all occupied intellectuals and journalists of the time.

Apart from the understaffing of the Archaeological Service (notwithstanding its highly symbolic role) and the neglect of monuments dating from historical periods other than antiquity, contentious issues touched upon at the time included the looting and illicit trafficking of ancient objects, the deep chasm between the preservation of antiquity, the modernization of the country and the urbanization of its spaces through new constructions, and conflicts between developers and archaeologists—a recurring subject until today. The dilemma "antiquity or development" has pervaded the public sphere ever since.

The comparative examination of two newspapers with differing ideological agendas reveals two different approaches to the meaning and public implementation of antiquity. During that politically unstable period, the sharp ideological ruptures between a state anti-Communist ideology and the Left were also reflected in divergent stances to ancient heritage. Thus, in the more conservative *To Vima,* antiquities are treated as a valuable source of knowledge and tourist income, enhancing the link between Greece and the (also fervently) anti-Communist West. On the other hand, the newspaper *I Avgi,* representing the intellectual Left whose supporters were often persecuted, advocated that Greeks should both protect and become inspired by ancient heritage in their social struggles for a better future. Yet according to the discourses promoted by *I Avgi,* such an engagement with the past should go beyond a sterile "archaeolatry," the worship of the ancestors, backed by the national educational system and the country's conservative forces. In the same vein, citizens should protect their heritage from the highly controversial and imperialist plans of the Western "allies" to invest in the country's wealth in order to serve their own interests.

Such an attitude became evident during the disputed reconstruction by the American School of the ancient Stoa of Attalos in the Athenian Agora. The project was deemed an "Americanization" of Greek heritage that ended up commercializing antiquities for tourist purposes. To a certain extent, this anti-Western rhetoric has reemerged in the current period of deprivation and crisis that began for Greece in 2010, a period identified by many as the new economic and political colonization of the country (Tziovas 2017). Not accidentally, the Acropolis, always a symbol of Eternal Greece, is presented in cartoons and unofficial discourses both now and in the period examined by Mouliou as being "for sale" to Western partners: once again, Greek archaeological heritage serves as a valuable source of cultural wealth used to pay off the country's immense economic debt.

From Exclusion to Gentrification: Antiquity and the Performance of Memory in Urban Spaces

The supremacy of ancient heritage over that of any other period has had critical consequences on cultural representations of "other" pasts in the country. In several places, the overpowering emphasis on national exceptionalism has led to the exclusion of countermemories (i.e., those who could not fit in the hegemonic versions of heritage), with this being a theme encountered in all subsequent chapters of this book.

Thessaloniki is such a case in question. Under Ottoman rule, it accommodated Greek-speaking Christians, Spanish-speaking Jews, Turkish-speaking Muslims, Slavs, Armenians, Vlachs, Levantines, and many other ethnic and religious groups. Although some material signs of their presence have survived, they became almost invisible through a long mnemonic process of indifference, perhaps guilt, and material and symbolic erasure. This fact is perhaps unsurprising considering that after the end of Ottoman rule in 1912 and especially during the Cold War, only classical monuments (even dating from Roman times, for the lack of older ones) and Byzantine churches could convincingly place the second largest Greek city on the national map.

However, since 2010, a different memory politics has emerged, aiming to change the conservative face of the city and its long-established attitudes to the past. In her contribution, Styliana Galiniki explores the emergence of this novel cultural framework, associated to a great extent, but not exclusively, with new people elected as local authorities. Through the lens of cultural geography, she examines what she calls "gentrification of local social memory" and its attempts to allow space, literally and metaphorically, to a multifaceted but silenced heritage.

Importantly, in 1991 thousands of protesters claimed their "ownership" of the Macedonian past and stigmatized "the forgery of Greek history" due to the appropriation by the Former Yugoslavian Republic of Macedonia of the name *Macedonia* and Greek archaeological heritage imagery (see Karpozilos and Christopoulos 2018). Considering that the archaeological finds of Vergina, associated with classical Greece and the kings of ancient Macedonia, have been endlessly reproduced alongside the image of Alexander the Great (i.e., constant reminders of the area's ancestral Hellenism), this new cultural policy in Thessaloniki associated with Mayor Yiannis Boutaris deserves special treatment. At the same time, there has been a rise in xenophobic and Far Right groups in Thessaloniki who have long venerated Alexander under his modern statue on the sea front, itself an "archaeologized" connection to a Hellenic past, whereas attempts in 2018 of the leftist Greek government to resolve the dispute between Greece and Former Yugoslav Republic of Macedonia over the use of the name "Macedonia" again led to extended demonstrations, this time combined with public reactions against economic austerity and the submission to international creditors.[15] The conflict between the two countries ended with the Prespa Agreement, signed in June 2018. In the agreement is an explicit clarification that the citizens of North Macedonia are not related to the ancient Macedonians. Despite this and the fact that the agreement stipulated the removal of any image of the "Vergina Sun" from public spaces in North Macedonia, the agreement was fervently criticized by a large part of the Greek population, not necessarily nationalist, especially in Northern Greece.

At first glance, gentrification here regards the management of public spaces of Thessaloniki through references to its multiethnic history—references that make visible other pasts and other people (cf. Ashworth, Graham, and Tunbridge 2007; Tunbridge 2008; Gnecco 2015). However, it also concerns the roles Thessalonians are willing to perform publicly, as well as the rebranding of the city's image for tourist consumption.

Nonetheless, this novel process does not take place in a vacuum. Nostalgic references to cosmopolitan Thessaloniki of the early twentieth century had become common in the last decade of the twentieth century in a rich publishing and cultural activity about the "good old days," as well as during some cultural festivals (especially when Thessaloniki acted as European Capital of Culture in 1997). Moreover, some Ottoman monuments (for example, the Hamza Bey, a mosque that was used as a porno cinema, and the Yeni Mosque, which interestingly served as an archaeological museum) have been, or are planned to be, restored and included in the cultural life of the city.

Galiniki contends at the outset that this new memory framework of mind occurs in a rather safe temporal context that does not put local national identity in "difficulty." In fact, more than 95 percent of Salonican Jews were exterminated during World War II, almost all Salonican Muslims were expelled after the population exchange with Turkey in 1923, the internationals who fought here in World War I are buried in the local foreign cemeteries, and many "others," haunting the city like ghosts (cf. Mazower 2004), have left a long time ago.

In any case, performing memory as "a social event" in Thessaloniki goes beyond references to a long-lost ethnic diversity. It also regards a collective attempt to redefine the content of this remembered heritage: "signs of memory" have been placed around the city informing citizens and visitors about events of significant symbolic value; since 2013, a march connects mnemonic sites of the Jewish deportation; and the abovementioned Yeni Mosque has been allowed to conduct prayer services during Ramadan. This perspective of local cultural memory, perhaps having been experienced long before its official employment, as Galiniki appositely remarks, has a complex impact on the use and representation of ancient heritage as well. The major project for the new sea front around the statue of Alexander (see the cover photo of this volume) challenges previous practices and encourages leisure and sociability; local museums and exhibitions are openly engaged with the multiethnic heritage of Thessaloniki on various occasions; artistic performances held in historic sites focus on relevant aspects of the Salonican past; even copies of the *Incantadas*, the Roman sculptures that stood in the yard of a Jewish house in the nineteenth century and were exported to the Louvre in 1864, have been received in public ceremonies as examples of a multilayered urban history after nearly 150 years of oblivion (Solomon and Galiniki 2018).

In the current polarizing times of crisis, one should not think that the reception of this new memory politics by local collectivities and a growing number of visitors is uncontested—how could that be? In May 2018, for example, Mayor Boutaris was physically attacked by Far Right citizens during a commemoration ceremony for the victims of the Pontic Genocide of 1919.[16] Galiniki argues that memory wars are always ready to explode in relation to the public use of local monuments, as happened in 2016 with the use of the restored Rotunda, a Roman, Byzantine, and Ottoman monument located at the buffer zone between a former mosque, a current church, and a valued World Heritage site (for an earlier contestation, see Stewart 2001). The recently rebranded, "gentrified" image of multicultural Thessaloniki seems to walk a tightrope between conflicting aspects of social memory and self-awareness on the one hand, and the positive effects of cultural tourism on local economy in the currently difficult time of austerity on the other. A new, difficult, and deeply ambiguous yet transformative process seems to have taken place that produces, contests, and at the same time reevaluates the city's reemerged heritage(s).

Antiquity as Burden and as Promise

Ancient monuments are not only a source of pride and repetitive affirmation of identity but also a serious burden. Often, the attachment to an almost sanctified past is seen as an obstacle to modernization, or even as a hypocritical cultural element that has alienated Greeks from their recent cultural traditions rooted, according to many, in the Ottoman times and not in an antiquity "imported" from and imposed by the West.

This gap between the past and the present, the need to compromise between the preservation of heritage traces, and the completion of works that are meant to improve a society's economy and living standards describe Greece's dilemmas since its early modern years. The conundrum of "antiquities versus development" or "the dead versus the living" entails selections and ambivalent decisions by citizens and authorities alike and often anticipates conflict.

At the heart of such oppositional encounters stands the separation of heritage sites from everyday community life, a basic aspect of heritage management in general. Michael Herzfeld, in his influential ethnography on the social impact of historic preservation of private houses (variously interpreted as Venetian or Ottoman) in the Cretan town of Rethymno (1991), and Anna Stroulia and Susan Buck Sutton, in their *Archaeology in Situ* (2010a), have contributed a great deal to the exploration of the relationship between authorities and local communities, the ways this division affects knowledge of the past, its perception as "property," and the interpretation of and attitudes toward historic heritage nationwide. In the language of the state bureaucracy, "protection" means visible spatial effects, fences, surveillance, alienation from one's own past, frequent violation of property rights and family values, imposition of unwanted hierarchies, a "national, official and monumental time" over "social time" (Herzfeld 1991), and inevitably appropriation of local heritage in the name of its global significance.

Greece can present a long list of cases of such "chasms between ancient and modern Greece" (Stroulia and Buck Sutton 2010b), between the lived and the preserved heritage. The expulsion of residents from their houses in order to excavate ancient monuments already dates to the nineteenth century: villagers of the settlement of Kastri, which was extended above the ancient sanctuary of Delphi, had to be removed in order to allow the French School to excavate the site, as did the people living around the Athenian Agora (Sakka, this volume). Similarly, official attempts to protect (or "purify" from later interventions) significant archaeological landmarks have equally significant repercussions on communities' lives and perceptions of both archaeological patrimony and the "antisocial" role of the state. The so-called *Kastroplikta*, a refugee settlement built after the Asia Minor War in the twenties that literally touched the Byzantine Walls of Upper Thessaloniki (Ano Polis), was scheduled to be demolished in 2010 in order to enhance the view of the Byzantine fortifications (Mirtsioti 2010), whereas the Anafiotika settlement at the foot of the Acropolis is still in the public eye.[17] Although the latter is now considered a picturesque and touristy corner in the historical center of Athens, it profoundly experiences bureaucratic ambivalence concerning the residents' proprietorial status and the management of the charming, oft-photographed houses (Caftanzoglou 2001).

However, the state is not always the unquestioned rescuer of antiquities. Indeed, it might find itself trapped in its own rhetoric as the main defender of archaeological heritage, especially when it has to preserve antiquities that impede large construction works and the associated interests of the involved building companies. This is, for example, the case of the discovery of the commercial heart of ancient and Byzantine Thessaloniki, the crossroad of the Roman cardo and decumanus that was discovered during the construction of the city's Metro station at Venizelou Street in 2012. After a ferocious meeting, the Central Archaeological Council decided to remove the discovered archaeological complex, characterized by specialists and heritage organizations all over the world as of invaluable significance ("a Byzantine Pompeii," Christides 2013), and at a later stage to have it transferred to a military camp at the edge of the city, in the context of what Wienberg calls "creative dismantling" (2014).[18] Archaeologists working for the Archaeological Service found themselves in a difficult position as they had to follow orders that contradicted both their own scientific views and the European conventions for the protection of archaeological heritage also signed by Greece. Their reactions together with those of international Byzantinologists, academics, local civil society collectivities, and the then local authorities caused heated public debates and powerful petitions that in 2015 led to the state's decision to preserve the antiquities in situ in the form of an open-air museum that could function as a new landmark of the city (Adam-Veleni and Mylopoulos 2018). This decision was received as a great victory for those who defended the coexistence of heritage preservation with the cultural and tourist development of Thessaloniki, whereas it was in alignment with the rhetoric of the Greek state as the major protector of Greek antiquities, as it appears for example in the question of the repatriation of the Parthenon Marbles. Nevertheless, four years later, in December 2019, the same decision was unexpectedly revised and reversed with (once again) the change of government, the gradual change of the composition of the Central Archaeological Council, and the diffusion of an argumentation about the delay that the preservation of antiquities would cause to the construction of the Metro.[19]

Thus, as one can expect, archaeological protection zones in Greece constitute a highly controversial battleground. In his chapter, Aris Anagnostopoulos examines these spatial and legal entities conceptualized by the Greek state in order to defend both the antiquities and its national values. Going beyond the evident oppositions "us versus them" and "communities versus state authorities," Anagnostopoulos approaches the law as a "flexible" concept that, in its inception, already allows space for its transgression. The ground on which the state exercises its idealized sovereignty is never as stable, fixed, and determinable as its officials wants us to believe through the use of a totalizing legislative language that promises social order and heritage protection. On the contrary, such spaces, always contested and always incomplete, are engaged in shifting relations of uncertainty and ambiguity.

To this end, Anagnostopoulos uses ethnographic observations from fieldwork: first the island of Poros, a touristy place off the coast of Argolis (northeast Peloponnese), where the archaeological protection zone has caused fierce conflict between the locals and the Archaeological Service (with the latter being accused of corruption as well as of the decline and abandonment of certain places because "it enforces the law"); and then Gonies, a barren, depopulated village on Mt. Psiloritis in Crete, where the notion of an archaeological protection zone has acquired a very different content, as we will see.

Here, the popular Foucauldian concept of "heterotopia" (Foucault 1986) is a key one in unfolding and understanding the heritage versus space dissonance (cf. Galiniki, this volume; Konstantinou, this volume). However, it does not connote a land of ruins colonized by the modern European imagination, as Leontis has so influentially argued in her *Topographies of Hellenism* (1995, 40–66): a domain of archaeological quests where modern Greeks were disciplined in order to respond to the colonial gazes on them (Hamilakis 2007, 85f) or an imaginary periphery that supported others' constructions of self (Plantzos, this volume). What is of interest for Anagnostopoulos in using the concept is basically its "utopian sediment" that emerges from his informants' narratives about archaeological zones. Behind every accusation of bureaucratic inertia and every complaint about the Archaeological Service and its inability "to do something" about the plethora of neglected and unappreciated antiquities lie the elements of this imaginary heterotopia that ancient Greece is or can be for modern Greeks. This utopian approach to the past informs the difference between the nation and its territory, an idealized law and its contradictory application, "the letter of the law" and its enforcement, the weight of ancient heritage and the impossibility of the Archaeological Service to operate as it is supposed to, and the disorder in contrast to a promised order. The very impossibility of the law to be applied in its entirety and the actual limitations of the Archaeological Service to efficiently protect the antiquities open up the chasm between a long-promised utopia and the reality of the everyday practice.

The same utopian element prompts the villagers of Gonies to seek the implementation of archaeologists' power in their largely abandoned area and the declaration of archaeological zones. Although the excavated sites in the area are few in number, their presence is highlighted in topical discourses about the different temporalities of the village. Protection zones then become a legislative as well as discursive tool that could help locals confront the contestation of their village's communal lands by energy companies who covet the area for profit.

No doubt, the heterotopic function of archaeological spaces is cause for not only straightforward conflict but also a potentially different future.

Landscapes

Cultural heritage and landscape constitute two interrelated analytical concepts, two corresponding ways of seeing the external world, both past and present (Tilley 1994; Bender 1998, 2002; Garden 2006). The "production" and multiple appropriations of an archaeological site, itself a human-made landscape, may tell us a lot about the ways social groups locate themselves in an environment, its history and materiality, while they remember, perform, and represent its diverse cultural content.

Katerina Konstantinou explores social contestation in relation to the management and the perceived meaning of a significant Greek cultural landscape, that of ancient Dodona in Epirus, northwestern Greece. In her ethnographic account, she examines how the site, the place of an acclaimed ancient oracle of Zeus, is socialized through human action (cf. Bender 1993, 11) and the use of a long-established academic discourse that saw the cradle of Greek civilization in ancient Epirus.

For people who live near the archaeological site or come from the area and from Epirus in general, Dodona is an emblematic landscape that plays a special role in their sense of place (cf. Convery, Corsane, and Davis 2012a, 2012b). As is the case of other archaeological sites in the country (see Solomon 2006), Dodona was connected to recent cultural idioms of Epirus, forming a four-thousand-year-old Greek tribal sequence. Through the interplay of archaeology with folklore studies, this poor, neglected, and harsh mountainous area near the sensitive Greek-Albanian border came to represent a crucial land for the nation's ancestry, a perception supported by local intellectual elites and members of Epirote institutions, such as the University of Ioannina, the Ioannina Archaeological Museum, and the Society of Epirote Studies (Gremotsis 2011).

Yet Dodona lacks impressive ancient remains, apart from the theater that dates from the later historical phases of the site. The site draws its significance from the remote antiquity of the area (praised even in ancient literary sources as remarkably old) and its evocative natural surroundings, whose sacredness has been broadly promoted to modern times. In this framework, the celebrated drama festival organized in its theater between 1960 and 1999 and its widespread appeal was seen—and is still remembered—by locals as a form of pilgrimage to an archetypal mnemonic place. Such perception of the site was a means to cope with the lack of imposing remains and also a response to the indifference with which their area had been treated until recently.

Sacredness, therefore, has escaped the strict chronological framework of antiquity, when Dodona united all Epirotes and all Greeks. It has become part of a local discourse on "primordiality." It utilizes the official landscape of the site, its assumed "energetic power," and the relevant narratives of researchers and local intellectuals (formed during the twentieth century) to present itself anew to archaeologists, state authorities, and a targeted audience of tourists.

Nevertheless, this process is far from uncontested. Inspired by the growing interest in archaeological ethnography, Konstantinou collects local voices and memories hitherto unheard. During her fieldwork, she found that the performances of the drama festival appeared to unite antiquity with a local theater tradition professed in the present. She cites the restoration of the theater condemned by the locals as "inauthentic" and its "non-traditional" aesthetics, the use of concrete in a "sacred" historical site, the gradual deterioration of the sets throughout the forty-year duration of the festival as having motivated local communities to oppose archaeologists, architects, and bureaucrats, often using the opponents' same argumentation on the significance of the site.

Finally, due to the construction of the Egnatia highway that had been planned to pass very close to the site, sound pollution also became a major issue in the heritage debate on Dodona. In a landscape represented by archaeologists as sacred, sound pollution would be unacceptable. The argument, in accordance with current literature calling for an interpretative sense of the past in the present made through a sensory understanding of archaeological remains (see Tilley 2019), was successfully used against the initial construction plans. Not accidentally, the exhibition on Dodona entitled "The Oracle of Sounds," which was held at the prestigious New Acropolis Museum in Athens in 2016, emphasized the soundscapes of the Epirote landscape (both historical and modern) and at long last placed Dodona on a widely acknowledged, national heritage scene.

The Heritage Gaze

As one could easily predict, references to the Acropolis of Athens are frequent in this book. Its celebrated association with Greek and international heritage values and identity discourses, its inclusion—due to its universal value—in the World Heritage Sites list since 1987, and its centrality in archaeology and the world history of art in matters of conservation and tourism management and in debates on heritage repatriation as related to the Parthenon Marbles controversy have made it (rather uncontestably this time) one the most visited, representative, experienced, and analyzed archaeological sites globally.

The fact that the history of Athens has evolved around this always visible rocky hill has rendered the gaze over it a central issue in decisions pertaining to its management. Especially after the establishment of the modern Greek state, the gaze over the Acropolis, perhaps more than a visit to it, became part of a broader cultural framework within which citizens, philhellenes, students, tourists, and art lovers have learned to appreciate and enjoy the view to the monument. Not surprisingly, this rather atemporal, culturally mediated view has been vastly commercialized in the tourist and leisure industry, offered for consumption by the "semiotic gaze" (Urry 2002) of infinite visitors as well as in the estate market.

In her chapter on the monument's cultural visibility, Andromache Gazi returns to 2007, when the decision to demolish two buildings from the 1930s, adjacent to the New Acropolis Museum, caused an extensive public controversy. The museum was then under construction, and the reason behind the decision taken by the Central Archaeological Council to demolish the buildings was that the two listed private properties would partially obstruct the view to the Acropolis from certain points of the museum and specifically from its restaurant terrace.

The legitimacy and ethical dimensions of such destruction relied at first on a hierarchy of value assigned to the competing heritages. "What is more important?" seems to have been asked in the case examined by Gazi: the view to a universally venerated monument—which the New Acropolis Museum is committed to research and promote—or some rather sophisticated houses bearing elements of modern architecture of the thirties?

Similar to the museumlike displays in the Athens Metro station discussed by Plantzos, emphasis on the visibility of the ancient heritage in the itineraries of everyday life becomes an important part of the narrated and mainly exposed self

(Watson and Waterton 2010). Both city residents and visitors are called on to bear witness, using their own eyes in a kind of repetitive "autopsy" (cf. Konstantinou, this volume) of a much-advertised visual dialogue between the museum and the emblematic cultural landscape of the sacred rock.

Yet the sacredness of the monument is subject to different perspectives (literally and metaphorically) of those who have the power to allow or impede the gaze to the site. Thus in 2019, such an "autopsy" was impeded by the announced construction of two multistory hotels in the highly valued surrounding area of the Acropolis. The process revealed severe gaps in current zoning laws. The two constructions, one reaching ten stories high, spurred the strong reaction of heritage organizations as well as of locals who claimed that "not everything is for sale" and that the buildings once completed would block the view to a UNESCO heritage site.[20]

Undoubtedly, the view to the Acropolis and especially to the Parthenon is highly appreciated not only in symbolic but also in economic terms. The Acropolis is ultimately a spectacle (Yalouri 2001; Loukaki 2008). Therefore, as the nation's museum par excellence, the New Acropolis Museum found itself obliged to protect such a valuable view, and to manipulate the visitors' view, at the expense of another heritage, that is, the listed interwar buildings seen as intruding into the realm of the monument's visibility. After all, the museum intends to be a new landmark of the city, that of a successfully Europeanized museum (Plantzos 2009, 2010, this volume), after decades of passionate discussions about its appropriate form, operation, museological study, and location. It could not but pay respect to the archetypal site whose movable objects it has been called on to house and display. Modernity, cultural visibility, and the classical aesthetic values met on the terrace of the museum's restaurant—perhaps another reminder of the sensory consumption of heritage in postmodernity.

Nevertheless, behind the decision for the demolition of the listed houses also lies a question of purification. As has been mentioned above and analyzed by Anagnostopoulos and Konstantinou in their respective contributions, the idea that classical heritage is "polluted" by historic remains of more recent periods is certainly a key one in understanding archaeological heritage management in the country. Even in 1974, it was suggested that the acclaimed theater of Dodona should be restored to resemble a "noble" classical-era Greek (not Roman) theater to recall the celebrated examples of theaters in southern Greece.

Unsurprisingly perhaps, the Acropolis itself has been deprived of most historic remnants dating after the classical period, as "matter out of place" (Douglas 1966). In relation to the issue, the Anafiotika quarter built in the nineteenth century, mentioned earlier, falls into this same category because it was considered "accumulated rubbish of unsightly dwellings" (Vikelas, in Caftanzoglou 2001, 122) and thus it had to be cleared away.

But as the Anafiotika story has shown, this game of heritage values changes over time: the area is now considered a nostalgic retreat for Athenians and tourists alike (Caftanzoglou 2010). The "social life of things" (Appadurai 1986) depends on malleable constructs of value and meaning. This is, after all, what happened with the two "intrusive" houses in front of the New Acropolis Museum: the mobilization of architects, archaeologists, and thousands of other citizens prevented the planned demolition, acknowledging the historic and aesthetic value of buildings less than a hundred years old as legitimate. Once again, the state bureaucracy contradicted itself by redeciding that its initial decision to list the houses as works of art was the right one.

Antiquity as Dark Heritage

With Thessaloniki once again the focus, Eleni Stefanou and Ioanna Antoniadou remind us that the dominance of classical imagery has silenced not only the city's multiethnic heritage, as shown already by Galiniki, but also its recent political history associated with some of its most important historical fortifications. This is the case of Eptapyrgio, or Yedi Kule, the Acropolis of the Roman, Byzantine, and Ottoman Thessaloniki, which in 1988 was proclaimed by UNESCO, together with a series of Byzantine churches (among which is the Rotunda mentioned above), as a single group of World Heritage Sites. The monument, which nowadays is essentially represented and promoted as a medieval fortification, houses the headquarters of the former local Department of Byzantine Antiquities (now part of the Ephorate of Antiquities of the City of Thessaloniki) and is open to the public.

However, before the Eptapyrgio was monumentalized, it had another, rather silenced phase in its life: for nearly a century, from 1890 to 1989, it was used as an Ottoman (and after 1913, a Greek) prison—indeed a very harsh one. In its spaces, countless men and women were imprisoned, tortured, and executed, including for political reasons, especially during the dark years of the Metaxas dictatorship (1936–1940), World War II, the Civil War, and the military junta (1967–1974).

Stefanou and Antoniadou turn their attention to one of these almost forgotten "communities of memory" (Booth 1999), whose members were imprisoned because of their political views and activities during the junta. Their stories, although inextricably bound with the history of the building, the city, and the country as a whole, seem to have been erased from the celebrated monument.

There are several reasons behind such neglect, among which stands the exaltation of Byzantine heritage, a highly ideologized field of archaeological inquiry, as mentioned earlier. More than this, however, the imprisonment and suffering of citizens for political reasons is still a matter of traumatic and largely silent memory that the deep political divides bequeathed by Cold War polarization make hard to tackle in public.

In their ethnographic research, Stefanou and Antoniadou criticize the representation of the monument only as a Byzantine fort. They walk with their informants through the former prison, at least in those parts that are accessible to visitors. The former detainees share their experiences. They explain the meaning, literally embodied, of the prison's spaces—its doors, yards, corridors, and staircases—and also events and moments that should be told and known to the public, at least alongside the display of the archaeological spolia.

In fact, this monument of celebrated ancient architecture is also an example of difficult heritage, in Sharon Macdonald's words, a monument that disrupts the present and "is also contested and awkward for public reconciliation with a positive, self-affirming contemporary identity" (2009, 1). This lack of positive meaning in the monument is essentially ignored by archaeologists, who are deeply criticized by the former political prisoners for distorting a painful truth. As Laurajane Smith has put it, "heritage is not necessarily a good thing" (2006, 58).

Undoubtedly, political prisoners' dissatisfaction with the underrepresentation of their experiences calls for the writing of the monument's fuller and more critical biography, one that will include the voices of the victims still alive. This biography will unite glorious and dark stories in the same narrative, stories of Byzantine architectural sophistication but also of human suffering and injustice. If communities matter in the heritage world, as Crooke (2008) has convincingly argued, a bottom-up "archaeology of internment" (Myers and Moshenska 2011) has to give them a say. The battle for the soothing of traumatic memories, and perhaps the protection of human rights in the present, also passes through the critical representation of those difficult though powerful and instructive heritage sites.

Antiquity and the Greek Crisis: Stimulating New Agency

In August 2014, the chief archaeologist of the Archaeological Service in Serres, Northern Greece, announced in a press conference the excavation of a huge circular tomb close to the site of Amphipolis, a major ancient port city in Macedonia. The news caused a great fuss in the media concerning the identity of the buried skeletons found there. Once again, Alexander the Great rather unwillingly participated as protagonist in the coverage of Amphipolis, because numerous hypotheses were put forward connecting the unearthed bones to him, his mother, his wife Roxane, his general Hephestion, and others. "Alexandromania" and an unprecedented treasure hunt were nourished by the excavator, the media, then Prime Minister Antonis Samaras, the Minister of Culture, the church, numerous bloggers who linked the mound to the Greekness of Macedonia, and thousands of people who followed the digging process on the news day by day. The prime minister and his wife paid a visit to the mound in a symbolic gesture recalling a similar trip made by the venerated right-wing PM Konstantinos Karamanlis in 1977, when he visited the excavations of the Macedonian tombs at Vergina. The case of Amphipolis was severely criticized by the Association of Greek Archaeologists, university teachers, and other archaeologists on the grounds of its dating and its political manipulation by the government just a few days before the national elections in January 2015 (Hamilakis 2014). The newly elected government soon put an end to this public discussion (as well as to its funding), and the story of Amphipolis passed into history until July 2019 and the return of the conservative party to power.

However, the case of Amphipolis is not simply an exaggerated case of an impressive archaeological discovery exploited by the media or the nationalist rhetoric of a right-wing government. It is also an intense social event whose intensity and passion is inextricably linked to the current economic crisis in Greece.

Thus, one can say that such excitement was strategically triggered by the then government as a means of distracting people from economic hardship and the need for more austerity measures that authorities had to take before the second (out of three by 2016) memorandum that the country signed in order to deal with its debt and avoid the omnipresent threat of an eventual declaration of bankruptcy. Nevertheless, this tale has more to tell us. As has been noted (Plantzos 2014a; Hamilakis 2015; cf. Hamilakis 2013), the excavation and the management of the associated narrative constituted an exercise of what Michel Foucault called bio-power, a term he used to describe "a number of phenomena that seems to be quite significant, namely, the set of mechanisms through which the basic biological features of the human species became the object of a political strategy, of a general strategy of power, or, in other words, how, starting from the eighteenth century, modern Western societies took on board the fundamental biological fact that human beings are a species" (Foucault 2007, 16).

The state's narrative regarding the assumed identity of the buried bodies was extensively implemented for the construction of bio-political distinctions between Greeks and non-Greeks in the contested territory of Northern Greece. Such distinctions, it can be argued, go beyond the claims of the "secular religion of archaeology" in the nineties (Hamilakis 2007), when the dispute over the ownership of the ancient Macedonian past and its heritage were debated. The management of Amphipolis proposed a different version of a patriotic archaeology conducted in front of TV cameras, debated on blogs and Facebook, or in the fighting comments published below every relevant newspaper article appearing on the web. The limits between specialist and unofficial discourses on classical heritage were drastically blurred. In this "archaeo-politics in the times of crisis" (Hamilakis 2015; Tziovas 2017), the ancient bones were capable of dividing people on the name of supposed racial differences. Such distinctions—hidden and embarrassing during the years of political correctness—are now disguised through the excuses of austerity and "thanatopolitics" (Papanikolaou 2013). It is in this context that foreign people's deaths, such as those of refugees and "illegal immigrants" (amassed for years in hot spots in Lesvos and elsewhere in the country under inhuman conditions that thoroughly contradict western concepts of civil rights; see Lévy 2020) are naturalized in a new, ostensibly justified construction of "otherness."

Thus the sites of traumatic memory discussed by Plantzos in his contribution, these "glossy" Westernized archaeo-spaces of our times, become more necessary than ever before, not only as antidotes to the melancholy of an never-ending recession but also as discursive arguments employed in a perceived new colonization of the country's past. In this case, Greeks appear undeserving of their glorious heritage. Their failure to adapt to global economic pressures and dictates verifies the neocolonial gaze according to which the famous Greek claim of continuity from antiquity to the present seems to have failed in practice (Tziovas 2014b, 14–16). Ancient heritage sparks a new, updated, anticolonization narrative. The extremes reached by the current entanglement in narratives and practices of debt and defaults present Europe in decline and Greece as its broken link (Michail-Matsas 2015). Alternatively, deployment of ancient legacy resuscitates old ideas on the continuing cultural debt to Greece (nourished both nationally and internationally), or it may more interestingly work as a source of artistic inspiration and agency.

This last category is what interests Eleana Yalouri and Elpida Rikou in their examination of the role of archaeological heritage in contemporary art projects in Athens. Considering the powerful and often "tyrannical" authority of the classical past on the present, the authors follow three different art projects related to Greek antiquity.

All three took place in highly symbolic archaeological sites in Athens. Indeed, two of them were housed in the Athenian Agora, a symbolic space associated with the birth of democracy. At the Roman Forum, the artist Tino Seghal presented a project on the idea of progress, Aemilia Papaphilippou set up an installation (accompanied by a performance) in the Athenian Agora, and Natasa Biza conducted a site-specific project that commented on the emblematic landscaping of the Agora with "ancient" plants in the fifties by the American School of Classical Studies. The first two projects were carried out under the aegis of NEON, a powerful private foundation with a significant role in the contemporary art scene that also aims at the reinvigoration of ancient sites through modern art interventions.

The authors placed their exploration within the also "difficult" field of contemporary art in Greece that, despite its attraction of public interest, remains rather timid and introverted. Again, the attachment to the past (ancient to more recent) and the repetitive comparison between Greek and Western art scenes weigh on the insecure present of the former. Interestingly, within the context of the economic crisis, Greek contemporary art has been exoticized as a place that may teach others and provide art responses to hot social issues, as the title *Learning from Athens* of the art exhibition *documenta 14* revealed, for the first time jointly organized between Kassel, Germany, and Athens. "Athens represents the uncertain future of Western European democracy," declared the artistic director of the 2017 documenta, Adam Szymczyk (Politakis 2014), and this rather sad affirmation becomes the stimulus for a productive process that may problematize artists and audiences alike (Rikou and Yalouri 2017).[21]

Yalouri and Rikou compare the different ways in which the three artists deal with the Greek antiquity inside its celebrated spaces. They discuss how these projects and the artistic and curatorial trends they represent challenge our established conceptions of our "difficult" relationship with its remains in the public spaces of everyday Athenian life. Undermining the status of antiquity as undisputed national and global heritage is not an easy task. Yet what seems to be at stake is a convincing answer to the question about the role a contemporary artist is supposed to play in this desired dialogue among people, people and public space, and public space and past "materialities." As the authors appositely argue, this dialogue can be produced not just by stressing "affinity, conformity, or continuity." On the contrary, it may be "one of divergence and/or contestation, underscoring paradoxes, differences, or even conflict." Eventually, new perspectives on the bond between the ancient past and an artistic present can be grounded on critical, in-depth approaches to hitherto uncontested meanings of heritage.

In Conclusion

Greek archaeological heritage is a contested terrain. Since the nineteenth century, almost all conflicts characterizing social reality in Greece and in Cyprus seem to have been linked to the use, and more generally the perception, of the two countries' ancient material culture.

As practiced heritage, antiquities have been deployed not simply as signs of Greek national identity but mainly as weapons in the expression and negotiation of social differences, disagreements, and clashes, either internally (i.e., within the two national domains) or on the international scene. Archaeological heritage is central to the relation between Greece, Cyprus, and the West, and it has been both the means to approach and resist the powerful Western "other," always according to time, context, ideology (right or left wing), and other social divides. In this enduring game, presented and analyzed in this book, social groups and their alliances have varied, as have the aims and objectives of those involved in the disputes around the interpretation and management of ancient material culture.

More than an unquestionable national treasure proudly offered to foreign (crypto-colonial or otherwise) gazes, archaeological heritage has also been employed in multiple games of social antagonism, cultural visibility, and appropriation. It has been variably "ours" and "theirs," significant and tyrannical, inclusive and exclusive, and even traumatic when referred to (a peripheral and unaccomplished) modernity, either claimed and pursued or unclaimed and rejected. In Greece, heritage sites objectify conflicts between communities and authorities (archaeologists, central and local governments), academics and artists; between the demands of an important past versus those of a humble and struggling present; and between the demands of everyday life versus those imposed by formal or hegemonic narratives regarding the significance, value, and representation of the ancient Greek past.

Conflicting uses of archaeological heritage are central to Greece during the current times of crisis and austerity, in which cultural values and human rights appear to be at risk. Because people feel attacked by global and often unclear political and economic interests, antiquity is evoked to counteract and assuage these feelings; it is also used to advocate a new decolonization process, or often as a source of inspiration in order to deal with the practical and moral consequences of the crisis. At the same time, it is also used as a governmentalization tool for the imposition of authoritative, even racist, bio-political strategies that polarize social groups and present ancient Greek heritage as being at the antipodes of solidarity, cultural exchange, and social coexistence in the present.

It becomes obvious that heritage contestation is not only a provocative research concept that enables interesting insights into different people's identities, ideas, attitudes, and uses of the Greek archaeological past across time and context. It is also a stimulus to follow changes in their perspectives and points of view, to subvert generalizing stereotypes about the homogeneity of national culture, and to explore polyphony and diversity—that is, the endless polysemy of heritage. As Greece itself becomes a site of conflict with social ruptures and struggles for a better future being inscribed on the surface of its heritage, this book is a way for those interested in Greece and its material past to critically engage with contemporary social and political issues in and about this area of the world.

ESTHER SOLOMON is Assistant Professor in Museum Studies at the University of Ioannina. She studied archaeology, museology, and social anthropology at the University of Ioannina, the Università Internazionale dell'Arte in Florence, the University of Sheffield, and the University College London. She worked as curator in several museums in Greece and abroad and has published extensively on public archaeology, museum representations, exhibition curating, and the social and political uses of the past in Greece.

Notes

1. On reactions from Syrian and other heritage scholars, see https://www.theguardian.com/world/2015/aug/24/palmyra-destruction-ancient-temple-baal-shamin-war-crime-un-isis, accessed July 29, 2016.

2. Accessed July 20, 2016, http://tracks.unhcr.org/2016/01/syrias-landmarks-restored-in-miniature/.

3. Accessed July 20, 2016, http://www.amth.gr/images/Raidestos/ΑΦΙΣΑ_SITE.jpg.

4. See for example the happening organized by the architect and activist artist Eleni Tzirtzilaki in a remote plot in Lesvos, where hundreds of unnamed refugees, drowned while trying to escape to the West, are buried. The recognition of this loss was made public through a special lament for the dead children from Syria that took place amid the humble, improvised tombs and their association with similar archaeological remains. Accessed June 1, 2016, http://nomadikiarxitektoniki.net/perpatontas.

5. According to Aristotle, "memory is like the imprint or drawing in us of things felt" (Forty 1999, 2). For a discussion of the understanding of time in archaeology and its pragmatic concern to study things "in an untensed and inhuman time of duration in which notions of past or present or future are irrelevant," see Tilley (2017, 10).

6. See also the declaration of the World Archaeological Congress (http://www.worldarchaeologicalcongress.org/about-wac/history/146-history-wac), cited in Silverman (2011b), and the manifesto of the Association of *Critical Heritage Studies* founded in 2012 (accessed July 25, 2016, http://archanth.anu.edu.au/heritage-museum-studies/association-critical-heritage-studies).

7. For example, at the conferences of the open forum *Dialogues in Archaeology*, which were held on the island of Lesvos (2016), the Greek gate for reception of refugees and asylum seekers from Asia, and Ioannina, Northwest Greece (2017), academics and heritage practitioners claimed a strong interest in the ephemerality of the material record in relation to the unprivileged groups of our times such as the refugees. They acknowledged the need to document forced migration and, most important, to engage with the broad social movements of our times (e.g., Hamilakis 2016, 2017). On the Ioannina *Dialogues in Archaeology*, see http://archdial17.conf.uoi.gr/2017/05/12/%CF%80%CF%81%CF%8C%CF%83%CE%BA%CE%BB%CE%B7%CF%83%CE%B7, accessed May 3, 2018.

8. The museological literature on the subject is extremely vast. See, for example, Karp and Lavine (1991), Handler and Gable (1997), Byrne (2008), Altayli and Viau-Courville (2018), and Solomon and Apostolidou (2018).

9. For example, in 2011, the European Heritage Label, an initiative designating heritage sites that represent a common European cultural identity and other initiatives and programs being planned or already undertaken by UNESCO, decided to draw on similarities and

common experiences rather than on differences, a trend aiming at integration and civic dialogue in an era of fundamentalism and the spread of hatred and violence in the European "family" (Innocenti 2015, 18).

10. Danforth (1984); Lowenthal (1988, 1998, 243–45); Morris (1994); Leontis (1995); Shanks (1996); Gourgouris (1996); Voutsaki (2003); Dyson (2006); Hamilakis (2007); Damaskos and Plantzos (2008); Plantzos (2008, 2014b); Loukaki (2008); Tziovas (2014a); Voutsaki and Cartledge (2017); Papadimitriou and Anagnostopoulos (2017).

11. See, for example, the constitution of the Athens Archaeological Society in 1837, which, only five years after the new state's independence, attributed the hitherto lack of archaeological research in the country to "the ignorance and barbarism of the despotic Turks" (Mazower 2008, 33).

12. See Konstantinou (this volume) for the relevant issue among archaeologists and local intellectuals in the region of Epirus over the "purification" of the ancient theater of Dodona.

13. At the end of her chapter, Sakka alludes precisely to this connection between archaeology and poetry: the archaeological discoveries at Asine in the Peloponnese triggered the writing of the emblematic poem "King of Asine" by George Seferis, Nobel Laureate in Literature. For a visual example of this Greek "essence" based on diachronic local themes and values encountered at the permanent exhibition of the Benaki Museum, see Plantzos, also in this volume.

14. For the "Greek refractions" of the fall from paradise, a pervasive social metaphor in comparisons between past and present, see Herzfeld (1987, 33). See also Konstantinou (this volume) for the comparison between a highly praised past and a humble present that has been made by the villagers living near the acclaimed theater of ancient Dodona in Epirus.

15. On the 2018 Greek rallies against the use of "Macedonia," their archaeological imagery, and the role they played in Far Right groups and the clergy, see https://www.reuters.com/article/us-greece-macedonia-protests/greeks-rally-against-use-of-macedonia-in-name-dispute-with-skopje-idUSKBN1FA0FY and https://www.nytimes.com/2018/02/04/world/europe/greece-macedonia-protest.html (accessed April 28, 2018).

16. The attack was associated with Boutaris's promotion of the city's multicultural past and his positive attitude toward Turks, Muslims, Jews, Albanians, gays, and other minorities. Accessed June 1, 2018, https://www.theguardian.com/world/2018/may/20/suspected-far-right-thugs-attack-mayor-of-thessaloniki-greece-at-rally.

17. On the political side of the demolition of the Kastroplikta settlement and the decided preservation of a few houses for tourist purposes, see the local residents' view at http://alterthess.gr/content/ekdilosi-gia-ta-kastroplikta, accessed May 4, 2018.

18. For an extensive coverage of the issue, the different phases and the arguments of the involved parties, see articles published on the local newspaper *Parallaxi* from 2013 to 2020. Accessed July 11, 2020. https://parallaximag.gr/?s=%CE%BC%CE%B5%CF%84%CF%81%CF%8C+%CE%92%CE%B5%CE%BD%CE%B9%CE%B6%CE%AD%CE%BB%CE%BF%CF%85, also Pantazopoulos 2019.

19. For the December 2019 revision, see the international appeal by Europa Nostra (accessed July 2, 2019, https://www.europanostra.org/europa-nostra-appeals-to-preserve-in-situ-the-antiquities-at-the-venizelos-metro-station-in-thessaloniki/). See also the relevant text published in May 2020 by The Association of Greek Archaeologists that started a new legal cause against the government's revisionist decision (accessed July 11, 2020, https://www.archaiologia.gr/blog/2020/05/27/%CE%BF-%CF%83%CE%B5%CE%B1-%CE%B3%CE%B9%CE%B1-%CF%84%CE%B7-%CE%B4%CE%B9%CE%B1%CF%84%CE%AE

%CF%81%CE%B7%CF%83%CE%B7-%CF%84%CF%89%CE%BD-%CE%B1%CF%81%CF%87%CE%B1%CE%B9%CE%BF%CF%84%CE%AE%CF%84%CF%89%CE%BD/).

20. Accessed July 2, 2019, https://www.theguardian.com/cities/2019/mar/08/not-everythings-for-sale-greeks-mobilise-as-new-hotels-obscure-acropolis-views-athens.

21. In this framework, the research project *Learning from documenta* coordinated by the authors of this chapter, Eleana Yalouri and Elpida Rikou, critically discussed political and epistemological aspects of documenta's presence in Athens. Accessed May 8, 2018, http://learningfromdocumenta.org/about.

References

Abu Khafajah, Shatha, and Arwa Badran. 2015. "From Heritage to Archaeology and Back Again." In *The Palgrave Handbook of Contemporary Heritage Research*, edited by Emma Waterton and Steve Watson, 91–112. Basingstoke: Palgrave Macmillan.

Adam-Veleni, Polyxeni, and Yannis Mylopoulos, eds. 2018. *The Metro-nome of Thessaloniki's History*. Athens: Hellenic Ministry of Culture, Hellenic Ministry of Infrastructures, and Attiko Metro S.A. Accessed July 11, 2020. https://parallaximag.gr/wp-content/uploads/2019/12/METRO-NTAS-for-web.pdf.

Altayli, Afşin, and Mathieu Viau-Courville, eds. 2018. *Museums and Contested Histories*, *Museum International* 70 (3–4), special issue.

Appadurai, Arjun. 1986. "Introduction: Commodities and the Politics of Value." In *The Social Life of Things. Commodities in Cultural Perspective*, edited by Arjun Appadurai, 3–63. Cambridge: Cambridge University Press.

———. 2008. "The Globalization of Archaeology and Heritage: A Discussion with Arjun Appadurai." In *The Heritage Reader*, edited by Graham Fairclough, Rodney Harrison, John Jameson, and John Schofield, 209–18. London: Routledge.

Arendt, Hannah, ed. 1968. *Walter Benjamin, Illuminations*. New York: Schoken.

Ashworth, Gregory J., Brian J. Graham, and John E. Tunbridge. 2007. *Pluralising Pasts: Heritage, Identity and Place in Multicultural Societies*. London: Pluto.

Bender, Barbara. 1993. "Introduction: Landscape, Meaning and Action." In *Landscape. Politics and Perspectives*, edited by Barbara Bender, 1–17. Oxford: Berg.

———. 1998. *Stonehenge. Making Space*. Oxford: Berg.

———. 2002. "Time and Landscape." *Current Anthropology* 43 (S4): 103–12.

Bender, Barbara, Sue Hamilton, and Christopher Tilley, eds. 2007. *Stone Worlds: Narrative and Reflexivity in Landscape Archaeology*. Walnut Creek, CA: Left Coast.

Bennett, Tony. 1988. "The Exhibitionary Complex." *New Formations* 4: 73–102.

Benton, Tim, ed. 2010. *Understanding Heritage and Memory*. Manchester: Manchester University Press.

Benton, Tim, and Clementine Cecil. 2010. "Heritage and Public Memory." In *Understanding Heritage and Memory*, edited by Tim Benton, 7–25. Manchester: Manchester University Press.

Bhabha, Homi K. 1994. *The Location of Culture*. London: Routledge.

Booth, James W. 1999. "Communities of Memory: On Identity, Memory, and Debt." *American Political Science Review* 93: 249–63.

Boswell, David, and Jessica Evans, eds. 1999. *Representing the Nation: A Reader. Histories, Heritage, Museums*. London: Routledge.

Bounia, Alexandra, and Theopisti Stylianou-Lambert. 2011. "National Museums in Cyprus: A Story of Heritage and Conflict." In *Building National Museums in Europe 1750–2010*. Conference proceedings from EuNaMus: European National Museums: Identity Politics, the Uses of the Past and the European Citizen. Bologna, April 28–30, 2011. EuNaMus Report No. 1. Accessed July 1, 2016. http://www.ep.liu.se/ecp/064/009/ecp64009.pdf.

Breglia, Lisa. 2006. "Complicit Agendas: Ethnography of Archaeology as Ethical Research Practice." In *Ethnographies of Archaeological Practice: Cultural Encounters, Material Transformations*, edited by Matt Edgeworth, 173–84. Lanham, MD: AltaMira.

Butler, Beverley. 2006. "Heritage and the Present Past." In *Handbook of Material Culture*, edited by Christopher Tilley, Webb Keane, Susanne Küchler, Michael Rowlands, and Patricia Spyer, 463–80. London: Sage.

Byrne, Denis. 2008. "Western Hegemony in Archaeological Heritage Management." In *The Heritage Reader*, edited by Graham Fairclough, Rodney Harrison, John Jameson, and John Schofield, 229–34. London: Routledge.

Caftanzoglou, Roxani. 2001. *Στη Σκιά του Ιερού Βράχου. Τόπος και Μνήμη στα Αναφιώτικα* [In the Shadow of the Sacred Rock: Place and Memory in Anafiotika]. Athens: Greek National Center for Social Research.

———. 2010. "Producing and Consuming Pictures: Representations of a Landscape." In *Archaeology in Situ: Sites, Archaeology and Communities in Greece*, edited by Anna Stroulia and Susan Buck Sutton, 159–78. Lanham, MD: Lexington.

Castaneda, Quetzil E., and Christopher N. Matthews, eds. 2008. *Ethnographic Archaeologies: Reflections on Stakeholders and Archaeological Practices*. Lanham, MD: AltaMira.

Christides, Giorgos. 2013. "Thessaloniki: Ancient Dilemma for Modern Greece." *BBC*, March 14, 2013. Accessed July 13, 2020. https://www.bbc.com/news/world-europe-21743758.

Clifford, James. 1999. "Museums as Contact Zones." In *Representing the Nation: A Reader. Histories, Heritage, Museums*, edited by David Boswell and Jessica Evans, 435–57, London: Routledge.

Convery, Ian, Gerard Corsane, and Peter Davis, eds. 2012a. *Making Sense of Place: Multidisciplinary Perspectives*. Woodbridge: Boydell and Brewer.

———. 2012b. "Introduction: Making Sense of Place." In *Making Sense of Place: Multidisciplinary Perspectives*, edited by Ian Convery, Gerard Corsane, and Peter Davis, 1–8. Woodbridge: Boydell and Brewer.

———. 2014. *Displaced Heritage: Responses to Disaster, Trauma, and Loss*. Woodbridge: Boydell and Brewer.

Creighton, Oliver H. 2007. "Contested Townscapes: The Walled City as World Heritage." *World Archaeology* 39 (3): 339–54.

Crooke, Elizabeth. 2005. "Dealing with the Past: Museums and Heritage in Northern Ireland and Cape Town, South Africa." *International Journal of Heritage Studies* 11 (2): 131–42.

———. 2008. *Museums and Community: Ideas, Issues and Challenges*. Abingdon: Routledge.

Damaskos, Dimitris, and Dimitris Plantzos, eds. 2008. *A Singular Antiquity: Archaeology and Hellenic Identity in Twentieth-Century Greece*. Athens: Benaki Museum.

Danforth, Loring M. 1984. "The Ideological Context of the Search for Continuities in Greek Culture." *Journal of Modern Greek Studies* 2: 53–85.

———. 1995. *The Macedonian Conflict: Ethnic Nationalism in a Transnational World.* Princeton, NJ: Princeton University Press.

Demetriou, Olga, and Murat Erdal Ilican. 2018. "A Peace of Bricks and Mortar: Thinking Ceasefire Landscapes with Gramsci." *International Journal of Heritage Studies.* DOI: 10.1080/13527258.2017.1413673. Accessed January 18, 2018. https://doi.org/10.1080/13527258.2017.1413673.

Douglas, Mary. 1966. *Purity and Danger: An Analysis of Concepts of Pollution and Taboo.* London: Routledge and Kegan Paul.

Dyson, Stephen L. 2006. *In Pursuit of Ancient Pasts. A History of Classical Archaeology in the Nineteenth and Twentieth Centuries.* New Haven, CT: Yale University Press.

Edgeworth Matt, ed. 2006. *Ethnographies of Archaeological Practice: Cultural Encounters, Material Transformations.* Lanham, MD: AltaMira.

Eyal, Gil. 2004. "Identity and Trauma: Two Forms of the Will to Memory." *History and Memory* 16 (1): 5–36.

Fairclough, Graham, Rodney Harrison, John Jameson Jr., and John Schofield, eds. 2008. *The Heritage Reader.* London: Routledge.

Forty, Adrian. 1999. "Introduction." In *The Art of Forgetting,* edited by Adrian Forty and Susanne Küchler, 1–18. Oxford: Berg.

Foucault, Michel. 1986. "Of Other Spaces." *Diacritics* 16: 22–27.

———. 2007. *Security, Territory, Population: Lectures at the Collége De France, 1977–78.* New York: Palgrave Macmillan.

Fragoudaki, Anna. 1997. "Οι Πολιτικές Συνέπειες της Ανιστορικής Παρουσίασης του Ελληνικού Έθνους" [The Political Consequences of the Ahistorical Presentation of the Greek Nation]. In *Τι Είν' η Πατρίδα μας; Εθνοκεντρισμός στην Εκπαίδευση* [What Is Our Country?: Ethnocentrism in Education], edited by Anna Fragoudaki and Thalia Dragona, 143–98. Athens: Alexandria.

Galiniki, Syliana. 2015. "Οι Χρήσεις της Αρχαιότητας στη Συγκρότηση της Ταυτότητας μιας Πόλης: Η Περίπτωση των Σύγχρονων Δημόσιων Γλυπτών της Θεσσαλονίκης" [The Uses of Antiquity in the Construction of a City's Identity: The Case of the Contemporary Public Sculptures of Thessaloniki]. PhD diss., National Technical University of Athens.

Galiniki, Styliana, and Esther Solomon. 2014. "'Voglio per lui la pace eterna': Διεκδικώντας την Ελληνική Αρχαιότητα στην Ύστερη Οθωμανική Θεσσαλονίκη (1872–1912)" ['Voglio per lui la pace eterna': Claiming Greek Antiquity in late Ottoman Salonica (1872–1912)]. Proceedings of the international conference: Thessaloniki on the Eve of 1912, Thessaloniki, September 21–23, 2012. Accessed July 26, 2016. http://tinyurl.com/h3jl9mo.

Garden, Mary Catherine. 2006. "The Heritage Scape: Looking at Landscapes of the Past." *International Journal of Heritage Studies* 12 (5): 394–411.

Gegner, Martin, and Bart Ziino, eds. 2012. *The Heritage of War.* Abingdon: Routledge.

Gnecco, Cristóbal. 2015. "Heritage in Multicultural Times." In *The Palgrave Handbook of Contemporary Heritage Research,* edited by Emma Waterton and Steve Watson, 263–80. Basingstoke: Palgrave Macmillan.

Gourgouris, Stathis. 1996. *Dream Nation: Enlightenment, Colonization and the Institution of Modern Greece.* Palo Alto, CA: Stanford University Press.

Graham, Brian, Gregory Ashworth, and John Tunbridge. 2000. *A Geography of Heritage: Power, Culture, and Economy.* Abingdon: Routledge.

Graham, Brian, and Peter Howard, eds. 2008. *The Ashgate Research Companion to Heritage and Identity.* London: Ashgate.

Gremotsis, Kostas. 2011. "Το Αρχαιολογικό Μουσείο Ιωαννίνων. Διερεύνηση Κοινωνικών, Ιστορικών και Ιδεολογικών Αναφορών" [The Archaeological Museum of Ioannina: Exploring Its Social, Historical and Ideological Perspectives]. MA diss., University of Ioannina.

Hadzic, Lejla, and Jonathan Eaton. 2017. "Rebuilding the Broken: Regional Restoration Camps as a Meeting Platform in the Western Balkans." In *Heritage and Peacebuilding*, edited by Diana Walters, Daniel Laven, and Peter Davis, 205–20. Woodbridge: Boydell and Brewer.

Haldrup, Michael, and Jørgen Ole Bærenholdt. 2015. "Heritage as Performance." In *The Palgrave Handbook of Contemporary Heritage Research*, edited by Emma Waterton and Steve Watson, 52–68. Basingstoke: Palgrave Macmillan.

Hall, Stuart. 2008. "Whose Heritage? Un-settling 'The Heritage,' Re-imagining the Post-nation." In *The Heritage Reader*, edited by Graham Fairclough, Rodney Harrison, John Jameson, and John Schofield, 219–28. London: Routledge.

Hammami, Feras, and Daniel Laven. 2017. "Rethinking Heritage from Peace: Reflections from the Palestinian-Israeli Context." In *Heritage and Peacebuilding*, edited by Diana Walters, Daniel Laven, and Peter Davis, 137–48. Woodbridge: Boydell and Brewer.

Hamilakis, Yannis. 2007. *The Nation and Its Ruins: Antiquity, Archaeology, and National Imagination in Greece.* Oxford: Oxford University Press.

———. 2013. *Archaeology and the Senses: Human Experience, Memory and Affect.* Cambridge: Cambridge University Press.

———. 2014. "Εθνική Θησαυροθηρία ή Κριτική Αρχαιολογία;" [National Treasure-Hunting or Critical Archaeology?]. *I Avgi*, August 24, 2014. Accessed July 30, 2016. http://www.avgi.gr/article/10812/3762556/ethnike-thesaurotheria-e-kritike-archaiologia-.

———. 2015. "Eternal Debts and Occult Economies: The Archaeo-Politics of the Contemporary Crisis." Inaugural professorial lecture at the University of Southampton, December 8, 2015. Accessed July 30, 2016. https://coursecast.soton.ac.uk/Panopto/Pages/Viewer.aspx?id=a70788c0-2b51-474e-8a19-1a67771ea658.

———. 2016. "Οι Αρχαιολογίες της Βίαιης Μετανάστευσης" [Archaeologies of Forced Migration]. Keynote speech, *Dialogues in Archaeology* 2, Lesvos, April 14, 2016.

———. 2017. "Για μια Αρχαιολογία της Σύγχρονης Μετανάστευσης" [Towards an Archaeology of Contemporary Migrations]. Keynote speech, *Dialogues in Archaeology* 3, Ioannina, June 1, 2017.

Hamilakis, Yannis, and Aris Anagnostopoulos, eds. 2009a. *Archaeological Ethnographies.* Special double issue, *Public Archaeology* 8 (2–3).

———. 2009b. "What Is Archaeological Ethnography?" In *Archaeological Ethnographies*, edited by Yannis Hamilakis and Aris Anagnostopoulos, 65–87, special double issue, *Public Archaeology* 8 (2–3).

Hamilakis, Yannis, and Fotis Ifantidis. 2016. *Camera Kalaureia: An Archaeological Photo-Ethnography.* Oxford: Archaeopress. Accessed July 9, 2020. https://www.researchgate.net/publication/305109376_Camera_Kalaureia_An_Archaeological_Photo-Ethnography_Mia_Archaiologike_Photo-Ethnographia.

Hamilakis, Yannis, and Nicoletta Momigliano, eds. 2006. *Archaeology and European Modernity: Producing and Consuming the "Minoans."* Padova: Botega d'Erasmo; *Creta Antica*, special issue.

Hamilakis, Yannis, and Eleana Yalouri. 1996. "Antiquities as Symbolic Capital in Modern Greek Society." *Antiquity* 70: 117–29.

———. 1999. "Sacralizing the Past: Cults of Archaeology in Modern Greece." *Archaeological Dialogues* 6 (2): 115–35.

Handler, Richard, and Eric Gable. 1997. *The New History in an Old Museum: Creating the Past at Colonial Williamsburg.* Durham, NC: Duke University Press.

Harloe, Katherine, Nicoletta Momigliano, and Alexandre Farnoux, eds. 2018. *Hellenomania.* London: Routledge.

Harrison, Rodney, 2008. "The Politics of the Past: Conflict in the Use of Heritage in the Modern World." In *The Heritage Reader*, edited by Graham Fairclough, Rodney Harrison, John Jameson, and John Schofield, 177–90. London: Routledge.

———, ed. 2010. *Understanding the Politics of Heritage.* Manchester: Manchester University Press.

———, ed. 2013. *Heritage. Critical Approaches.* Abingdon: Routledge.

Harvey, David. 2008. "The History of Heritage." In *The Ashgate Research Companion to Heritage and Identity*, edited by Brian Graham and Peter Howard, 19–36. London: Ashgate.

———. 2015. "Heritage and Scale: Settings Boundaries and Relations." *International Journal of Heritage Studies* 21 (4): 577–93.

Hastaoglou, Vilma. 2008. "Νεωτερικότητα και Μνήμη στη Διαμόρφωση της Μεταπολεμικής Θεσσαλονίκης" [Modernity and Memory in the Shaping of Postwar Thessaloniki]. In *Η Θεσσαλονίκη στο Μεταίχμιο: Η Πόλη ως Διαδικασία Αλλαγών* [Thessaloniki on the Verge: The City as a Change Process], edited by Grigoris Kafkalas, Lois Labrianidis, and Nikos Papamichos, 151–98. Athens: Kritiki.

Hekimoglou, Evangelos. 2012. "The Local Historiography of Thessaloniki and the Issue of Multicultural Coexistence." Paper presented at the international conference: The Holocaust in Thessaloniki, Council of Europe, October 16–17, 2012. Accessed May 8, 2018. https://www.academia.edu/4359704/%CE%A4he_Local_Historiography_of_Thessaloniki_and_the_Issue_of_Multicultural_Coexistence.

Herzfeld, Michael. 1982. *Ours Once More: Folklore, Ideology, and the Making of Modern Greece.* Austin: University of Texas Press.

———. 1987. *Anthropology through the Looking-Glass: Critical Ethnography in the Margins of Europe.* Cambridge: Cambridge University Press.

———. 1991. *A Place in History: Social and Monumental Time in a Cretan Town.* Princeton, NJ: Princeton University Press.

———. 1997. *Cultural Intimacy: Social Poetics in the Nation-State.* London: Routledge.

———. 2002. "The Absent Presence: Discourses of Crypto-Colonialism." *South Atlantic Quarterly* 101: 899–926.

———. 2003. "Pom Mahakan: Humanity and Order in the Historic Center of Bangkok." *Thailand Human Rights Journal* 1: 101–19.

———. 2006. "Spatial Cleansing: Monumental Vacuity and the Idea of the West." *Journal of Material Culture* 11 (1–2): 127–49.

———. 2009. *Evicted from Eternity: The Restructuring of Modern Rome.* Chicago: University of Chicago Press.

———. 2012. "Whose Rights to Which Past? Archaeologists, Anthropologists, and the Ethics of Heritage in the Global Hierarchy of Value." In *Archaeology and Anthropology: Past, Present and Future*, edited by David Shankland, 41–64. London: Berg.

Hodder, Ian. 1998. "The Past as Passion and Play: Catalhoyuk as a Site of Conflict in the Construction of Multiple Pasts." In *Archaeology under Fire: Nationalism, Politics and Heritage in the Eastern Mediterranean and the Middle East*, edited by Lynn Meskell, 124–39. London: Routledge.

Holtorf, Conelius, and Troels Myrap Kristensen. 2014. "Heritage Erasure: Rethinking 'Protection' and 'Preservation.'" *International Journal of Heritage Studies* 21 (4): 313–17.

Innocenti, Perla. 2015. *Cultural Networks in Migrating Heritage: Intersecting Theories and Practices*. London: Routledge.

Jenkins, Ian. 1992. *Archaeologists and Aesthetes in the Sculpture Galleries of the British Museum 1800–1939*. London: British Museum Press.

———. 2003. "Ideas of Antiquity: Classical and Other Ancient Civilizations in the Age of the Enlightenment." In *Enlightenment—Discovering the World in the Eighteenth Century*, edited by Kim Sloan with Andrew Burnett, 168–77. London: British Museum.

Just, Roger. 1989. "Triumph of the Ethnos." In *History and Ethnicity*, edited by Elizabeth Tonkin, Mayron McDonald, and Malcolm Kenneth Chapman, 71–88. London: Routledge.

Kakampoura, Rea. 2006. "Λαογραφικά Αρχεία και Εθνική Ταυτότητα. Μια σχέση αλληλεπίδρασης" [Folklore Archives and National Identity: A Relationship of Interaction]. *Kritiki Diepistimonikotita* 2: 108–135.

Karafoulidou, Vicky. 2018. *". . . της Μεγάλης Ταύτης Ιδέας." Όψεις της Εθνικής Ιδεολογίας, 1770–1854* [. . . of this Great Idea. Aspects of National Ideology, 1770–1854]. Athens: Polis.

Karp, Ivan, and Steven D. Lavine, eds. 1991. *Exhibiting Cultures: The Poetics and Politics of Museum Display*. Washington, DC: Smithsonian Institution.

Karpozilos, Kostis, and Dimitris Christopoulos. 2018. *10+1 Ερωτήσεις & Απαντήσεις για το Μακεδονικό* [10 +1 Questions and Answers on the Macedonian Issue]. Athens: Polis.

Kirshenblatt-Gimblett, Barbara. 1998. *Destination Culture: Tourism, Museums, and Heritage*. Berkeley, CA: University of California Press.

Knapp, Bernard A., and Sophia Antoniadou. 1998. "Archaeology, Politics and the Cultural Heritage of Cyprus." In *Archaeology under Fire: Nationalism, Politics and Heritage in the Eastern Mediterranean and the Middle East*, edited by Lynn Meskell, 13–43. London: Routledge.

Kotsakis, Kostas. 1991. "The Powerful Past: Theoretical Trends in Greek Archaeology." In *Archaeological Theory in Europe*, edited by Ian Hodder, 65–90. London: Routledge.

———. 1998. "The Past Is Ours." In *Archaeology under Fire: Nationalism, Politics and Heritage in the Eastern Mediterranean and the Middle East*, edited by Lynn Meskell, 44–67. London: Routledge.

Küchler, Susanne 1999. "The Place of Memory." In *The Art of Forgetting*, edited by Adrian Forty and Susanne Küchler, 53–72. Oxford: Berg.

LaFreniere, Kelsey. 2012. "Commemorating the Holocaust and Communism: The Politics of Hungarian Public Memory." Honors theses. Paper 27. Accessed July 27, 2016. http://scarab.bates.edu/cgi/viewcontent.cgi?article=1053&context=honorstheses.

Layton, Robert. 2008. "Conflict in the Archaeology of Living Traditions." In *The Heritage Reader*, edited by Graham Fairclough, Rodney Harrison, John Jameson, and John Schofield, 256–73. London: Routledge.

Layton, Robert, Peter Stone, and Julian Thomas, eds. 2001. *Destruction and Conservation of Cultural Property*. London: Routledge.

Leontis, Artemis. 1995. *Topographies of Hellenism: Mapping the Homeland.* Ithaca, NY: Cornell University Press.

Lévy, Bernard-Henri. 2020. "Lesbos: La Honte de l'Europe." *Paris Match*, July 1, 2020. Accessed July 9, 2020. https://www.parismatch.com/Actu/International/Lesbos-la-honte-de-l-Europe-1692083.

Logan, William, and Keir Reeves. 2009a. "Introduction. Remembering Places of Pain and Shame." In *Places of Pain and Shame: Dealing with "Difficult Heritage,"* edited by William Logan and Keir Reeves, 1–14. London: Routledge.

———, eds. 2009b. *Places of Pain and Shame: Dealing with "Difficult Heritage."* London: Routledge.

Logan, William, Máiréad Nic Craith, and Ullrich Kockel, eds. 2015. *A Companion to Heritage Studies.* Chichester: Wiley-Blackwell.

Loukaki, Argyro. 2008. *Living Ruins: Value Conflicts.* Aldershot: Ashgate.

———. 1988. "Classical Antiquities as National and Global Heritage." *Antiquity* 62: 726–35.

Lowenthal, David. 1988. "Classical Antiquities as National and Global Heritage." *Antiquity* 62: 726–35.

———. 1998. *The Heritage Crusade and the Spoils of History.* Cambridge: Cambridge University Press.

Macdonald, Sharon. 2009. *Difficult Heritage: Negotiating the Nazi Past in Nuremberg and Beyond.* London: Routledge.

———. 2013. *Memorylands: Heritage and Identity in Europe Today.* London: Routledge.

Massey, Doreen. 2005. *For Space.* London: Sage.

Mazower, Mark. 2004. *Salonica, City of Ghosts: Christians, Muslims and Jews, 1430–1950.* New York: Knopf.

———. 2008. "Archaeology, Nationalism and the Land in Modern Greece." In *A Singular Antiquity: Archaeology and Hellenic Identity in Twentieth-Century Greece*, edited by Dimitris Damaskos and Dimitris Plantzos, 33–41. Athens: Benaki Museum.

Meskell, Lynn, ed. 1998. *Archaeology under Fire: Nationalism, Politics, and Heritage in the Eastern Mediterranean and the Middle East.* London: Routledge.

Michael-Matsas, Savvas. 2015. "Greece: The Broken Link." *Critique: Journal of Socialist Theory* 43 (3–4): 313–27.

Mirtsioti, Giota. 2010 "Κατεδαφίζονται τα Καστρόπληκτα" [Kastroplikta Settlement Is Being Demolished]. *Kathimetini*, January 16, 2010. Accessed July 28, 2016. http://www.kathimerini.gr/382063/article/epikairothta/ellada/katedafizontai-ta-kastroplhkta.

Morris, Ian. 1994. "Archaeologies of Greece." In *Classical Greece: Ancient Histories and Modern Archaeologies*, edited by Ian Morris, 8–47. Cambridge: Cambridge University Press.

Mouliou, Marlen. 2008. "Museum Representations of the Classical Past in Post-war Greece: A Critical Analysis." In *A Singular Antiquity: Archaeology and Hellenic Identity in Twentieth-Century Greece*, edited by Dimitris Damaskos and Dimitris Plantzos, 83–109. Athens: Benaki Museum.

Myers, Adrian, and Gabriel Moshenska, eds. 2011. *Archaeologies of Internment.* New York: Springer.

Myrogiannis, Stratos. 2012. *The Emergence of a Greek Identity (1700–1821).* Newcastle upon Tyne: Cambridge Scholars.

Nelson, Robert S., and Margaret Olin, eds. 2003. *Monuments and Memory, Made and Unmade.* Chicago: University of Chicago Press.

Nikolentzos, Konstantinos. 2003. *Όψεις της Διαχείρισης της Αρχαιολογικής Πολιτικής. Οι Σχέσεις του ΥΠ.ΠΟ με τις Ξένες Αρχαιολογικές Σχολές και την εν Αθήναις Αρχαιολογική Εταιρεία.* [Aspects of the Management of Archaeological Policy: Relations between the Ministry of Culture, the Foreign Archaeological Schools and the Archaeological Society at Athens]. Athens: National School of Public Administration and Local Government. Accessed July 31, 2016. http://www.ekdd.gr/ekdda/files/ergasies_esdd/14/2/504.pdf.

Papadimitriou, Nikos, and Aris Anagnostopoulos, eds. 2017. *Το Παρελθόν στο Παρόν. Μνήμη, Ιστορία και Αρχαιότητα στη Σύγχρονη Ελλάδα* [The Past in the Present. Memory, History and Antiquity in Contemporary Greece]. Athens: Kastaniotis.

Papanikolaou, Dimitris. 2013. "Η Καλή Ζωή στην Αποικία. Σωφρονισμός, Βιοπολιτική, Θανατοπολιτική" [Nice Life in the Colony: Correction, Bio-Politics, Thanatopolitics]. *Tehnientos*, May 2, 2013. Accessed July 30, 2016. http://tinyurl.com/goaksju.

Pantazopoulos, Yannis. 2019. "Η Σύγκρουση για τις Αρχαιότητες στο Μετρό της Θεσσαλονίκης" [The Conflict over the Antiquities of the Thessaloniki Metro]. *Lifo*, December 17, 2019. Accessed July 11, 2020. https://www.lifo.gr/articles/archaeology_articles/251383/i-sygkroysi-gia-tis-arxaiotites-sto-metro-tis-thessalonikis-poies-einai-ti-lene-oi-emplekomenoi.

Plantzos, Dimitris. 2008. "Archaeology and Hellenic Identity, 1896–2004: The Frustrated Vision." In *A Singular Antiquity: Archaeology and Hellenic Identity in Twentieth-Century Greece*, edited by Dimitris Damaskos and Dimitris Plantzos, 10–30. Athens: Benaki Museum.

———. 2009. "Η Κιβωτός και το Έθνος: ένα Σχόλιο για την Υποδοχή του Νέου Μουσείου Ακροπόλεως" [The Ark and the Nation: A Comment on the Reception of the New Acropolis Museum]. *Sihrona Themata* [Current Issues] 106: 14–18.

———. 2010. "'Il n'y a pas de hors texte': Το Μουσείο της Ακρόπολης και τα Απόνερα του Ιδεαλισμού" ["Il n'y a pas de hors texte": The Acropolis Museum and the Wake of Idealism]. *Tetradia Mousiologias* 7: 23–29.

———. 2014a. "Amphipolitics." *The Athens Review of Books* 55. Accessed July 25, 2016. http://athensreviewofbooks.com/?p=1333.

———. 2014b. "Dead Archaeologists, Buried Gods: Archaeology as an Agent of Modernity." In *Re-Imagining the Past: Antiquity and Modern Greek Culture*, edited by Dimitris Tziovas, 147–64. Oxford: Oxford University Press.

Politakis, Dimitris. 2014. "Documenta 14: Τι Έχει να μας Μάθει η Αθήνα;" [Documenta 14: What Does Athens Have to Teach Us?]. *Propaganda*, October 15, 2014. Accessed July 30, 2016. http://popaganda.gr/documenta-14-ti-tha-mas-mathi-athina-2017/.

Rikou, Elpida and Eleana Yalouri. 2017. "Learning from documenta: A Research Project between Art and Anthropology." In *On Curating* 33, edited by Nanne Buurman and Dorothee Richter. Accessed May 4, 2018. http://www.on-curating.org/issue-33-reader/learning-from-documenta-a-research-project-between-art-and-anthropology.html#.WuxxuZe-lPZ.

Roberts, Catherine, and Philip R. Stone. 2014. "Dark Tourism and Dark Heritage: Emergent Themes, Issues and Consequences." In *Displaced Heritage: Responses to Disaster, Trauma and Loss*, edited by Ian Convery, Gerard Corsane, and Peter Davis, 9–18. Woodbridge: Boydell and Brewer.

Rowlands, Michael. 2002. "Heritage and Cultural Property." In *The Material Culture Reader*, edited by Victor Buchli, 105–14. Oxford: Berg.

Sakka, Niki. 2002. "Αρχαιολογικές Δραστηριότητες στην Ελλάδα (1928–1940): Πολιτικές και Ιδεολογικές Διαστάσεις" [Archaeological Activities in Greece (1928–1940): Political and Ideological Aspects]. PhD diss., University of Crete.

Sandell, Richard, ed. 2002. *Museums, Society, Inequality*. London: Routledge.

Sather-Wagstaff, Joy. 2011. *Heritage That Hurts: Tourists in the Memoryscapes of September 11*. Walnut Creek, CA: Left Coast.

Scott, James, C. 1985. *Weapons of the Weak: Everyday Forms of Peasant Resistance*. New Haven, CT: Yale University Press.

Shankland, David. 1996. "The Anthropology of an Archaeological Presence." In *On the Surface: The Re-opening of Çatalhöyuk*, edited by Ian Hodder, 349–57. Cambridge: MacDonald Institute.

———, ed. 2012. *Archaeology and Anthropology: Past, Present and Future*. London: Berg.

Shanks, Michael. 1996. *The Classical Archaeology of Greece: Experiences of the Discipline*. London: Routledge.

———. 2008. "Archaeology and Politics." In *The Blackwell Companion to Archaeology*, edited by John Bintliff, 490–508. Oxford: Blackwell.

Shanks, Michael, and Cristopher Tilley. 1992. *Reconstructing Archaeology: Theory and Practice*. London: Routledge.

Silverman, Helaine, ed. 2011a. *Contested Cultural Heritage: Religion, Nationalism, Erasure and Exclusion in a Global World*. New York: Springer.

———. 2011b. "Contested Cultural Heritage: A Selective Historiography." In *Contested Cultural Heritage. Religion, Nationalism, Erasure and Exclusion in a Global World*, edited by Helaine Silverman, 1–50. New York: Springer.

———. 2015. "Heritage and Authenticity." In *The Palgrave Handbook of Contemporary Heritage Research*, edited by Emma Waterton and Steve Watson, 69–88. Basingstoke: Palgrave Macmillan.

Sloan, Kim 2003. "'Aimed at Universality and Belonging to the Nation': The Enlightenment and the British Museum." In *Enlightenment—Discovering the World in the Eighteenth Century*, edited by Kim Sloan with Andrew Burnett, 12–25. London: British Museum.

Smith, George, Phyllis Messenger, and Hilary Soderland, eds. 2010. *Heritage Values in Contemporary Society*. Walnut Creek, CA: Left Coast.

Smith, Laurajane. 2004. *Archaeological Theory and the Politics of Cultural Heritage*. London: Routledge.

———. 2006. *Uses of Heritage*. London: Routledge.

Smith, Laurajane, and Emma Waterton. 2009. *Heritage, Communities and Archaeology*. London: Duckworth.

Smith, Laurajane, and Gary Campbell. 2015. "The Elephant in the Room: Heritage, Affect and Emotion." In *A Companion to Heritage Studies*, edited by William Logan, Máiréad Nic Craith, and Ullrich Kockel, 442–60. Chichester: Wiley-Blackwell.

Solomon, Esther. 2006. "Knossos: Social Uses of a Monumental Landscape." In *Archaeology and European Modernity: Producing and Consuming the "Minoans,"* edited by Yannis Hamilakis and Nicoletta Momigliano, 163–82. Padova: Botega d'Erasmo; *Creta Antica*, special issue.

———. 2007. "'Multiple Historicities' on the Island of Crete: The Significance of Minoan Archaeological Heritage in Everyday Life." PhD diss., University College London.

———. Forthcoming. "Minoan Columns and the 'Knossian Red': Thoughts about the Reproduction of the Past in the Present of Crete." In *Replica Knowledge: Histories,*

Processes and Identities. International Conference at the Tieranatomisches Theater of the Humboldt University, Berlin, February 2–4, 2017, edited by Felix Sattier and Anna Simandiraki-Grimshaw.

Solomon, Esther, and Eleni Apostolidou, eds. 2018. "*Museums, Museum Education and 'Difficult' Heritage.*" Special issue, *MuseumEdu* 6. Volos: University of Thessaly. Accessed July 23, 2019. http://museumedulab.ece.uth.gr/main/en/node/431.

Solomon, Esther, and Styliana Galiniki. 2018. "Las Incantadas of Salonica: Searching for 'Enchantment' in a City's Exiled Heritage." In *Hellenomania*, edited by Katherine Harloe, Nicoletta Momigliano, and Alexandre Farnoux, 271–310. London: Routledge.

Sørensen, Marie Louise Stig, and Dacia Viejo-Rose, eds. 2015. *War and Cultural Heritage. Biographies of Place.* Cambridge: Cambridge University Press.

Stewart, Charles. 1994. "Syncretism and a Dimension of Nationalist Discourse in Modern Greece." In *Syncretism/Anti-Syncretism: The Politics of Religious Synthesis*, edited by Charles Stewart and Rosalind Shaw, 127–43. London: Routledge.

———. 2001. "Immanent or Eminent Domain? The Contest Over Thessaloniki's Rotonda." In *Destruction and Conservation of Cultural Property*, edited by Robert Layton, Peter Stone, and Julian Thomas, 182–98. London: Routledge.

Stolcke, Verena. 1995. "Talking Culture: New Boundaries, New Rhetorics of Exclusion in Europe." *Current Anthropology* 36: 1–26.

Stroulia, Anna, and Susan Buck Sutton, eds. 2010a. *Archaeology in Situ: Sites, Archaeology and Communities in Greece.* Lanham, MD: Lexington.

———. 2010b. "Archaeological Sites and the Chasm between Past and Present." In *Archaeology in Situ: Sites, Archaeology and Communities in Greece*, edited by Anna Stroulia and Susan Buck Sutton, 3–50. Lanham, MD: Lexington.

Stoneman, Richard. 2010. *Land of Lost Gods: The Search for Classical Greece.* Rev. ed. London: I. B. Tauris.

Tilley, Christopher. 1994. *A Phenomenology of Landscape: Places, Paths and Monuments.* Oxford: Berg.

———. 1999. *Metaphor and Material Culture.* Oxford: Blackwell.

———. 2001. "Ethnography and Material Culture." In *The Sage Handbook of Ethnography*, edited by Paul Anthony Atkinson, Amanda Coffey, Sara Delamont, John Lofland, and Lyn H. Lofland, 258–72. London: Sage.

———. 2017. *Landscape in the Longue Durée: A History and Theory of Pebbles in a Pebbled Heathland Landscape.* London: UCL.

———. 2019. "How Does It Feel? Phenomenology, Excavation and Sensory Experience: Notes for a New Ethnographic Field Practice." In *Handbook of Sensory Archaeology*, edited by Jo Day and Robin Skeates, e-book. London: Routledge.

Tilley, Christopher, Webb Keane, Susanne Küchler, Mike Rowlands, and Patricia Spyer, eds. 2006. *Handbook of Material Culture.* London: Sage.

Tolia-Kelly, Divya P., Emma Waterton, and Steve Watson, eds. 2017. *Heritage, Affect and Emotion: Politics, Practices and Infrastructures.* New York: Routledge.

Trigger, Bruce. 1989. *A History of Archaeological Thought.* Cambridge: Cambridge University Press.

Tunbridge, John. 2008. "Whose Heritage to Conserve? Cross-Cultural Reflections on Political Dominance and Urban Heritage Conservation." In *The Heritage Reader*, edited by Graham Fairclough, Rodney Harrison, John Jameson, and John Schofield, 235–44. London: Routledge.

Tunbridge, John, and Gregory Ashworth. 1996. *Dissonant Heritage: The Management of the Past as a Resource in Conflict*. Chichester: John Wiley.
Tziovas, Dimitris, 1989. *Οι Μεταμορφώσεις του Εθνισμού και το Ιδεολόγημα της Ελληνικότητας στο Μεσοπόλεμο* [The Metamorphoses of Ethnicity and the Ideological Construction of Greekness in the Inter-war Period]. Athens: Odisseas.
———, ed. 2014a. *Re-Imagining the Past: Antiquity and Modern Greek Culture*. Oxford: Oxford University Press.
———. 2014b. "Introduction: Decolonizing Antiquity, Heritage Politics and Performing the Past." In *Re-Imagining the Past: Antiquity and Modern Greek Culture*, edited by Dimitris Tziovas, 1–26. Oxford: Oxford University Press.
———, ed. 2017. *Greece in Crisis: The Cultural Politics of Austerity*. London: I. B. Tauris.
Urry, John. 2002. *The Tourist Gaze*. London: Sage.
Voutsaki, Sofia. 2003. "Archaeology and the Construction of the Past in Nineteenth-Century Greece." In *Constructions of the Greek Past: Identity and Historical Consciousness from Antiquity to the Present*, edited by Hero Hokwerda, 231–55. Groningen: Egbert Forsten.
Voutsaki, Sofia, and Paul Cartledge, eds. 2017. *Ancient Monuments and Modern Identities. Towards a Critical History of Archaeology in 19th and 20th century Greece*. London: Routledge.
Walters, Diana, Daniel Laven, and Peter Davis, eds. 2017. *Heritage and Peacebuilding*. Woodbridge: Boydell and Brewer.
Waterton, Emma, and Steve Watson, eds. 2015a. *The Palgrave Handbook of Contemporary Heritage Research*. Basingstoke: Palgrave Macmillan.
———. 2015b. "Heritage as a Focus of Research: Past, Present and New Directions." In *The Palgrave Handbook of Contemporary Heritage Research*, edited by Emma Waterton and Steve Watson, 1–17. Basingstoke: Palgrave Macmillan.
Watson, Steve, and Emma Waterton, eds. 2010. *Culture, Heritage and Representation: Perspectives on Visuality and the Past*. Aldershot: Ashgate.
Wienberg, Jes. 2014. "Four Churches and a Lighthouse—Preservation, 'Creative Dismantling' or Destruction." *Danish Journal of Archaeology* 3 (1): 68–75.
Winter, Tim. 2014. "Material Culture and Contested Heritage in Tourism." In *The Wiley Blackwell Companion to Tourism*, edited by Alan A. Lew, C. Michael Hall, and Allan M. Williams, 368–77. Chichester: John Wiley and Sons
Yalouri, Eleana. 2001. *The Acropolis: Global Fame, Local Claim*. London: Berg.
———. 2010. "Η Δυναμική των Μνημείων: Αναζητήσεις στο Πεδίο της Μνήμης και της Λήθης" [The Dynamics of Monuments: Quests in the Field of Memory and Oblivion]. In *Αμφισβητούμενοι Χώροι στην Πόλη: Χωρικές Προσεγγίσεις του Πολιτισμού* [Contested Spaces in the City: Spatial Approaches to Culture], edited by Kostas Yannakopoulos and Yannis Yannitsiotis, 349–80. Athens: Alexandria.
Young, James. 1993. *The Texture of Memory: Holocaust Memorials and Meaning*. New Haven, CT: Yale University Press.

Part I

Between Nationalism, Colonialism, and Crypto-Colonialism: Historical Perspectives and Current Implications

1 Hellas *Mon Amour*

Revisiting Greece's National "Sites of Trauma"

Dimitris Plantzos

For Lack of Anything Else

In *The Archaeologist*, originally published in 1903, Greek novelist Andreas Karkavitsas presents Greece as a fledgling nation-state in a lethal entanglement with its once glorious past (Karkavitsas 2002).[1] In the story, two brothers are trying to protect the land they have inherited from their famed ancestors; one brother is clever and pragmatic, and the other ("the archaeologist") is devoted to the study of the past and its tangible remains. Whereas the latter believes that only the promotion of their common heritage will help them survive in a hostile world, the former urges his brother to "live in the present" and stop dreaming of bygone days of glory. The archaeologist's foreign friends are interested only in the antiquities hidden on his land, and they encourage him to devote himself exclusively to the study of the past and the promotion of his property's archaeological wealth. At the end of the novel, the archaeologist is killed when a marble statue he has excavated collapses and crushes him during the wedding of his younger brother, who then lives happily ever after with his peasant wife.

Karkavitsas's protagonist, Aristodemus, an archaeologist by conviction and not by trade, is described as a victim of his own archaeolatry as well as of the disingenuous Graecophilia of his foreign friends, who style themselves with ancient Greek names, read old books, and rob archaeological sites in an attempt to construct a cultural genealogy for themselves. The Westernized Aristodemus seeks his own identity, as well as that of his nation, in the foreign books he reads. He is contrasted with the illiterate peasant girl Elpida ("Hope"), the protagonist's brother's fiancée, who (according to the text) could not possibly survive "under the eyeglasses" of the knowledgeable foreign men, but knows the truth of her origins as they have been transmitted to her from generation to generation.

To a great extent, *The Archaeologist* is an allegorical parody of the *Altertumswissenschaft* (science of antiquity or classical studies) movement and the way

Greece found itself trapped in a colonial premise. Meticulous study of the classical past in all its manifestations—texts, facts, artifacts—emerged in the eighteenth century as a necessary nation-building apparatus expected to "instill self-discipline, idealism, and nobility of character" in a rising European middle class of public servants and bureaucrats (Marchand 1996, 19). In Germany in particular, this practice turned into nothing less than a cultural obsession. Greece and Rome were in effect colonized by this aggressive pursuit of historical education, turning the study of classical heritage into a device by means of which to discriminate between the classically educated upper classes and the ignorant commoners (Toner 2013). In Greece, archaeophilia (i.e., the love of things ancient) was often deployed as a yardstick for patriotism (Plantzos 2008).

Presented in *The Archaeologist* as a valuable piece of farmland, Greece is also described as a country threatened with extinction at the hands of its persistently hostile neighbors. In the novel, the Turks and the Bulgarians are thinly disguised as such unfriendly "friends," divided from Aristodemus's family by centuries-old feuds. The Germans, the British, and the French are portrayed as well-educated archaeophiles who compliment the protagonist on his cultural heritage and advise him on its management but are there to further their own cultural and political interests. Throughout the nineteenth century, Greek ruins were appropriated by foreign archaeological expeditions led primarily by the French and the Germans. These groups often insisted on their rights to export a selection of archaeological finds made on Greek soil to their countries of origin. Fierce debates between Greece and several European states over the ownership of artifacts ensued, as well as vociferous discussions within Greece itself (Kalpaxis 1996). In the novel, Aristodemus's Greece is in dire need of any help it can get from powerful foreigners, and its glorious past is presented as the only reason they would think of offering Greece their support in return. Obliging to his friends and impatient with members of his own household who fail to see the importance of such heritage, Karkavitsas's hero tries to strengthen the ties of his land's archaeological finds to the minds and hearts of these eloquent dilettantes: "a rare manuscript each and some marbles from our digs" are his parting gifts to them, in the hope that "the ancestors will remind you a bit of their successors" (Karkavitsas 2002, 85).

What Karkavitsas is describing in his novel, therefore, is his country's past as an intellectual colony. Greece as a modern nation-state was constructed from scratch, based on a neoclassical model aiming at the creation of a brave new political and cultural world. What this entailed was a systematic colonization of Greece's classical past as, in the words of Neni Panourgiá, "the gaze towards the future passes through a re-articulation, a re-formation and repossession of an antique ideality" (Panourgiá 2004, 167). According to this scholar, "what was at stake [in the establishment of neoclassicism as the Greek cultural modality par excellence], not only in Greece but throughout Europe, was the institution of modernity itself and in that process what we encounter in Greek neoclassicism is the process of transformation of place into space: Greece became the European pla(y)cespace" (Panourgiá 2004, 177). At the same time, I would add, Greece became Europe's heterotopic site of origins as well as cultural playground.[2] Greece has been endowed ever since with the practice of aestheticizing its past, now quite stereotypical, as a new form of governmentality, as a tool by means of which to forge and discipline the national subject. However, to Karkavitsas and many other Greek intellectuals active across the entire span of the twentieth century, this process was quite traumatic because it promoted Greece's Hellenic past over its more recent Byzantine and folk cultures—its very "soul," as these are called in *The Archaeologist*. More to the point, it rendered Greece and its citizenry into the cultural (and political) domain of other nations: philhellenism, Graecophilia and other such modern vices allowed Greece's foes, disguised as friends, to forge and discipline the inhabitants of Greece into modern supranational subjects, expected to commit themselves to Europe's political projects at the same time they were curating Europe's archaeological past.

This agenda is illustrated at one point in *The Archaeologist*, when the protagonist's foreign friends assure him that what the Greeks have to do is to "dig the soil and amass every stone belonging to the age [of the ancients]. To open museums and schools, and nothing else" (Karkavitsas 2002, 18). In his novel, therefore, Karkavitsas put forward what he believed to be a new strategy for the nation: to redefine Greece's temporality as a living culture rather than a fossilized essence suitable only for museums and libraries. Consequently, he urged his contemporaries to promote national continuity rather than neoclassical revival.

By the time Karkavitsas was writing his novel, however, all major Athenian museums, and many regional ones, were already up and running: the National Archaeological Museum, the Acropolis Museum, the Numismatics Museum, and the Epigraphic Museum in Athens, as well as the museums at Olympia, Sparta, Epidaurus, and so on. Four museums were founded in the year 1900 alone: Corinth, Thera, Chalkis, and Mykonos. From 1903 to 1906, nine more were planned to be added, three every year, including the museums at Delphi, Nauplion, Delos, Heraklion, and Volos (Gazi 2008). These museums did what museums are expected to do across the globe: they collected, conserved, preserved, displayed, and explained archaeological artifacts in their domain as tangible evidence substantiating the nation's long, linear, uninterrupted, and exceptional history over the millennia (fig. 1.1). Their tactics and their rhetoric reflect Western expectations of the Greeks as curators of their past, as well as the Greeks' own pride in securing the job.

By the mid-1920s, however, a new attitude toward the collecting and displaying of national treasures was emerging, as can be demonstrated by the case of

Fig. 1.1. Corinth, the Archaeological Museum in the 1910s. Courtesy of American School of Classical Studies at Athens.

Fig. 1.2. Athens, the Benaki Museum; classical and medieval galleries. Photo by D. Plantzos.

the Benaki Museum (first established in 1926), where Greek—indeed, Hellenic—culture is perceived as an organic entity, its lifetime spanning from time immemorial (in fact, from a time before Hellenism itself) to the threshold of the third millennium (fig. 1.2). This narrative persists to the present day: according to the museum's official guidebook, published in 2000, its visitors "will follow, step by step, the historical development of Hellenism as it unfolds through the millennia" (Delivorrias 2000, 27). Describing Greek history as an "exciting journey" and a "true epic," this text explains how modern Greece undertakes its own archaeology: as a soul-searching exercise dealing with the traumas of the past, ultimately confirming Greek exceptionalism. The museum's website, moreover, claims that its collections illustrate "the character of the Greek world through a spectacular historical panorama."[3] According to the same blurb, the time span covered by the exhibition runs "from antiquity and the age of Roman domination to the medieval Byzantine period, from the fall of Constantinople (1453) and the centuries of Frankish and Ottoman occupation to the outbreak of the struggle for independence in 1821, and from the formation of the modern state of Greece (1830) down to 1922, the year in which the Asia Minor disaster took place." Clearly, according to this text, only the contributions of the Hellenes to Greek culture and art are considered legitimate throughout the history of the nation; all others are portrayed as barbarian conquerors waiting to be charmed by the Greek spirit rather than being likely to advance it. The now refurbished permanent exhibition at the museum spans from Cycladic art to a Karagöz screen and figures, a specter (as its Cycladic counterpart) of another culture familiarized by the Greeks through tradition, translation, and inertia. The collection is scattered around the museum's branches and satellite buildings and includes the two Nobels and the one Lenin prize won by Greeks, all for poetry; one of the very few Greek Oscars (for *Zorba the Greek*); and other such national memorabilia. It is a Hellenic panorama indeed, exploring as well as exploiting the nation's past for whatever it's worth, and at the same time displaying Greece as either a traumatic adventure in the unfriendly seas of world history, or as a response to an unforgiving, albeit forgetful, colonial gaze inspecting modern Greece from a Western viewpoint.

The success of this policy is confirmed by the public's enthusiastic embrace of the museum's continuous appeals for funding and donations; bequests of single items or entire collections are the top source of enrichment for its holdings. What started in the 1920s as a top-down attempt to construct an audience responsive to cultural coaching has now, a century later, created a driving force behind the museum's often improvised, largely countertheoretical, and defiantly old-fashioned strategies at interpreting contemporary Greece through its material past. For in the last thirty years or so, we have come to realize that rather than serving as mere illustrators of a people's "character," museums create a nation's past through a complicated, though quite intelligible, system of narratives they deploy on its behalf (Hooper-Greenhill 1992; Bennett 1995). We now understand that discovery, classification, interpretation, and conservation are far from self-evident procedures; they construct both the nation's past and the nation itself as the guardian of that past. In the words of Benedict Anderson, "museums, and the museumizing imagination, are both profoundly political" (Anderson 1991, 178). Through careful selection of certain elements of the past and the elimination of others, museums engage in a rather unsophisticated play of historical remembering, as well as forgetting, in order to produce a viable national identity. More than constructing a nation's sense of itself, museums tend to construct their own viewers, be they nationals or tourists, as subjects of a logocentric, elitist, privileged discourse bequeathed by the Enlightenment. In their efforts to construct their visitors as subjects of their own rhetoric, museums are thus able to forge and promote a hegemonic version of national identity based on what are seen as appropriate narratives regarding the nation's past.

The fashion through which modern Greece chooses to display its classical heritage illustrates the persistent ambivalence in the way the country faces the world to the present day, as well as the strategies deployed by contemporary Greeks to claim classical tradition as their national property. As Stathis Gourgouris has observed, contemporary Greek culture "becomes characteristically insular, experiencing itself as both superior and inferior to Western culture, being both xenophobic and xenomanic, believing itself to be the most privileged and the most oppressed" (Gourgouris 1996, 276). Reiterating modern Greece's connection to its classical past—stereotypically advertised as Europe's own genealogy—creates a pattern of repetitive reenactment, what Sigmund Freud described as an inexplicably persistent history of suffering, and what he clinically termed as "trauma." In a seminal study of historical trauma as both experience and reference, Cathy Caruth theorizes that trauma is "unclaimed experience" or history no one talks about, in order to suggest that visiting and revisiting "the site of trauma"—the place where it all happened—creates new modes of seeing and of listening (Caruth 1996, 56).

Before describing what, in my view, constitutes Greece's modern "sites of trauma," I would like to dwell a bit on one of the main examples used by Caruth in her study: Alain Resnais's 1959 film *Hiroshima Mon Amour*, which she finds "opens up the question of history . . . as an exploration of the relation between history and the body" (Caruth 1996, 26). As it becomes clear through her work, history in that film transcends the concerns of what we see and what we perceive (what can be summarized as "the body" in the line quoted above), as well as the ethics of choosing what to tell (remember) and what not to tell (forget). My interest in Caruth's argument and the film is due to a long sequence at the beginning of the film that concerns the museum in Hiroshima, a sort of "museum of national trauma," which seems to fall outside Caruth's interests (she does not discuss it much in her paper) but would be very interesting for us to discuss here.

In *Hiroshima Mon Amour*, scripted by Marguerite Duras, the viewer witnesses a long, frustrated dialogue between a French actress and a Japanese architect, respectively identified only as *she* and *he*. She finds herself in Hiroshima for a short, thirty-six-hour period in order to participate in an anti-war film project. The two strangers have a brief affair, and the movie follows them through their separation. Besides being a contemplation on the atomic bombing of Hiroshima in 1945, the film dwells on the tension between memory and oblivion, identity and anonymity, and presence and absence, all staged in a bleak landscape of abandonment, defeat, and loss. Despite the film's title, Hiroshima is not really loved by anyone; as a cultural landscape, it has been rendered into a site of conflict claimed by two opposing sides, with one accusing the other of neglect and forgetfulness:

> HE: You saw nothing in Hiroshima. Nothing.
>
> SHE: I saw everything. Everything.
> (Duras 1961, 15)

Thus runs the film's opening dialogue of recriminations between the two former lovers, until the Japanese man accuses the French woman of "not being endowed with memory." According to Marguerite Duras, herself born in what at the time was French Indochina (now Vietnam), memory is the privilege of the colonized whereas oblivion is the crime of the colonizers. Being seen is being remembered, accepted, and recognized, and topographical landmarks help a country to be seen. The film's opening sequence moves among the venues where the town's memory is kept alive: the hospital, where the bomb's victims are treated; and the museum, where the bombing itself is documented. The woman remembers:

> Four times at the museum. Four times at the museum in Hiroshima. I saw the people walking around. The people walking around, lost in thought, among the photographs, the reconstructions, for lack of anything else. The photographs, the photographs, the reconstructions, for lack of anything else. The explanations, for lack of anything else. Four times at the museum in Hiroshima. I watched the people. I myself, lost in thought, looked at the scorched metal. The twisted metal. Metal made as vulnerable as flesh. Human flesh, suspended, as if still alive, its agony still fresh. Stones. Charred stones. Shattered stones. (Duras 1961, 17)

Although Caruth's thesis has been criticized, mostly on empiricist and essentialist grounds, as an "intellectual project of thinking against the grain of Western culture" (Kansteiner and Weilnböck 2010), I still find her definition of cultural trauma—as an experience consisting of an incident of severe physical and mental injury followed by a belated series of symptoms bearing no causal relationship to the original injury—both relevant and compelling. I would therefore like to suggest that Greek archaeological spaces, both museums and sites, operate as "sites of trauma," as the placescapes where the unlived experiences of an imagined past have been revived.

Behind their neoclassical façades, Greek museums built in the years after the liberation and until as late as the 1950s strove to treat the material remains of the Classical past in the ways devised by Western archaeology: meticulous taxonomies, arcane terminologies, essentialist readings, and linear narratives (see fig. 1.1). As already mentioned, the European museum has been deployed within Western societies both as a disciplinary tool and an apparatus for control and surveillance (Hooper-Greenhill 1992; Bennett 1995). Exported beyond the West, the museum functioned as a vehicle for hierarchies and genealogies produced in the West. In the words of Elliot Colla, working on the ways Egyptology as an academic discipline has been used to construct modern Egyptian identities in and out of Egypt, "*artifact* is both a useful label for classifying proper objects of study and a powerful concept that helps to move the horizon of interpretation beyond that of the immediate present" (Colla 2007, 61). Taking material remains of an earlier culture found on Greek soil and turning them into classifiable, collectable, and readable artifacts satisfied the sensibilities of a European elite constructing its own identity on these very artifacts. At the same time, this process, defined by Colla as "artifaction," enabled the repossession of the past, which also meant repossessing the present (Colla 2007, 121–65). It also proved that the Greeks (like the Egyptians, the Indians, or the Siamese at about the same time) were as "modern," "metropolitan-like," and "Western" as anybody. Therefore the relationship of the modern Greek state to classical culture appears to be quasi-metaphysical; already in 1834, the first Greek archaeological law stipulated that antiquities "have been produced by the ancestors of the Greek people" (Voudouri 2008, 126) and were thus taken to be more than just works of historical and aesthetic significance; they were testimonials regarding the indigenous aspect of Hellenic culture. As such, the Greek authorities believe that Greek antiquities stand out compared to any other cultural remains as bearers of a significance that is unique. In a resolution by the Central Archaeological Council in 1963, for example, every remnant of Classical Greek culture was recognized as "unicum," therefore superior to any other work of European or global art and presumably superior to any remains of other cultures found in Greece itself (Voudouri 2008, 125–39).

Museums and sites in contemporary Greece work hard to attract the gaze of the tourist and earn the visitor's appreciation: objects (duly cleaned, restored, and cased according to the appropriate artifaction techniques), signs, and reconstructions—"for lack of anything else"—repeat stories of mourning and loss and relate the trauma of temporality as a belated experience, as an experience forever "unclaimed." However, this very effort to repackage the past as spectacle (in the sense first exploited by Heidegger) in order to suggest Greece's genealogies as well as the world's debt to Greece inaugurates the forgetting of Greece's singularity by forgetting its referential specificity (Caruth 1996, 32); it has already become "classical," "global," and "atemporal." Think of *Hiroshima Mon Amour* once again: the lines of the man in the beginning of the film are the complaints of every Greek, Egyptian, Indian, or Japanese, every local who feels that his or her culture is not really appreciated. While the visitors protest that "they have seen it all," he or she knows "they have seen nothing." The performance of one's "cultural authenticity" remains unnoticed (Dicks 2003, 16–40).

In many instances, cultural patrimony is used by countries in the periphery of the West—be they former colonies such as Egypt or "crypto-colonies" such as Greece,[4] eternally struggling under the shadow of the West—in order to compensate for real or imaginary "national shortcomings." Greek demands for the return of the Elgin Marbles are a case in point (see Hamilakis 2007, 243–86): abducted from Athens by members of the Western elites who were infused with the spirit of neoclassical dilettantism, the "marbles" are now housed in London, in the metropolitan museum par excellence, where they are displayed alongside archaeological remains from the entire world; they appear as objects of world culture and as documents of Britain's imperial force, now heavily subdued. The Greek campaign for the return of the Parthenon or the Elgin Marbles has often become a quasi-postcolonial battle: Greece seems desperate to affirm its cultural supremacy against its "allies," who constantly question its efficiency as a modern state.

For a culture to achieve its decolonization, it needs to attract the colonizer's gaze in the first place. Such conflicts over who controls cultural visibility are waged every time a peripheral culture feels attacked by the appropriation strategies deployed by the metropolis. Intensive restorations of sites and monuments, such as in Olympia, Epidaurus, and the Acropolis itself, create simulacra of ruins—antique rather than ancient—for the gratification of the tourists' need to commemorate their actual presence on the site through the taking of pictures or videos, as well as the Greeks' need to appear worthy of modernity and of their Hellenic past.

In such performances of a modern ethos, Greek archaeological sites and museums utilize strategies, technologies, and narratives taken from the colonial archive in order to reaffirm their allegiance to Western modernity. When neoclassicism seemed to be losing its erstwhile attraction, archaeology in Greece underwent an intensive modernization process, from changes in the appearance of its museums to bold technological advancements in excavation, conservation, reconstruction, and monument enhancement. In that respect, no Greek museum

Fig. 1.3. Athens, the Acropolis Museum; the Parthenon Gallery. Photo by D. Plantzos.

is more "national" than the new Acropolis Museum. As I have argued elsewhere (Plantzos 2011), this museum employs an aggressive and improvised "technology of enchantment" (cf. Gell 1998, 74; see also Wengrow 2007). By directly referring to the salvationist and conservationist tactics of the world's massive metropolitan institutions such as the British Museum, the Acropolis Museum has been conceived as a weapon in Greece's effort to claim centrality in the world cultural system; its exhibits are aesthetically "modernized," treated as ends in themselves as well as excerpts of a wider narrative that appears at once nationalist, exceptionalist, and anti-colonial.

The exhibition of the Parthenon Marbles in the Acropolis Museum's top-floor gallery reads like an exploration of national trauma (fig. 1.3). The remaining pieces are shown next to copies of their missing "brothers and sisters"—"human flesh, suspended, as if still alive, its agony still fresh," shattered marble exhibited next to plaster replicas "for lack of anything else." "The reconstructions," the French woman is heard saying in *Hiroshima Mon Amour*, "have been made as authentically as possible. The illusion, it's quite simple, the illusion is so perfect that the tourists cry" (Duras 1961, 18). The Parthenon Marbles are then offered to our gaze, displayed as the relics of a by now sanctified Hellas, as the holy stigmata of national exceptionalism. For the Acropolis Museum and its rhetoric, the gaps in its display function as a repetitive reenactment of a traumatic event—the unexpected and overwhelmingly violent interruption of the nation's historical continuum (Caruth 1996, 91)—while at the same time pinpointing with merciless precision the essence of their traumatic absence. What for the West is arguably the beginning of its reconnection with its classical genealogy, is for the Greeks the beginning of their separation from theirs (like the Hiroshima bombing for the Europeans signifies the end of the war rather than the beginning of Japanese suffering). Heritage is deployed as a weapon not against colonialism or globalization but against a metropolis that appears to be monopolizing modernity. Greek museums westernize their exhibits in order to attract the gaze of the West or, in the case of the Acropolis Museum, re-Elginize the Parthenon Marbles in order to tell the world they can be better at this. Classical Hellas is thus represented as a site of conflict and as Greece's national treasure—as well as its passport to modernity.

Described as cases of peripheral (post)modernity, these developments are, according to this kind of rhetoric, the result of "incomplete" or merely inadequate modernization, where modernity is injected from the top down in the form of narratives constructed by colonialism, Orientalism, and corporate capitalism. Such "always already postmodern" cultural situations (Buell 1994, 324–43; esp. 327), idiosyncratic or peripheral as they may be, have been produced through an effort to come up with a modernity for the periphery of the Western world, to reshuffle hitherto accepted time-and-place frames by means of an attempted "re-centering" of the globalization flow (Iwabuchi 2002). However, the tendency to reappropriate Classical culture or persistently yearn for archaeological modernities and any other such emblems of colonial rule, desire, and discipline creates unexpected and quite paradoxical gaps in the course of disseminating a European cultural heritage. This is what Homi Bhabha has theorized as "colonial mimicry" in order to embrace "those ideological correlatives of the western sign—empiricism, idealism, mimeticism, monoculturalism . . . that sustain a tradition of . . . 'cultural' authority" (Bhabha 1994, 150). In the words of Bhabha, "the desire to emerge as 'authentic' through mimicry . . . is a final irony of partial representation" (Bhabha 1994, 126). To put it differently, modernity does not always, if ever, look quite the same when one moves away from the metropolis.

The repetition, on behalf of the colonized, of the colonial signs—invariably "taken for wonders"—involves a changing of their nuances, a translation that eventually becomes politically subversive. However, I find that the articulation of such a counternarrative, by way of a critique of the master narrative and its exclusion of peripheral stories, is absent in most Greek museums, "national" or otherwise. Nevertheless, the trauma of the hitherto unlived, "unclaimed" experiences of the Classical informs our exhibitions of the nation's past even though they seem entirely oblivious to the fact. The mechanical regurgitation of Western "empiricism, idealism and monoculturalism" (Bhabha 1994, 150) can do very little to supply and support cultural identities that are not predisposed to becoming perpetual consumers of modernity.

Although Homi Bhabha's notion of mimicry has been criticized as a narrative that is itself essentialist, elitist, Eurocentric, and coming from a privileged, bourgeois, academic higher ground (anticipated in Spivak 1988; see Friedman 1997), as my own argument may seem to be doing, I am convinced that neither he nor I are guilty of perpetually defining the non-West as "Other" while establishing the West as "Subject," despite our postcolonial rhetoric. According to Bhabha, "the problem of cultural interaction emerges only at the significatory boundaries of cultures, where meanings and values are (mis)-read or signs are misappropriated" and, as a result, "culture only emerges as a problem, or a problematic, at the point at which there is a loss of meaning in the contestation and articulation of everyday life, between classes, genders, races, nations" (Bhabha 1994, 50). Therefore, when I argue that contemporary Greeks (impossibly taken as a whole, at the same time imaginary and imagined) construct their antiquity as a means to appease the perils caused by a traumatic modernity, I try to locate their speech outside the logocentric European paradigm, not to constitute it within its margins. In doing so, I investigate precisely the point where everyday life in contemporary Greece becomes the field wherein meanings get to be articulated and identities become contested. I would think the inherent irony of such projects in self-archaeology goes to great extent in soothing the pains of loss and incomplete mourning created by the realization of the temporality of the present and the nostalgia for a past that was never lived.

Even though several of my examples so far have been drawn from Greece's earlier days as an independent state, I find that the attitudes I have studied in this chapter are most evident in the postwar period: it was only after the German occupation of Greece between 1941 and 1944 and the bloody Civil War that ensued (1946–1949) that the country emerged as a highly polarized and largely undemocratic society in the early 1950s, and the Greeks felt the need to reassess their cultural and political affiliations with the West. What for the Greek Right (the victors of the Civil War) was their political and ideological ally and their spiritual homeland became a cultural adversary for the Left. Intriguingly, classical antiquity was enlisted by both camps at the same time as the key to the West's hearts (and state treasuries) and as a formidable weapon against its political and cultural supremacy. What I read as Greece's traumatic relation with its classical past was intensified from its years of westernization that followed the conflicted 1940s and up to its accession into the European Economic Community (the precursor of the European Union) in 1981. The year 1981 also happened to bring a major shift in Greek politics, namely the rise of the socialists to power. PASOK, the socialist party that was to govern the country largely for the next couple of decades, and Andreas Papandreou (1919–1996), its charismatic leader, adopted, especially for the greater part of the 1970s and 1980s, a fundamentally Third World rhetoric drawn from worldwide anti-Western (or, more accurately, anti-American) movements that had been active since the 1960s in places such as Cuba and Vietnam. These movements were later to be transferred to European soil via anti-regime movements emerging from Spain, Greece, and so on (Kornetis 2015). Soon, anti-Westernism in Greece acquired a highly vocalized, performative trope by far transcending the confines of PASOK or its political satellites. Within this climate, the display of antiquities both at home and abroad was promoted as a formidable weapon against "the enemy" and in effect a platform for Greek exceptionalism (Mouliou 2008; Plantzos 2011). This new strategy revised the scheme promoted by Karkavitsas in the early twentieth century; whereas he castigated archaeolatry as a sign of Greece's foreign dependency, archaeolatry (in its newly packaged, xenophobic version) was now adopted precisely as a means to counter Western intrusionism.

The severe sovereign debt crisis that has hit Greece since 2009 and the ensuing economic recession have fueled anti-European feelings even further. The combined intervention by the European Union, the European Central Bank, and the International Monetary Fund (internationally dubbed, and locally loathed as, the "Troika") was seen as mainly neocolonial warfare against a nation that deserved better treatment (Liakos 2013; Triandafyllidou, Gropas, and Kouki 2013; see also Yalouri and Rikou, this volume). In a bitter twist of events, classical antiquity was deployed by Greece's fierce critics as a weapon against what they insisted were the country's chronic deficiencies, from clientelism and tax evasion to bureaucracy and state corruption (Talalay 2013; Tziovas 2014, 13–16; see also Plantzos 2017). At this critical, significatory junction of cultural contestation and misappropriation, certain sectors in Greek society, encouraged by several political factions (on either side of the now almost obsolete Right/Left divide) and systematically goaded by the media, turned to antiquity or Greek tradition at large as a means to reaffirm national exceptionalism. As Greek antiquity once again became a hotly debated topic, whereby modern Greeks were invariably accused by their European allies for both their inefficiency in managing their classical heritage and their misappropriation of it in the first place, it seemed inevitable that archaeology would reemerge in the country's day-to-day life as an antidote to the economic recession and its moral implications.

Public Displays of Archaeology

Greece's archaeology of national trauma is nowhere more evident than in the heart of its largest cities—in those hubs of metropolitan modernity where urban

Fig. 1.4. Athens, city center; part of the classical fortification preserved in situ, under a glass pyramid. Photo by D. Plantzos.

life is abruptly and somewhat brutally interrupted in order to allow glimpses of the distant past to seep through. Whereas museums and organized archaeological sites are well-defined areas where the informed, and most likely paying, public is allowed to interact with carefully laid out and expertly interpreted material remains of a past that is deemed important in the present (as discussed in the first part of this chapter), the scraps of ancient ruins preserved in the corners of our streets or squares constitute a different sort of sensory reminder of the nation's antiquity and its primeval ties to its land. Archaeological preservation is part of a modern state's duties in the interests of humanity, and there are well-defined sets of often strict, most likely international, rules specifying what needs to be kept where and how.

Inevitable as it may be, the modern habit of preserving bits of antiquity within the urban grid allows Greece to exercise this particular sort of archaeology with a vengeance (figs. 1.4 to 1.6). Be they well groomed and tidy, allowed to fall into disrepair and eventual ruin, successfully incorporated into modern buildings purposefully designed to accommodate the leftovers of their predecessors, or (more often) awkwardly placed under massive new constructions that

Fig. 1.5. Athens, city center; part of a classical street and cemetery preserved "in situ," as part of a public square. Photo by D. Plantzos.

Fig. 1.6. Athens, city center; antiquities preserved "in situ" in a residential area. Photo by D. Plantzos.

seem to ignore them, Greece's incidental antiquities serve a strategic purpose. On the one hand, for the unsuspecting foreigner, they act as an eloquent reminder of the land's antiquity and hopefully its commitment to a modernity that has recognized the pursuit of history and its material traces as one of its fundamental values. Next to the country's expertly and heavily reconstructed archaeological sites, its own urban streets themselves act as its "modern signature," combining the rights to a spectacular classical heritage with the will and the ability to manage it successfully (cf. Leontis 1995, 40–66; Plantzos 2011).

On the other hand, the ruins preserved within Greece's modern urban centers are there to interact with the country's own citizens. They are there to remind them of antiquity's metaphysical grip and to recreate antiquity as an ever-present ontology. Across the globe, rescue archaeology is more often asked to reconcile the need for urban expansion with the interests of archaeological research and the conservation of material heritage (Williams 2014; 2015). In Greece, these parallel narratives inevitably came into conflict with one another as massive modernizing projects, such as the building of a subway train system in Athens in the 1990s and currently in Thessaloniki, or the massive venues erected mostly in Athens for the 2004 Olympic Games, seemed to demand the country choose between its glorious past and a highly promising future. In all these instances, the demands of the present are juxtaposed with the allure of a past, which becomes needier by the second. Behind this conflict hides the frustration over who is to control the narratives through which one may define the past and control the present. This is hardly original and far from being a Greek privilege. What does constitute a certain Greek singularity, however, is the very way in which the past, through its archaeological manifestations, becomes available in the present, as well as the roles it is allowed to perform within and in regard to it.

The display of antiquities is a central feature of most Athens metro stations (figs. 1.7 to 1.8) so much so as to make one wonder whether this "sacralization" of urban space was not in fact the reason behind the metropolitan railways construction in the first place (Hamilakis 2001). In a city where metro stations look like museums and museums often copy the practical aspects of a metro station (see Plantzos 2011), space becomes a commodity of particular significance, a place where the past is revived in order both to be inscribed onto the daily routines of the Athenians and to impress the tourists, who are usually hungry for visualized history. Metro stations in Athens may be seen to be doing what its museums perhaps fail to do: a casual trip reveals "the people walking around, lost in thought." Then there are the objects themselves: vases and sculptures ("shattered stones"); bits of buildings, tools, jewelry, and weapons ("the twisted metal"), sometimes in the original but more often in reproduction lest they be pinched or vandalized; charts and graphs ("the photographs, the photographs, the reconstructions"). These objects are curated in specially designed, museum-like cases and panels with wall texts and itineraries designed by the state Archaeological Service to promote the material remains of Greece's classical past on the one hand, and to imply the modern state's ability to turn them into world renowned "star exhibits" on the other hand. Crypto-colonial mimicry—the need to appear as Hellenic as Western imagination ever wanted Greece to be, and at the same time as modern as no one ever thought Greece could become—thus turns urban spaces into monuments in and of themselves. As if the country's hundreds of museums were not enough to monumentalize its fabulous temporalities, it seems there is an urgent need to turn its capital's pharaonic metro stations into museums in themselves, often designed by the same museographers and always employing the same artifaction techniques to inscribe national time into national space. The outcome of this artifaction project, and as a result the artifact itself, is this new, performative way of looking at Greek archaeology and becoming part of it.

The classical past is therefore revived in the present both as a paradigm and as a promise: Greece's constituent archaeolatry informs and controls the quotidian movement of its citizens, an intervention disguised as the prospect of a spectacular future. Greeks find themselves organized as archaeophilic bodies in their metropolitan everyday comings and goings, as faithful carriers of a splendid (albeit imported) tradition, and as the worthy recipients of a much coveted inheritance. At the same time, this pride in one's past is expressed in the form of silent anguish against the trauma of that same past's neglect by the nation's friends and foes alike. It seems that although the nation's archaeologists (or indeed the nation itself as its own archaeologist par excellence) followed the advice sarcastically attributed by Karkavitsas to his country's supposed allies: to strive for their nation's archaeological visibility and not much else. They eventually discovered that public displays of archaeology tend to work as disciplinary tools at home rather than for an international audience that is invariably accused of "having seen nothing, nothing." As Caruth observed, it is precisely through that sort of seeing "from the site of trauma" that a spectator may indeed become a witness (Caruth 1996, 56).

But what lies in Greece to be witnessed? Among the Athens metro displays, pride of place must be accorded to the archaeological stratigraphy sections constructed in some of the stations (chiefly Syntagma, Acropolis, Monastiraki, and Dafni) (fig. 1.7).

Appearing as an imaginative cross between tedious scientism and abstract interior design, those brightly colored, sculpture-like tableaux invite the gaze of the traveler (fig. 1.8) or indeed the visitor to the station in order to turn her or him into a witness of Greek history turned into spectacle. Though presumably accurate scientifically, these sections are obviously human-made, representing what was discovered—including remains of buildings, pits, tombs, and pottery sherds stuck in their archaeological context. As the successive time periods of

Fig. 1.7. Athens, a stratigraphy section displayed at Dafni metro station. Photo by D. Plantzos.

Fig. 1.8. Athens, antiquities and a stratigraphy section displayed at Syntagma metro station. Photo by D. Plantzos.

each locality are exhibited, piled up one on top of the other, they are meant to serve as a poignant reminder of what Greece had to lose in order to embrace modernity—however good the Greeks may have proved to be at the job—while at the same time revisiting the site of trauma where this transition became more demanding. The temporalities of the Greek nation, already mythical or in the process of becoming mythologized, are thus collapsed into a voracious present, even when they appear as no more than dusty displays cramped in the corner of a metropolitan railway station meant to serve hundreds of thousands of commuters on a daily basis.

Similarly, those "rescued" scraps of antiquities preserved in situ in the margins of the modern city grid, in this peculiar no man's land between public and private space often occupying the edges of our squares or the basements or our buildings, claim the gaze of the passerby wishing to chart contemporary Greece as an ancient nation—or rather a historical site where classical materialities are still in force, even when viewed from a distance. Even when rotting at the side of our streets, covered in wild foliage and completely illegible, under long-faded signs meant to provide them with the appropriate if often incomprehensible scholarly documentation, those necessary places of archaeological contemplation, with their wire fences and forbidding locks, remind us of the past's antiquity through the monumentalization of the present. They become a game with time, in effect striving to cover the painful distance between reality and its representation.

This forceful representation of Greek modernity is constructed in a heavily aestheticized fashion in the Athens metro: the underground's technical achievement, one for which the Greeks felt collectively proud when the service first opened to the public (cf. Hamilakis 2001), is emphatically mirrored by its luxurious construction (massive spaces, shiny marble surfaces, daring pyramid-shaped glass skylights, and so on) and its strict policies against buskers, or even eating and drinking on the premises for fear of soiling or littering. (The relentless recession since 2009, and the reduction of their own staff owing to drastic budget cuts, has forced the metro authorities to become somewhat less vigilant against beggars, who often now patrol the trains while in motion but remain unseen in the stations themselves.) Stations therefore remain museum-like, both in their effort to offer a sterilized environment to their day-to-day users as well as in their art displays. A number of contemporary Greek artists (many from the diaspora, such as Takis, Chryssa, and Stephen Antonakos) are featured in stations closely associated with them (such as Alekos Fassianos's personal ties with the Metaxourgio station area). Whereas most of these artists wish to represent modern Greece as a truly Western society, in line with artistic and cultural developments elsewhere, classical tradition often creeps in to remind us of its stronghold over collective Greek sensibilities. Dimitris Mytaras's *Dexileos* (2000) is the best example of this

Fig. 1.9. *Dexileos* by D. Mytaras (2000; det.), displayed at Dafni metro station. Photo by D. Plantzos.

phenomenon (fig. 1.9): displayed over the main wall of the ticket concourse of Dafni Station, with smaller installations elsewhere on the premises, the work is a large tableau in relief, "deconstructing" the well-known image from a fourth-century-BC grave stele erected in the Keramikos for a young Athenian rider who fell in battle. The modern work plays with the forceful poise of the youth on his horse spearing his enemy in the moments of triumph prior to his death, as well as with the lettering of the accompanying inscription. As a public display of the way modern Greeks attempt their own national archaeology—as emotive attachment to the material remains of an ancient past they persistently perceive as theirs—Mytaras's *Dexileos* confirms the nation's infatuation with the graceful motifs of classical sculpture as a way of reinforcing the day-to-day commuters' commitment to their country's past. To Hellenize modern Greek space, therefore, this display and others like it simultaneously produce a territorialized version of classical antiquity that is specific to Greece and its inhabitants. The artifact produced here, then, is personal time itself and its everyday applications. Commuters are inscribed with the fragmented image of their fallen ancestor as repetitive reenactment of their nation's traumatic history, as well as a visual reminder that the repossession of the past through its own materiality is necessary in order to repossess the present.

Seemingly Seamless

The examples discussed so far suggest that in contemporary Greece the relation to the past is perceived as a traumatic revisiting precisely because of the precariousness of this relation in the first place. On the threshold of the Greek twentieth century, the disdain expressed by Karkavitsas for his protagonist in *The Archaeologist* reveals its author's frustration with his compatriots' persistent mimicking of Western-born archaeolatry and fetishist archaeology. In the traumatic decades that followed, Greeks felt the need to reaffirm their cultural identity in the face of political and financial adversity, and classical antiquity was enlisted as their most far-reaching weapon. In this process, the relation to the country's past acquired a strikingly materialist quality in Greece as the fledgling nation adopted its patrons' archaeological zeal to impress them with its newly imported scientific skills. Greece's representation of itself remains largely archaeological, as a result of a crypto-colonial effort to mimic attitudes and traits seen abroad, admired and loathed at the same time. As a result, the classical past acquires a forbidding territoriality excluding all non-Greeks, alienating even those living in the country itself. Although these claims are meant to rescue classical antiquity and its material remains from their Western-born hijackers and their museums, they end up creating an exclusionary realm, archaeolatric and archaeopathic at the same time, wherein only Greek-born individuals are expected to feel at ease with this kind of crassly constructed and heavily materialized Hellenic distinctiveness.

Material antiquities play a significant role in this process even when their presence is merely hinted at. Take, for example, the way Greek passports are decorated. Although traveling documents are not really expected to carry any nonpractical features, some countries have chosen to embellish theirs. Canada, for instance, opted for natural and human-made landscapes that become fully visible only under UV lights, thus safeguarding the document's validity. Greek passports, on the other hand, offer a full range of ancient Greek artifacts, some even predating Greek civilization itself: Cycladic figurines of the third millennium BC, Cretan antiquities of the second millennium BC, classical Hellas with its Olympic Games revived (or indeed reinvented) by Western modernity, marble-built temples and open-air theaters, the gold ossuary from Vergina and the astrolabe from Antikythera, two Byzantine churches, a bridge dating from the Ottoman period, and a monumental wire bridge (albeit one funded by the European Commission and built by a French company) inaugurated in 2004 suggestive of Greece's successes in modernization. In the heart of this archaeological extravaganza, where the bureaucracy of travel is unexpectedly subjected to a rather unsubtle game of biopolitics, stands—what else?—the Parthenon (fig. 1.10). Poised in its familiar three-quarter view, the half-ruined temple is represented alone and cleansed from the noise of its own history, not quite in its former glory

Fig. 1.10. Sutured: the Parthenon centerfold in a Greek passport.

though not exactly in its present state either. Artifaction techniques are thus incorporated into a state-authorized strategy for the production of the national subject. In effect, the passport's holder emerges as the outcome of a double artifaction process, and she or he appears to be the sum of buildings or things imagined as archaeological artifacts of cardinal national significance in the first place.

The decision to embellish Greek passports with illustrations of archaeological sites and artifacts is relatively recent. It dates back to 2006, when, in view of the rise of international terrorism and the need for augmented security in travel, the issuing of passports was transferred from municipalities to the police (Plantzos 2008, 25). As safety of transportation became a top priority internationally, with biometric data and microchips added to travel documents as a means to monitor the national subject and keep suspects of terrorism under surveillance, Greek police chose (quite anonymously it seems, and without consulting with any other authorities in the country) to enforce a national sense of belonging to Greek citizens, in effect a rehashed cultural identity stereotypically based on the materiality of a museumized classical past. As Greeks traveling abroad surrender their passports to border police—a momentary gesture, presumably leaving no recollection of the fanciful archaeological assemblage to the unsuspecting officer—they are expected to feel proud of a heritage successfully claimed in the face of any challenger. The document's thirty-odd pages inscribe on the body and the spirit of its bearers their Hellenic pedigree and the unsurpassable culture that goes with it while at the same time confirming their lonely trajectory in a world where Hellenes are few and far between. In addition, crypto-colonial mimicry is well employed here; all chosen sites and objects are meant to trigger admiring recollections to those imaginary foreigners, but the document's frontispiece is a monochromatic rendition of Philipp von Foltz's 1852 oil painting *Pericles' Funeral Oration*, a neoclassical creation that imagines how Athens and its most famous statesman might have looked back in the day.[5] Accepting an image generated by the neoclassical imagination as Greece's iconic representation, even in the age of machine-readable passports, confirms Greece's crypto-colonial condition as the weakest link in a relentless game of cultural appropriation.

The Parthenon centerfold (fig. 1.10) is sutured in place with blue-and-white thread. This naive gesture, devised by some anonymous state officer back at the beginning of the current millennium, carries more depth than it betrays at first sight. In psychoanalysis, a suture is a narrative technique through which the symbolic and the imaginary are stitched together, in the same way bodily tissues are sutured after an injury to avoid infection and enable healing (Heath 1977–78, 60). In semiotics and (with quite spectacular results) cinema theory, the suture metaphor has been used to describe the traumatic realization that utterances create in their subject as both present and absent, in the sense that signifiers are a priori excluded from their own representations (Miller 1977–78).[6] A suturing device—in the case of Greek passports, the literal stitching together of the idealized image of the Parthenon and the very document that validates a Greek subject's national identity—tries to relate a sense of absence and want to the structure of which they are integral parts, stitching together a fantasy of being once again unified (and unique). By suturing the Parthenon to the heart of the Greek passport, state authorities construct their subjects as signifiers inserting themselves into the symbolic register. The blue-and-white thread suturing a thoroughly modern image of classical antiquity onto the heart of the most official document of Greekness constructs both the subject of this symbolic address (its Greek holder) and the tangible presence of a traumatic national absence. The state document thus represents its holder's cultural genealogy even where this genealogy is not known or where it is doubted by strangers. Through this facile, perhaps random or improvised gesture, the nation, imagining itself as the agent of its own self-representation, attempts the salutary suturing of a gaping national wound, the deep trauma effected by the violent separation of the collective imaginary from its highly mythologized (though mostly by others) classical past.

By touching the blue-and-white thread in the middle of her or his passport and gazing at the Parthenon in a state that is neither past nor present, the contemporary Greek citizen is constructed (and not only on a symbolic level) as a modern subject par excellence—that is, as the agent, a symbolic iteration, from which she or he is frustratingly absent. As Stuart Hall and others have shown, identities are not states of being but processes, indeed points of suture "between, on the one hand, the discourses and practices which attempt to 'interpellate,' speak to us or hail us into place as the social subjects of particular discourses, and on the other hand, the processes which produce subjectivities, which construct us as subjects which can be 'spoken'" (Hall 2000, 19). The examples discussed in this chapter illustrate this production of national subjectivities to which quotidian life in Greece seems to be utterly devoted. Conceived in the field of cultural difference, and produced through the technologies of colonial mimicry, the sites I revisited in the preceding pages question foreign, cultural, and political authority as an act of resistance (or a promise of eventual emancipation). At the same time, they intervene in the country's everyday life, creating their viewers as national subjects organized round day-to-day performances of cultural identification, whether conscious or not.

Classical antiquity—or rather its ghostly apparition, imagined, celebrated, and recycled, abroad as well as at home—is always here, though its overbearing presence is by and large experienced as a traumatic absence. The contrived "archaeologies of Greekness" discussed in this chapter are meant to enable contemporary Greeks to relate the trauma of temporality as a belated though forever unclaimed experience, as a performance of mourning for a present that is past no more.

DIMITRIS PLANTZOS is Professor of Classical Archaeology at the National and Kapodistrian University of Athens. He is the author of *Greek Art and Archaeology: 1200–30 BC* (Lockwood Press, 2016) and co-editor (with T.J. Smith) of *A Companion to Greek Art* (Wiley-Blackwell, 2012).

Notes

Parts of this chapter were presented, in earlier drafts, at the Modern Greek Seminar run by the subfaculty of Byzantine and Modern Greek Studies of the University of Oxford and at the Norwegian Institute at Athens. I am grateful to Dimitris Papanikolaou and Zarko Tankosic for the respective invitations, as well as to Delia Tzortzaki and Marlen Mouliou, who discussed aspects of this work with me. I am also grateful to Esther Solomon, who asked me to rework my earlier paper into a chapter for this volume and encouraged me to develop my ideas with her customary thoughtfulness and grace.

1. On the novel, see Plantzos (2014); Diamandi (2008); Politi (1988).

2. On the subject of Greece as a classical heterotopia of ruins, see Leontis (1995, 40–66); Hamilakis (2007, 85–99).

3. See http://goo.gl/bgXNSA, accessed June 7, 2015.

4. The concept of crypto-colonialism, introduced by Michael Herzfeld with regard to Greece, Thailand, and other such "buffer zones" between the colonies proper and the Western metropolises, may be particularly useful when introducing postcolonial analysis into Greek cultural studies; see Herzfeld (2002) and cf. Plantzos (2012; 2014). On contemporary Greece as a country at the crossroads between the two most dynamic projects of Western modernity, colonialism and nationalism, see Hamilakis (2009).
5. See http://goo.gl/ClkdmC, accessed January 12, 2016.
6. See also Heath (1981, 106); Silverman (1983, ch. 5); Browne (1975–76); Hall (2000).

References

Anderson, Benedict. 1991. *Imagined Communities. Reflections on the Origin and Spread of Nationalism*, 2nd ed. London: Verso.

Bennett, Tony. 1995. *The Birth of the Museum: History, Theory, Politics*. London: Routledge.

Bhabha, Homi. 1994. *The Location of Culture*. London: Routledge.

Browne, Nicholas. 1975–76. "The Spectator-in-the-Text: The Rhetoric of Stagecoach." *Film Quarterly* 29 (2): 26–38.

Buell, Frederic. 1994. *National Culture and the New Global System*. Baltimore: Johns Hopkins University Press.

Caruth, Cathy. 1996. *Unclaimed Experience. Trauma, Narrative, and History*. Baltimore: Johns Hopkins University Press.

Colla, Elliot. 2007. *Conflicted Antiquities. Egyptology, Egyptomania, Egyptian Modernity*. Durham, NC: Duke University Press.

Delivorrias, Angelos. 2000. *A Guide to the Benaki Museum*. Athens: Benaki Museum.

Diamandi, Maria. 2008. "The Archaeologist in Contemporary Greek Novel." In *A Singular Antiquity: Archaeology and Hellenic Identity in Twentieth-Century Greece*, edited by Dimitris Damaskos and Dimitris Plantzos, 383–99. Athens: Benaki Museum.

Dicks, Bella. 2003. *Culture on Display: The Production of Contemporary Visitability*. Maidenhead: Open University Press.

Duras, Marguerite. 1961. *Hiroshima Mon Amour. A Screenplay by Marguerite Duras for the Film by Alain Resnais with an Introduction and Notes by the Author*. New York: Grove.

Friedman, Jonathan. 1997. "Global Crisis, the Struggle for Cultural Identity and Intellectual Porkbarelling: Cosmopolitans Versus Locals, Ethnics and Nationals in an Era of Dehegemonization." In *Debating Cultural Hybridity*, edited by Pnina Werbner and Tariq Modood, 70–89. London: Zed.

Gazi, Andromache. 2008. "'Artfully Classified' and 'Appropriately Placed': Notes on the Display of Antiquities in Early Twentieth-Century Greece." In *A Singular Antiquity: Archaeology and Hellenic Identity in Twentieth-Century Greece*, edited by Dimitris Damaskos and Dimitris Plantzos, 67–82. Athens: Benaki Museum.

Gell, Alfred. 1998. *Art and Agency: An Anthropological Theory*. Oxford: Oxford University Press.

Gourgouris, Stathis. 1996. *Dream Nation: Enlightenment, Colonization and the Institution of Modern Greece*. Stanford, CA: Stanford University Press.

Hall, Stuart. 2000. "Who Needs 'Identity?'" In *Identity: A Reader*, edited by Paul du Gay, Jessica Evans, and Peter Redman, 15–30. London: Sage Publications.

Hamilakis, Yannis. 2001. "Antiquities Underground." *Antiquity* 75: 35–36.
———. 2007. *The Nation and its Ruins: Antiquity, Archaeology, and National Imagination in Greece*. Oxford: Oxford University Press.
———. 2009. "Indigenous Hellenisms/Indigenous Modernities: Classical Antiquity, Materiality, and Modern Greek Society." In *The Oxford Handbook of Hellenic Studies*, edited by George Boys-Stones, Barbara Graziosi, and Phiroze Vasunia, 19–31. Oxford: Oxford University Press.
Heath, Stephen. 1977–78. "Notes on Suture." *Screen* 18 (4): 48–76.
———. 1981. *Questions of Cinema*. Basingstoke: Macmillan.
Herzfeld, Michael. 2002. "The Absent Presence: Discourses of Crypto-Colonialism." *South Atlantic Quarterly* 101:899–926.
Hooper-Greenhill, Eilean. 1992. *Museums and the Shaping of Knowledge*. London: Routledge.
Iwabuchi, Koichi. 2002. *Recentering Globalization: Popular Culture and Japanese Transnationalism*. Durham, NC: Duke University Press.
Kalpaxis, Thanasis. 1996. "Επιρροές της Γαλλογερμανικής Αντιπαράθεσης του 19ου αιώνα στην Κατασκευή της Εικόνας της Αρχαίας Ελλάδας" [Influences of Franco-German Confrontation of the Nineteenth Century on Building the Image of Ancient Greece]. In *Ένας Νέος Κόσμος Γεννιέται: Η Εικόνα του Ελληνικού Πολιτισμού στη Γερμανική Επιστήμη κατά τον 19ο αιώνα* [A New World Is Born: The Image of Greek Culture in German Science in the Nineteenth Century], edited by Evangelos Chrysos, 41–58. Athens: Akritas.
Kansteiner, Wulf, and Harald Weilnböck. 2010. "Against the Concept of Cultural Trauma." In *A Companion to Cultural Memory Studies*, edited by Astrid Erll and Ansgar Nünning, 229–40. Berlin: De Gruyter.
Karkavitsas, Andreas. 2002. *Ο Αρχαιολόγος* [The Archaeologist]. Athens: Estia.
Kornetis, Kostis. 2015. "'Cuban Europe'? Greek and Iberian Tiersmondisme in the 'Long 1960s.'" *Journal of Contemporary History* 50 (3): 486–515.
Leontis, Artemis. 1995. *Topographies of Hellenism: Mapping the Homeland*. Ithaca, NY: Cornell University Press.
Liakos, Antonis. 2013. "Greek Narratives of Crisis." *Humaniora. Czasopismo Internetowe* 3 (3): 79–86. Accessed April 25, 2016. http://goo.gl/hqILcL.
Marchand, Suzanne L. 1996. *Down from Olympus: Archaeology and Philhellenism in Germany, 1750–1970*. Princeton, NJ: Princeton University Press.
Miller, Jacques-Alain. 1977–78. "Suture (Elements of the Logic of the Signifier)." *Screen* 18 (4): 35–47.
Mouliou, Marlen. 2008. "Museum Representations of the Classical Past in Post-war Greece: A Critical Analysis." In *A Singular Antiquity: Archaeology and Hellenic Identity in Twentieth-Century Greece*, edited by Dimitris Damaskos and Dimitris Plantzos, 83–109. Athens: Benaki Museum.
Panourgiá, Neni. 2004. "Colonizing the Ideal: Neo-Classical Articulations and European Modernities." *Angelaki* 9 (2): 165–76.
Plantzos, Dimitris. 2008. "Archaeology and Hellenic Identity, 1896–2004: The Frustrated Vision." In *A Singular Antiquity: Archaeology and Hellenic Identity in Twentieth-Century Greece*, edited by Dimitris Damaskos and Dimitris Plantzos, 10–30. Athens: Benaki Museum.

———. 2011. "Behold the Raking Geison: The New Acropolis Museum and Its Context-Free Archaeologies." *Antiquity* 85: 613–30.

———. 2012. "The *Kouros* of Keratea: Constructing Subaltern Pasts in Contemporary Greece." *Journal of Social Archaeology* 12: 220–44.

———. 2014. "Dead Archaeologists, Buried Gods: Archaeology as an Agent of Modernity in Greece." In *Re-imagining the Past: Antiquity and Modern Greek Culture*, edited by Dimitris Tziovas, 147–64. Oxford: Oxford University Press.

———. 2017. "Amphipolitics: Archaeological Performance and Governmentality in Greece under the Crisis." In *Greece in Crisis: The Cultural Politics of Austerity*, edited by Dimitris Tziovas, 65–84. London: I. B. Tauris.

Politi, Jina. 1988. "The Tongue and the Pen." In *The Greek Novel AD 1–1985*, edited by Roderick Beaton, 42–53. London: Croom Helm.

Silverman, Kaja. 1983. *The Subject of Semiotics*. Oxford: Oxford University Press.

Spivak, Gayatri Chakravorty. 1988. "Can the Subaltern Speak?" In *Marxism and the Interpretation of Culture*, edited by Cary Nelson and Lawrence Grossberg, 271–313. Besingstoke: Macmillan.

Talalay, Lauren E. 2013. "Drawing Conclusions: Greek Antiquity, the €conomic [*sic*] Crisis, and Political Cartoons." *Journal of Modern Greek Studies* 31: 249–76.

Toner, Jerry. 2013. *Homer's Turk: How Classics Shaped Ideas of the East*. Cambridge, MA: Harvard University Press.

Triandafyllidou, Anna, Ruby Gropas, and Hara Kouki, eds. 2013. *The Greek Crisis and European Modernity*. Basingstoke: Palgrave Macmillan.

Tziovas, Dimitris. 2014. "Decolonizing Antiquity, Heritage Politics, and Performing the Past." In *Re-imagining the Past: Antiquity and Modern Greek Culture*, edited by Dimitris Tziovas, 1–26. Oxford: Oxford University Press.

Voudouri, Daphne. 2008. "Greek Legislation Concerning the International Movement of Antiquities and Its Ideological and Political Dimensions." In *A Singular Antiquity: Archaeology and Hellenic Identity in Twentieth-Century Greece*, edited by Dimitris Damaskos and Dimitris Plantzos, 125–39. Athens: Benaki Museum.

Wengrow, David. 2007. "Enchantment and Sacrifice in Early Egypt." In *Art's Agency and Art History*, edited by Robin Osborne and Jeremy Tanner, 28–41. Oxford: Blackwell.

Williams, Tim D. 2014. "Archaeology: Reading the City through Time." In *Reconnecting the City: The Historic Urban Landscape Approach and the Future of Urban Heritage*, edited by Francesco Bandarin and Ron van Oers, 19–46. Oxford: Wiley-Blackwell.

———. 2015. "Preservation in Situ: Not an Ethical Principle, but Rather an Option amongst Many." In *Fernweh: Crossing Borders and Connecting People in Archaeological Heritage Management*, edited by Monique H. van den Dries, Sjoerd J. van der Linde, and Amy Strecker, 38–41. Leiden: Sidestone.

2 Archaeology and Politics in the Interwar Period

The Swedish Excavations at Asine

Niki Sakka

This chapter discusses the ongoing interaction of Greek and foreign archaeologists in the light of the best-known Swedish excavation site in Greece: Asine, in the northeastern Peloponnese. The Asine project represents an important case study that enables fuller understanding of the dynamics of both the Swedish scientific activity in Greece and the broader tradition of the foreign archaeological institutes that provided reference for Swedes. Further, it offers insights into the operation of institutionalization processes, collaborations, negotiations, contradictions, and social networks that have influenced the management of archaeological heritage in Greece, underscoring links between past and contemporary culture. In the following discussion, my interpretation of management will follow Firth, who defines it as "a process by which contested issues are resolved in favor of specific values" (Firth 1995, 52).

Encounters of Greek and Foreign Archaeology

Heritage management in Greece has been considered a national enterprise since the establishment of the Greek state. The foreign archaeological schools, operating in the country from as early as the late nineteenth century, have been actively involved in shaping this management. Their successive projects—conditioned by the wider sociopolitical, economic, and intellectual context and by the rich interlacing of collective and individual entities, institutional policies, and academic priorities—have decisively influenced the development of archaeology and a number of related disciplines in Greece.[1]

Reflective accounts of foreign institutions have led to their diverse roles being conceptualized in novel ways. Much of the recent literature focuses on the interactions between foreigners and locals, arguing that Greek archaeologists should be—though they have not always been—partners in an exchange relationship (Hamilakis 2008). The process of developments in the field is approached as a product of the interrelation of Greek and foreign academic traditions, cultures, and interpersonal ties, all of which are deeply affected by the "powerful impact of the landscape" (Smith and Kitromilides 2009, 4). The histories of the foreign institutions and the personal histories of their members are, thus, perceived as "part and parcel of the story of modern Greece" (Beaton 2009, 221; see Mouliou, this volume).

Encounters can take a variety of forms entailing mutual borrowings but also conflicts. Throughout history, Western countries have been deeply involved in the story of Greece as a modern nation, the balance of power being invariably unequal. In this context, the foreign archaeological institutions, whether or not they are officially associated with their respective governments, cannot always be expected to be disinterested.[2] State support, translated into economic and political profit, has been important to their advancement and to the individuals' professional futures. Perhaps the clearest example of foreign archaeologists' political involvement in Greece relates to espionage and intelligence before and during the two World Wars, raising serious ethical questions and revealing the complex relationship between intellectuals and public life (Clogg 2009; Allen 2011; Lalaki 2013). Their engagement with Greece also included philanthropic activities, associated with "the struggle" of "the archaeologists to understand their own role in a modern landscape," and was used to encourage the shaping of a larger political and social network (Davis and Vogeikoff-Brogan 2013, 6). Thus, the American School of Classical Studies' philanthropic involvement in the development of Greece's social infrastructure through the participation of its members in the American Red Cross (1918–19), the Refugee Settlement Commission (1922–28), and the Marshall Plan (1948–52), besides being a genuine expression of the ethos of American volunteerism, also helped build social credit that would later be converted into political power (Davis 2013).

Over the years, this web of interdependencies would result in both innovations and real losses, institutional expansion, and the rise of nationalistic scholarship. Government funding, channeled through the institutions to a limited number of well-placed archaeologists, resulted in considerable gains in specialized knowledge and quite often in valuable methodological innovations, but only rarely would this encourage innovative interpretations (Trigger 1997). Nonsymmetrical power relationships would allow binary distinctions to be made between Greek and "other" archaeologists. Acknowledgment of the scientific worth of foreign schools and of their role in locating Greece within a European network of intellectual institutions did not exclude perceiving them as colonial outposts serving their countries' political agendas (Smith and Kitromilides 2009, 1).

The evolution of the multidimensional relationships between Greek and foreign archaeology is best illustrated in the histories of late nineteenth-century and early twentieth-century large-scale excavations. Excavations at Olympia,

Delos, Delphi, Knossos, Corinth, and the Athens Agora, among other sites, were regarded as national projects that created international prestige and scholarly status, often reflecting the tensions within European nation-states.

After complex negotiations, the Greek-German Convention of April 13 and 25, 1874 on the excavations at Olympia (ratified by Law 541/1875) became the first international regulation of a long-term excavation project (Marchand 1996, 81–84; Voudouri 2010, 549–551). The regulation recognized absolute state ownership of the finds, tried to determine state policy toward the foreign schools, and consolidated Greece's decision to control the export of antiquities (Dyson 2006, 75, 83–85).

Still, the convention invoked the concept of reciprocity, defined by Gouldner (1960, 164) as "a mutually contingent exchange of benefits between two or more units." Article 6 provided "doubles où *répétitions*" for the Germans "in commemoration of [Greek-German] mutual work" and in recognition of German sacrifices. According to Keohane (1986, 8), "even genuinely reciprocal relationships are not power-free: strong and weak actors practicing reciprocity face different opportunity costs, and the international structure of power helps to establish what values are regarded as equivalent." German claims were based on the assumption—shared by all the foreign schools and never abandoned—that Greece, as a financially weak state with limited technical resources, could not cope with the increasing needs of its monuments in terms of protection, conservation, and research.[3] Through the acquisition of antiquities, the economic capital invested in the archaeological enterprises would subsequently be converted to political and ideological capital to the benefit of those who administered it (Bourdieu 1990; Hamilakis and Yalouri 1996). The clause provoked strong reaction within Greece. For those who considered the antiquities "inalienable wealth" (Yalouri 2001, 101–107) that could not be given away, the unequal exchange violated widely held values (Amandry 1992, 91; Dasios 1992, 131). In the wider political and diplomatic climate of the time, the clause was interpreted as an expression of not only "mechanisms of reciprocity" but also of "relations of subordination" (Lévi-Strauss 1944, 267), and it has never since been repeated in legal documents. However, the pattern persisted, albeit in modified form.

Compensatory arrangements, such as a "donation" of selected material to foreign excavators at the discretion of the Archaeological Council, helped control the tensions and asymmetries.[4] Greek archaeologists seem to have internalized the "norm of reciprocity which morally obliges [them] to give benefits to those from whom [they have] received them" (Gouldner 1960, 174). This conceptual framework evolved from the realistic view of experienced field archaeologists that out of the large amount of archaeological material packed in barely accessible store rooms, a limited number could be of value if given to foreign archaeological institutions. This view made such donations acceptable without creating any commoditization connotations. "Reciprocity involves conforming to generally accepted standards of behavior" which, however, are consistent with practices of self-interest (Keohane 1986, 4, 21). The exchange (conduct of a systematic excavation and concession of finds) was further justified insofar as display of antiquities abroad allowed the circulation of the Greek past and promoted its study.[5] In the long run, the practice of explicitly donating antiquities was gradually abandoned. Instead, finds are temporarily displayed in an increasing number of international, sometimes touring, exhibitions, whereas Law 3028/2002 (article 25) allows reciprocal exchange with other museums and the renewable loan of antiquities.

In 1891, lengthy negotiations between the Greeks, the French, and the Americans over the so-called Great Excavation at Delphi would illustrate the tendency of the Greek state to explicitly exchange the symbolic capital of antiquities for political and economic profit. The permit granted to the French School was linked to trade policy—a commercial agreement between the two countries concerning the reduction of French import duties on Greek currants (Amandry 1992; Dasios 1992). The project would evolve into the most visible French archaeological program in Greece; at the same time, it would help consolidate the Greek national identity and the claim to continuity with concrete material evidence. In this context, the need to remove the modern settlement of Kastri, which had grown up over the ancient sanctuary, to a new location was not questioned by the establishment (Skorda 1992). Some decades later, the dream of revealing the ancient civic and commercial center of Athens—the main locus of democracy (i.e., the Agora)—would be prioritized over the reactions of local residents, most of them refugees, who were obliged to abandon their houses and received little compensation for the expropriation (Sakka 2008; Hamilakis 2013a).

The histories of "great digs" are also histories of missed opportunities. At the time, foreign academic institutions did not welcome the idea of cooperation with the host institutions. On the one hand, the Greek-German Convention of 1874 recognized that both countries should have publication rights over the excavation results (article 7), although no joint publication was launched. On the other hand, the Greek-French contract on Delphi granted exclusive right of publication to the French government (Law 1974/1891, article 4). Likewise, the intention of Greece to promote the Agora excavations as a joint Greek-American project met with strong resistance from the American side (Hamilakis 2013a).[6] In an era when archaeological work was embedded in nationalistic and, in Herzfeld's term, crypto-colonial logic (Herzfeld 2002), collaboration with Greek archaeologists was limited almost entirely to the provision of the excavation permits and to official supervision of the foreign projects, funded exclusively by foreign resources. In this climate, it is not surprising that tensions arose. The contrast with recent decades, when an increasing number of joint archaeological projects and publications has helped consolidate a better-balanced relationship, underscores the omissions that had dominated the field (Davis 2013).

Fig. 2.1. The harbor of ancient Asine. The arrival of the excavation supplies (1922). (Asine Collection of Museum Gustavianum in Uppsala.) Courtesy of Swedish Institute at Athens.

The present chapter discusses the ongoing interaction between Greek and foreign archaeologists in the light of the Asine excavations. Research started in 1922 and, after an interruption of some four decades, went on until the late 1980s. Facets of the earlier excavations (1922–30) will be explored, focusing on the interplay between the local and global forces that shaped the archaeological project itself as well as its political profile. Histories are recreated from archival records, newspaper reports, and examination of the legal framework of the excavations.

The Asine Excavations in Historical Perspective

The Asine project was initiated in a period when Sweden was becoming a modern nation (Lundberg 1985). Between 1890 and 1930, significant Swedish innovative industries related to increased demand for mechanization and engineering skills, coupled with iron, steel, wood, and pulp exports, added to a growing national economy and to the rise of the new Swedish middle class (Smångs 2008; Schön 2008). Together with this late (at least by Western standards) but rapid industrialization and urbanization, the first decades of the twentieth century also saw the democratization of Sweden (Tilton 1974, 562). The king and conservative leaders, fearing that Sweden might follow the example of Russia, Germany, and

Austria-Hungary, were forced to renounce their opposition to liberal development, a process that in 1918–21 resulted in the right to vote for all citizens, as well as the firm establishment of parliamentary government. As Timothy Tilton has written, "Swedish democracy had triumphed without a revolution—but not without the *threat* of revolution" (Tilton 1974, 568). In turn, democratization led the way to social reforms and the extension of education to the masses (Acemoglu and Robinson 2000, 1168, 1180, 1192). Meanwhile, the dissolution of the union of Norway and Sweden in 1905 and "the establishment of an independent kingdom of Norway based upon race and national ideals" ("The Dissolution of the Union of Norway and Sweden," 1907, 441) had aroused strong nationalistic sentiments.

Sweden's cultural policy was built against this background with the financial support of the state and favored stability, tradition, democracy, and the consolidation of the Swedish national identity (Widén 2011, 885; Hegardt and Källén 2011, 110–113). As industrialization spread across the Western world, intellectuals were turning to the past, seeking purity and simplicity in order to avoid the "corruptions of later times" (Gillman 2010, 57). Greek antiquity, long invoked in the name of international values, was accordingly engaged in the shaping of norms and the negotiation of interests. Thus, in 1909 the first chairs of classical archaeology and ancient history in Swedish universities were created, establishing a base for the development of a strong classical tradition. Earlier, in 1894, pioneer excavations had been carried out by Samuel Wide and Lennart Kjellberg, in the Poseidon sanctuary at Kalaureia, Poros (see Anagnostopoulos, this volume), and at Aphidna in Northern Attica (Hägg 2002; Wells 2002). Material from the excavations and travels of Wide, Kjellberg, Axel Boëthius, and Einar Gjerstad in Greece and Cyprus (see Bounia et al., this volume), together with the collection of sherds donated by the Greek archaeologist Valerios Stais, formed the nucleus of several public collections in Sweden, including those of Lund and Uppsala Universities. In 1920, a room in the Gustavianum, once the principal building of Uppsala University, was redesigned to serve as a museum of the Institute of Ancient Culture and Society (Nordquist 1978).

It is within this cultural-economic climate that the Asine project was conceived and implemented as a result of collaboration between the Crown Prince of Sweden Gustavus Adolphus (future King of the Swedes from 1950 to 1973), the Universities of Lund and Uppsala, the French School at Athens, and the Greek authorities. Following the tradition of the house of Bernadotte, which had long had a prominent role in art and culture in Sweden, Adolphus was devoted to the classics and humanities.[7] Throughout his life, he participated in several archaeological expeditions and became one of the founders of the Swedish Institute of Classical Studies in Rome in 1925 and its first chairman of the board (Encyclopaedia Britannica n.d.).

In 1920, while traveling in Greece with his uncle Prince Eugen, Adolphus visited Asine in the company of well-known Greek numismatist Ioannis Svoronos. The Hellenistic fortification walls Adolphus saw stimulated his interest and prompted him to organize the excavation project. The French archaeologists, who were encouraged by Svoronos and had conducted preliminary fieldwork on the site, surrendered their excavation rights to the Swedes. Axel W. Persson, one of the foreign members of the French School in Athens at the time, deployed all his powers of persuasion "for which he was renowned" to convince the French (Wells and Penttinen 2005, 23).

In the autumn of the same year, the Greek Archaeological Council approved the prince's request to conduct excavations in Asine at his own expense, and the Greek government granted the permit in the spring of 1921.[8] In the next few months, Gustavus Adolphus helped organize a high-powered excavation committee and became its chairman. By that time, the Swedish state, universities, public institutions, limited companies, and individuals had collected the necessary funds (Frödin 1938, 9–10). This was the first time that the Swedes had undertaken a major archaeological project in the Mediterranean, where long before, British, French, and German scholars had established clear archaeological "spheres of interest" (Silberman 1990, 101–2). Adolphus's involvement proved a deciding factor in its implementation (Wells 2002, 13).

Five excavation campaigns took place in 1922, 1924, 1926, and 1930 under the direction of Persson, associate professor of Lund and Uppsala Universities, and Otto Frödin, experienced excavator and keeper of Stone Age and Bronze Age antiquities in the Statens Historiska Museum (Frödin 1938; Wells 2002, 13).

For Swedish archaeologists, the Asine excavations were "not only . . . of enormous importance for the study of [their] own prehistory" but also a means of boosting the country's academic and cultural prestige by contributing, before it was "too late . . . to [the] research in the classical period of Ancient Greece," which at that time was "being conducted with great energy by various nations."[9] Some three years later, the American School of Classical Studies at Athens would negotiate the excavation of the Ancient Agora of Athens, using almost the same reasoning (Sakka 2008; Hamilakis 2013a). Swedes were building on the long-established view of archaeology as a landscape where European states were negotiating their relative position and each other's status. Moreover, in a period when competition among countries in the international, industrialized society was increasingly becoming part of archaeological and museum practice (Dyson 2006, 167–68), Sweden was portraying itself as a model for other countries to follow (Oakes 2001, 69–70): Swedish scholars would pioneer "on sites with Mycenaean remains" a "very precise method, characterized by maximum carefulness and planning" that would solve many problems otherwise unsolvable "in the manner excavations have been carried out down there so far."[10]

Fig. 2.2. Asine, work near the fortifications. (1926. Asine Collection of Museum Gustavianum in Uppsala.) Courtesy of Swedish Institute at Athens.

Fig. 2.3. Excavation of a Mycenaean chamber tomb on Barbouna Hill. Axel W. Persson on the right, in a white helmet. (1922 or possibly 1926. Asine Collection of Museum Gustavianum in Uppsala.) Courtesy of Swedish Institute at Athens.

Interestingly, Antonios Keramopoulos, then ephor of antiquities of Argolid, Corinthia, and Arcadia, outlined the expectations for the Asine project in a letter to then minister of education Theodoros Zaimis, stating that "no one can foretell if valuable finds or remarkable works of art will be unearthed but anyhow the field methodology will provide a model of excavation research."[11] It seems that Greek archaeologists, though energetic and skillful excavators themselves, nevertheless expressed their admiration for foreign field techniques, having perhaps internalized the stereotypes about the authority of foreign scholarship over the years.

For their part, the Swedes at the time do not seem to have evaluated the potentially positive impact of the Asine project on the development of Swedish archaeological practice. The key role of the excavation would only be acknowledged in writing considerably later, in the first decade of the twenty-first century when Robin Hägg, Berit Wells, and Penttinen would review the Asine field as a training dig for a whole generation of scholars who thereby gained specialized knowledge (Wells 2002, 13–16; Hägg 2002, 11; Wells and Penttinen 2005, 31). This seemingly unilateralist view, widely held in the thirties, could not but affect the future handling of the project.

However, communication can develop in many contexts. While seeking other justifications for the Asine project, one could list its potential for furthering trade. Although Greece was at the time beyond the sphere of significant Swedish business interests, it was not completely outside their scope. In 1934, almost thirteen years after the Asine project was initiated, the commercial links between the two countries resulted in the inauguration of the Hellenic-Swedish Chamber of Commerce in the presence of Gustavus Adolphus. On that occasion, both Adolphus and Georgios Pesmazoglou, the then Greek finance minister, underlined the positive impact on economic cooperation of the intellectual interaction between Greece and Sweden (*Kathimerini* 1934, 4).

Last but not least, a further decisive incentive for the Asine excavations seems to have been the expectation that they might generate valuable and highly desirable artifacts to enrich the Swedish universities' collections, perhaps in the hope of increasing interest in classical studies and promoting the eternal values embedded in antiquities. Such considerations were far from unique at the time. The American archaeological expedition to Colophon in Anatolia was dispatched in 1922 with the goal of, among other things, excavating objects that would enrich the collections of the Fogg Museum of Harvard University (Davis 2003, 150–52). In any case, Swedish demands, officially expressed already in 1922, and the underlying assumptions about the place of modern Greece in international politics would become entangled in a series of tense controversies in a period when the Greek state was concentrating on westernization and development. "Earthen made pots" were bound to become "a queer cause of strained international relations," as J. Balfour, a senior official in the British Foreign Office, would note with surprise.[12]

The Tangible Past Matters

Soon after the end of the 1922 field season, "the Swedish Mission . . . applied to the Ministry [of Education] for permit to receive from the [Asine] finds as many as the [Greek] Government was considering useless for the State Museums."[13] Selecting artifacts proved a difficult task because "the restored vases were few while the amount of sherds . . . was enormous . . . The Swedish Mission, understanding that difficulty," withdrew its original application and asked for the transport of all the finds from that year's expedition to Sweden as a loan for three years for conservation, restoration, and study. Their justification for the revised demand—in reality, a disguised form of their original one—was the lack of a Swedish Institute in Greece, which would have facilitated the final publication of the excavation. Consequently, they argued that they were at a disadvantage by comparison with other foreign schools.

Nikolaos Kyparissis, director of the Archaeological Service, presented the case to the Archaeological Council. Kyparissis emphasized the meticulous methods employed in the excavations and the importance of the scientific results but stressed that the finds were "totally insignificant as far as their actual value was concerned." Furthermore, he concentrated on the expected gains for Greece, claiming that granting permission "could both accelerate the studies of Greek antiquity in Sweden and assist the Swedish mission to secure rich resources for continuing the excavations and perhaps for establishing a Swedish or Scandinavian Institute that would greatly honor our country." Employing antiquities as "ambassadors of the nation" was—and still is—a recurring feature of the discourse on the Greek past and its enhancement (Hamilakis 2007, 200). There followed a thorough discussion. Christos Tsountas, a professor at the University of Athens, was the only member of the council who expressed his doubts about the concession on the grounds that it would be difficult to reject similar demands in the future.

The meeting of the Archaeological Council took place at a time of significant instability in the political and economic arenas, in the aftermath of the Asia Minor disaster of 1922, which affected all subsequent developments in Greece. In such difficult circumstances, "the Council, bearing in mind the minor significance of the finds up to then . . . the absence of a Swedish Institute . . . and the excavators' inability to study the finds at the site" unanimously approved the Swedish application, suggesting that a decree should be issued to legalize the concession.[14]

The resulting benefits to the Swedes were unprecedented, "violating active Greek legislation," as Konstantinos Kourouniotis, director of the Archaeological

Service (1925–33), would pointedly comment in a later report. In that report, in contrast to his former attitude on the issue (as we will see below), Kourouniotis would clearly distinguish between the export of artifacts from an ongoing and unpublished excavation, as was the case with Asine, and the prevailing informal Greek policy of "donating, after the final conclusion of an excavation conducted by a foreign country a few, totally unimportant, samples of the finds that are of no use to the Greek museums."[15]

A similar permit concerning the finds after 1922 and up to 1926 was issued in April 1926, and the material was taken to Uppsala.[16] Because exported material was not inventoried, the agreement was to be based on mutual trust.[17] This time the relevant decree clarified that the antiquities should be repatriated at Sweden's expense, and any future finds should be conserved and studied in a Greek public museum.

Such handlings have direct implications for the prestige of the archaeological authorities. The decision of the Archaeological Council, the highest decision-making body in Greece on all matters pertaining to archaeological work and whose opinion was widely trusted, did not comply with the law, so its authority and standing was bound to be undermined. Yet deviation from the law, even when not for personal gain, creates structural problems: established archaeological norms are devalued in the eyes of those who have benefited from the decision, and at the same time, it creates a basis for further demands.

In May 1929, instead of returning the antiquities in accordance with the provisions of the 1926 legislative decree, the Swedes asked the Greek government to send an archaeologist to Sweden in order to select from the material already conserved the artifacts that could be conceded to them.[18] This time the Swedish mission did not hesitate to use its political capital to assure its goal: its request was addressed to the Ministry of Foreign Affairs and not, as before, to the Ministry of Education, the only competent authority for the export of antiquities.

By the end of 1929, a three-member committee composed of the archaeologists Antonios Keramopoulos, professor at the University of Athens; Nikolaos Kyparissis; and I. Stefanou, secretary to the Greek embassy in Berlin, was sent to Uppsala.[19] In line with the current academic, strictly positivist reasoning, state scholars were connecting "discourse to the eye"; they were promoting observations and reason as the only valid way to reach "objective" conclusions (Plantzos 2008, 262–63). The committee recorded and photographed a total of 371 artifacts. However, in their official report, they clarified that because the greater part of the ceramics consisted of fragments still not conserved (over four thousand cardboard boxes), it was premature to select what could remain in Sweden. Still, they expressed doubts that the astounding volume of sherds would be thoroughly sorted, classified, and conserved after transportation to Greece. They suggested that Greek staff who would lack the personal interest of the actual excavator could not easily accomplish such a demanding task. Though such concerns were in alignment with the Swedish position, it was not explicitly accepted by the committee.

The meeting of the Archaeological Council on February 1, 1930, took place in a different sociopolitical context. Greece's domestic conditions had improved under the stable Liberal government of Venizelos, which was encouraging the modernization of the state (Mavrogordatos 1983, 37–38). Venizelos was promoting a series of long-overdue constitutional and administrative reforms, including the reorganization of archaeological policy through measures aiming at, among other things, introducing stricter controls over foreign archaeological schools (Sakka 2012). The new rationale was explicitly expressed by the Codified Law 5351/1932, which remained in force until June 2002 and limited the number of excavations that could be conducted by foreign institutions to three per year. Perhaps thanks to this new self-assurance, the council adopted a more rigid attitude. It questioned its previous weaker performance and demanded the restitution of all material previously transported to Sweden.[20]

Discussion continued on February 15 following the involvement of the Greek Ministry of Foreign Affairs that characterized the council's decision as "strict" and likely "to give rise to serious complaints on the part of the Swedish government."[21] The council perceived the involvement as a disrespectful intrusion of diplomacy into the sphere of archaeological policies, and it unanimously approved the proposal of its chairman, Georgios Papandreou, minister of education (1930–32)[22] that its earlier decision of February 1 be implemented. Unwilling to make concessions, Papandreou stated that the council should not endorse former violations of the archaeological laws. At stake were the social prestige of the establishment and the self-image of archaeological institutions.

Before long, the Swedish embassy once again approached the Greek Ministry of Foreign Affairs, appealing for a year's extension on the export permit.[23] The British ambassador at Athens, Patrick Ramsay, who was obviously on easy terms with his Swedish colleague, Baron Jonas M. Alströmer, reported that "as according to the Swedish Minister," the finds consisted "of a very large number of earthenware jars (600) of little or no archaeological value to the Greeks, the Swedish government [was] reluctant to go to the expense of so large a shipment both ways."[24] During the new round of negotiations, Alströmer "raised the question with Mr. Venizelos, only to be told that, as Prime Minister of Greece, he was much too occupied with important affairs of State to consider old pots and vases."[25]

On April 4, the council approved the extension of the export permit, endorsing Kourouniotis's opinion that the Archaeological Service "would be released from the most laborious and very expensive work of studying and reassembling the sherds."[26] However, in its next meeting, it reversed its earlier pronouncement by majority vote after an intervention by one of its members, Sokratis Kougeas, then professor of ancient history at the University of Athens.[27] The council demanded once more the return of the antiquities but suggested that the Greek state should cover the cost of transferring the material.[28] Only Kourouniotis and Panagiotis Kastriotis supported the Swedish demands, on the grounds that "the emergent love . . . of the Swedes in Greek antiquities . . . would be invigorated." It is in such choices and responses to foreign attitudes that contradictions and structural dilemmas of modern Greek life become evident: "stern morality" against "a relaxed attitude to violations of the norm" according collective and personal motives, and perception of archaeology as an objective discipline while supporting national pursuits (Kourelis 2008).

On January 8, 1931, the daily press published without further comment a telegram from the Swedish ambassador in Bucharest, according to which the steamboat conveying the Asine finds from Sweden was on its way to Piraeus (*I Proia* 1931, 6). Indeed, on January 12, Kourouniotis informed the council that some 270 boxes had arrived from Sweden.[29] In early December of the same year, Persson, invoking the restitution of the Asine material at the Nauplion Museum, requested the possible exchange of antiquities between Greece and Sweden.[30] Decisions were promptly taken.[31] The agreement was signed by Papandreou on December 16, 1931.[32]

The incident received further publicity on the occasion of the visit of Prince Adolphus and his family to Greece in 1934. D. M. Kalapothakis, chief press officer of the Greek Ministry of Foreign Affairs, sent to the director of *Eleftheron Vima*, a widely circulated Greek newspaper, a letter on the Asine question. Kalapothakis stated that a number of officials in the Ministry of Foreign Affairs and the Archaeological Service had been in favor of conceding the antiquities to Sweden. Kalapothakis condemned the Archaeological Council's resolution as backward and monolithic, adding that the dispute had "jeopardized" Greco-Swedish relations (*Eleftheron Vima* 1934, 1–2). Oddly, the publication of the letter, which appeared on the front page of the paper under the heading "Scholarship and Bureaucracy," produced no reaction in Greek society and was not followed by any kind of sophisticated debate. Although usually sensitive to issues concerning the export of antiquities, public opinion did not react this time (Petrakos 1982, 79–92; Hamilakis and Yalouri 1996; Solomon 2007, 167–77). The ethics of providing artifacts as a reward for the Swedish excavation project were not questioned. Was this lack of concern because the Greek public had long been (and indeed to some extent still is) trained to appreciate above all the spectacular masterpiece? In this respect, humble sherds get little credit. Another parameter to be considered is that Sweden did not rank in public consciousness among the great foreign powers that exerted a dominant influence over Greece, threatening its dignity and hurting its national pride.

On September 27, 1934, after the import of Swedish Stone Age objects was complete according to the 1931 agreement, the Archaeological Council authorized the export of some 223 boxes of antiquities designated as being "of no use" to the Greek state museums, for distribution to Swedish universities.[33]

According to current theoretical approaches, the values ascribed to archaeological material are socially and historically constructed, changeable, and fluid (Appadurai 1986; Darvill 1995, 40–43). In the thirties, experts acting on behalf of the state valued the Asine artifacts on their "use value"—that is, on the basis of their ability to offer some kind of return (Darvill 1995, 43–44). They designated as "useless" those finds that were not useful for studying, interpreting, and cross-dating the archaeological strata and the architectural remains, those whose absence would not compromise the integrity of important bodies of material, and those that would not be displayed in public museums.[34] The material from Asine was not singularized as a unit. It was the research and scientific potential merged with the aesthetic, artistic, and educational values of specific artifacts that rendered them singular and put them in a cognitive space from which they could communicate manifold meanings to diverse publics, both national and international (cf. Kopytoff 1986).

The 1931 agreement and the following exchange of antiquities put an apparently dignified end to the dispute for both parties. Yet the conflict seemed to leave its mark on the practice of Swedish archaeology in Greece for the next few decades. The excavations at Asine were interrupted in 1930 and did not resume until 1970, after a lapse of forty years. The Swedish Archaeological Institute at Athens was not established until 1947. On the other hand, it is perhaps not coincidental that in May 1931, in anticipation of the new Law 5351/32, the Archaeological Council decided to retract from the relevant draft the article allowing the concession of duplicate items to "Greek and foreign scientific Institutions that were carrying out excavations."[35] Although there is no clear connection between the Asine case and the drafting of the legislation, the members of the council could not but have been influenced by this case. The 1922 and 1926 export permits had created bad precedents, encouraged other foreign schools to demand equal treatment, and vindicated the concerns Tsountas had expressed at the time. In this light, it could be assumed that supplanting established practice with legislation must have seemed rather clumsy to those responsible for the management of the national cultural capital. Once again, the state bureaucracy maintains "a thoroughly inflexible mask" while pursuing a wide range of goals, always "on condition of relative concealment or at least discretion" (Herzfeld 2008, 48, 43).

The story of the Greek-Swedish dispute is one of different interpretations attached to shared situations by different actors at different times and in different sociopolitical contexts. It is a story of tensions and compromises, or to rephrase Appadurai, "what linked value and exchange" in the social life of the

Asine collection was "politics (in the broad sense of relations, assumptions, and contests pertaining to power)" (Appadurai 1986, 57).

From the Swedish perspective, the whole matter fitted well within the logic of a long-established code of scientific and political ethics concerning the acquisition of antiquities, as analyzed earlier. Although engaged in the excavation project on their own initiative, the Swedes subsequently addressed the issue of their concrete reward from the Greek state. In the publication of the Asine excavations, Frödin wrote that after lengthy negotiations, the Asine Committee had received part of the finds in recompense for the "great financial sacrifices" made by Sweden for the exploration of the site. He even presented the Greek reservations as the result of the "political conditions then prevailing in Greece," contextualizing archaeological practice within the wider framework of local political structures without questioning the legitimacy of the Swedish demands (Frödin 1938, 12). Achieving the concession of antiquities by violating Greek law and codes of practice was viewed in an almost neocolonial attitude, as if Greece had a moral obligation to the country that was revealing its past. Frödin's perspective illustrates the way Westerners have analyzed modern Greece: neither primitive nor civilized, with a glorious ancient past and a less-than-glorious present.

The Greek approach to handling of the dispute was a shifting compromise between the global character of classical heritage and Greece's local need for maintaining control over it as its legitimate "owner" while at the same time emphasizing its uniqueness (Leontis 1995; Yalouri 2001). Rigid implementation of legislation, reactions to the disrespectful Swedish attitude, and affirmation of the state archaeologists' hegemonic position in the protection and management of antiquities on behalf of the nation can be contrasted with a certain flexibility, seen in the overall pattern of reciprocity and embedded in the context of the implicit benefits of interaction with the West and in the increasingly realistic approach to the curation challenges posed by the voluminous body of the Asine material.

Historians and anthropologists have dealt with the processes of nation-building in Greece and the reinvention of the past. At the same time, they have pointed to the marked difference in the attitudes toward classical antiquity as a shared legacy of Western culture and Greece's position on the margins of Europe. Herzfeld calls this duality *disemia*, "the formal or coded tension between official self-presentation and what goes on in the privacy of collective introspection" (Herzfeld 1997, 14). The Asine case reflects this pattern of pairs of codes that, according to Herzfeld, defines Greek identity. Binary verbal and behavioral elements are manifested in several instances: in the comparison between Greek and Swedish field methods, in the intentionally flexible evaluation of antiquities as "ambassadors" and as "useless" for the state museums, in the conflicting positions of the Greek Ministry of Foreign Affairs and those of the Archaeological Service, in the ways Greeks and Swedes interpreted or dismissed the Greek law for their own ends, and in the ability of archaeologists and state officials to transform their discourse according to historical circumstances and personal interests.

The Asine case—a story of authority and subversion, of collaborations and tensions, of colonial behaviors deliberate or unconscious—embodies the complex interaction between national and foreign scholars, politicians, and diplomats. It highlights the way the highly praised artifacts are variously used and reused by different audiences. While directing our gaze to the structuring factors of Greek archaeology, it also summarizes the multiple stories of foreign archaeologies in Greece. It works as a paradigm that confirms antiquity is not singular but rather contested, open to divergent actions, readings, and expectations as a source of competing claims and counterclaims.

Life around the Excavation

There are many ways of conceptualizing the story of the Asine excavations. Meanings may also emerge from the variety of relationships between the members of the Swedish excavation team and the local community, and from the archaeological site's integration with the present. Archaeological practice in Greece, including tensions between archaeologists and local residents, is often thought to create isolated, demarcated sites, accessible only under conditions that deepen the past-present divide (Stroulia and Buck Sutton 2010).

Yet information extracted from Persson's publications and from the catalogues of two retrospective exhibitions (Nordquist 1988; Wells 1998) indicates that Swedish archaeologists in the 1920s had developed what could be described as quite a warm relationship with local communities that went beyond the limits of the archaeological sites themselves.

Accounts of a more personal nature and photographs understandably represent the Swedish perspective, creating a subjective picture of the atmosphere of the excavation. Nevertheless, these accounts reveal a rather active interest in the social lives of the locals, even within the structures of work hierarchies: "we have only pleasant memories of our intercourse with [the Dendra villagers] except that their attention and interest was sometimes a slight hindrance to the smooth course of the work" (Persson 1931, 10). Daily interaction and participation in feasts (Wells 1998, 50, 87, 93–95, 97) created a long-term engagement that seems to have emerged organically: "Many times we have taken part in [the villagers'] sorrows, and been asked for good advice at Evangelos's coffee-shop" (Persson, in Nordquist 1988, 34). Such memories may fit a pattern of academic elitism among Swedish scholars who, for example, present themselves as being asked for advice by the locals and not vice-versa, but they also speak of sharing of feelings and experiences.[36] Villagers, named in familiar terms, were not just seen as excavation workmen or providers for the excavation team. "A more capable cook and a more honest and upright man than young Orestes is not to be found in the whole of Greece" (Persson 1931, 9). "The honest fisherman Aristides and Evangelos, our friend the taverner," shared a special bond with the Swedish archaeological team, warmly welcoming it each time.[37]

Ghosts and spirits of the past pervaded archaeologists' and locals' everyday lives, created bonding experiences around the excavation field (cf. Yalouri 2014), helped found a "Swedish-Greek alliance," and strengthened the locals' sense of belonging to a place, engendering strong emotions and serving economic interests.[38] Both seasonal workmen (who were professionally involved in the excavations) and locals were deeply concerned about the ruins: "on the whole, [the laborers] were hard-working and conscientious and as the work proceeded they became extremely interested. This is equally true also of the other villagers, men, women, and children" (Persson 1931, 9). Archaeological work soon became part of the community's daily reality, and the finds were a source of local pride: "It was customary for the villagers to meet outside the scene of our work to discuss the day's happenings" (Persson 1931, 14). The discovery of the impressive Dendra gold cup captivated both archaeologists and villagers: "When we brought the cup up out of the pit, loud cries of joy arose. Long live Sweden! Long live Greece! . . . we knew that it was one of the great moments of our lives" (Persson 1931, 14), albeit no doubt for different reasons. Western intellectuals placed major emphasis on the archaeological value of the find: the bowl was "bigger than the Vaphio cups!" (Persson 1931, 14). For locals, it might have been the firm link, conscious or subconscious, with the ancestral past that provoked powerful emotional reactions and inspired quasi-religious respect: "people from well nigh the whole of Argolis made pilgrimages to Dendra" (Persson 1931, 18). For both parties, the embodied interaction with antiquities generated memories: after being cleaned up, the cup "was filled with red Nemean wine and passed round the company" (Persson 1931, 15).

Although the process was open to all social actors, it was the popular archaeologies, reproduced in Persson's writings, that ascribed major significance to such ritual practices, empowering alternative readings of ancient artifacts. "Old Dimitri, the innkeeper at Mycenae who several times . . . walked the three hours' distance from Mycenae . . . was invited to drink wine [from the gold bowl]. He raised the cup to his lips with trembling hands. When he had drunk, he said with tears in his eyes: 'I am fortunate! Twice has God let me drink from gold cups, in Vaphio in 1889, when I was with Tsountas, and again today. Now I can die content!'" (Persson 1931, 18). Dimitris's inner, spiritual qualities and intuitive knowledge of the past are qualities recognizable in the villagers portrayed by Greek novelists such as Andreas Karkavitsas in *The Archaeologist* (1903) and Ilias Venezis in *Galini* (1939). In Plantzos's words, both writers were arguing for an

Fig. 2.4. Villagers visiting Dendra Tholos Tomb. (Summer 1926.) Courtesy of Swedish Institute at Athens.

"'un-scientific,' non-academic archaeology, based on an idiosyncratic, national metaphysics" (Plantzos 2014, 160; see also this volume), which Persson seems to have embraced despite being an agent of Western modernity himself. Sensorial intimacy with archaeological finds, shaped on the border of official archaeology and bureaucratic restrictions, was thought to create pleasantly lived experiences and to promote meaningful dealings with the past (Hamilakis 2013b, 44–46).

Rather than dismissing local folk practices—such as the actual use of the cup or the organization of "banquets" in tholos tombs (Wells 1998, 80)—as trivial, the Swedish archaeologists, following rituals that were quite familiar at the time, validated the distinctive engagement with the past, the deeper appreciation of its materiality, and its emotional reception. Western scholarship expanded to accommodate popular performances and improvised appropriations of antiquity, acknowledging their importance for the living culture. Next to the nineteenth-century and early twentieth-century museographical tradition of the glass display case, which prioritized visual experience, the power of sentiment and the multisensorial appreciation of ancient relics were claiming their position. Examples include Sophia Schliemann's famous photo wearing the jewelry of "Priam's Treasure," and Tsountas's stimulating answer to the question posed by one of his students on the existence or not of a base in Vaphio's cups: "When they were found I used them to drink wine" (Karouzou 1974). Tangible past merges with present, fragments of antiquity are made personal, and consciousness of the past extends through touch, sounds, smells, actions, and feelings (Lowenthal 1985, 238–59).

Besides intangible values, the eight-year Swedish project provided economic advantages for the local community mainly through employment. At that time, the promotion of the archaeological site as a tourist destination was not included in the project's perspectives, even though cultural tourism was a developing industry. In the long term, however, even though the archaeological site has never acquired a prominent position on mass tourism itineraries, Tolon, situated one kilometer from the Acropolis of Asine, was once a fishing village but has developed into a seaside resort where Swedish travel agencies send their customers (Styrenius 1998, 53). Thus, it confirms the way in which a place can sometimes exercise power and fascination over not only those excavating its past but also their fellow countrymen, creating strong and lasting bonds.

The past is imbued with meaning and agency in the present. Almost a century ago, the ruins of Asine brought together in many different ways the absent "king of Asine," Swedish and Greek archaeologists, and the local people. They naturalized the values that ancient Greece represented inside and outside the country and negotiated tensions between local and Western interests. The ghosts of the past were revived in excavations, in lived experiences of tangible artifacts, in cups filled with red Nemean wine, in memories, in expectations, in emotions, and in the collective imaginaries of nations. The terracotta, male, bearded head that was found in the Mycenaean settlement on the northwestern slope of Asine's acropolis blurred the lines between past and present and gave new life to

> the king of Asini
> we've been searching for so carefully on this acropolis
> sometimes touching with our fingers his touch upon
> the stones.[39]

NIKI SAKKA is an archaeologist at the Ephorate of Antiquities of Athens, Hellenic Ministry of Culture. She has participated in many excavations in Greece and was actively involved in the project of the enhancement of the archaeological site of Lykeion, Athens. Her research interests include the archaeology of Athens, the archaeological policy of the Greek state, and its political, social, and cultural implications in Greece and abroad.

Notes

1. An early version of this text was presented at the Eighth Annual Meeting of the European Association of Archaeologists in Thessaloniki, September 24–29, 2002. I sincerely

thank Thanasis Kalpaxis for his helpful comments on that version. The text has benefited from the suggestions of the late Berit Wells. I wish to express my gratitude to Esther Solomon for inviting me to contribute to this volume and for her valuable comments and thoughtful suggestions. I am particularly grateful to Aris Anagnostopoulos for allowing me to read and refer to his unpublished paper presented at the Friends of the Historical Archive of the Greek Archaeological Service on November 10, 2014, introduced by Arto Penttinen (Anagnostopoulos 2014). I would also like to express my gratitude to Eleana Yalouri for her acute observations and advice and, most important, the insights she has shared with me. Further thanks are due to Elena Kountouri, then director of the Directorate of the Management of the National Archive of Monuments, Documentation and Protection of Cultural Goods, for facilitating my access to the archives, and to the very helpful staff of the Directorate, especially Sofia Fragoulopoulou. I am thankful to Arto Penttinen, director of the Swedish Institute at Athens (hereinafter SIA), both for his suggestions and for allowing me to reproduce photos published in Wells (1998). The originals of photos one to three are kept in the Asine Collection of Museum Gustavianum in Uppsala, Sweden; the original of the fourth photo is kept in the Archive of the SIA (hereinafter ASIA).

2. The École Française d'Athènes (1846), the Deutsches Archäologisches Institut (1874), the British School of Athens (1886), the Österreichisches Archäologisches Institut (1908), and the Scuola Archeologica Italiana di Atene (1909), to mention only the most long established ones, were funded and supported by their respective governments. The American School of Classical Studies at Athens (1881) is a nonprofit institution, not directly linked to the US government.

3. In the memorandum submitted to the Prussian Foreign and Education Ministries for permission and funding to excavate Olympia, Ernst Curtius wrote that the Greeks possessed "neither the interest nor the means" to conduct a major excavation (Marchand 1996, 81).

4. Department of the Management of Historical Archive of Antiquities and Restorations (Hellenic Ministry of Culture and Sports), Box 778b, Report of the Director of the Archaeological Service, August 23, 1930, unsigned.

5. In 1939, on the occasion of the export of five classical sculptures to the New York World's Fair, journalists wrote celebratory articles in which they emphasized that the exhibit triggered lectures and articles that rekindled the American interest in Greece (Eleftheron Vima 1940, 4).

6. Jack Davis, former director of the ASCSA, contrasts American philanthropic activities with the institution's unwillingness to invest in academic collaborations with Greek archaeologists and in educational programs on contemporary Greece (Davis and Vogeikoff-Brogan 2013, 6–7; Davis 2013, 34).

7. Gustavus Adolphus's mother, Victoria of Baden, took a keen interest in Egyptology. In 1892–95, she donated to Uppsala University various antiquities obtained from excavations conducted under her auspices in the Nile Valley (Starck 1974, 11–12).

8. Department of the Management of Historical Archive of Antiquities and Restorations, Acts of the Archaeological Council (hereinafter AAC) 1915–1924, Meeting 98, November 10, 1920.

9. Frödin in Dagens Nyheter, June 7, 1922, as cited in Nordquist (1988, 29).

10. Stockhoms-Tidningen, April 27, 1921, as cited in Nordquist (1988, 28). Cf. Styrenius (1998, 55).

11. ASIA, Asine file, document 276, Keramopoulos to Zaimis, March 26, 1922, as cited by Anagnostopoulos (2014).

12. PRO, FO 371/14391, Ramsay to Henderson, Confidential (n. 248), May 9, 1930, 21–22.

13. The quotations and information in this and the following paragraphs come from Department of the Management of Historical Archive of Antiquities and Restorations, AAC 1915–1924, Meeting 153, October 21, 1922.

14. The decree would be published in the Government Gazette on November 12, 1922.

15. Department of the Management of Historical Archive of Antiquities and Restorations, Box 778b, unsigned report of the Director of the Archaeological Service, August 23, 1930.

16. Legislative Decree, April 26, 1926.

17. Department of the Management of Historical Archive of Antiquities and Restorations, AAC 1924–1934, Report of A. Keramopoulos, N. Kyparissis, and I. Stefanou to the Ministry of Education, December 20, 1929, read at Meeting 309, February 1, 1930.

18. Information in this paragraph comes from the Department of the Management of Historical Archive of Antiquities and Restorations, AAC 1924–1934, Meeting 289, May 22, 1929.

19. The quotations and information in this paragraph come from the Department of the Management of Historical Archive of Antiquities and Restorations, AAC 1924–1934, Meeting 309, February 1, 1930.

20. Department of the Management of Historical Archive of Antiquities and Restorations, AAC 1924–1934, Meeting 309, February 1, 1930.

21. The quotations and information in this paragraph come from the Department of the Management of Historical Archive of Antiquities and Restorations, AAC 1924–1934, Meeting 310, February 15, 1930.

22. Georgios Papandreou (1888–1968), a close associate of Venizelos from the outset, supported the educational reform of 1929 to 1932, a turning point in the history of modern Greek education. Under Papandreou, the Ministry of Education undertook the construction of 3,167 new schools, following a loan taken out with a Swedish company (Dimaras 2006, 335–36).

23. Department of the Management of Historical Archive of Antiquities and Restorations, AAC 1924–1934, Meeting 320, April 4, 1930.

24. PRO, FO 371/14391, Ramsay to Arthur Henderson, Confidential (n. 248), May 9, 1930, 21–22.

25. PRO, FO 371/15237: 28, Patrick, Ramsay to Arthur Henderson, Annual Report on Greece for 1930, C882/882/19, 28.

26. Department of the Management of Historical Archive of Antiquities and Restorations, AAC 1924–1934, Meeting 320, April 4, 1930.

27. The quotations and information in the rest of the paragraph come from the Department of the Management of Historical Archive of Antiquities and Restorations, AAC 1924–1934, Meeting 321, April 7, 1930.

28. On May 15, 1930, the Greek Ministry of Foreign Affairs paid the Swedes 5,940 Swedish kroners to cover the expenses of the committee that was sent to Uppsala (ASIA, Asine file, document 404, as cited by Anagnostopoulos 2014).

29. Department of the Management of Historical Archive of Antiquities and Restorations, AAC 1924–1934, Meeting 351, January 12, 1931.

30. Department of the Management of Historical Archive of Antiquities and Restorations, AAC 1924–1934, Meeting 377, December 8, 1931.

31. Department of the Management of Historical Archive of Antiquities and Restorations, AAC 1924–1934, Meeting 378, December 14, 1931.

32. Document published in Wells (2002, 14–15).

33. Department of the Management of Historical Archive of Antiquities and Restorations, AAC 1924–1934, Meeting 15, September 27, 1934. On the current state of the Asine material, see Nordquist and Hägg (1996).

34. Department of the Management of Historical Archive of Antiquities and Restorations, AAC 1924–1934, Report of A. Keramopoulos, N. Kyparissis, and I. Stefanou to the Ministry of Education (Berlin, December 20, 1929), read at Meeting 309, February 1, 1930; AAC 1924–1934, Meeting 320, April 4, 1930; Meeting 378, December 14, 1931.

35. Department of the Management of Historical Archive of Antiquities and Restorations, AAC 1924–1934, Meeting 360, May 29, 1931.

36. Persson's emotional attachment to Greece may be deduced by his humanitarian work during World War II. Together with his wife, Elsa Segerdahl, he participated in the mission of International Red Cross in the Peloponnese in 1943–1944 (Papakongos 1977). Thanks go to Arto Penttinen for this reference.

37. Persson in Svenska Dagbladet, June 19, 1924 (see Nordquist 1988, 33–34).

38. Ibid.

39. George Seferis, *The King of Asini*, translated by Edmund Keeley and Philip Sherrard. Seferis won the Nobel Laureate for Literature in 1963 and was one of the most influential Greek poets. He was a main advocate of the Generation of the Thirties, whose modernism was characterized by a fascination with "Greekness," or the effort, "in short, to establish 'the real' Greek tradition." When interviewed by Keeley, Seferis responded to a question on the relation of a Greek poet to his particular historical tradition as follows: "Greece is a continuous process. In English the expression 'ancient Greece' includes the meaning of 'finished,' whereas for us Greece goes on living, for better or for worse; it is in life, has not expired yet. That is a fact" (Seferis 1970).

References

Acemoglu, Daron, and James A. Robinson. 2000. "Why Did the West Extend the Franchise? Democracy, Inequality, and Growth in Historical Perspective." *Quarterly Journal of Economics* 115: 1167–99.

Allen, Susan Heuk. 2011. *Classical Spies: American Archaeologists with the OSS in World War II Greece*. Ann Arbor, MI: University of Michigan Press.

Amandry, Pierre. 1992. "Ανασκαφές στους Δελφούς και Κορινθιακές Σταφίδες: Ιστορία μιας Διαπραγμάτευσης" [Excavations at Delphi and Corinthian Currants: The Story of a Negotiation]. In *Δελφοί: Αναζητώντας το Χαμένο Ιερό* [Delphi: In Search of the Lost Sanctuary], edited by Olivier Picard, 77–126. Athens: B. Giannikos and B. Kaldis.

Anagnostopoulos, Aris. 2014. *1920–1940, Δύο Δεκαετίες Σουηδικών Ανασκαφών στην Αργολίδα: Ζητήματα της Μεταφοράς Ευρημάτων στη Σουηδία και ένα «Χαμένο» Αρχείο του Μεσοπολέμου*. [1920–1940: Two Decades of Swedish Excavations in the Argolid: Aspects of the Transport of Finds in Sweden and a "Lost" Archive of the Interwar Period]. Paper presented at the Friends of the Historical Archive of the Greek Archaeological Service on November 10, 2014.

Appadurai, Arjun. 1986. "Introduction: Commodities and the Politics of Value." In *The Social Life of Things: Commodities in Cultural Perspective*, edited by Arjun Appadurai, 3–63. Cambridge: Cambridge University Press.

Beaton, Roderic. 2009. Epilogue to *Scholars, Travels, Archives: Greek History and Culture through the British School at Athens.* Proceedings of a Conference Held at the National Hellenic Research Foundation, Athens, 6–7 October 2006 *(BSA Studies 17)*, edited by Michael Llewellyn-Smith, Paschalis M. Kitromilides, and Eleni Calligas, 217–21. London: British School at Athens.

Bourdieu, Pierre. 1990. *The Logic of Practice.* Stanford, CA: Stanford University Press.

Clogg, Richard. 2009. "Academics at War: The British School at Athens during the First World War." In *Scholars, Travels, Archives: Greek History and Culture through the British School at Athens.* Proceedings of a Conference Held at the National Hellenic Research Foundation, Athens, 6–7 October 2006 *(BSA Studies 17)*, edited by Michael Llewellyn-Smith, Paschalis M. Kitromilides, and Eleni Calligas, 163–77. London: British School at Athens.

Darvill, Timothy. 1995. "Value Systems in Archaeology." In *Managing Archaeology*, edited by Malcolm A. Cooper, Antony Firth, John Carman, and David Wheatley, 40–50. London: Routledge.

Dasios, Fotis. 1992. "Η Περιπέτεια της Σύμβασης από Ελληνικής Πλευράς (1881–1891)" [The Adventure of the Convention from the Greek Side (1881–1891)]. In *Δελφοί: Αναζητώντας το Χαμένο Ιερό* [Delphi: In Search of the Lost Sanctuary], edited by Olivier Picard, 127–41. Athens: B. Giannikos and B. Kaldis.

Davis, Jack L. 2003. "A Foreign School of Archaeology and the Politics of Archaeological Practice: Anatolia, 1922." *Journal of Mediterranean Archaeology* 16 (2): 145–72.

———. 2013. "The American School of Classical Studies and the Politics of Volunteerism." In *Philhellenism, Philanthropy, or Political Convenience? American Archaeology in Greece*, edited by Jack L. Davis and Natalia Vogeikoff-Brogan, special issue, *Hesperia* 82 (1): 15–48.

Davis, Jack L., and Natalia Vogeikoff-Brogan. 2013. Introduction to "Philhellenism, Philanthropy, or Political Convenience? American Archaeology in Greece," edited by Jack L. Davis and Natalia Vogeikoff-Brogan, special issue, *Hesperia* 82 (1): 1–14.

Dimaras, Alexis. 2006. "Modernization and Reaction in Greek Education during the Venizelos Era." In *Eleftherios Venizelos: The Trials of Statesmanship*, edited by Paschalis M. Kitromilides, 319–45. Edinburgh: Edinburgh University Press.

Dyson, Stephen L. 2006. *In Pursuit of Ancient Pasts: A History of Classical Archaeology in the Nineteenth and Twentieth Centuries.* New Haven: Yale University Press.

"The Dissolution of the Union of Norway and Sweden." 1907. *American Journal of International Law* 1: 440–44.

Encyclopaedia Britannica. "Gustav VI Adolf (King of Sweden)." n.d. *Encyclopaedia Britannica.* Accessed July 23, 2019. http://www.britannica.com/EBchecked/topic/249843/Gustav-VI-Adolf.

Firth, Antony. 1995. "Ghosts in the Machine." In *Managing Archaeology*, edited by Malcolm A. Cooper, Antony Firth, John Carman, and David Wheatley, 51–67. London: Routledge.

Frödin, Otto. 1938. Introduction to Otto Frödin and Axel W. Persson, *Asine. Results of the Swedish Excavations 1922–1930*, edited by Alfred Westholm, 9–24. Stockholm: Esselte Aktiebolag.

Gillman, Derek. 2010. *The Idea of Cultural Heritage.* Rev. ed. Cambridge: Cambridge University Press.

Gouldner, Alvin W. 1960. "The Norm of Reciprocity: A Preliminary Statement." *American Sociological Review* 25: 161–78.

Hägg, Robin. 2002. "Swedish Archaeology in Greece, 1894–1994." In "*Peloponnesian Sanctuaries and Cults*. Proceedings of the Ninth International Symposium at the Swedish Institute at Athens, 11–13 June, 1994, edited by Robin Hägg, 9–13. Stockholm: Swedish Institute at Athens.

Hamilakis, Yannis, and Eleana Yalouri. 1996. "Antiquities as Symbolic Capital in Modern Greek Society." *Antiquity* 70: 117–29.

Hamilakis, Yannis. 2007. *The Nation and Its Ruins: Antiquity, Archaeology, and National Imagination in Greece*. Oxford: Oxford University Press.

———. 2008. "Decolonizing Greek Archaeology: Indigenous Archaeologies, Modernist Archaeology and the Post-Colonial Critique." In *A Singular Antiquity: Archaeology and Hellenic Identity in Twentieth-Century Greece*, edited by Dimitris Damaskos and Dimitris Plantzos, 273–84. Athens: Benaki Museum.

———. 2013a. "Double Colonization: The Story of the Excavations of the Athenian Agora (1924–1931)." In *Philhellenism, Philanthropy, or Political Convenience? American Archaeology in Greece*, edited by Jack L. Davis and Natalia Vogeikoff-Brogan, *Hesperia* 82 (1): 153–77.

———. 2013b. *Archaeology and the Senses: Human Experience, Memory, and Affect*. Cambridge: Cambridge University Press.

Hegardt, Johan, and Anna Källén. 2011. "Being through the Past: Reflections on Swedish Archaeology and Heritage Management." In *Comparative Archaeologies: A Sociological View of the Science of the Past*, edited by Ludomir R. Lozny, 109–35. New York: Springer-Verlag.

Herzfeld, Michael. 1997. *Cultural Intimacy: Social Poetics in the Nation-State*. New York: Routledge.

———. 2002. "The Absent Presence: Discourses of Crypto-Colonialism." *South Atlantic Quarterly* 101: 899–926.

———. 2008. "Archaeological Etymologies: Monumentality and Domesticity in Twentieth-Century Greece." In *A Singular Antiquity: Archaeology and Hellenic Identity in Twentieth-Century Greece*, edited by Dimitris Damaskos and Dimitris Plantzos, 43–54. Athens: Benaki Museum.

Keohane, Robert O. 1986. "Reciprocity in International Relations." *International Organization* 40: 1–27.

Kopytoff, Igor. 1986. "The Cultural Biography of Things: Commoditization as Progress." In *the Social Life of Things: Commodities in Cultural Perspective*, edited by Arjun Appadurai, 64–91. Cambridge: Cambridge University Press.

Kourelis, Kostis. 2008. "Musings on Architecture and Archaeology." *Singular Antiquity 4: Herzfeld*. Accessed May 20, 2016. http://kourelis.blogspot.gr/2008/09/singular-antiquity-4-herzfeld.html.

Lalaki, Despina. 2013. "Soldiers of Science—Agents of Culture: American Archaeologists in the Office of Strategic Services (OSS)." In *Philhellenism, Philanthropy, or Political Convenience? American Archaeology in Greece*, edited by Jack L. Davis and Natalia Vogeikoff-Brogan, *Hesperia* 82 (1): 179–202.

Leontis, Artemis. 1995. *Topographies of Hellenism: Mapping the Homeland*. Ithaca, NY: Cornell University Press.

Lévi-Strauss, Claude. 1944. "Reciprocity and Hierarchy." *American Anthropologist* 46: 266–68.
Lowenthal, David. 1985. *The Past is a Foreign Country.* Cambridge: Cambridge University Press.
Lundberg, Erik. 1985. "The Rise and Fall of the Swedish Model." *Journal of Economic Literature* 23: 1–36.
Marchand, Suzanne L. 1996. *Down from Olympus: Archaeology and Philhellenism in Germany, 1750–1970.* Princeton, NJ: Princeton University Press.
Mavrogordatos, George Th. 1983. *Stillborn Republic: Social Coalitions and Party Strategies in Greece, 1922–1936.* Berkeley, CA: University of California Press.
Nordquist, Gullög C. 1978. "The History of the Collection." In *From the Gustavianum Collections in Uppsala, 2, 1978: The Collection of Classical Antiquities: History and Studies of Selected Objects. Acta Universitatis Upsaliensis Boreas* 9: 11–36.
———. 1988. *Fragments of Axel W. Persson.* Exhibition at the Swedish Institute at Athens, June 1–24, 1988. Athens: Swedish Institute at Athens.
Nordquist, Gullög C., and Robin Hägg. 1996. "The History of the Asine Excavations and Collections, with a Bibliography." In *Asine III: Supplementary Studies on the Swedish Excavations 1922–1930*, edited by Robin Hägg, Gullög C. Nordquist, and Berit Wells, 11–18. Stockholm: Swedish Institute at Athens.
Oakes, Leigh. 2001. *Language and National Identity: Comparing France and Sweden.* Amsterdam: John Benjamins.
Papakongos, Kostis. 1977. *Αρχείο Πέρσον: Κατοχικά Ντοκουμέντα του ΔΕΣ Πελοποννήσου* [The Persson Archive: Occupation Documents of IRC in the Peloponnese]. Athens: Papazisis.
Persson, Axel W. 1931. *The Royal Tombs at Dendra near Midea.* Lund: C. W. K. Gleerup.
Petrakos, Vasileios. 1982. *Δοκίμιο για την Αρχαιολογική Νομοθεσία* [Treatise on the Archaeological Legislation]. Athens: Publications of the Arheologikon Deltion [Archaeological Bulletin] 39.
Plantzos, Dimitris. 2008. "Time and the Antique: Linear Causality and the Greek Art Narrative." In *A Singular Antiquity: Archaeology and Hellenic Identity in Twentieth-Century Greece*, edited by Dimitris Damaskos and Dimitris Plantzos, 253–72. Athens: Benaki Museum.
———. 2014. "Dead Archaeologists, Buried Gods: Archaeology as an Agent of Modernity in Greece." In *Re-imagining the Past: Antiquity and Modern Greek Culture*, edited by Dimitris Tziovas, 147–64. Oxford: Oxford University Press.
Sakka, Niki. 2008. "The Excavation of the Ancient Agora of Athens: The Politics of Commissioning and Managing the Project." In *A Singular Antiquity: Archaeology and Hellenic Identity in Twentieth-Century Greece*, edited by Dimitris Damaskos and Dimitris Plantzos, 111–24. Athens: Benaki Museum.
———. 2012. "Αρχαιολογική Πολιτική της Κυβέρνησης Βενιζέλου, 1928–32: Σχέδια, Προτάσεις και Θεσμικές Ρυθμίσεις" [Archaeological Policy of Venizelos's Government, 1928–32: Plans and Constitutional Reforms]. In *Ελευθέριος Βενιζέλος και Πολιτιστική Πολιτική* [Eleftherios Venizelos and Cultural Policy], edited by Tasos Sakellaropoulos and Argyro Vatsaki, 92–110. Athens: Benaki Museum and National Research Foundation "Eleftherios Venizelos."
Schön, Lennart. 2008. "Sweden—Economic Growth and Structural Change, 1800–2000." In EH.Net Encyclopedia, edited by Robert Whaples. Accessed May 20, 2016. http://eh.net/encyclopedia/sweden-economic-growth-and-structural-change-1800-2000.

Seferis, George. 1970. "The Art of Poetry n. 13. Interviewed by Edmund Keeley." *The Paris Review* 50. Accessed May 20, 2016. http://www.theparisreview.org/interviews/4112/the-art-of-poetry-no-13-george-seferis.

Silberman, Neil Asher. 1990. "The Politics of the Past: Archaeology and Nationalism in the Eastern Mediterranean." *Mediterranean Quarterly* 1: 99–110.

Skorda, Despina. 1992. "Η Ανασκαφή των Δελφών και οι Έλληνες Αρχαιολόγοι (1863–1881)" [The Excavation of Delphi and the Greek Archaeologists (1863–1881)]. In *Δελφοί: Αναζητώντας το Χαμένο Ιερό* [Delphi: In Search of the Lost Sanctuary], edited by Olivier Picard, 61–71. Athens: B. Giannikos and B. Kaldis.

Smångs, Mattias. 2008. "Business Groups in Twentieth-Century Swedish Political Economy: A Sociological Perspective." *American Journal of Economics and Sociology* 67: 889–914.

Smith, Michael Llewellyn, and Paschalis M. Kitromilides. 2009. Introduction to *Scholars, Travels, Archives: Greek History and Culture through the British School at Athens.* Proceedings of a Conference Held at the National Hellenic Research Foundation, Athens, 6–7 October 2006 *(BSA Studies 17)*, edited by Michael Llewellyn Smith, Paschalis M. Kitromilides, and Eleni Calligas, 1–12. London: British School at Athens.

Solomon, Esther. 2007. "'Multiple Historicities' on the Island of Crete: The Significance of Minoan Archaeological Heritage in Everyday Life." PhD diss., University College London.

Starck, Sylvia. 1974. "The Victoria Museum—An Introduction." In *From the Gustavianum Collection in Uppsala, Acta Universitatis Upsaliensis Boreas* 6: 11–14.

Stroulia, Anna, and Susan Buck Sutton. 2010. "Archaeological Sites and the Chasm between Past and Present." In *Archaeology in Situ: Sites, Archaeology and Communities in Greece*, edited by Anna Stroulia and Susan Buck Sutton, 3–50. Lanham, MD: Lexington.

Styrenius, Carl-Gustaf. 1998. *Asine. En Svensk Utgrävningsplats I Grekland.* [A Swedish Excavation Site in Greece]. Stockholm: Medelhavsmuseet.

Tilton, Timothy A. 1974. "The Social Origins of Liberal Democracy: The Swedish Case." *The American Political Science Review* 68: 561–71.

Trigger, Bruce. 1997. "Book Reviews. Down from Olympus: Archaeology and Philhellenism in Germany, 1750–1970, edited by Suzanne L. Marchand. Princeton University Press, 1996." *Bulletin of the History of Archaeology* 7: 43–44. Accessed May 20, 2016. http://doi.org/10.5334/bha.07211.

Voudouri, Daphne. 2010. "Law and the Politics of the Past: Legal Protection of Cultural Heritage in Greece." *International Journal of Cultural Property* 17: 547–68.

Wells, Berit. 1998. *Life Around an Excavation. Η Ζωή Γύρω από μία Ανασκαφή.* Athens: Swedish Institute at Athens.

———. 2002. "The Prehistory of the Swedish Institute at Athens." In *New Research on Old Material from Asine and Berbati in Celebration of the Fiftieth Anniversary of the Swedish Institute at Athens*, edited by Berit Wells, 9–22. Stockholm: Swedish Institute at Athens.

Wells, Berit, and Arto Penttinen. 2005. *On Site: Swedish Archaeologists in Greece.* Athens: Motivo.

Widén, Per. 2011. "National Museums in Sweden: A History of Denied Empire and a Neutral State." In *Building National Museums in Europe 1750–2010.* Conference Proceedings from EuNaMus, European National Museums: Identity Politics, the Uses of the Past and the European Citizen, Bologna 28–30 April 2011, edited by Peter Aronsson and Gabriella Elgenius, 881–902. Linköping: Linköping University Electronic Press. Accessed May 20, 2016. http://www.ep.liu.se/ecp_home/index.en.aspx?issue=064.

Yalouri, Eleana. 2001. *The Acropolis: Global Fame, Local Claim.* Oxford: Berg.

———. 2014. "In the Spirit of Matter: Reconnecting to Antiquity in the Greek Present." In *Re-imagining the Past. Antiquity and Modern Greek Culture*, edited by Dimitris Tziovas, 165–85. Oxford: Oxford University Press.

Archival Sources

1. Department of the Management of Historical Archive of Antiquities and Restorations (Hellenic Ministry of Culture and Sports): Acts of the Archaeological Council 1915–1924; 1924–1934. Boxes 559, 778b.
2. "Eleftherios K. Venizelos." Digital Archive, Benaki Museum. Accessed May 20, 2016. http://www.venizelosarchives.gr/index.asp.
3. Public Record Office (PRO), FO 371.
4. Archives of the Swedish Institute at Athens, Asine file.

Greek Daily Press

Eleftheron Vima. "Τα Περίφημα 'Συντρίμματα' από τας Σουηδικάς Ανασκαφάς. Μια Πρότασις του κ. Δ. Μ. Καλοποθάκη" [The Famous "Sherds" from the Swedish Excavations: A Proposal by Mr. D. M. Kalapothakis]. September 22, 1934, 1–2.

I Proia. 1931. "Απόδοσις Αρχαιοτήτων" [Return of Antiquities]. January 8, 1931, 6.

M. P. 1940. "O Αμερικάνικος Τύπος διά την Ελληνικήν Γλυπτικήν" [The American Press on Greek Sculpture]. *Eleftheron Vima*, February 12, 1940, 4.

Kathimerini. 1934. "O Διάδοχος της Σουηδίας Ενεκαινίασε το Ελληνοσουηδικόν Επιμελητήριον. Θερμοί Λόγοι του υπέρ της Ελλάδος" [The Crown Prince of Sweden Inaugurated the Hellenic-Swedish Chamber of Commerce: Warm Words on Greece]. September 28, 1934, 4.

Karouzou, Semni. 1974. "Χρήστος Τσούντας. Ένας Ήρωας της Αρχαιολογικής Έρευνας" [Christos Tsountas, A Hero of the Archaeological Research]. *To Vima*, December 31, 1974, as cited in *O Mentor* 28 (1993): 178–83.

Legislation

Law 541/1875. "Περί κυρώσεως Συμβάσεως μεταξύ Ελλάδος και Γερμανίας περί αρχαιολογικών ανασκαφών εν Ολυμπία" [On the Ratification of the Convention between Greece and Germany on the Archaeological Excavation at Olympia]. *Efimeris tis Kiverniseos* [Government Gazette, hereinafter FEK], 59/15-11-1875.

Law 1974/1891. "Περί κυρώσεως συμβάσεως περί αρχαιολογικής ανασκαφής εν Δελφοίς" [On the Ratification of the Convention on the Archaeological Excavation at Delphi]. FEK 126/A'/6-5-1891.

Legislative Decree, November 9, 1922. "Περί δανεισμού των εκ των ανασκαφών της Ασίνης ευρεθεισών αρχαιοτήτων εις την ενεργούσαν τας ανασκαφάς Σουηδικήν Επιτροπήν" [On the Loan of the Asine Archaeological Finds to the Swedish Committee]. FEK 232/A'/12-11-1922.

Legislative Decree, April 26, 1926. "Περί των εν Ασίνη αρχαιολογικών ευρημάτων υπό της ενεργούσης τας εκεί ανασκαφάς Επιτροπής εκ Σουηδών" [On the Asine

Archaeological Finds from Excavations Conducted by the Swedish Committee]. FEK 144/A'/5-5-1926.

Law 5351/1932. "On Antiquities," codified by the Presidential Decree of August 9/24, 1932. FEK 275/A'/24-8-1932.

Law 3028/2002. "Για την προστασία των Αρχαιοτήτων και εν γένει της Πολιτιστικής Κληρονομιάς" [On the Protection of Antiquities and Cultural Heritage in General]. FEK 153/A'/28-6-2002.

3 Contested Perceptions of Archaeological Sites in Cyprus

Communities and Their Claims on Their Past

Alexandra Bounia, Polina Nikolaou, and Theopisti Stylianou-Lambert

Introduction

Cyprus has often been used as an example par excellence to discuss issues of contested heritage. Emphasis has been mainly placed on the ethnic dimensions of heritage construction and consumption, and to its political use related to territorial and national claims of the two main communities of the island, the Greek Cypriots and the Turkish Cypriots. The nature of archaeological remains and historical monuments makes them a suitable focus for the lodging of claims and counterclaims relating to cultural supremacy over the land. In addition, almost all historical accounts regarding archaeology in Cyprus start with an extensive reference to the illicit digging and trading of antiquities that took place during the late nineteenth century, within the colonial frame of mind. In this narrative, the foreign colonial regimes in Cyprus, the British and the Ottoman Empires, and foreign consuls, such as the infamous Luigi Palma Di Cesnola,[1] are those responsible for depriving the island of large numbers of artifacts, today forming the collections of museums around the world. The theme of illicit pillaging and trading of antiquities has also become central in the cultural war between the two communities in subsequent periods, and the debate continues to this day, with the Greek Cypriots accusing the Turkish Cypriots of inadequate protection of the cultural heritage of the island on their part and the Turkish Cypriots returning the culpability, referring to the Muslim monuments of the southern part.[2] These accounts are usually presented as one-sided stories of victimization (Stylianou-Lambert and Bounia 2016).

In this chapter, we intend to introduce a rather different perspective. We will focus on antiquity as a multilayered contested terrain in which multiple actors and multiple perspectives are at play. We will argue that, instead of focusing on stories of victimization, we should understand the development of the interest in antiquities as a complex relational and political process negotiated in the different spaces in which archaeology was practiced—a process that has been determined by the changing interests of various stakeholders, the construction of the (colonial) self and the other, and the rise of national identity and nationalism. The first part of this chapter will present in brief the construction of the (colonial) archaeological space as a relational and political process. Then we will focus on the conflicting perceptions of archaeological space by different groups of individuals, more specifically Cypriot natives, local intellectual elites, colonial rulers, and other foreigners. We will argue that the interest in antiquities, archaeology, and the past in the late nineteenth and early twentieth centuries in Cyprus has been a complex interplay between various understandings of the land, the right to its ownership, and the symbolic significance of its "treasures." These ideas continue to influence Cyprus to this day, as we will argue in the epilogue.

The Construction of the Archaeological Space in Cyprus

The concept of heritage as a situated process and practice (which has been emphasized in the past decade by the work on critical heritage), in conjunction with the relational notion of place, can provide the critical tools for positioning archaeology in its political, social, and cultural milieu (Graham, Ashworth, and Tunbridge 2000; Harvey 2015a). However, this literature tends to follow a structural hierarchy of scale when the mechanisms through which "dissonant" heritage operates (Tunbridge and Ashworth 1996)—universal approaches for the protection of ancient monuments and local and national claims—appear to be, as Harvey (2015b) argues, more elusive and less structural than nation-states or local places.

This conceptual framework can be enhanced by the work done by human geographers on the concept of place and their arguments to abandon the idea that place as a locus is a preexisting natural register with essential identities and boundaries. Of particular help is Doreen Massey's seminal and influential work on place. Massey's (2005, 9) three propositions on place reconceptualize it as a dynamic notion that is never finished or closed with fixed boundaries: first, it is the product of interactions with different scales (from the local to the global); second, it is a sphere of coexisting heterogeneity; and third, space, as a product of interrelations with material practices, is always under construction. In Massey's words, a place is "a meeting place, where the difference of a place must be conceptualized more in the ineffable sense of constant emergence of uniqueness out of (and within) the specific constellations of interrelations within which that place is set" (2005, 69). Drawing from Massey's work, Harvey (2015b, 584) suggests examining the competing claims over heritage in terms of the content and nature of their respective expressions of relationality instead of understanding them through the essential organizational settings of scale. Put differently, if one views heritage as a relational process, then the elements of context and contingency, in the form of different spatial and temporal interrelations of power locally articulated, come to the fore as essential analytical tools. In this chapter, when we talk about places, we refer to the archaeological sites of the field and the museum as fluid temporal and spatial constructions embedded in specific sociohistorical contexts.

The relational view of archaeology and space can facilitate the understanding of different and competing colonial politics that were at play in the Mediterranean region because it offers the opportunity to examine the relation between colonial governments and the preservation of the past (Moro-Abadia 2006, 13). First, it disrupts the modern-bounded concepts of space that were the hallmarks of colonial histories; second, it helps to transcend the general homogenizing tendency of postcolonial theory that obscures the diversity and materiality of the colonial experience and thus becomes vague and ahistorical (Eagleton 1998; Harvey 2015b; Nash 2002; Shohat 1992).

In correlation with the new imperial histories, colonial culture is perceived not as a homogeneous diachronic discourse but as a diverse and multifaceted phenomenon that should be situated in specific temporal, spatial, and sociopolitical contexts (Lester 2001; 2006; Shohat 1992). In this line, imperial histories have been reconsidered from an alternative geographical perspective; attention is given to the special characteristics of different imperial sites and networks (Lester 2001). Similarly, Stoler and Cooper (1997, 4) argue that social transformations—both in the colonies and metropolises—were constructed through "global patterns and local struggles," and as such they treat colonies and metropolises "in a single analytic field."

This geographical perspective of colonial histories is useful to the examination of the history of heritage and archaeology because it gives space for the "small stories," such as the non-elite quotidian practice and the social and cultural plurality, and to the different sites in which archaeology as a science was practiced (Lorimer 2003, 300; Liebmann 2008). The use of heritage for political purposes is carried out not only from top to bottom, from the government to the people, but also from bottom to top. In fact, often there is an inner path, where ideas from above give directions to communities, which in turn reroute interest in specific fields. As Crooke (2010) mentions, participation in a community is locally defined as an interaction that takes place in a self-designated identity field and involves some form of community hierarchy. The incentives of engagement in activities are multileveled and can be based upon standard and well-recognized interests, personal relationships with a specific area or origin, and the desire of performing cultural identity and personal or communal interests. By adopting this interdisciplinary and contextual approach, we can bring forward the complicated entanglements of global and local forces that conditioned Cypriot archaeology. This is essential for understanding the use of heritage on the island.

Conflicting Perceptions of Archaeological Spaces

In the late nineteenth and early twentieth centuries, the local and global context of Cypriot archaeology was constituted by an amalgam of imperialism, local colonial governments, elitism, scientific expertise and narratives, local populations, and social exclusion. In the case of Cyprus, there is a constant interaction between authorities and the local people regarding the use of heritage for political purposes. The quest we find in private archival correspondence, as well as in the writings of various antiquarians (such as Reinach 1891) for a more systematic "historical and educational" study of the material culture of the past, is also a quest related to the need to anchor the nation in the past on behalf of its people (see also Trigger 1995; Leriou 2007a). Leriou (2007a, 566) argues that Cypriot archaeology has been (and continues to be) defined by the culture-historical approach, which was introduced at the end of the nineteenth century, when Cypriot antiquities started being systematically classified and used to reconstruct the island's history and culture. Consequently, the material remains of the past were understood as having direct associations with ethnic identities and, as such, performances around them as having an immediate impact on political causes.

As the following sections will show, archaeological sites and findings in nineteenth-century Cyprus were perceived in different ways by natives, local intellectuals, and colonial rulers. These often conflicting perceptions influence what archaeological findings mean and how they are narrated and used.

Natives and Archaeological Sites in the Field as an Everyday Space

According to Nick Shepherd (2003) "native labor" is at the heart of colonial political economy. Archaeological research was in need of a socially diverse population, and this can be viewed on the social structure of archaeological operations in the field in the late nineteenth century. To perform excavations, a broad public participation was necessary, including laborers who could dig, field assistants who could negotiate with the diggers, and museum archaeologists or antiquarians who organized the process. Until recently, these "minor figures" (Lorimer 2003, 200) or "marginal people" (Clifford 1988) were silenced by the dominant narratives of the mythical age of exploration that favored heroic individuals—in this case, the dilettantes and antiquarians at the beginning, and the eminent archaeologists later on. Minor figures such as laboratory assistants or non-European assistants in colonial settings, or even instruments, were ignored in favor of the individuality of the main "hero," the antiquarian or archaeologist (Camerini 1996; Turner 1997). Nevertheless, a closer look at the minor figures of the archaeological record offers another view of European empires distant from the simplistic, one-way models (Nikolaou 2013, 159; 2015) and allows for a more nuanced understanding of the politics of archaeology.

Cypriot people were closely involved in all aspects of the colonial archaeological process. They were the diggers, the field assistants, and in certain cases the initiators of the effort (i.e., local intellectuals who developed their own interest in antiquities and their own agendas). Despite the recurrent allegations by prominent scholars, such as Professor John Myres (1914, xv–xvi), that "The Cypriot peasantry have ever treated the relics of their ancestors with a levity and cupidity rare even in the Levant," this view is only part of the story.

A closer look at the writings of dilettantes and antiquarians who participated in this early stage of Cypriot "archaeology" provides the reader with interesting stories. Cypriot villagers of both the main ethnic communities of the island were employed and often left alone to do their work with limited supervision in most of the late nineteenth century, whereas their employers would only visit the sites to record and collect the artifacts the villagers discovered. With few exceptions, it was not the archaeological process—which in this period was starting to emerge as a field-based scientific endeavor—that was of interest to them, but the "results" in the form of material remains. This approach is resonant with the imperial/global and colonial/local contexts in which archaeology operated in this period: first, archaeological excavations in the Eastern Mediterranean were largely sponsored by European museums, whose foremost aim was to adorn their galleries with artifacts from classical civilizations; second, in Cyprus, excavating for "antiquities" was for a certain elite class, a "fashionable amusement of the day" (Myres 1914, xiv).

Reinach (1891), for instance, recounts an interesting story regarding Max Ohnefalsch-Richter, one of the most well-known foreign archaeologists working on the island in the late nineteenth century, and his relation with the native workers. In October 1880, Ohnefalsch-Richter had started excavations in the area of Larnaca on behalf of the British Museum. The results were not satisfactory, and consequently the workers, who wanted to continue working in the area because this allowed them to stay close to their families and in more comfortable conditions during the winter, took advantage of the absence of the archaeologist himself and put some "ancient vases decorated with concentric circles" among the finds of the site. Astonished by the fact that archaic objects were found next to Roman ones, Ohnefalsch-Richter wrote an article about them in the journal of the German Archaeological Institute only to realize his mistake four years later. Reinach claims that this was the first, but not the last, time that the workers managed to trick the German archaeologist and lead him to erroneous conclusions.

The story, which is one of the many that can be found in texts of the nineteenth century, allows for a series of conclusions regarding both the tactics of these early archaeologists/antiquarians and the playful, human, and practical understanding of their work by the natives.

The interest of the local population in the antiquities of their land took various forms. Another well-known antiquarian, Sir Hamilton Lang,[3] records his own experiences. Lang claims that the villagers in Dali became quite extraordinary at discovering tombs. At the beginning, they discovered them by accident, as in the case of the well of Laksha Nicoli, but later on they became quite professional in that they had enough knowledge to charge high prices to collectors willing to acquire the objects the villagers had found (Lang 1878, 331–32).

> In 1868, after a torrential rain, some peasants of Dali were passing along the base of a hillside to the north of their village on the summit of which is a well which gets the name of Laksha Nicoli. They found evidently washed down from the hillside, a few pieces of ancient pottery in perfect preservation, and one of them representing a duck. The peasants at once thought that more might be found where these came from, and they set to work to turn over the ground on the hillside. To their surprise they got into tombs, and extracted pieces of pottery in great number, and some lances in bronze. News of the discovery soon spread, and as the villagers were in much distress, having lost most of their crops from the ravages of locust, they repaired in great numbers to the pottery-diggings. (1878, 331)

This interest seems to be fed by financial gains. Furthermore, Lang (1878, 338) argues, "Thus five young men who were working in the hope of gaining a shilling or two a day stumbled upon a treasure which brought them about 800 pounds." But in some other instances, financial gain was not enough, or even tempting. After having inspected the collections kept in the house of local villagers, Hogarth (1889, 106) complains that during his visit to the village of Marion, he did not manage to acquire an object that had attracted his attention because "the jealous owner would neither permit a near inspection nor sell his treasure."

The laws enacted by the Ottoman authorities in 1869 and 1874 regarding the restrictions of the excavation and exportation of archaeological artifacts[4] only served to make collecting practices more complicated, and the regulations imposed by the British authorities after 1878 did not effectively control how archaeology was conducted in Cyprus. Illicit digging of antiquities was a pursuit for Cypriots of all ethnic backgrounds and religions, and a thriving market of antiquities was established. Lang (1878) claims that in Dali, the peasants were led in their pursuit chiefly by two men: Hasen, a Turk of Dali, and the old Hagge Georgi (probably of Greek origin, judging by the name). The former was General Cesnola's middleman, and as Lang (1878, 333) argues, "he had an extraordinary aptitude for such work." The latter was working for Lang and, according to the man, "had wonderful luck."

Fig. 3.1. Some of the Turkish workers of Cesnola. Courtesy of Bank of Cyprus Cultural Foundation.

The role of the middlemen, or chief workers, is further illuminated by a September 6, 1897 letter written by Antonio Grigori, who signs himself as superintendent of the British excavations on the island.[5] He asks the archaeologists of the British Museum to introduce him to the British governor so that he can ask for a job because he had been jobless for months. He further asks for five or six pounds to sustain him until he gets a new excavation to supervise. The mere fact that he writes this letter indicates his role in the chain of interest regarding antiquities.

In other words, native Cypriots of both ethnic backgrounds seem to have perceived and understood archaeological sites as local, familiar, everyday places that could unveil valuable artifacts in more or less the same way that their land would grow crops to maintain their livelihood.

Local Intellectuals and the Construction of Archaeology as a Space of National Significance

In contrast, prominent educated members of both communities adopted a rather different understanding and rhetoric. They understood archaeology and the past as a terrain for the construction of their "national self" and the promotion of their political goals. Greek intellectuals took advantage of the European interest in the "classical past" and used it to develop national claims that supported union (*enosis*) with Greece. The Muslim community also realized the importance of the past in the politics of the present, and at the beginning, it supported the efforts toward the common protection of Cypriot heritage and the establishment of the Cyprus Museum. The community gradually turned its interest to the medieval heritage that supported a multicultural narrative for the island and thus better suited their claims on it.

The role of the Greek intellectual community in the early interest in antiquities is rather complex. On the one hand, the Greek community was actively engaged in the collection and dealing of antiquities, and it used these entities to encourage foreign interest in the island's antiquities, thus aiming to support the connection of Cyprus with Greece and Europe. On the other hand, these intellectuals expressed a strong desire for the archaeological finds to stay in Cyprus and establish local collections and museums to educate the public. This double/ambivalent approach continues to characterize the (Greek) Cypriot cultural policy up to the present day (Karageorghis 2004).

Several archival documents reveal the involvement of Greek Cypriots in the collection and dealing of antiquities as well as the use of the latter to encourage foreign interest in the island and support toward its connection to Greece. Various letters written by prominent Greek Cypriots and addressed mainly to the archaeologists of the British Museum offer various ancient objects for sale.[6] For instance, the merchant Caridis, a partner in the London-based company Caridi, Taylor, and Co., writes in 1889 to the keeper of the British Museum, C. Smith, on behalf of his friend F. Partides, who had offered to sell the museum some Cypriot antiquities. There seems to be a negotiation of the price, which ends in the mutual satisfaction of both parties.[7] In another series of letters dated 1896, A. Mavrogordato writes to the new keeper of the British Museum, A. S. Murray, about a stone seal in the possession of one of his friends. Despite the fact that the owner of the seal considers it "a real treasure," the price offered and the opinion of the specialist do not support this belief.[8]

Gradually, the interest in selling artifacts became less and less appealing and gave rise to the desire to protect antiquities and discourage their exportation. This is the attitude of many intellectual Greek Cypriots, such as Demetrios Pierides (1811–1895). Pierides, a prominent member of the Greek Cypriot community, served as a consul of Great Britain in Larnaca (1845–1850) and was a member of the Legislative Council (1884–1885); he was also a keen antiquarian and collector. He was an interlocutor for foreign scholars and antiquarians who visited the island during his lifetime. Sir Hamilton Lang claimed that Pierides was his "coadjutor in all connected with antiquities" and his "instructor from his superior, nay, very exceptionably profound antiquarian and philological knowledge" (Lang 1878,

Fig. 3.2. Demetrios Pierides. Courtesy of Pierides Foundation.

332). Reinach (1891, 170) claimed that Pierides was "un de plus intelligent collectionneurs de Chypre," ("one of the most intelligent collectors of Cyprus") and J. T. Wood described Pierides as "the most obliging and useful man."[9] But Pierides was also one of the founding members of the Cyprus Museum and an active supporter of its establishment.

Similarly, in a letter to the Greek archaeologist Panayiotis Kavvadias, another intellectual, N. Katalanos, the editor of the Greek Cypriot newspaper *Evagoras*, blamed the lack of a specific policy for the protection of antiquities by the British colonial government for having led everybody on the island, "people of the city and peasants, illiterate and well-educated, to take advantage of the country's sacred heirlooms and to think that there is no problem in using them to make a profit."[10] Katalanos, like other similarly minded Greek Cypriot intellectuals, had a different purpose in mind when it came to antiquities: a national aim.

The antiquities as material proof of origin—in this case, Hellenism—were used by Greek Cypriot intellectuals to support the demand of enosis, strengthen Greek identity, and establish links with mainland Greece. As Leriou argues

(2007a, 573), ethnic groups often select certain parts of their material culture and employ them as emblematic *indicia* to highlight their differentiation from other groups and thus set their boundaries. This practice is exactly what happened in the case of Greek Cypriots. Antiquities became a central part of their ever-growing national identity, and as such, they became a matter of politics and conflict. The transfer of antiquities (the insignia of their Greek identity) to the British Museum and other European institutions—as part of British imperialist and scientific policy—gradually became a problem for them and occasionally infuriated them. For instance, ardent supporter of enosis, journalist, and politician Nikolaos Lanitis wrote an article published in the Athenian newspaper *Estia* in 1896 expressing both the interest of the local community of intellectuals for the ancient monuments as evidence of their national identity and their frustration at the export of antiquities by British archaeologists to British museums, despite the fact that the epistemological orientation of the British Museum's work in Cyprus in the 1890s supported his claims. Moreover, he emphasized the point that Greek Cypriot intellectuals spoke on behalf of the whole community and thus claimed for this community a special relation with specific material remains.

> The illegal antiquities' traders who turn to Cyprus should rest. . . . If indeed the apostles of various archaeological societies and representatives of the glorious British Museum are honest workers of science, their work and the resulting findings will not be harmed if our ancestral heirlooms stay in Cyprus, to which they belong according to all natural and ethical laws, taking into account all their limitations and versions. The recent important findings of the Cyprus excavations by Dr. Murray were unearthed here . . . the objects that had just been born from the paternal land, which affectionately protected them in order to display them the great day of Enosis, as foolproof exhibits of common descent, to our brothers of the same blood. The real workers of science can very well do their work in the Cyprus Museum. . . . The voice of the Greek groups of the island, powerful because they are right, needs to be heard and it is necessary the honorable and honest citizens, who care for national pride, to raise a shout of ultimate protest against such an injustice. . . . Let's fight for the sacred heirlooms of our great ancestors, since by doing so we fight for our honor, our national pride.

In other words, Greek Cypriots used the ideas and liberties given by the British in order to empower their Hellenic identity, thus supporting their political claims. It is within this framework that this complex relationship with antiquities developed: efforts to promote Cypriot archaeology internationally, even at the expense of the protective laws (as in the case of the support given to the Swedish Archaeological Expedition [1927–1931] to export antiquities at the expense of the 1905 legislation that prohibited it; cf. Sakka, this volume), were combined with strong voices against their exportation and for their protection on the island, through the establishment of the Cyprus Museum (Stylianou-Lambert and Bounia 2016).

Fig. 3.3. Exportation of antiquities by the Cyprus Exploration Fund in 1890, with the participation of large numbers of people of all groups. Courtesy of Trustees of the British Museum.

The Cyprus Museum was established on June 15, 1882, as the result of a petition approved by the British high commissioner of the island, Sir Robert Biddulph (Stanley-Price 2001; Pilides 2009, 63). The petition was signed by the archbishop of Cyprus and both the cadi and the mufti of Cyprus (i.e., the leaders of the main religious communities).[11] The petition was justified with the following reasons: first, a museum would have a very positive influence on the mind and the taste of the people; secondly, it would help promote the study of the history and antiquities of the island and attract intellectuals and scholars. It was further argued that the museum would be under the supervision of the government of Cyprus and would be considered a national institution. The museum opened its doors to the public nine years after the initial decision was made, on May 16, 1891 (Merrillees 2005). In its early years, two conflicting claims can be evidenced: although the British government in London did not give substantial funds for its formation, the museum was in effect a colonial apparatus of power for controlling Cypriot archaeology because the government's share of the findings from excavations would be housed there; in addition, it was the place where the local claims over Cyprus's national past and future could be debated. The

Cyprus Museum in these early years was heavily dependent on subscription fees, which in turn showed that wealthy members of both communities supported the institution. However, the existing subscribers' lists shows that by the late 1880s, the number of Greek Cypriot subscribers was significantly larger than those of the Turkish Cypriot community.[12] For instance, in 1883, out of twenty-nine subscribers, just five appear to be from the Muslim community, prominent among which were the cadi and the mufti.[13]

Cultural identity is commonly associated with the importance that people attach to specific historical monuments. The Greek Cypriot community focused on the "classical past" and the "classic museum," as the Cyprus Museum was called by George Jeffery (Pilides 2009), but monuments of different periods were also present on the island. The more the Greek community turned to the classical past to support its national arguments, the more the Muslim community felt alienated and estranged from it (Hardy 2010). As Sian Jones (2005, 96) notes, the reformulation of the official representations of national heritage is a process that plays an integral part in the ways in which those "pushed to the edges" seek to reclaim a space for themselves. As was natural, the Muslim community felt more comfortable with the Ottoman past. The Venetian, Frankish, and Ottoman heritage was not subject to claims or interest by the Greek community, and at the beginning, it was located only marginally in the region of interest of Europeans. In other words, it was the most appropriate to attract the attention of the Turkish Cypriot community.

The first to express interest in the reuse and the deterioration of the medieval monuments of Cyprus was George Jeffery (1855–1935). As the curator of monuments, Jeffery criticized the change of use and damages as unacceptable by European standards. He also shared the belief that true protectors of the monuments were the people, and therefore he argued the education of the population would mean the gradual reduction of threats to the monuments (Pilides 2009). At first, Jeffery attributed the lack of interest in medieval monuments to the lack of education on the part of the Cypriots. Later, he understood that there was no lack of interest in the monuments, but the focus was on those monuments representing "classical antiquity." In other words, it was a "selective" interest with which he was dealing. Jeffery initially expressed his interest in preserving medieval heritage through the establishment of a small museum for Venetian findings in Famagusta in 1903, and then two years later through the establishment of a medieval museum in Nicosia. To this effort, he found support from the Evkaf, a Muslim institution established in 1571 as a public benefit foundation to promote education, restoration of historical and cultural preservation, and economic and social development. The denial by the Greek authorities to offer Jeffery the Church of St. Nicholas for his museum was soon to be remedied by the Evkaf, which provided Jeffery with a small building next to the Turkish Lyceum. The

Architectural Museum, or Musée Lapidaire as it was and is still named, opened in 1928 and was partly funded by the Evkaf. In a letter dated November 14, 1928, addressed to the minister of the colonies, Jeffery thus presents his newly established museum.

> The history of the Lusignan dynasty of Cyprus is without a parallel in any other country, and at the same time its relationship to medieval Europe inspires an interest in every European nation, and also amongst the Turks.
>
> The architectural remains in the Musée are almost exclusively from ancient buildings used as mosques, medresses, etc. They are, therefore, regarded by the Moslems [*sic*] as almost inalienable Moslem property and a list of them is deposited in the Evkaf office. It is the earnest desire of the Moslem community that the Musée—the construction of which is partly paid by the Evkaf funds—should remain in the charge of the C.A.M. [Curator of Ancient Monuments] and the Delegates of the Evkaf. (Quoted in Pilides 2009, 675)

The appropriation of this cultural period from one of the ethnic communities of the island is very clearly set out in the excerpt from the letter. It is also clear that the "colonial discourse" was already formulated in terms of the medieval monuments. These monuments were part of European heritage, and therefore it was perfectly natural for Europeans to develop an interest in them. On the other hand, the Muslim population of the island, whose presence is not documented in ancient tradition but in medieval tradition (the sixteenth century, and more specifically 1571, a time when the island became part of the Ottoman territory) and who had continued to use these monuments, giving them other meanings, shared interest in this heritage. The Muslims considered this heritage their own, or at least more of their own compared to the classical one that had been adopted by the Greek Cypriot community.

Foreigners, Colonial Rulers, and Archaeological Sites as Scientific Spaces

The discussion in the previous sections has already made apparent the important role the British colonial politics played in the development of the locals' understanding of archaeology and the past. In the summer of 1878, the Ottoman Empire ceded the administration of Cyprus to the British Empire as part of the Convention of Defensive Alliance. The arrival of the British on the island was a peaceful invasion of administrators, and by the early 1880s, the island became "the backwater in Britain's overseas imperium" (Holland and Markides 2006, 164). The island never acted as a naval base, and this fact was evident in the lack of fortifications, which were noticeable in other key British colonies in the region such as Malta and Gibraltar (Varnava 2009). The status of Cyprus within the British Empire remained ambiguous until the first decades of the twentieth century. In 1914, legal advisors of the Foreign Office described the island as a "bit of Turkey in British occupation, under British administration" (Markides 2006, 19); only in 1925 did Cyprus become an official British colony. This ambivalent position of Cyprus on the British imperial map becomes evident in the attitudes toward the regulation of Cypriot archaeology.

In accordance with imperial ideology, the British had expressed a strong interest in classical heritage, which they considered to be the cradle of European civilization. This view was widely used to legitimize British (but also European in general) colonization. The self-defined paternalistic mission of the British Empire as a perceived, superior civilization that should govern the "uncivilized" was evidenced in Cyprus not only in the necessary administration of the supposedly primitive inhabitants but also in the regulation of the preservation of the material remains due to the "inadequacy" of Cypriots (Stanley-Price 2001). The acquisition of the island was publicized as part of a larger regional development for the benefit of Asia Minor under English patronage in collaboration with the Ottoman Empire (Holland and Markides 2006). For the British officials, the primitive character of Cypriot material culture provided proof of the island's primitive population and undeveloped character. Foreign officials residing on the island reinforced these imaginative geographies, describing Cypriots as sagacious and dishonest, whereas the island's orientalist character was evidenced by palm trees and camels and in the perceived, peculiar style of the discovered antiquities, which did not exactly fit the shape and form of classical artifacts (Knapp and Antoniadou 1998). In Cyprus, however, things were relatively more complex. The global scale of British imperial politics was intersected with the local colonial conditions and with the aspirations of the local population, as described earlier.

Furthermore, there was a gradual change of attitude on behalf of the colonial powers from the early interest and support of the late nineteenth century that encouraged the Greek character of Cypriot antiquities to a completely different perspective in the 1930s, which brought forward a local Eteocypriot[14] group of people to counterbalance the rising Greek voices for enosis with Greece (Given 1998). The idealization of classical Greece became part of the methodologies used by the colonial powers to establish a good relationship with part of the local population. This relationship changed in the process, when the Greek Cypriot population used exactly the same frame of mind (i.e., their affinity with classical Greek antiquity) to argue for their enosis with Greece. It is this exemplification of the notion of archaeology and heritage as a pedagogical and policy tool that we see in other national contexts as well (Harvey 2015a; Tolia-Kelly 2010).

Despite this political use of archaeology by the colonial authorities in Cyprus, claims against the limited efforts made by the colonial government for the protection of the heritage of the island were made even by British archaeologists. Sir John Myres,[15] who was among the first who studied Cypriot archeology in the nineteenth century, criticized the government for failing to spend any funds on maintaining and properly storing the collection of the Cyprus Museum (Myres and Ohnefalsch-Richter 1899, vi–vii; Merrillees 2005, 15, 18). Similarly, Reinach (1891, 169) argued that unlike France, which had spent more than one hundred thousand francs to support archaeological work in Tunisia, Britain had done almost nothing for Cyprus.

The efforts of regulating and constraining the archaeological explorations in Cyprus were conducted not as part of a wider imperial project but by individuals of the local British government. Col. Falkland Warren, chief secretary of the island in 1880, sent a circular order that informed the various commissioners that everything that lay underneath the soil was governmental property, including tombs, whether regarded as antiquities or monuments.[16] In 1887, all excavations by private individuals were prohibited by Sir Henry Bulwer, the high commissioner of Cyprus. In essence, these regulations affirmed the territory of the island as the property of the Cyprus government and thus of the British Empire. Given (2001) claims the reasoning behind the control of excavations on the island is the ideological force of archaeology and the colonial need to control the sources of information and interpretation that derive from it. The Cyprus government not only regulated the sources of archaeological information (i.e., excavations) but also authorized its members for the interpretation of the past in terms of documenting the island's history (Given 2001; see for example Cobham 1894). These regulations could also be interpreted as "the absolute territorial definition of sovereignty" (Silvern 2002, 38).

Nevertheless, local politics were interspersed with broader imperial geopolitical tensions. The Cyprus government, through the Legislative Council, members of which were representatives of the local communities, voted for stricter bills that prohibited the exportation of antiquities. However, the British government in London opposed the enactment of stricter conditions, as explained by the secretary of state, because these conditions would not allow any exportation of antiquities. In the secretary of state's opinion, no museum would want to excavate in a country that forbade the exportation of antiquities.[17] For example, despite the opposition of the local government, the British government in London gave permission to the Royal Berlin Museum to excavate and export antiquities in 1894 because "it was anxious to meet the German Emperor's views."[18] Exportation of antiquities thus became a tool of cultural politics as well, not only by the Cypriot people but also by the colonial forces.

The British imperial interpretations of the island and their colonial administration gave the space to the local communities to articulate their claims over archaeology. The Greek Cypriots considered Britain a large philhellenic force that would free them from the "barbarian" Ottoman rule and allow their union with Greece. At first, the British intellectuals who visited the island in different capacities emphasized the Greek character of Cyprus as much as possible. John Myres stressed the "Greek character" of Cyprus's past and thus offered support to those who wanted the unification of Greece and Cyprus. He was a devoted admirer of the Greek world and had received a classical education. The nineteenth-century scientific view that the archaeological material reflected the ancient ethnic group of the people on the island was a key component of his work (see also Leriou 2007b), which also influenced the development of Cypriot archaeology and the views of many of his contemporaries. The keeper of the British Museum at the turn of the previous century, A. S. Murray, also viewed Cyprus as the easternmost extension of the Mycenaean world. It is precisely this community, which consisted of British philhellenes, archaeologists, and antiquarians, that supported the idea of the creation of the Cyprus Museum as an academic space to collect and study the material remains of the land. Claims over the ownership of Cyprus's heritage were made in the sessions of the Legislative Council by Turkish Cypriot and Greek Cypriot members through the discussions on the enactment of stricter regulations on the exportation of artifacts. In the sessions held in the 1890s, some members considered this topic to be a more pressing matter than the preservation of ancient buildings.[19] However, it was the British and the European "discovery" of the medieval period, through Jeffery, that encouraged and promoted a different valuation of the archaeological remains—one that the Muslim community found more interesting and appropriate for its own claims.

Cypriot antiquities were thus made a special arena for contested claims: on the one hand for the refusal of the British sovereignty over Cyprus (mainly by Greek Cypriots), and on the other hand for the justification of British rule by the local (British) authorities. Given (1998) has suggested that colonial authority used archaeology in order to control the development of Greek Cypriot nationalism. Through the governor of the island from 1926 to 1932, Sir Ronald Storrs, the authorities encouraged and promoted the discovery of an ancient autochthonous population, whose presence would make ancient Cypriots less Greek and indeed repressed by the Greeks. The Swedish archaeologists started digging in the island from 1927 discovered the Eteocypriots and used them as a political tool. Despite the lack of evidence that would support a conscious collaboration between the colonial authorities and the Swedes, and irrespective of the archaeological and historical merit of such claims, there is no doubt that archaeology could and would be used for such a political claim (see also Scott 2002; Leriou 2007b). Storrs, who is reported to have been ordered to foster a sense of "Cypriot patriotism" to counteract Greek nationalism (Scott 2002; Given 1998), also made accusations against Greek Cypriots. He wrote in his memoir that the historic record of Cyprus had been compromised by the removal of all Phoenician artifacts predating the Mycenaean colonization from Cyprus Museum: "none has survived the determination of the Greek majority that Cyprus shall possess proofs of none but Hellenic origin" (Storrs 1939, 488). Even though this accusation may refer to the rearrangement of the collection from the old museum building to the new one, it is also quite telling of a culture war in progress, using monuments, museums, and archaeology to justify political aspirations.

Despite the complexity of the relation among politics, archaeology, local communities, and the colonial rulers, there seems to be one common thread that connects them: an effort on behalf of the British and the other foreigners to endorse an academic, neutral, scientific aura to their understanding and approach to the Cypriot past.

Epilogue

This chapter aimed to address heritage issues in Cyprus as a multileveled contested territory. The relation between archaeology, communities, and the past in Cyprus is embodied within the various sites in which archaeology as a science operates: the field, the museum, government offices, and newspaper articles. These sites were not homogeneous or bounded but were simultaneously characterized by the multiscale nexus of universal/imperial ideas of heritage as expressed in the colonial attitudes toward antiquities on the island, the shifting position of Cyprus on the British imperial map, and the strong wish to claim responsibility for the local cultural heritage by local agents, which was influenced by the changing European archaeological narratives. It is our understanding that conflict regarding heritage is a perpetual process located in the way different groups of individuals perceived the spaces of archaeological sites and situated within these fluid spatial and temporal configurations. In many ways, these perceptions continue to influence Cypriot archaeology and Cyprus's relation to the past until this day. These narratives were embodied in the armed struggles for union with Greece that took place in 1931 and from 1955 to 1959. In addition, even after the formation of the Republic of Cyprus in 1960, there were ongoing struggles between the two ethnic communities which led to the military operation by Turkey in 1974 and the subsequent division of the island that continues to this day. Although there are continuing efforts at reconciliation and the borders between the two parts of the island opened in 2003, the current narratives (both in national museums and in terms of the illegal trafficking of antiquities) express the conflicted perceptions of the archaeology of the island formed since the late nineteenth century (Stylianou-Lambert and Bounia 2016). The relation to the past and the use of material remains continue to be used to make and remake claims to the land.

In our discussion regarding the nineteenth century, native Cypriots of both ethnic groups seem to have understood archaeological sites as familiar, local, and their own to use for their livelihood. This perception is not uncommon today, when the discovery of archaeological artifacts is suppressed by the villagers or owners of the land where these discoveries have been made because it would be "inconvenient"[20] for them to report such findings to the authorities. This understanding, which has class conflict at heart, is often used as an argument against allegations regarding illicit trading of antiquities by Turkish Cypriots before and after 1974 (Hardy 2010, 203).

In contrast, Cypriot intellectuals of the nineteenth century saw these sites and artifacts as spaces full of meaning that would allow them to construct national identities. This premise is true for both sides of the island. These intellectuals initiated and supported the creation of national museums, many of which exist to this day, such as the Cyprus Museum and the Musée Lapidaire; the former is in the southern part of Cyprus, and the latter is in the northern part. Today, these museums, and also the new ones that have been established by official bodies and individuals along these lines, make the same national claims using material culture and the past to educate Cypriots, with each museum making choices about which part of the past to promote (Stylianou-Lambert and Bounia 2016).

Finally, colonial rulers and other foreign archaeologists saw the archaeological sites as neutral, scientific spaces that would enrich the Western understanding of the world with their treasures. They organized scientific expeditions, published academic accounts, and collected in a calculated manner, which reconfigured the antiquities as objectified knowledge. As their perceptions of archaeological sites and findings conflicted with those of the natives and with those of the local intellectuals, they tried to educate the natives and change their perceptions of archaeological findings. It is interesting to notice that today the museums around the world housing Cypriot archaeological collections place them within a scientific archaeological discourse that, by creating a perceived neutral context, moves them away from any possible political position. For example, the British Museum's Cypriot collection is in the Greek and Roman Department, with some objects in the Ancient Levant Galleries; the Cypriot collection of the Louvre resides in the Department of Near Eastern Antiquities (Levant); and the collection of the Metropolitan Museum of Art is part of the Greek and Roman Art. In none of the institutions is there any reference to the contested nature of antiquity on the island or the continuous division of the land.

ALEXANDRA BOUNIA is Professor of Museology at the Department of Cultural Technology and Communication of the University of the Aegean. She studied archaeology and history of art at the University of Athens (Greece) and museum studies at the University of Leicester (UK). She edited *Collector's Voice: Ancient Voices* (Ashgate, 2001) in collaboration with Prof. Susan Pearce, and she is the author of *The Nature of Classical*

Collecting: Collectors and Collecting 100 BCE-100 ACE (Ashgate, 2004), *Behind the Scenes of the Museum: Museum Collections Management* (in Greek, Patakis, 2009), and, together with Theopisti Stylianou-Lambert, *Political Museum: Power, Conflict and Identity in Cyprus* (Routledge 2016).

POLINA NIKOLAOU, PhD, is a historical-cultural geographer who works on the history and theory of museums and collections and on the history of archaeology. Building on her PhD thesis, "The Diaspora of Cypriot Antiquities and the British Museum, 1860–1900," her current research interests are the conceptual and historical aspects of the relationship between knowledge, space, and antiquities and between the concept of archaeological provenance and museums. She also provides consulting services in exhibitions and historical research projects.

THEOPISTI STYLIANOU-LAMBERT is Associate Professor in the School of Fine and Applied Arts at the Cyprus University of Technology and the founder and coordinator of its *Visual Sociology and Museum Studies Lab*. Her research interests include museum studies and visual sociology. She has published widely on museums and photography, is the coauthor of *The Political Museum* (Routledge, 2016), and is the editor of *Museums and Visitor Photography* (MuseumsEtc, 2016), *Museums and Photography: Displaying Death* (coeditor, Routledge, 2016), *Photography and Cyprus: Time, Place, Identity* (coeditor, I. B. Tauris, 2014), and *Re-envisioning Cyprus* (coeditor, University of Nicosia Press, 2010).

Notes

1. Luigi Palma di Cesnola (1832–1904) was a soldier, diplomat, and amateur archaeologist. He was the US consul in Larnaca (1865–1871). In the periods 1865–1872 and 1873–1876, he undertook many excavations and amassed a very large collection of artifacts that he exported and sold to the Metropolitan Museum of Art through a complex process of negotiation (both legal and illegal) with the Ottoman authorities. He then became the director of the museum (1879) until his death. Cesnola's activities in Cyprus made him one of the most notorious collectors and dealers of antiquities in the world. For Cesnola's activities on the island, see Nikolaou (2015).

2. This chapter is based on extensive archival and bibliographical research conducted by the authors, two Greek Cypriots and a Greek national, between 2012 and 2016. Nikolaou's work has resulted in the submission of her thesis on the diaspora of Cypriot antiquities (Nikolaou 2013), and Stylianou-Lambert and Bounia's work is published in a volume on the museums of Cyprus (Stylianou-Lambert and Bounia 2016).

3. Sir Hamilton Lang (1836–1913) was a merchant, financier, and collector. He was appointed to Larnaca as a manager of the local brand of the Imperial Ottoman Bank and

served as an acting vice-consul for Britain. He developed an interest in collecting Cypriot antiquities. Much of his collection was purchased by the British Museum in 1872–73; other items were loaned at first and then donated to the Glasgow Art Gallery and Museum, as well as the Louvre and various museums in Germany.

4. For a detailed discussion of this legislation, see Stanley-Price (2001).

5. Letter from A. Grigori to unknown recipient (September 6, 1897), British Museum, Greek and Roman Department Archives, Original Letters, Vol. 1896–1897.

6. Letters from A. Louisides to unknown recipient (1896), British Museum, Greek and Roman Department Archives, Original Letters, Vol. 1896–1897.

7. Letters from Caridi to C. Smith (1888–1889), British Museum, Greek and Roman Department Archives, Original Letters, Vol. 1888.

8. Letter from A. Mavrogordato to A. S. Murray (June 13, 1896), British Museum, Greek and Roman Department Archives, Original Letters, Vol. 1896–1897.

9. Letter from J. T. Wood to C. T. Newton (March 22, 1879), British Museum, Greek and Roman Department Archives, Original Letters, Vol. 1879–1882.

10. Letter from N. Katalanos (?) to P. Kavvadias (September 13, 1896), General Directorate of Antiquities Athens-Greece, Directorate of the Management of the National Archive of Monuments, Documentation and Protection of Cultural Good, Box 486 (1887–1911), Folder Cyprus 1896.

11. The role of the cadi is juridical, and the role of the mufti is religious. A mufti is an Islamic legal expert. See also Bouleti (2015).

12. Lists of subscriptions and donations to the Cyprus Museum (1883–1884, 1889), Cyprus State Archives, Folder SA1/2089/86. Lists of subscribers to the Cyprus Museum (1889–1895), Cyprus State Archives, Folder SA1/645/1895.

13. The percentage of Greek Cypriots and Turkish Cypriots during the 1960 constitution of the Republic of Cyprus was 77.1 percent and 18.2 percent, respectively. However, the percentage of Turkish Cypriots to the Greek Cypriot population during the British colonial period is estimated between 25–30 percent (Hatay 2007).

14. According to the Swedish excavators, the Eteocypriots were the native group of people living on Cyprus before the Mycenaean colonization of the island. For a detailed discussion of the political use of this "invention," see Given (1998).

15. Sir John Linton Myres (1869–1954) was an archaeologist and the first Wykeham professor of Ancient History at the University of Oxford. He conducted excavations in Cyprus, wrote the first guide to the Cyprus Museum, and catalogued the collection of Cesnola.

16. Circular Order sent by F. Warren to the District Commissioners (September 11, 1880), Cyprus State Archives, Folder SA1/5919/1880.

17. Letter from A. H. Young (Chief Secretary) and Sir William Haynes Smith (High Commissioner of Cyprus) (May 15, 1899), in minute papers page 3, Cyprus State Archives, Folder SA1/1154/1899.

18. Telegram from Secretary of State to W. Sendall (January 4, 1893), Cyprus State Archives, Folder SA1/81/1894.

19. Minutes of meetings on the Ancient Monuments Bill (1899), National Archives at Kew, Colonial Office: Cyprus, Sessional Papers, Folder 69/12 Legislative Council (1899).

20. For example, when archaeological findings are discovered during the construction of a building, all work has to stop so that the Department of Antiquities can evaluate the site.

References

Bouleti, Eleni. 2015. "Early Years of British Administration in Cyprus: The Rise of Anti-Colonialism in the Ottoman Muslim Community of Cyprus, 1878–1922." *Journal of Muslims in Europe* 4: 70–89.

Camerini, Jane. 1996. "Wallace in the Field." *Osiris* 11: 44–65.

Clifford, James. 1988. *The Predicament of Culture.* Cambridge, MA: Harvard University Press.

Cobham, Claude D. 1894. *An Attempt to a Bibliography of Cyprus.* 3rd ed. Nicosia: Government Print Office.

Crooke, Elizabeth. 2010. "The Politics of Community Heritage: Motivations, Authority Control." *International Journal of Heritage Studies* 16 (1–2): 16–29.

Eagleton, Terry. 1998. "Postcolonialism and 'Postcolonialism.'" *Interventions* 1 (1): 24–26.

Given, Michael. 1998. "Inventing the Eteocypriots: Imperialist Archaeology and the Manipulation of Ethnic Identity." *Journal of Mediterranean Archaeology* 11 (1): 3–29.

———. 2001. "The Fight for the Past: Watkins vs. Warren (1885–6) and the Control of Excavation." In *Cyprus in the 19th Century AD: Fact, Fancy and Fiction*, edited by Veronica Tatton-Brown, 255–60. Oxford: Oxbow.

Graham, Brian, Gregory J. Ashworth, and John E. Tunbridge. 2000. *A Geography of Heritage.* London: Hodder Arnold.

Hardy, Sam. 2010. "Interrogating Archaeological Ethics in Conflict Zones: Cultural Heritage Work in Cyprus." PhD diss., University of Sussex.

Harvey, David C. 2015a. "Landscape and Heritage: Trajectories and Consequences." *Landscape Research* 40: 911–24.

———. 2015b. "Heritage and Scale: Settings Boundaries and Relations." *International Journal of Heritage Studies* 21: 577–93.

Hatay, Mete. 2007. "Is the Turkish Cypriot Population Shrinking?" *PRIO Cyprus Center Report 2/2007.* Nicosia: PRIO. Accessed July 18, 2016. https://www.prio.org/Global/upload/Cyprus/Publications/Is%20the%20Turkish%20Cypriot%20Population%20Shrinking.pdf.

Hogarth, David George. 1889. *Devia Cypria: Notes of an Archaeological Journey in Cyprus in 1888.* London: Henry Frowde, Amen Corner E.C.

Holland, Robert F., and Diana W. Markides. 2006. *Britain and the Hellenes.* New York: Oxford University Press.

Jones, Sian. 2005. "Making Place, Resisting Displacement: Conflicting National and Local Identities in Scotland." In *The Politics of Heritage*, edited by Jo Littler and Roshi Naidoo, 94–114. London: Routledge.

Karageorghis, Vassos. 2004. *The A. G. Leventis Foundation and the Collections of Cypriot Antiquities in Museums Abroad.* Athens: AG Leventis Foundation.

Knapp, Bernard. A., and Sophia Antoniadou. 1998. "Archaeology, Politics and the Cultural Heritage of Cyprus." In *Archaeology under Fire*, edited by Lynn Meskell, 13–43. London: Routledge.

Lang, Robert. H. 1878. *Cyprus: Its History, Its Present Resources, and Future Prospects.* London: Macmillan.

Leriou, Anastasia. 2007a. "Locating Identities in the Eastern Mediterranean during the Late Bronze Age–Early Iron Age: The Case of 'Hellenized' Cyprus." In *Mediterranean Crossroads*, edited by Sophia Antoniadou and Anthony Pace, 563–91. Athens: Pierides Foundation.

———. 2007b. "The Hellenization of Cyprus: Tracing Its Beginnings (an Updated Version)." In *Patrimoines Culturels en Méditerranée Orientale: Recherché Scientifique et Enjeux Identitaires*, edited by Sylvie Müller Celca and Jean-Claude David, 1er atelier (November 29, 2007): *Chypre, une Stratigraphie de l' Identité*. Lyon: Recontres scientifiques en ligne de la Maison de l' Orient et de la Mediterranée.

Lester, Alan. 2001. *Imperial Networks*. London: Routledge.

Liebmann, Matthew. 2008. "The Intersections of Archaeology and the Postcolonial Studies." In *Archaeology and the Postcolonial Critique*, edited by Matthew Liebmann and Uzma Z. Rizvi, 1–20, Lanham, MD: Altamira.

Lorimer, Hayden. 2003. "Telling Small Stories: Spaces of Knowledge and the Practice of Geography." *Transactions of the Institute of British Geographers* 28 (2): 197–217.

Markides, Diana. W. 2006. "Cyprus 1878–1925: Ambiguities and Uncertainties." In *Britain in Cyprus: Colonialism and Post-Colonialism 1878–2006*, edited by Hubert Faustmann and Nicos Peristianis, 19–33. Mannheim: Bibliopolis.

Massey, Doreen, 2005. *For Space*. London: Sage.

Merrillees, Robert. S. 2005. *The First Cyprus Museum in Victoria Street, Nicosia*. Nicosia: Moufflon.

Moro-Abadia, Oscar. 2006. "The History of Archaeology as a 'Colonial Discourse.'" *Bulletin of the History of Archaeology*, 16 (2): 4–17. Accessed July 18, 2016. http://www.archaeologybulletin.org/articles/abstract/10.5334/bha.16202.

Myres, John. L. 1914. *Handbook of the Cesnola Collection of Antiquities from Cyprus*. New York: Metropolitan Museum of Art.

Myres, John L., and Max Ohnefalsch-Richter. 1899. *A Catalogue of the Cyprus Museum*. Oxford: Clarendon.

Nash, Catherine. 2002. "Cultural Geography: Postcolonial Cultural Geographies," *Progress in Human Geography* 26 (2): 219–30.

Nikolaou, Polina. 2013. *The Diaspora of Cypriot Antiquities and the British Museum (1860–1900)*. PhD diss., University of Exeter.

———. 2015 "Archaeology, Empire and the Field: Exploring the Ancient Sites of Cyprus, 1865–1876." In *Spaces of Global Knowledge: Exhibition, Encounter and Exchange in an Age of Empire*, edited by Diarmid F. Finnegan and Jonathan Jeffery Wright, 39–55, Farnham: Ashgate.

Pilides, Despo. 2009. *George Jeffery: His Diaries and the Ancient Monuments of Cyprus*, Vols. 1–2. Nicosia: Department of Antiquities, Republic of Cyprus.

Reinach, Salomon. M. 1891. *Chroniques d'Orient. Documents sur les Fouilles et Découvertes dans l'Orient Héllenique de 1883 à 1890*. Paris: Librairie de Firmin-Didot.

Scott, J. (2002). "World Heritage as a Model for Citizenship: The Case of Cyprus." *International Journal of Heritage Studies* 8 (2): 99–115.

Shepherd, Nick. 2003. "'When the Hand That Holds the Trowel Is Black': Disciplinary Practices of Self-Representation and the Issue of 'Native' Labor in Archaeology." *Journal of Social Archaeology* 3 (3): 334–52.

Shohat, Ella. 1992. "Notes on the 'Post-Colonial.'" *Social Text* 31–32: 99.

Silvern, Steven E. 2002. "State Centrism, the Equal-Footing Doctrine, and the Historical-Legal Geographies of American Indian Treaty Rights." *Historical Geography*, 30: 33–58.

Stanley-Price, Nicholas P. 2001. "The Ottoman Law on Antiquities (1874) and the Founding of the Cyprus Museum." In *Cyprus in the Nineteenth Century AD: Fact, Fancy and Fiction*, edited by Veronica Tatton-Brown, 267–75. Oxford: Oxbow.

Stoler, Ann-Laura and Frederick Cooper. 1997. "Between Metropole and Colony: Rethinking a Research Agenda." In *Tensions of Empire: Colonial Cultures in a Bourgeois World*, edited by Louise A. Stoler and Frederick Cooper, 1–56, London: University of California Press.
Storrs, Sir, R. (1939). *Orientations*. London: Reader's Union Ltd.
Stylianou-Lambert, Theopisti, and Alexandra Bounia. 2016. *The Political Museum: Power, Conflict and Identity in Cyprus*. Walnut Creek, CA: Left Coast.
Tolia-Kelly, Divya P. 2010. "Narrating the Postcolonial Landscape: Archaeologies of Race at Hadrian's Wall." *Transactions of the Institute of British Geographers* 36 (1): 71–88.
Trigger, Bruce G. 1995. "Romanticism, Nationalism and Archaeology." In *Nationalism, Politics and the Practice of Archaeology*, edited by Philip L. Kohl and Clare Fawcett, 263–79. Cambridge: Cambridge University Press.
Tunbridge, John E., and Gregory Ashworth. 1996. *Dissonant Heritage: The Management of the Past as a Resource in Conflict*. Hoboken, NJ: John Wiley and Sons.
Turner, Frank M. 1997. "Practicing Science: An Introduction." In *Victorian Science in Context*, edited by Bernard Lightman, 283–89. London: University of Chicago Press.
Varnava, Andrekos. 2009. *British Imperialism in Cyprus 1878–1912*. Manchester: Manchester University Press.

Archival Sources

Circular Order sent by F. Warren to the District Commissioners (September 11, 1880), Cyprus State Archives, Folder SA1/5919/1880.
Letter from J. T. Wood to C. T. Newton (March 22, 1879), British Museum, Greek and Roman Department Archives, Original Letters, Vol. 1879–1882.
Letters from Caridi to C. Smith (1888–1889), British Museum, Greek and Roman Department Archives, Original Letters, Vol. 1888.
Letters from A. Louisides to unknown recipient (1896), British Museum, Greek and Roman Department Archives, Original Letters, Vol. 1896–1897.
Letter from A. Mavrogordato to A. S. Murray (June 13, 1896), British Museum, Greek and Roman Department Archives, Original Letters, Vol. 1896–1897.
Letter from N. Katalanos (?) to P. Kavvadias (September 13, 1896), General Directorate of Antiquities Athens-Greece, Directorate of the Management of the National Archive of Monuments, Documentation and Protection of Cultural Good, Box 486 (1887–1911), Folder Cyprus 1896.
Letter from A. Grigori to unknown recipient (September 6, 1897), British Museum, Greek and Roman Department Archives, Original Letters, Vol. 1896–1897.
Letter from A. H. Young (Chief Secretary) and Sir William Haynes Smith (High Commissioner of Cyprus) (May 15, 1899), in minute papers page 3, Cyprus State Archives, Folder SA1/1154/1899.
Lists of subscriptions and donations to the Cyprus Museum (1883–1884, 1889), Cyprus State Archives, Folder SA1/2089/86.
Lists of subscribers to the Cyprus Museum (1889–1895), Cyprus State Archives, Folder SA1/645/1895.
Minutes of meetings on the Ancient Monuments Bill (1899), National Archives at Kew, Colonial Office: Cyprus, Sessional Papers, Folder 69/12 Legislative Council (1899).
Telegram from Secretary of State to W. Sendall (January 4, 1893), Cyprus State Archives, Folder SA1/81/1894.

4 Pressed On in Press

Greek Cultural Heritage in the Public Eye: The Post-War Years

Marlen Mouliou

Introduction

In today's participatory culture of digital crowdsourcing social media, news and opinions are fashioned and spread quickly; they are often liked, debated passionately, and eventually buried in multiple layers of digital data debris. This intriguing modern stratigraphy of public voices on myriad matters is certainly fascinating to study. The different uses of the past have their own share in this constant production of public views. For instance, the infamous Amphipolis case dominated mass and social media in Greece in recent years.[1] Although it is not the only such example, it vividly illustrates current attitudes and trends.

But are these only contemporary practices in the media world? Haven't antiquities and heritage management in Greece always been pressed on in the press and placed under scrutiny in the public eye? Hasn't the press, in the pre-digital era, been an initiator of public knowledge and opinions about archaeology and cultural heritage and their uses in Greece? Nonetheless, a critical analysis of the role of the press in public debates and critical controversies on such matters has not been systematically pursued, although a broader research on the uses of the past in Greece has been extensive.[2]

This chapter argues that Greek antiquities and the management of cultural heritage have always been in the public eye in Greece. Thus, it sets out to demonstrate why and how the press embarked on formulating public views on archaeological matters during the early post-war era (from the end of the civil war to the dark years of dictatorship, 1948–1967). This is a very interesting period of the post–civil war, "anti-Communist state" in Greece, whereby the country was obliged to take ideological sides within the wider Cold War doctrine that brought a profound divide of the world between West and East (Judt 2010, 121). For the country, this has been a period of "stunted," "mutilated," and "supervised" democracy, with many critical subversions, transitions, and changes

Fig. 4.1. The fragility of democracy in Greece in the post-war years. Cartoon. (Newspaper *To Vima*, July 14, 1963.) Courtesy of Historic Archives, *To Vima*.

during which Greek political parties and society at large experienced constant polarizations and instability (Kostis 2013, 783). At the same time, Greece struggled to recover its destroyed social infrastructure, rehabilitate its economy based on external financial aid, and attract capital investments that would be instrumental in developing key domains of domestic production.

Yet the Greek case must not be seen in isolation. Tony Judt, in his seminal book *Postwar: A History of Europe since 1945*, remarked that immediately after the end of the war, Europeans faced a "Himalayan task" to recover the immensely damaged economy of the continent (Judt 2010, 82). He also noted that an economic disaster could be a powerful stimulus to rapid reformations and growth in certain economic and social sectors. This observation is particularly relevant to the Greek case.

Table 4.1. Frequencies and percentages of newspaper articles per year, for the period 1950–1967. (Statistics: M. Mouliou).

	To Vima		*I Avgi*	
	Number of articles	**%**	**Number of articles**	**%**
1950	30	2%	—	—
1951	26	2%	—	—
1952	70	5%	—	—
1953	116	9%	4	2%
1954	102	8%	—	—
1955	103	8%	—	—
1956	89	7%	5	3%
1957	79	6%	17	9%
1958	68	5%	10	5%
1959	61	5%	10	5%
1960	57	4%	14	8%
1961	94	7%	14	8%
1962	77	6%	33	18%
1963	53	4%	19	10%
1964	67	5%	13	7%
1965	64	5%	15	8%
1966	56	4%	19	10%
1967	79	6%	12*	7%
SUM	1291		181	

*The sample ends in April 1967, as the newspaper closed down straight after the military coup.

Taking as a premise that the mass media are producers and disseminators of meanings about contexts of public social life and that the Greek press has been meticulous in covering cultural matters during this critical period, this chapter aims to reflect on how certain ideological conflicts shaped different and often heated public discourses on Greek archaeology and heritage management in Greek society.

Different opinion makers who regularly authored articles in the Greek press have expressed various discourses that have been remarkably rich in references to archaeology, at least in the two national and, for most of their lifetime, daily morning newspapers,[3] which will be used as sources for the purposes of this study.[4] A corpus of a bit less than 1,500[5] articles of all types and sizes, dated mainly between 1950–1967 from *To Vima* and *I Avgi,* has been the reservoir this chapter draws from, together with a few revealing text samples from the years 1946 and 1948.

The texts published in these newspapers have been short articles[6] (i.e., reports on archaeological explorations, openings of new museums and redisplays, urgent rescues of cultural heritage), serial articles of an antiquarian nature, and essays of known authors (archaeologists, philologists, literary writers). Their objective was to formulate a kind of archaeological education systematically for lay readers and enhance the national imaginary on the importance and contribution of ancient Greek civilization to the shaping of the modern world in the Cold War era. Their key role was thus to create a certain kind of awareness upon the aesthetic, symbolic, scientific, and economic values of the past and its material culture.[7]

It is far from original to note that since the formation of the modern Greek state, the relationship of the Greeks to their past and cultural heritage has been determined by the supremacy of the ancient versus modern Greek culture. In the context of this chapter, the focus will be on how geopolitical and epistemological battlefields, locally and globally, were intertwined to create specific print media discourses for Greek archaeological heritage, which would enlighten, "educate,"[8] and influence readers before the boom of the mass media era. The role of Greek cultural heritage within the broader ideological agenda of the Greek rehabilitation project in the early post-war period can thus be explored along the lines of the following two broader questions.

How were the American Marshall Plan aid, the Cold War doctrine, state rhetoric, and the struggles of Greece to rehabilitate its economy and society within an ideologically divided world reflected in the Greek press during this period? How were the ancient past and other layers of historical memory pressed on in key press circulations?

The analysis of actual newspaper sources that can provide answers to these questions will be deployed along a flexible chronological axis in order to assess their timeliness and relevance to political, social, cultural, and archaeological matters that took shaping during the early post-war period.

Greek Archaeological Heritage in the Early Post-War Years: Press Discourses within the Marshall Plan Context (1948–1952)

The Historical and Political Context

The year 1947 was one of crisis throughout Europe, and it signposted a radical turning point in the continent's recovery (Judt 2010, 3). After a decisive trip to Moscow and other European capitals, US Secretary of State George C. Marshall realized that the initiative for the recovery of the continent should come from the United States; thus, his eminent recovery plan took shape. By the time the Marshall Plan was completed in 1952, the United States had spent approximately 13 billion dollars, an amount equivalent to 201 billion dollars today, to rehabilitate seventeen countries (beneficiaries). When the so-called Porter Mission visited

Greece in early 1947 to assess how the US aid would be distributed in the country, one of its members noted in the mission's diary that "Greece is the strangest country of the world. It is the only country whereby destruction of material goods continues whilst the other countries are being rehabilitated. . . . It is the only country whereby everything happens without any plan and the common good is not taken into consideration" (Stathakis 2011, 295–96). This rather ardent statement indicates outsiders' perceptions about Greece during that period despite its resourceful natural beauties and archaeological wealth. In 1948, Marshall's European Recovery Program (ERP) was introduced into Greece, which as a beneficiary of 649 million dollars eventually became the sixth largest recipient of this aid in Europe (Zachariou 2001, 153, Report 1951).[9] The aid focused on three pillars of the Greek economy, namely agriculture, shipping, and tourism, with tourism being directly connected to Greece's two main resources: good climate and archaeological heritage.

The publication *Greece Calling* was an early post-war insightful source. The eighty-page document of state propaganda, published in 1948 in Athens under the auspices of the Information Division of the Greek Reconstruction Claims Committee, reveals the broader mindset within which the newspaper narratives under study took shape. In a way, it sets the frame through which we can attempt to decodify the newspaper agenda by bringing forward, for public consumption, various matters related to antiquity. Written in English as an official document designed to reach mainly US authorities and officials, it stands out as a monument of Greek state policy, outlining the key domains Greece aimed to rehabilitate in order to rebuild its economy. Within this intended scope, it used the legacy of the heroic Greek past, both ancient and recent (e.g., the Greek War of Independence and the exemplary Greek resistance during World War II), as a way to explain why humanity should pay tribute to the small and shattered land of Greece. It mirrored the values placed by state officials upon the archaeological heritage and ancient past of the country, which endured struggles for world liberty and civilization throughout its long history. From the official rhetoric rich in meanings, symbolism, and undertones imprinted in this publication, some telling examples are worthy of special mention for their direct references to the epic contribution of Greece to the world and the heroic genealogy of Greek heritage as shaped by lands, monuments, personalities, and institutions. Moreover, their significance is consolidated by the fact that they focus on the prominence of this heritage to the Greek rehabilitation project and its relevance to the then nascent tourism "industry."[10]

The first inner page of the booklet set the tone of a rhetoric that would unfold throughout its pages. It consisted of an ancient epigraphy-like visual that defined what Hellas should be for the world via an uninterrupted genealogy of celebrated names.[11] In this genealogy, emphasis was clearly placed upon the classical past, democracy, poetry, philosophy, and humanism together with the Greeks' acts of sacrifice as a way to safeguard freedom, the most precious of values and gifts, as the text asserted. The introductory article, "The Voice of Greece," set the tone of the post-war Greek politics and diplomatic agenda toward the ancient Greek past, Byzantium (but less so), and the more recent heroic acts of Greek people during wartime. Signed by Sophocles Venizelos, then president of the Information Division of the Greek Reconstruction Claims Committee, it outlined the ideas behind the monumental synopsis of Greek glory by presenting Greece's values to the world and stressing its current need for urgent rehabilitation through foreign aid. This mindset and political agenda was served by the following texts of the booklet. Some of them, with a distinctly lyrical tone, abound on references to ancient Greece and culture and create imageries of the country's past and post-war future through "touring" in places "where the ideal 'Greece' is still more vivid" (*Greece Calling* 1948, 39). A. Londos, then secretary general for touring, stressed in his own statements in the booklet that Greece, with "such an abundance of assets," could certainly become "a country especially suitable for touring." His list of Greece's qualities included "her varied natural beauty," the "exceptional climate," and her "historical interest and her great importance in the progress of civilization, which have made her known to the whole world for centuries. . . . Her abundant national treasures, remnants of which one encounters at every bend of the road, are very important tourist factors" (*Greece Calling* 1948, 53).

This state discourse would have been widely known then and would have, to some extent, adopted or debated in the contemporary press.

An Overview of the Press Agenda

The primary mission of the newspaper *To Vima* was to discuss ancient monuments as authentic and powerful national symbols and as sacred landscapes of memory building that could spur notions of respect, understanding, and protection of the ancestral past. As expected, the ancient world took up the lion's share in the press coverage.

The Bronze Age (or Pre-Hellenic civilization, as it was called in the early postwar articles) was not less popular; on the contrary, in the years 1950–1952, it attracted more media coverage by *To Vima* than the typically popular classical past as a result of the remarkable discoveries of the "Pre-Hellenic civilization" in Mycenae during the early 1950s.

However, after a careful look at the whole sample under study, it is noticeable that *I Avgi* focuses more on the ideological connections of the past with the present (29%) and the protection of the cultural heritage (12%). This is worth noting, especially when compared to the less impressive 9 percent and 4 percent, respectively of corresponding samples from *To Vima*.

Table 4.2. Frequencies and percentages of newspaper articles for the period 1950–1967 according to the different temporalities presented in them. (Statistics: M. Mouliou).

	To Vima						*I Avgi*	
	Total corpus of articles (1950–1967)		**Corpus of articles (1950–1952)**		**Corpus of articles (1953–1967)**		**Total corpus of articles (1953–1967)**	
Palaeolithic-Mesolithic	26	2%	2	0%	24	2%	1	1%
Neolithic	19	2%	0	0%	19	2%	2	1%
Bronze Age	291	23%	41	32%	250	21%	28	16%
Geometric to Late Classical	522	40%	31	25%	491	41%	66	36%
Roman	49	4%	4	3%	45	4%	9	5%
Byzantine	118	9%	17	13%	101	9%	9	5%
Ottoman	2	0%	0	0%	2	0%	2	1%
Some of all periods	77	6%	9	7%	68	6%	8	4%
After the War of Independence	6	0%	2	2%	4	0%	3	2%
Present time in relation to the past	111	9%	11	9%	100	9%	53	29%
No chronological references	69	5%	9	7%	60	5%	—	—

During the early post-war period when the Marshall Plan was in effect, quite a few articles in *To Vima* focused on the archaeological research conducted by the American School of Classical Studies, mainly in the Athenian Agora. This interest was surely not unintentional within the wider political climate of the time. In most cases, the tendency was to publish articles that focused on the quest for new archaeological discoveries, unearthed treasures, spectacular finds, and unique "big-dig" experiences. The spotlight on golden rarities or sculptural masterpieces coexisted with other commentaries on different types of findings whose evidential, rather than aesthetic or artistic, status was also very important. The word *treasure* has been frequent in the press language, but as a way to pay tribute to the scientific, historical, and symbolic value of varied remnants of the past. Less frequent but still present have been notices on the history of Greek archaeology, its eminent personalities and "heroic" pioneers, the archaeological methodology and the differences between systematic and rescue fieldwork, and its distinction from romanticism. Other texts signed by leading intellectuals aimed at informing and cultivating the readers on a variety of intellectual matters inspired by ancient lands.

Quite a fair number of articles approached ancient monuments as tourist dreamlands for the betterment of the present. Print media also focused on the ethical responsibilities of the state to protect cultural property in its totality; provide the means for its proper research, documentation, and conservation; and create the foundations for its constructive appreciation by the Greek and international public. When government officials ran short of these expectations, the press put out statements of political opposition and occasionally resistance against the oblivious state. Topics of discussion included the need for the reorganization of museums in the country (especially their operation in key touristic areas, display policies, and museum typology), the repatriation of cultural property, the required alertness of the Greek state against illicit traffic of antiquities and museum thefts, and the reformation of the Greek Archaeological Service and the improvement of its resources.

From this wide range of textual material, we shall pinpoint articles that explicitly or implicitly touched on critical matters with strong ideological bearings for Greek politics and identity dilemmas, challenges, and conflicts.

The Past as a Contested Present in the Early Post-War Press

While civil war passions carried on, *To Vima* published articles with explicit allusions to enemies and allies. These references focused on the symbolic importance of repatriating antiquities looted from Greece during the Nazi occupation and the prevalence of such honorable efforts against alternative suggestions that would favor the payment of war compensations from the conquerors. They also stressed the damages of antiquities during the occupation not only by listing them but also by implying the almost possessive right of every Greek citizen over them. Some commentaries touched upon the damages caused by the illicit trafficking of antiquities and the looting of archaeological sites by local villagers in order to serve the international art market. Interestingly, the looting was presented as a kind of unequal struggle of poor Greece (and poor Greeks) against thirsty and rich foreign museums supported by their states, which admired the ancient heritage of Greece but deprecated its modern occupants. In an article entitled "The Art World" [*Ο κόσμος της τέχνης*], written in 1946 by Marinos Kalligas, an art historian, later director of the National Gallery, and regular columnist for the newspaper, references to the pride, sensitivity, and responsibility of the Greeks toward their ancestral past and its safeguarding abound together with feelings of anger and revulsion for the numerous and irreperable damages, literal and symbolic, effected upon Greek antiquities during the war. Kalligas's frustration was triggered by the realization that poor Greek villages were forced to become looters of antiquities in order to escape poverty, and thus he advocated the enforcement of implementing compensations and "the right to reclaim the

Table 4.3. Frequencies and percentages of newspaper articles for the period 1950–1967 according to the different broad categories of topics presented in them. (Statistics: M. Mouliou).

	To Vima						*I Avgi*	
	Number of articles	**%**	**1950–1952**	**%**	**1953–1967**	**%**	**Number of articles**	**%**
Archaeological fieldwork in Greece conducted by Greeks	258	28%	25	20%	233	20%	26	14%
Archaeological fieldwork in Greece conducted by foreigners	175	14%	8	6%	167	14%	13	5%
Archaeological fieldwork abroad but of Greek interest	73	6%	10	8%	63	5%	5	3%
Archaeological fieldwork abroad/ history of other countries	73	6%	8	6%	65	6%	22	12%
Archaeological museum work in Greece (permanent museums)	72	6%	8	6%	64	5%	14	8%
Archaeological museum work in Greece (temporary exhibitions and loan exhibitions abroad)	21	2%	3	2%	18	2%	4	2%
Archaeological museums abroad	10	1%	2	2%	8	1%	—	—
Archaeology as science	6	0%	0	0%	6	1%	1	1%
Archaeology and other disciplines	2	0%	0	0%	2	0%	1	1%
Archaeological visits	109	8%	5	4%	104	9%	14	8%
Heritage management	48	4%	5	4%	43	4%	7	4%

(*Continued*)

Table 4.3. (*continued*)

	To Vima						I Avgi	
	Number of articles	**%**	**1950–1952**	**%**	**1953–1967**	**%**	**Number of articles**	**%**
Protection of cultural property	54	4%	5	4%	49	4%	22	12%
Portraits/ biographies	32	2%	2	2%	30	3%	4	2%
Modern people and the past	24	2%	3	2%	21	2%	5	3%
Hellenism	2	0%	1	1%	1	0%	1	1%
Classics/humanism	11	1%	5	4%	6	1%	2	1%
The ancient world	58	4%	5	4%	53	5%	2	1%
The indebtedness of the modern world to ancient Greece	6	0%	1	1%	5	0%	1	1%
The Byzantine world	33	3%	4	3%	29	2%	1	1%
Book reviews/article reviews/research result reviews/ debates	65	5%	12	10%	53	5%	12	7%
Description of individual artifacts/ monuments	58	4%	2	2%	56	5%	13	7%
Repatriation of cultural property	12	1%	0	0%	12	1%	7	4%
Popular themes	17	1%	0	0%	17	1%	1	1%
History	9	1%	0	0%	9	1%	—	—
Bronze Age world	51	4%	12	10%	39	3%	—	—
The museum generally/ museology	8	1%	0	0%	8	1%	—	—
Collections/ collecting/ collectors	2	0%	0	0%	2	0%	—	—
Illicit traders	—	—	—	—	—	—	4	2%
None of the above	2	0%	0	0%	2	0%	—	—

stolen antiquities and ask for similar ones in case some are not traced" (Kalligas 1946, 1–2).

A couple of years later, the same author joined other commentators who cheerfully greeted the reopening of three galleries at the National Archaeological Museum at the dawn of the postwar reformation (Kalligas 1948; see also Vanderpool 1950). He assigned a symbolic meaning to this reopening and hinted at the risks hidden in the new Communist ideology and the polarization caused by the Greek civil war. The museum reopening was thus related to the necessity for national resurrection and the urgent need for a strengthening of the nation's collective conscience and unity because "it provide[d] the opportunity to weigh up [the symbolic representation of the classical and European] values, and judge whether it is worth fighting for their survival or instead for their replacement by other values which represent a new state of affairs" (Kalligas 1948, 2).

In the early 1950s, the press turned its interest to subjects such as the challenging relationship between the ancient and Byzantine past within contemporary Greek society, discussed either in conjunction with certain political ideologies of the time or alongside the emerging and progressively vital dilemmas concerning the management of modern cultural heritage. The problematic coexistence of different historical periods in the material body of archaeological remains and modern cities, together with a problematization of different value-laden hierarchies upon them recurrently, came to the fore.[12] In an essay written soon after Law 1469/1950, "On the Protection of a Special Category of Buildings and Works of Art Dated after 1830" [*Περί προστασίας ειδικής κατηγορίας οικοδομημάτων και έργων τέχνης μεταγενέστερων του 1830*], was put in force, Evangelos Papanoutsos condemned "the indifference and contempt with which [modern Greeks] often approach the most recent intellectual and cultural achievements traced in the monuments of our modern history" and noted that if Greeks "are told that a building or a sculpture or a painting are 'old' works of art, then our mind relates them immediately to ancient Greece. We surpass with distinct ease even the Byzantine Middle Age" (Papanoutsos 1950). His critical assessment of the ambivalent evaluation of the diverse Greek pasts concluded with overt disappointment that "it is not a reasoned construction, a product of teaching but a diffused feeling among the masses of Greek people the belief that a monument has historical value only if it is very old with more than 1000 years on his physical body" (Papanoutsos 1950). On the other hand, two years later, Kalligas condemned the destruction of important monuments of thirteenth and forteenth centuries in Crete as a result of the Greek state's carelessness. He reproached the "irrational" purchase of the Maximos's Megaron,[13] a neoclassical mansion of the early twentieth century, for thirty thousand golden liras, perceived at the time as unnecessary expense even if the purchase was completed at a price favorable to the state. In a distinctively harsh tone, he criticized his fellow Greek citizens for their "Neohellenic fault to destroy with mania their old monuments," despite their aesthetic and historical significance, in order to replace them with new structures of ambiguous taste. Kalligas touched upon a recurrently contentious issue, the "fruitless battle of the archaeologists who try to save the monuments against the ostensibly 'progressive' mindset of a few pretentious and deceptively forward looking engineers" (Kalligas 1952), and thus brought to the fore the need for the endorsement of a more visionary, much less shortsighted positioning on the valuation of cultural heritage in the present.

Ideological battles over the value of different layers of Greek history and their material expressions were hence not uncommon, but another scientific rivalry emerged in 1952 and progressively gathered momentum: the rivarly between the Minoan and Mycenean civilizations and their positioning in the long line of the glorious ancestral past. The excavations and findings in Mycenae during that year have perhaps caused this peculiar competition, but the motives behind the rivalry must have been deeper beyond the materiality of ancient ruins, rooted to human passions. Spyridon Marinatos, excavator of prehistoric Akrotiri in Thera and professor of archaeology at the National and Kapodistrian University of Athens, wrote a series of articles in order to defend Minoan archaeology, noting among other things that "it is premature, to say the least, to deny the supremacy of Crete in favor of Mycenae" (Marinatos 1952a, 1952b). In the coming years, this peculiar prehistoric rivalry became heated continually through numerous newspaper writings composed by Greek and foreign archaeologists after the discovery of new excavation findings, the publication of new books, or Palmer's explicit critical review on theories and interpretations about the Minoan civilization as put forward by its excavator, Sir Arthur Evans.[14]

There have also been burgeoning dilemmas regarding the perils of lending Greek antiquities abroad in view of the nonexistent legal framework that would define the terms and conditions of their exportation and loan. The matter arose after a proposal to organize an exhibition of Greek antiquities in the United States. On the one hand, it was considered tempting for material and symbolic reasons because it would potentially invigorate the Greek economy and enhance the national morale and pride of the Greek diaspora in America. On the other hand, it was also considered dangerous. The reasoning was that it would set unique and irreplaceable works of art at risk and thus create a precedent for the necessary movement of Greek museum collections outside national borders without having any prior proof that traveling exhibitions would, in reciprocity, help Greek museums solve their numerous problems (Kalligas 1953). It is well known that this provocative subject would be feverishly reignited in 1977 when new legislation (Act No 654/1977) allowed the export of Greek antiquities for temporary exhibitions abroad and opened up numerous possibilities for the implementation of a series of touring exhibitions to foreign museums all around the globe (Mouliou 1996; 2008, 96, 104; Hamilakis and Yalouri 1996; Solomon 2007). When the act was enforced, however, it caused controversy and ethical dilemmas across the spectrum of Greek society, beyond the usual circles of politicians, intellectuals, and archaeologists to different local communities whose agendas were also interesting and diverse.

Other sensitive subjects for public debate during the early postwar period were related to political, epistemological, and institutional matters, such as the thorny geopolitics of the past related to the discussion regarding the contruction of an archaeological museum in Thessaloniki and the significance of this project within the wider context of the impassioned Macedonian Issue,[15] or the declining status of classical studies in the world.[16] Occasionally, matters of transparency in public administration were also reported, either to set up public debate concerning controversial issues on the management of the Service for the Management of Archaeological Resources (the predecessor of the Archaeological Receipts Fund) or to reveal a peculiar rivalry[17] between university professors and archaeologists of the Archaeological Service over high key positions in the state administrative hierarchy or the institutional move of heritage management services to the Ministry of Education or the Ministry of Presidency.

When the Marshall Funds period came to a close, the final report *The Marshall Plan in Greece* (July 1948–January 1952), written in Greek, described in detail the results of the Marshall Aid during the period 1948–1952 and stressed the importance of the Greek "Tourism Industry" in the rehabilitation process of the country. Its rhetoric and main argument were not dissimilar to a case addressed four years earlier in the *Greece Calling* document. Some general information on the use of funds for the recovery of museums was also put forward. The report claimed that the museums of the country had reopened.[18] Yet we know that their recovery and reorganization lasted much longer, and this surely was a contentious issue often tackled by the press in the next post-war phase.

When Greece Was Called to Change: Greek Archaeological Heritage and the Press after the Marshall Plan in the Cold War Era (1953–1967)

The Historical and Political Context

From 1953 to 1965, Greek politics was defined by the absolute domination of right-wing conservative parties, the fluid and fragile alliances between the divergent political parties of the Center, the marginalization of the Left, and the displacement of many dissident citizens. In search of new economic partners and capital investors from abroad, the Greek governments set out to change the country through an ambitious program of public works and reconstruction of all infrastructure under Konstantinos Karamanlis's leadership. They consolidated Greece's strong alliance with the United States and were compelled to manage a difficult relationship with neighboring Turkey. The European Economic Alliance became a constant chapter of the state national agenda. The year 1965 stands out as a critical one for Greek politics because the ambivalent leadership of the Greek king and the gradual immersion of the country into new turbulent waters of political instability led to the overthrow of the parliamentary regime in 1967.

Not a Singular Agenda: The Debated Presence of Heritage Issues in the Post-War Press

During this period, press narratives on archaeological research and classical education remained consistent in *To Vima*, which reinforced its mission to educate its readers and provide updates on "the work of the archaeological spade" and the methodology of the archaeological discipline. There is also evidence suggesting the intention of the newspaper to moderate ideological and scientific variances by giving the floor to both Greek and foreign archaeologists to present either research findings or weekly guided tours to different museums and archaeological sites around the country. This latter practice, established in 1955 with the introduction of a regular column, the so-called "Sunday Guided Tours" ["*Ξεναγήσεις της Κυριακής*"], aimed at cultivating the historical memory of the citizens and their civic conscience on the value of ancient and modern Greek culture. Concurrently, the debate on the need to promote and enhance the management of the archaeological heritage in order to better support the touristic development of the country within the global tourism market gathered momentum.[19] The opening of more museums, the increase of public expenditure for cultural productions, and the effort to create cultural infrastructures around the country were often in the headlines of the press. The slow reorganization of museums, the poor management of the archaeological sites, the meager salaries of the archaeologists, and the gradual shrinkage of this crucial scientific sector were issues for concern in the pages of newspapers.[20]

In *I Avgi* and its archaeological coverage, we can trace another approach that is openly oppositional, both to the political status quo and the conservative governmental agendas and to Western foreign powers' crypto-colonial presence in Greece (Herzfeld 2002; Hamilakis 2007, 2008). It seems that the newspaper often promoted a discourse of resistance against improper practices by the state and the West and adopted a campaigning tone with ethical underpinnings for the protection, management, and dissemination of Greek cultural heritage. Its articles put special emphasis on the protection of the archaeological heritage by the Greek state for the benefit of all Greek citizens and on the importance of this heritage for modern Greeks as an eternal source of education, inspiration, and prosperity. One of its early pieces,[21] driven by the disastrous effects of the massive earthquake in Zakynthos and Kefallonia, laments "the loss of national treasures, relics and works of art" and stresses the duty of the Greek people to continue the labors of culture because "these labors are interlinked with the roots of their national existence and constantly enlighten the Greek peoples' search for a better life." The article sets the tone for other opinion pieces on the protection of cultural heritage published in the years to come. Archaeology and antiquities are often presented as signs and symbols of Greek identity not only for modern Greece but also for other territories beyond modern national borderlines and promoted as valuable educational assets for modern Greeks. One such article[22] highlights one of the most problematic issues of modern Greek history, the Cyprus Issue, in order to denounce the colonial agenda and regime of the British Empire on the island and reaffirm its Greekness, proven by its ancient monuments, its archaeological museum, and the continuous archaeological discoveries that stand as solid evidence that "the Cypriots are not of any obscure origin but they are Greeks, with Greek consciousness and Greek culture" (see Bounia et al., this volume). Occasionally, as a reaction to specific breaking news, antiquities are discussed as sacred public goods at risk of becoming commercial products that serve the interests of foreign investors and partners of corrupt and irresponsible Greek state officials.

During this period, some sensitive cases of public cultural works connected to the classical past and its monumental material and immaterial heritage were also thoroughly discussed by the press. One such case was related to the erection of a modern monument in Thermopylae, a memorial dedicated to the heroic battle fought there in 480 BC by Leonidas, the Spartan warrior-king, and his small force of three hundred men against the massive army of the Persian king. The project was proposed to the Greek state by the Greek-American organization the Knights of Thermopylae, founded in 1951 in the United States by an ex-president of the American Hellenic Educational Progressive Association (AHEPA) and three hundred elite Greco-Americans. According to *To Vima*,[23] the main purpose of the Knights of Thermopylae was "the embellishment and national development of historic, archaeological and touristic sites of Greece, through funds provided by members of the Organization." This specific project, their first one in Greece, was presented in a public ceremony on June 30, 1955, in the presence of the king of Greece, the Greek governement, and many representatives of the Greek establishment, including archaeologist Spyridon Marinatos, who was also a member of two committees commisioned to coordinate the project and the preparation of all adjunct events that signposted its completion. Some months after the inauguration of the monument, Kalligas, urged by the news that another similar project would be realized in Thessaloniki—this time involving the making of a monument to Alexander the Great (see Galiniki, this volume)—wrote a critical review in *To Vima* to explain why the Thermopylae project had been a bad example to follow. He expressed his disdain for the aesthetic quality of the monument (or rather, the lack of it) and spoke of "artistic paradoxes," arguing that the erection of sculptural monuments of national significance in public spaces should be decided by a committee of experts and not left to the decision-making of politicians or ignorant benefactors (Kalligas 1955). Although his discontent was not openly related to the semiforeign nature of the funding source, it did raise a valid point about transparency in state functions by setting specific institutional rules and standards on the use of public space, independent of political circumstances.

The connecting thread between this case and another perhaps more well-known controversial example, the reconstruction work of the Stoa of Attalos II in the Ancient Agora of Athens, was the American origin of the funding sources and the complex micropolitical entanglements of both undertakings. In 1949, with the approval of the Greek authorities, the American School of Classical Studies decided to reconstruct the Stoa of Attalos II, a project that was regarded as "a terrific challenge" as "the most monumental and daring undertaking to which the School had ever committed itself."[24] The undertaking was also perceived as "a contribution of the first rank to classical scholarship and as an expression of American friendship for Greece" (Meritt 1984, 63). The inauguration ceremony took place on September 3, 1956, in the presence of the Greek royal family, the Greek prime minister, many ministers, the leaders of the opposition parties, many visiting scholars, and hundreds of ordinary people. For Greek state officials, the site and its museum represented a diachronic paragon, as valuable and significant as "a text of Platonic philosophy, a passage from the Bible, a school or a church."[25] The Greek state expressed its immense gratitude to the researchers from the American School who had resurrected the site and contributed decisively to the revival of the birthplace of democracy and to the protection of universal freedom, justice, and solidarity. For the American government, the reconstruction project and the creation of the museum was "the American people's debt of honor to ancient Athens . . . the symbol of Democracy, the most valuable ideological inheritance of Ancient Greece." Thus the reconstructed Stoa became "a living monument and dedication to "the voice of freedom . . . representing common ideals between the US and Greece."[26]

During the summer of 1956, in connection with the celebrations of the seventy-fifth anniversary of American School of Classical Studies at Athens and the inauguration of the reconstructed Stoa of Attalos issue, the announcement of special "archaeological festivals" had its own share in the media coverage, indicating the gradual weaving of stronger interconnecting threads between tourism and the enhancement of archaeological heritage in Greece, along the lines of the pre-1950s *Calling Greece* manifesto. The reporter from *To Vima* received the news positively, stressing that "these festivities will once more bring Greece closer to the international intellectual world. Its antiquities which come to light will be a serious challenge to the world of intellect and art in favor of Greece's recognition as a land whose cultural light and spirit offer it every right to be considered as a race with the most beautiful and numerous traditions, thanks to their eternal expression and radiance."[27]

However, enthusiasm for the resurrection of the ancient monument was not unanimous. The heated arguments among exponents and opponents of the project focused on matters such as scientific accuracy, contemporary site management, ideology, and international politics. One of the most forceful opponents was Anastasios Orlandos,[28] who objected to the idea of reconstructing the Stoa and requested a public reading of a statement he authored during the inauguration ceremony in order to present his critical arguments. With another public letter entitled "Should the Stoa of Attalos Be Reconstructed or Only Restored" and subtitled "A Scientific Polemic" and "The Whiteness of the Monument Is Temporary," Spyridon Marinatos counterargued for the rightness of the project and the feebleness of Orlandos's argumentation: "The restoration is a work of necessity for the rescuing of a monument. It is not always 'beautiful' though; otherwise a shepherd's boots and trousers that are full of patches and stitches could also be considered beautiful" (Marinatos 1956).

The coverage of this polemical issue by the Leftist *I Avgi*[29] was pursued differently, with deeper ideological and political undertones. Apart from the criticism on the aesthetic side of the project and the daring execution of an extensive reconstruction project just below the Acropolis promontory, the argument of the newspaper focused on the lack of adequate archaeological material evidence and the poor choice of reconstruction of a monument instead of restoration, which was also preferred by the scientific community. Above all, the newspaper noted that the reconstructed Stoa represented a reinforcement of the dominant state ideology and of the rhetoric of Western (American) imperialism and capitalism. This notion was exemplified by the personification of American donors as modern analogues of Hellenistic rulers who demanded the inscription of their names in commemorative panels placed on the walls of the reconstructed monuments. The newspaper decried the complete "Americanization" of the monument and characterized it as "Stoa of American Order."

A third case that attracted media attention and was covered in quite different ways between the two newspaper sources was the "Sound and Light" show, implemented for the first time on the "Sacred Rock" of the Acropolis in the spring of 1959. *To Vima* provided fairly informative and laudatory coverage, creating anticipation and excitement about this new kind of art, "the art of lyrically interpreting landscapes, monuments, legends and history."[30] *I Avgi*, in contrast, took an openly oppositional stance and perceived the project as encapsulating the power game between Greece and its Western allies. It spoke of the surrender of

Fig. 4.2. "Worthy of your glorious ancestors . . ." by US President Dwight Eisenhower. Cartoon. (Newspaper *To Vima*, December 20, 1959.) Courtesy of Historic Archives, *To Vima*.

the Greek state to foreign (in this case, French) business monopolies and of Konstantinos Karamanlis's personal agenda and ambitious vision as the new Pericles through a series of public works. In other words, the "Sound and Light" was criticized as nothing less than a showcase for the projection of personal, political, and financial self-interests of Greek politicians and foreign investors under the pretext of touristic development and social progress that would presumably create some new jobs opportunities for the Greek people.

During the same period, the issues of illicit trafficking of antiquities and the repatriation of the Parthenon Marbles made their appearance and remained popular with a mounting intensity of coverage in the press.[31] In 1957 and 1958, *I Avgi* published a series of articles under the general heading "Modern Elgins" [*Σύγχρονοι Ελγίνοι*] in order to address controversial matters regarding the protection of Greek archaeological heritage.[32] Its approach was more critical than simply informative when compared to the spirit of most articles published in *To Vima*. Gleaning the issues from this series, we note that some drew attention to the inertia of the Greek government to claim the return of the Marbles from the British government, and others expressed deep concern for the growing phenomenon of clandestine excavations in archaeological sites because "Modern

ΠΑΤΡΙΩΤΙΚΗ ΑΥΤΟΘΥΣΙΑ

Ἀνεχώρησε προχθές ὁ κ. Μαρκεζίνης εἰς Λονδῖνον, ὅπου εὑρίσκεται καὶ ὁ κ. Τσάτσος.

ELGIN MARBLES
ΕΛΓΙΝΕΙΑ ΜΑΡΜΑΡΑ

MAC SPIRO

—Ἑλληνικόν κλασικόν κάλλος δέν θέλετε, σέρ; Ἐπιστρέψατε εἰς τήν Ἑλλάδα τά μάρμαρα καί... κρατῆστε ἐμᾶς!...

Fig. 4.3. "Patriotic Self-sacrifice": proposing the repatriation of the Elgin Marbles to Greece and the "donation" of two Greek politicians. Cartoon. (Newspaper *To Vima*, December 17, 1961). Courtesy of Historic Archives, *To Vima*.

Elgins are invisible to the authorities but very visible to the villagers who thrive as beehives." The lack of state efficiency in the organization of archaeological matters in Greece and the monstrous state bureaucracy was to be condemned because it "dispose[s] half of its budget for the . . . military protection of the 'Greco-Christian civilization' [and] does not seem to be similarly eager to save, safeguard and promote the treasures of our ancient civilization in this land." The newspaper condemned the lack of systematic monitoring from the state, the impunity of the foreigners, and the barbarity of ignorant contractors, and it sarcastically stated, "the foreigners remain the absolute lords in our homeland . . . Funding for archaeology is so limited that the Greek archaeologist-civil servant must persuade the state that he will discover at least a Parthenon or at least another statue of Hermes by Praxiteles in order to be able to conduct an excavation." The newspaper mused, "What if there was some tidiness in our land, what if we had a proper archaeological organization, museums, tourism and more critically if there was a spirit for the proper development of our natural and artistic treasures?" According to this critique, two main benefits would result if strategic actions were taken: first, the country would be assured a huge income via the tourist industry, and second, it would systematically pursue an essential educational campaign so that Greek citizens could better understand, value, and enjoy their cultural heritage. Both observations have still not lost their significance for Greek society sixty years later.

In 1958, *I Avgi* rebuked the anachronistic and unproductive type of ancestor worship, as promoted by an equally anachronistic and conservative school system that was responsible for building negative connections between the Greeks and archaeological remnants of their past. According to the newspaper article, "The ancestor mania and the bombastic teaching of history provided by the school lead to the incurable repulsion of youngsters towards ancient Greek civilization and their cultural heritage, for they perceive it more as a torturous process than as a study of humanity."[33] Today, these dramatic observations continue to sound timely.

Quite a few articles brought to the fore the difficult coexistence of different stratigraphies of the past with the present, as mentioned earlier. Some articles focused on the need to safeguard the aesthetic and physical intergrity of the Acropolis in the late 1950s through a holistic landscaping of the area surrounding the archaeological site. Other articles focused on the archaeology of modern life and discussed the responsibilty of the state to rescue the diverse material culture of preindustrial popular culture, then at high risk due to rapid urbanization and technological modernization of the country.[34] Dimitrios Loukatos (1957a, 1957b), a scholar of folk studies, wrote alarming texts proposing the urgent organization of folk art museums in order "not to forget that there is another more recent heritage of our great grand fathers, the neohellenic, which, although poor in prize-giving and modest in artistic achievements, is nonetheless wealthy in terms of human and national significance and closely connected with the Greek psyche, much more than the distant ancient past" (Loukatos 1957a, 3). He envisioned that such a type of museum would not represent the Athenian bourgoisie but instead support local agricultural communities whose self-esteem and pride could be further encouraged. In his words, "even those with high political bearings could take a breath of national pride in this type of Museum, of course if they still retain in their souls some of their folk and provincial conscience" (Loukatos 1957b, 3). As Ioannis Kontis, director of antiquities and restorations, admitted with honesty, the Greek Archaeological Service concentrated all its care and effort on the protection and enhancement of monuments of the classical past. Hence, many medieval monuments "were reminders of a period of occupation and thus had to disappear. Under the pretext of 'national reasons' which in truth is used to cover up simplistic and dangerous historical views and often ruthless personal interests, many monuments of Western artistic style have been sacrificed which would otherwise be true ornaments for our country today."[35]

In the 1960s, Athens's rapid urbanization and lack of respect for the architectural monuments of the recent past caused the extensive destruction of many neoclassical buildings that dated to the nineteenth century. This fact was often criticized in the contemporary press. One of the hundreds of buildings that were put at risk, but fortunately was spared, was Villa Ilissia, hosting the Byzantine and Christian Museum, whose key location was considered by the then Karamanlis government as ideal for the erection of new edifices for the courts or a new cultural center. The coverage of the press revealed strong oppositions by intellectuals who claimed the "rescue of the few beautiful remnants of this recent past."[36]

In 1965, when Athens's uncontrolled urbanization was well under way, *I Avgi* welcomed a proposal from the Municipal Council for the foundation of a city museum, an institution for the history, culture, and social development of the Greek capital from the Byzantine period to today. The museum would cover a very long historical period that, according to the newspaper, was left "neglected, unjustly treated and unknown, because it has never received the honors of a museum presentation."[37] The article predicted that such an initiative would be warmly welcomed by all citizens and emphatically noted that the municipality of Athens should no longer neglect this important matter.

A year and a half later, just three weeks before the military coup of April 21, 1967, the press extensively covered the realization of the First Archaeological Congress. The congress would bring to the fore diverse, contentious issues with the operation of the Archaeological Service, many of which continue to exist in later periods. These matters were outlined under three main axes: museum problems, the protection of archaeological sites, and illicit trafficking of antiquities. The newspaper reporter concluded that "despite recent efforts and achievements, the Archaeological Service remains inadequately equipped and without proper organization in order to face and fight not only the problems set by a country in rapid development but also the current demands of a developing science. Thus, the Archaeological Service cannot stand against the bulldozers, the machine-driven land cultivation, the looters or the polluting factories relying only on an outdated archaeological law and the zeal of a dedicated but inadequate personnel."[38]

Today, one of the few remaining arrows that the Greek Archaeological Service has in its quiver is a modernized and effective archaeological law. Yet it seems that the current economic crisis and its resulting effects raise perilous challenges that undermine the absolute power of the archaeological law as a vehicle to regulate the development of the country without concurrently putting the integrity, protection, and enhancement of Greece's unique cultural heritage at risk.

Harvesting, Digesting, Reflecting

In this chapter, I have tried to navigate through extensive territories of newspaper sources and their varied ideological landscapes on archaeological heritage valuation in early post-war Greece. In addition, the aim was to elucidate the contexts within which these landscapes have been produced and to harvest their material bearings in order to assess their significance during the time when they were first produced. If we were to classify this harvesting, label it, and place it in different containers of meaning making, the generic categories that emerge have global, regional, and local strands.

Antiquities as study resources and heritage symbols have been implictly and explicitly vested with political meanings in order to supplement Cold War narratives and signpost the ideological and cultural superiority of the West within a deeply divided world shaped by allies and enemies. In this global power game, modern Greece was left weakened and powerless, having placed its hope for resurrection in the generous "kindness" and support of the West and in its own rich ancient heritage. This patrimony has often been used as a national flag to reassert the territorial and intellectual precedence of Greece in the Aegean and Balkan region, especially when geopolitical disputes of varied intensity were imminent and eventually ignited. The result has been a polemic defensiveness toward any rhetoric that is at odds with the dominant national one.

Complex, multilayered stratigraphies of memory, hegemonic pasts, and value-driven approaches to material culture seem to be a dominant and recurrent denominator in the readings of many newspaper clippings. This problematic relationship with the different Greek pasts has in fact been anticipated. Coming to terms with the "thickness" of time that characterizes Greece and Greek culture has been not an ephemeral but rather an enduring challenge. Encouraging and formulating a kind of archaeological education for lay readers through the press as a way of setting the foundation stones for a less strained, more respectful, constructive, and eventually loving relationship of the Greeks with their heritage has not been an easy or a sustainable undertaking. As a significant and challenging issue in modern Greece, the stratigraphies of memory and the hegemonic superiority of the glorious classical past over other pasts are at stake, and therefore the state and the citizens alike must come to terms with difficult coexistence of material remnants, respect these remnants with maturity, and value them all for their different historical bearings.

The country had to develop its infrastructure and economy at the speediest pace and was called on to change. It was forced to exploit opportunities, build a new national brand through tourism, open up to the world, and perhaps invest in culture—an unfulfilled national vision that was perhaps never formulated as one. Within this frame, the different pasts dueled each time with different set priorities. The use of (mostly) archaeological heritage as an asset for the country's development and economic progress, mainly through the tourist industry in a service-based world, was anticipated and frequently served by the press. This material valuation seemed to have been driven by not only certain state policies but also different parties within and outside the country that were involved in the gradual shaping of Greece into a tourist destination, a branded product for international consumption.

Not less interconnected has been the drive of the newspapers to comment on national cultural policies and processes for the protection and enhancement of Greek heritage, in order to either showcase and applaud the heroic achievements and charismatic personalities of key cultural thinkers and practitioners in Greece or to criticize the state for its inefficiency, wrong-footedness, or lack of vision and investment in archaeological resources. In some way, the management of antiquities and cultural heritage at large has been perceived as a testing ground for the preparedness and efficacy of the Greek governments to build a modern European state that would be, on the one hand, well received and respected by the larger European family of nation-states and the American rulers and, on the other hand, mature and responsible enough to raise educated and conscientious citizens.

Intellectual and institutional divides between different national and international bodies related to Greek archaeology and its study, protection, and management (e.g., the Archaeological Service, universities, foreign archaeological schools, private entities, and individuals) add more strands and colors to the fabric of the post-war, archaeological resource management debate and its exposure to the public domain. Ultimately, the power struggle between the old and the new, its intersection with everyday life, and its impact on shaping public opinion and practices regarding the value and management of archaeological heritage in post-war Greece are what cuts across most of the newspaper sources under study. No doubt, this archival material provides a valuable reservoir of news, opinions, and approaches of early post-war, heritage-management, public literature with its own historical merit. As stated earlier, the aim in the context of this study was to provide an overview of the issues at stake and draft a road map for understanding the uses of the past during the early post-war period.

Yet apart from its historical significance, this road map can also be of use when reflecting on heritage management issues beyond the early post-war years. Similar grand narratives and discourses endured and shaped distinct categories of Greek cultural politics in later periods of modern Greece. These discourses have fed debates on the value of Greek antiquities on global, regional, and local levels. Greek antiquities have often been perceived as key formulators of modern Greek national identity, as stepping stones for the shaping of a rather ethnocentric and singular reading of the Greek past, and as a long-lasting passport for Greece's presence in European and international political affairs. They have acted not only as protagonists in a compelling story of national pride but also as well-crafted shields against any entity—state, private, or individual—that would question Greece's legacy and contemporary position in the world. The need for change, modernization, and development has been a constant demand and challenge for a country whose fragile economy has always been an open wound at risk of infection. Thus cultural heritage and its management came to reflect long-lasting divides between myriad entities: the present and the past and their multiple temporalities; state and private interests; politicians and cultural practitioners; discourses of authority (governmental, state, epistemological, or other) and civic voices expressed in a collective or individual manner; dedicated keepers of the material remnants of the past (i.e., archaeologists) and other parties or individuals whose relationship to the remnants of the past has been conditioned according to their own interests and drives; the archaeologists themselves and their internal differences; a bureaucratic status quo and a flexible management model that is difficult to enforce; the perception of antiquities as public goods and their counterreading as commercial products with prominent economic value; and their perception as sacred relics worshipped as such and other more liberating interpretations as cultural teasers and resources for personal meaning making.

In an article entitled "The Knowledge of Our Prehistory" [*I gnosi tis proistorias mas*], published in 1957 by *I Avgi*, we read the following insightful comment: "We seek education as not only an ornament but also a way to serve the practical needs of our life and our immediate environment. Real and appropriate education must be based on knowledge of the historic fate of Greece and of the historic fate of all humanity" (Papaioannou 1957, 1). In the early post-war press, a special vision to understand the meanings and values of Greek heritage and disseminate them to a wider public has been traced with diverse intensity on many different occasions through the discussion of certain contentious cases of the uses of the past in the present. The purpose was primarily to combat ignorance and encourage a special education on archaeological matters for the Greek lay public. In our contemporary digital world, the relationship of modern Greeks with their past, its multiple temporalities, and its current readings within the time and space of modern Greek history, as well as the global history of humanity, remains complex and challenging. Resources for tracing and analyzing these factors have grown to gigantic proportions. However, studying their own significance and impact is a challenge for the future.

Acknowledgments

I wish to express my gratitude to Esther Solomon for challenging me to return to archival material I partly studied years ago and set it anew under the microscope in order to assess its value in discussing provocative uses of the past in Greece in the post-war years. I am also grateful to Esther for her constructive comments on this work, her unlimited patience during the writing of this chapter, and her continuous friendship. My thanks go to the Historical Archive of Piraeus Bank

Group Cultural Foundation (especially to Dr. Eleni Beneki) and to the Directorate of the Management of the National Archive of Monuments, Documentation and Protection of Cultural Goods and its always helpful staff for facilitating my access to archival material related to the Marshall Plan. Finally, I extend my thanks to *To Vima* for granting me permission to reproduce the cartoons that visually supplement this chapter.

MARLEN MOULIOU is Assistant Professor of Museology at the National and Kapodistrian University of Athens and Coordinator of the Postgraduate Program in Museum Studies at the same university. From 2010 to 2016, she served as secretary and then chair of the International Committee for the Collections and Activities of Museums of Cities (CAMOC). She has written widely in Greek and also in international books and journals, and she coedited a number of publications, among others: *Memory Narrates the City: Oral History and Memory in the Urban Context* (Plethron, 2016); *Our Greatest Artefact: The City: Essays on Cities and Museums about Them* (with Ian Jones and Eric Sandweiss, CAMOC-ICOM, 2012). She is also the editor of *Museums and Museology in Modern Society: New Challenges, New Relationships* (*Archaeology and Arts Journal*, 2014–2015).

Notes

1. There has been a huge number of commentaries on the discovery of a monumental Macedonian tomb at Amphipolis in Northern Greece in the summer of 2014 and the multiple perspectives in its interpretation by archaeologists, politicians, and the public at large (see Plantzos 2017). A Google search using "Amphipolis" as a keyword currently generates no less than 397,000 results, a number that reveals an intense interest in the case and perhaps generally on current uses of the past in Greece.

2. From a remarkably diverse academic literature on the subject, here is a short selection of publications written in English: Brown and Hamilakis (2003); Hamilakis and Ifantidis (2013); Hamilakis and Anagnostopoulos (2009); Hamilakis and Momigliano (2006); Hamilakis and Rainbird (2004); Hamilakis (2007); Damaskos and Plantzos (2008); Plantzos (2012, 2014); Solomon (2006, 2007).

3. The newspaper *To Vima* [The Tribune] was founded in 1922 to advocate traditional central-liberal ideas, and the newspaper *I Avgi* [The Dawn] was founded in 1953 to represent the intellectual Left.

4. The collection of this newspaper material was conducted many years ago in the context of another comprehensive research project (Mouliou 1997). During that period, the archives of the newspapers were not digitized, and in particular those of the newspaper *I Avgi* were minimally organized. Many of its daily issues were missing. Thus, the sample under study does not represent its entire coverage on archaeological and cultural affairs.

In contrast, the newspaper *To Vima* had very orderly archives, which were studied in an exhaustive manner for the purpose of the aforementioned research project and also for this text. Reasons that stand as justifications for the selection of these newspapers are their longevity and enduring role as traditional platforms of archaeological dissemination in the public sphere, their intellectual value, and their diversified interest in other social and cultural domains.

5. More precisely, 1,291 articles from the newspaper *To Vima* during 1950–1967 and 181 articles from the newspaper *I Avgi* from August 16, 1953, to April 2, 1967.

6. In *To Vima*, most of these articles are short to medium size (only 6% of the total sample has been long articles), whereas in *I Avgi* the percentage of long feature articles is much higher (around 33%).

7. From a vast literature on heritage values, see de la Torre (2002); Mathers, Darvill, and Little (2005); Carman (1996); Clark (2006); Cleere (1989); Darvill (1995); Lipe (1984); and Smith (2006).

8. According to Evangelos Papanoutsos, leading Greek pedagogue, philosopher, and author of many such educationally purposed articles in the newspaper *To Vima*, the missionary approach of the press was indispensable in view of the poor cultural education of the average Greek citizen at the time (see e.g., Papanoutsos 1950, 1957).

9. For the implementation of the Marshall Plan in Greece, see also Sfikas (2011) and Vetsopoulos (2007).

10. For an overview of the tourist industry in Modern Greece, see Aesopos (2015) and Vlachos (2016).

11. Olympus—Homer—Athens—Marathon—Democracy—Delphi—Amphictyony—Pericles—Parthenon—Socrates—Plato—Alexander—Constantinople—Justinian—Saint Sophia—El Greco—Missolongi—Venizelos—Palamas—Skra—Sangarios—Pindus—El Alamein—Rimini.

12. For a discussion on the multitemporality of the past, see Hamilakis (2013), Hamilakis and Ifantidis (2013), and Hamilakis and Theou (2013).

13. After the war, Maximos Megaron was temporarily used as the residence of the US ambassador in Athens, but after its purchase by the Greek state in 1952, it was used as a guesthouse for important foreign guests. In 1982, it became the seat of the Greek prime minister's office.

14. Leonard Robert Palmer was a professor of comparative linguistics at the University of Oxford. His work contested Arthur Evans's dating of Minoan archaeological finds from Crete. In mid-1960, he published a series of articles relevant to this debate in *To Vima* (see e.g., July 5, 1960, 1, 5; July 6, 1960, 1, 5; July 7, 1960, 1, 5).

15. See *To Vima*, December 7, 1950, 3.

16. This could be traced in articles focusing on the symbolic significance of the Acropolis for Greece and humanity alike or on the end of classical education in Europe and the need for redefining classical studies and their relevance to the contemporary world. See *To Vima*, October 7, 1951, 1–2 and February 10, 1952, 3.

17. These are complex issues involving some key personalities of post-war archaeological heritage management, such as Ch. Karouzos, M. Kalligas, R. Agathoklis, A. Orlandos, and N. Kontoleon. For the sources that give all the details of such rivalries between archaeologists of the Archaeological Service and the universities, see *To Vima*, September 28, 1948, 3; June 11, 1952, 3; June 17, 1952, 3; August 18, 1960, 1; and August 24, 1960, 3–4.

18. Documents retrieved from the Historical Archives of the Greek Archaeological Service testify that at the end of 1949, the Central Archaeological Council decided to allocate 27.13 billion drachmas from the Marshall Funds for the rehabilitation of many Greek museums (Ref. No. 107/49, December 29, 1949). In this document, we read that the council allocated 4.5 billion drachmas for the interior redisplay of all museums and another 19 billion drachmas for the rehabilitation of six museums. The lion's share was given to the National Archaeological Museum (7 billion drachmas) and the Museum of Thessaloniki (5.5 billion drachmas). The remaining four museums were the National Gallery (1.7 billion drachmas); the Museum of the Acropolis (1.3 billion drachmas); the Museum of Heraklion, Crete (2 billion drachmas); and the Museum of Corfu (1 billion drachmas). Provisions for funds ranging from fifteen thousand to five hundred million drachmas were also allocated to eighteen more archaeological museums, depending on their size and needs.

19. In 1953, Marinatos comments on the role of antiquities in tourism (*To Vima*, March 21, 1953, 3) for the first time. Many more articles that follow focus on the perils threatening the Acropolis (*To Vima*, August 9, 1953, 3), the urgent need for the reopening of the National Archaeological Museum (*To Vima*, September 3, 1953, 3), museums in key tourist locations such as Rhodes (*To Vima*, May 19, 1954, 3), and generally the lack of museum infrastructure (*To Vima*, October 6, 1957, 1, 6; September 23, 1962, 5).

20. See *To Vima*, October 9, 1957, 1, 5, whereby it is reported that archaeologists are paid the minimum salary rate (1,750 drachmas per month starting salary), whereas their highest wages are very meager compared to the work requested by them (up to 3,200 drachmas). The article claims that the payment rates for museum and archaeological wardens are also very little (only 500 drachmas).

21. See *I Avgi*, August 16, 1953, 5.

22. See *I Avgi*, September 5, 1953, 2.

23. *To Vima*, June 19, 1955, 3.

24. Meritt (1984, 178–82). See also Mauzy (2006, 31–75); Liaska (2013); Sakka (2008, 2013); Mouliou (2008).

25. From the inaugural speech of then secretary of state K. Tsatsos. See *To Vima*, September 2, 1956, 3; *I Avgi*, September 17, 1958, 24.

26. Extract from the inaugural speech of President Eisenhower. See *To Vima*, September 4, 1956, 3–4.

27. See *To Vima*, June 16, 1956, 4.

28. Anastasios Orlandos was then director of restorations of ancient monuments and responsible for many restoration projects of ancient and Byzantine monuments in Greece during the post-war period.

29. *I Avgi*, August 3, 1957, 1, 5.

30. This coverage was signed by the music composer of the show; see P. Petridis in *To Vima*, March 21, 1959, 1–2.

31. See *To Vima*, May 9, 1954, 1; November 22, 1957, 3; May 28, 1961, 3.

32. In 1957, *I Avgi* included more than a dozen opinion pieces on this issue. All the articles were written by R. Raftopoulos. See a sample in *I Avgi*: July 28, 1957, 1, 5; July 31, 1957, 1, 5; August 2, 1957, 1, 5; August 4, 1957, 5.

33. See *I Avgi*, September 14, 1958, 5–6.

34. See *To Vima*, September 29, 1957, 3–4; January 8, 1958, 3. Cf. *To Vima*, April 12, 1959, 5–6.

35. See *To Vima*, July 5, 1964, 5; July 7, 1964, 3; July 8, 1964, 3.

36. See *To Vima,* February 11, 1962, 7; February 18, 1962, 5; June 8, 1963, 4.
37. See *I Avgi*, October 3, 1965, 5.
38. *To Vima,* March 30, 1967, 2.

References

Aesopos, Yannis, ed. 2015. *Tourism Landscapes: Remaking Greece.* Athens: Domes.

Brown, Keith, and Yannis Hamilakis, eds. 2003. *The Usable Past: Greek Metahistories.* Lanham, MD: Lexington.

Carman, John. 1996. *Valuing Ancient Things: Archaeology and Law.* Leicester: Leicester University Press.

Clark, Kate, ed. 2006. *Capturing the Public Value of Heritage.* The Proceedings of the London Conference January 25–26, 2006. London: English Heritage.

Cleere, Henry, ed. 1989. *Archaeological Heritage Management in the Modern World.* London: Unwin Hyman.

Damaskos, Dimitris, and Dimitris Plantzos, eds. 2008. *A Singular Antiquity: Archaeology and Hellenic Identity in Twentieh-Century Greece.* Athens: Benaki Museum.

Darvill, Timothy. 1995. "Value Systems in Archaeology." In *Managing Archaeology*, edited by Malcolm Cooper, Antony Firth, John Carman, and David Wheatley, 40–50. London: Routledge.

de la Torre, Marta, ed. 2002. *Assessing the Values of Cultural Heritage: Research Report.* Los Angeles: The Getty Conservation Institute. Accessed July 24, 2019. http://www.getty.edu/conservation/publications_resources/pdf_publications/pdf/assessing.pdf.

Final Report. 1952. *Το Σχέδιον Μάρσαλ στην Ελλάδα. Ιούλιος 1948–Ιανουάριος 1952* [The Marshall Plan in Greece. July 1948–January 1952]. Athens: Special Financial Mission of the Organization for Common Security.

Greece Calling. 1948. Athens: Information Division of the "Greek Reconstruction Claims Committee."

Hamilakis, Yannis. 2007. *The Nation and Its Ruins: Antiquity, Archaeology and National Imagination in Greece.* Oxford: Oxford University Press.

———. 2008. "Decolonizing Greek Archaeology: Indigenous Archaeologies, Modernist Archaeology and the Post-colonial Critique." In *A Singular Antiquity: Archaeology and Hellenic Identity in Twentieth-Century Greece*, edited by Dimitris Damaskos and Dimitris Plantzos, 273–84. Athens: Benaki Museum.

———. 2013. *Archaeology and the Senses: Human Experience, Memory and Affect.* Cambridge: Cambridge University Press.

Hamilakis, Yannis, and Aris Anagnostopoulos, eds. 2009. *Archaeological Ethnographies.* Special double issue of *Public Archaeology* 8 (2–3).

Hamilakis, Yannis, and Fotis Ifantidis. 2013. "The Other Acropolises: Multi-Temporality and the Persistence of the Past." In *Oxford Handbook of the Archaeology of the Contemporary World*, edited by Paul Graves Brown, Rodney Harrison, and Angela Piccini, 758–81. Oxford: Oxford University Press.

Hamilakis, Yannis, and Nicoletta Momigliano, eds. 2006. *Archaeology and European Modernity: Producing and Consuming the "Minoans."* Padova: Botega d'Erasmo; *Creta Antica*, special issue.

Hamilakis, Yannis, and Paul Rainbird. 2004. "Interrogating Pedagogies: Archaeology in Higher Education." In *Education and the Historic Environment*, edited by Don Henson, Peter Stone, and Mike Corbishley, 47–54. London: Routledge.
Hamilakis, Yannis, and Efthimis Theou. 2013. "Enacted Multi-temporality: The Archaeological Site as a Shared, Performative Space." In *Reclaiming Archaeology: Beyond the Tropes of Modernity*, edited by Alfredo Gonzalez-Ruibal, 181–94. London: Routledge.
Hamilakis, Yannis, and Eleana Yalouri. 1996. "Antiquities as Symbolic Capital in Modern Greek Society." *Antiquity* 70: 117–29.
Herzfeld, Michael. 2002. "The Absent Presence: Discourses of Crypto-Colonialism." *The South Atlantic Quarterly* 101: 899–926.
Judt, Tony. 2010. *Postwar. A History of Europe since 1945*. London: Vintage.
Kalligas, M. 1946. "Οι Ζημιές των Αρχαίων από την Κατοχή" [The Damages of Antiquities during the War Occupation]. *To Vima*, June 27, 1946, 1–2.
———. 1948. "Το Άνοιγμα του Εθνικού Αρχαιολογικού Μουσείου" [The Opening of the National Archaeological Museum]. *To Vima*, January 15, 1948, 2.
———. 1952. "Δια τα Μνημεία μας" [On Our Monuments]. *To Vima*, January 5, 1952, 1–2.
———. 1953. "Ο Δανεισμός Αρχαιοτήτων δια την Έκθεσιν Ελληνικής Τέχνης εις Αμερικήν" [The Loan of Antiquities for the Exhibition of Greek Art in America]. *To Vima*, April 13, 1953, 3.
———. 1955. "Είναι Απαραίτητος ο Έλεγχος για τα Εθνικά Γλυπτικά Μνημεία. Ο Λεωνίδας των Θερμοπυλών και Άλλα Χειρότερα" [Necessary to Impose a Control over National Sculptural Monuments. Leonidas of Thermopylae and Other Worse Cases]. *To Vima*, November 30, 1955, 3.
Kostis, Kostas. 2013. *Τα "Κακομαθημένα Παιδιά" της Ιστορίας. Η Διαμόρφωση του Νεοελληνικού Κράτους, 18ος–21ος αιώνας* [The "Spoiled Children" of History: The Formation of the Modern Greek State, Eighteenth–Twenty-First Century]. 3rd ed. Athens: Polis,
Liaska, Maria. 2013. "Το Μουσείο της Αρχαίας Αγοράς στη Στοά του Αττάλου. Η Ανακατασκευή της Στοάς και η Πρώτη Έκθεση του Μουσείου" [The Museum of Ancient Agora in the Stoa of Attalos: The Reconstruction of the Stoa and the First Exhibition of the Museum]. In *Αρχαιολογικές Συμβολές. Τόμος Β: Αττική* [*Archaeological Contributions Vol. 2: Attica*], edited by Stavroula Oikonomou and Maria Dogka-Toli, 79–93. Athens: Museum of Cycladic Art.
Lipe, William. 1984. "Value and Meaning in Cultural Resources." In *Approaches to the Archaeological Heritage*, edited by Henry Cleere, 1–11. Cambridge: Cambridge University Press.
Loukatos, D. 1957a. "Προβάλλει Επείγουσα η Ανάγκη να Οργανωθή και η Αρχαιολογία της Σύγχρονης Ζωής μας" [Urgent Need to Organize the Archaeology of Our Contemporary Life]. *To Vima*, November 10, 1957, 3–4.
———. 1957b. "'Ατομα και Οργανώσεις Πρέπει ν' Αρχίσουν από Τώρα την Συλλογήν και Φύλαξιν του Υλικού που Χάνεται" [Individuals and Organizations Must Start Now Collecting and Safekeeping the Material That Is Being Lost]. *To Vima*, November 12, 1957, 3.
Marinatos, S. 1952a. "Ο Επιστημονικός Ανταγωνισμός Συνέχεια Προϊστορικής Αντιζηλίας" [Scientific Antagonism as a Continuation of a Prehistoric Rivalry]. *To Vima*, October 26, 1952, 3.

———. 1952b. "Υποθέσεις που Διανοίγει το Μέγαρον του Βαθυπέτρου" [The Megaron in Vathypetron Opens up New Hypotheses]. *To Vima*, October 28, 1952, 1–2.

———. 1956. "Έπρεπε να Ανακατασκευασθή ή μόνον να Αναστηλωθή η Στοά του Αττάλου" [Should the Stoa of Attalos Have Been Reconstructed or Only Restored?]. *To Vima*, September 11, 1956, 2.

Mathers, Clay, Timothy Darvill, and Barbara Little, eds. 2005. *Heritage of Value, Archaeology of Renown: Reshaping Archaeological Assessment and Significance*. Gainesville, FL: University Press of Florida.

Mauzy, Craig. 2006. *Agora Excavations. 1931–2006. A Pictorial History*. Athens: The American School of Classical Studies.

Meritt, Lucy Shoe. 1984. *History of the American School of Classical Studies at Athens, 1939–1980*. Princeton, NJ: Princeton University Press.

Mouliou Marlen. 1996. "Ancient Greece, Its Classical Heritage and the Modern Greeks: Aspects of Nationalism in Museum Exhibitions." In *Nationalism and Archaeology*, edited by John Atkinson, Iain Banks, and Jerry O' Sullivan, 174–99. Glasgow: Cruithne.

———. 1997. *The Writing of Classical Archaeology in Post-war Greece (1950 to the Present); The Case of Museum Exhibitions and Museum Narratives*. PhD diss., University of Leicester. Accessed July 24, 2019. https://lra.le.ac.uk/handle/2381/7661.

———. 2008. "Museum Representations of the Classical Past in Post-war Greece: A Critical Analysis." In *A Singular Antiquity: Archaeology and Hellenic Identity in Twentieth-Century Greece*, edited by Dimitris Damaskos and Dimitris Plantzos, 83–109. Athens: Benaki Museum.

Papaioannou, M. 1957. "Η γνώση της Προϊστορίας μας" [The Knowledge of Our Prehistory]. *I Avgi*, July 30, 1957, 1, 5.

Papanoutsos, E. 1950. "Τα Νέα μας Μνημεία" [Our New Monuments]. *To Vima*, September 18, 1950, 1–2.

———. 1957. "Κείμενα και Μνημεία. Πνευματικά Ζητήματα" [Texts and Monuments. Spiritual Matters]. *To Vima*, December 19, 1957, 1–2.

Plantzos, Dimitris. 2012. "The Glory That Was Not: Embodying the Classical in Contemporary Greece." *Interactions. Studies in Communication and Culture* 3 (2): 147–71.

———. 2014. "Dead Archaeologists, Buried Gods: Archaeology as an Agent of Modernity in Greece." In *Re-imagining the Past. Antiquity and Modern Greek Culture*, edited by Dimitris Tziovas, 147–64. Oxford: Oxford University Press.

———. 2017. "Amphipolitics: Archaeological Performance and Governmentality in Greece under the Crisis." In *Greece in Crisis. The Cultural Politics of Austerity*, edited by Dimitris Tziovas, 65–84. London: I. B. Tauris.

Report. 1951. *Η Αμερικανική Βοήθεια προς την Ελλάδα (1945–1951)* [The American Aid to Greece (1945–1951)]. Athens: Mission for the Management of Financial Aid in Greece.

Sakka, Niki. 2008. "The Excavation of the Ancient Agora of Athens: The Politics of Commissioning and Managing the Project." In *A Singular Antiquity: Archaeology and Hellenic Identity in Twentieth-Century Greece*, edited by Dimitris Damaskos and Dimitris Plantzos, 111–24. Athens: Benaki Museum.

———. 2013. "A Debt to Ancient Wisdom and Beauty: The Reconstruction of the Stoa of Attalos in the Ancient Agora of Athens." In *Philhellenism, Philanthropy, or Political*

Convenience? American Archaeology in Greece, edited by Jack L. Davis and Natalia Vogeikoff-Brogan, special issue, *Hesperia* 82 (1): 203–27.

Sfikas, Thanassis. ed. 2011. *Το Σχέδιο Μάρσαλ. Ανασυγκρότηση και Διαίρεση της Ευρώπης* [The Marshall Plan: The Rehabilitation and Division of Europe]. Athens: Patakis.

Smith, Laurajane. 2006. *Uses of Heritage*. London: Routledge.

Solomon, Esther. 2006. "Knossos: Social Uses of a Monumental Landscape." In *Archaeology and European Modernity: Producing and Consuming the "Minoans,"* edited by Yannis Hamilakis and Nicoletta Momigliano, 163–82. Padova: Botega d'Erasmo; *Creta Antica*, special issue.

———. 2007. *Multiple "Historicities" on the Island of Crete: The Significance of Minoan Archaeological Heritage in Everyday Life*. PhD diss., University College London.

Stathakis, Giorgos. 2011. "Το Δόγμα Τρούμαν και το Σχέδιο Μάρσαλ στην Ελλάδα" [The Truman Doctrine and the Marshall Plan in Greece]. In *Το Σχέδιο Μάρσαλ. Ανασυγκρότηση και Διαίρεση της Ευρώπης* [The Marshall Plan: The Rehabilitation and Division of Europe], edited by Thanassis Sfikas, 295–312. Athens: Patakis.

Vanderpool, E. 1950. "Η Συστηματική Ανασυγκρότησις του Αρχαιολογικού μας Μουσείου" [The Systematic Rehabilitation of our Archaeological Museum]. *To Vima*, March 16, 1950, 3.

Vetsopoulos, Apostolos. 2007. *Η Ελλάδα και το Σχέδιο Μάρσαλ. Η Μεταπολεμική Ανασυγκρότηση της Ελληνικής Οικονομίας* [Greece and the Marshall Plan: The Post-War Rehabilitation of the Greek Economy]. Athens: Gutenberg.

Vlachos, Angelos. 2016. *Τουρισμός και Δημόσιες Πολιτικές στη Σύγχρονη Ελλάδα 1914–1950. Η Ανάδυση ενός Νεοτερικού Φαινομένου* [Tourism and State Policies in Modern Greece 1914–1950: The Emersion of a Modern Phenomenon]. Corfu: Economia.

Zachariou, Stelios. 2001. "Struggle for Survival: American Aid and Greek Reconstruction." In *The Marshall Plan: Fifty Years After*, edited by Martin Schain, 153–63. New York: Palgrave.

Part II

Spatial Metaphors and Ethnographic Observations: Heritage, Memory, and Dissonance

5 The Gentrification of Memory

The Past as a Social Event in Thessaloniki of the Early Twenty-First Century

Styliana Galiniki

THESSALONIKI, THE SECOND largest Greek city after Athens, is located in the northern region of Greece, Macedonia. It has recently claimed an envious position on the international stage: *National Geographic* included Thessaloniki in its top worldwide tourist destinations for 2013, referring to it as a "bolt of Greece lightning," and in 2014, *fDi Intelligence* magazine selected it from among forty-six midsized cities as the one with the greatest future potential for human capital and lifestyle.[1] Also, Yiannis Boutaris, the city's mayor from 2010 until 2019, was named one of the ten best mayors in the world in 2014;[2] *The Guardian* proclaimed him "a beacon of hope for Greece" (Leach 2014), and noted that in a country ravaged by the greatest postwar economic crisis, the mayor of Thessaloniki set an example for politically driven development. One of Boutaris's most noteworthy accomplishments lay in the fact that he managed to boost Thessaloniki's tourism industry by using the city's multicultural past as a "selling point" for Jewish and Turkish visitors (Patikas 2013, 39–42).

Boutaris's election in 2010 with the support of the Center and the Left marked the end of an era for the city of Thessaloniki. For over thirty years, not only the municipality but also the broader administrative region (prefecture) was in the hands of right-wing elected officials, who had been blamed for public policies of dubious aesthetic, accused of wasting public funds (see Christodoulou 2013), and known for encouraging or supporting in various ways xenophobic and nationalistic attitudes and populist practices, thus tarnishing the city's image and profoundly affecting the residents' identity (Tzanelli 2011). As early as the beginning of the nineties, the city's municipal authorities had instigated the organization of public demonstrations on the conflict with the neighboring North Macedonia (then FYROM)[3] regarding the right to use the name *Macedonia* and thus benefit from the cultural capital associated with its ancient past. From then onward, and until the first decade of the twenty-first century, Thessaloniki became a venue for annual events in honor of Alexander the Great, organized not only by far-right nationalist groups and parties but also by the regional authorities themselves. For decades, nationalists with overtly neo-Nazi affinities, far-right political figures, priests and the metropolitan bishop, populist local officials, and representatives of a certain nationalist intelligentsia used the contemporary statue of Alexander the Great, located on the Thessaloniki seafront, as a springboard for their gradual penetration into the social sphere. Moreover, they used the statue as a stage, an urban theater where the city's identity could be "performed" in the character that the dominant national discourse had assigned to it.[4] Thessaloniki became known, at least within Greece, as a bastion of nationalism and conservativism (Loizides 2015, 41–68; Galiniki 2015, 423–27).

By vowing to change the city's identity, Boutaris won the election as "the Apostate" (Angelos 2015, 158), willing to take on the city's conservative forces. His most revolutionary accomplishment was the fact that he used his position as an elected local official in order to implement politics of memory that were in contrast with the previously dominant narrative of the city's past (Angelos 2015, 158–88; Sintès and Givre 2015). By promoting multiculturalism as the element that best summed up the identity and guaranteed the prosperity of Thessaloniki, Boutaris succeeded in rescuing, not so much from oblivion as from silence,[5] Thessaloniki's "other" past—that of its past residents of other religions and ethnicities. He did not simply remind us of the fact that the city was known for centuries as the "Jerusalem of the Balkans," or that Kemal Atatürk was born in Thessaloniki. Through public declarations, symbolic gestures, and spatial practices, he did not attempt to hide the city's past "but, rather, celebrated the Ottoman and Jewish past of his hometown" (Loizides 2015, 152).

This was not the first time that multiculturalism entered the vocabulary of local elected officials. However, never before had it become a systematic policy focused on an attempt to reapproach the local cultural heritage and redefine its content. This process focused on practices that activated material remnants of that "other," more recent past (especially urban and religious architectural elements) or that, by assigning substance to and creating a space for immaterial things (emotions, stories, memories), transformed Thessaloniki's public space into a monument of absence. Until recently, the dominant narrative used archaeological remnants or their more recent reproductions as evidence of the city's Hellenism; these relics are now being reinterpreted as evidence of the city's multicultural nature.

A crucial factor in the promotion of multiculturalism as an element of the city's identity was the municipality's effort to rescue Thessaloniki from financial and social decline by tapping into the global tourism market. In the context of the so-called *city break tourism*, cities such as Thessaloniki are ideal destinations for short, low-cost holidays (Patikas 2013). In an effort to sell a destination, one can't leave its culture untouched because that is precisely where one can find the elements that could be used to promote a special local identity. On the contrary, as noted by Kearns and Philo (1993, 3), there is a conscious and deliberate manipulation of culture and history in order to underline the authenticity of certain local customs and traditions.

Neoliberal policies create competition between cities in an effort to attract investors and tourists; in many such cases, multiculturalism and, in particular, multiethnicity and ethnic diversity appear to be the one element that can restore the image of a city in decline—for example, due to deindustrialization (Paddison 2013)—by turning it into a place of openness and a consumer haven (Athanasiou 2014). However, showcasing a city's multiculturalism involves dealing with complex issues that are intrinsically linked to a certain version of collective memory and identity. In most modern nation-states, multiculturalism has been a sign of "otherness;" it has reflected a contested heritage and has been marginalized in order to make room for the construction of a unified, national conscience, a coherent identity. The multiculturalist imperative appears to challenge collective oblivion as it creates a space reserved for the public expression of marginalized groups and undesirable identities. Yet in many cases, it can also function as another mechanism for oblivion because it is often promoted as a means of covering up other, more unpleasant versions of the past. For example, many cities in eastern and central European countries have showcased their multiculturalism as an important element of their identity, aiming to win over the international tourism market by projecting a democratic—and thus sufficiently European—image. Yet this was a coping strategy aiming to obfuscate or reject the recent Communist past of the countries in question.[6]

The case of Thessaloniki is particularly interesting because the city is ever haunted by its multicultural identity: "it has turned its back on it, and is still in search of a new one" (Tzimou 2015). In this city of ghosts, as Mark Mazower (2004) called it, where various different communities with distinct features have coexisted for centuries, a new politics of memory attempted to redefine multiculturalism by transforming it from an "undesirable heritage" into a desirable and dominant one by giving a voice not to marginalized groups but to their ghosts—to identities that no longer exist in the real world. As the "living dead" in Markos Meskos's poem (1986, 14), they "return to Saloniki in the light of dawn / a melancholic, long forgotten old song / at the Depots and the Coulé café, under a breeze that's both foreign / and of today." This is an optimistic return because to the question "What do you think?" the poet answers, "I think I'll love again."[7]

Thus, if multiculturalism is a mechanism for the production of memory and oblivion, the memory of an "other past" in modern-day Thessaloniki was sought by an "other present." Multiculturalism was associated with spatial practices that redefine the material deposit of the past and emerged as a form of gentrification of memory.[8] Through performances of memory during Boutaris's mayoralty, multiculturalism was reclaimed as an alternative expression of the collective self, as an alternate identity, as an urban "hetero-identity," and as a role the city wished to play. Monuments took part in the social experience by breaching reality with their "heterotopic" quality (Foucault 1997). They allowed social actors to assume an imagined identity through the experience of memory as a social event by taking on the role of an actor or a spectator (Galiniki 2015). In the case of Thessaloniki, it was the city itself that played this game by trying on different roles.

By studying the recent politics of memory in Thessaloniki's public space and the various ways of dealing with the material remnants of the city's ancient and more recent past, this chapter reflects on whether the valorization of cultural heritage as an economic development tool can contribute to collective self-awareness, especially in a time when multiculturalism is at risk of turning from a European value into a European minefield.

From Substance to Absence: Desirable and Undesirable Fragments of History

Since 2011, Thessaloniki has been introduced to the international public as a "mosaic city" where "colorful, irregular, insignificant fragments of history and fortune . . . move about and resettle in its sandbox," transmitting "with modesty and confidence the city's message and identity: many stories, one heart."[9] According to the city brand promoted by the local authorities under Boutaris, Thessaloniki may not have "a world famous monument or a perfect face," but it does "have everything on an everyday scale, and you'll love it for that. . . . Its wealth is not a rare object on a pedestal; it is a heavy-laden chest where 2,300 years' worth of stories are kept and treasured."[10]

The history of Thessaloniki is a history of counter-identities not only because various cultural groups have had to coexist but also because each of these groups was forced to adopt a new identity with every change of regime, adapting or abandoning its customs and traditions and sometimes even mourning its losses. The city proved to be exceptionally adaptable to change, possibly because, in spite of the original trauma of the advent and establishment of a conqueror, its strategically significant geographic position always guaranteed it a privileged status.

Back in 315 BC, when the city was founded by King Cassandros—who named it after his wife, Alexander the Great's sister—Thessaloniki was a diverse space because it involved the mandatory removal and establishment of inhabitants from other regional settlements (Strabo cited in Adam-Veleni 2001, 80). In Roman times, the city evolved into a cosmopolitan center because its harbor and network of roads attracted merchants, philosophers, artists, armies, and ambitious leaders from all over the Mediterranean and the Balkan Peninsula, as well as products, religions, mentalities, and ideas. The city continued to thrive when the center of the Roman Empire moved east and Constantinople became its capital.[11] When "co-reigning" (*simvasilevousa*) Thessaloniki of the Byzantine Era was conquered by the Ottomans in 1430, it retained its strategic significance through five centuries of their rule. That period sealed the multicultural character of Selanik, as the Ottomans called it. Thessaloniki became home to not only Muslim Turks and (mainly Greek) Christians but also thousands of Jews who sought refuge in Thessaloniki toward the end of the fifteenth century after being chased out of Spain and other parts of southern and central Europe. These three communities—of which the Jewish was the most populous—coexisted and enjoyed unequal privileges; they lived in relatively separate sections of the city organized around their religious centers, without excluding the possibility of spatial and social interaction in their everyday lives however. Their way of life and social practices were characterized by a kind of "antagonistic tolerance" (Hayden 2002).[12] This social comingling intensified in the second half of the nineteenth century thanks to a series of reforms, known as Tanzimat, undertaken by the Ottoman Empire in order to become modernized, which allowed for the expression, construction, and performance of the city's numerous cultural identities based on ethnic rather than religious differences. At the time when it was fervently expected that the empire would fall apart and be replaced by independent nation-states in the Balkan Peninsula, the elites of all three communities started systematically working to reinforce their respective communities' ethnic self-awareness.

In 1912, when Thessaloniki was included in the Greek state, the city represented otherness because of its multicultural identity. Even the city's ancient past was an indication of otherness because the only visible monuments were not of the glorious classical period but of the Roman conquest, and only its surviving Byzantine monuments offered Greeks of the south a reassuring confirmation that Thessaloniki did fit into the national narrative. Besides, Macedonia's ancient past was itself, if not an otherness, at least a singularity in a state whose very existence was founded on the classical ideal of the democratic Athens of the pre-Christian fifth century.

The city's newly Greek administration tried to tame the city's otherness through a strategy of very early gentrification of public space, whose aim was to Hellenize it. This process was further assisted by a fire in 1917 that destroyed the majority of the city center, mostly affecting Jewish neighborhoods, and their reconstruction was certainly not a priority for the "new city plan" established, as requested by the Venizelos government, by the French city planner Ernest Hébrard (Lagopoulos 2005; Karadimou-Yerolympou 1995; Galiniki 2015, 165–70; Galiniki, forthcoming). On the contrary, the city center was redesigned in order to create functional zones and showcase Roman and Byzantine monuments. Until this point, Thessaloniki's only connection to the golden period of its ancient Macedonian past—the time of Alexander the Great—was its name, but this connection was forged anew through place names, city planning, and architecture.

The "cleansing" of urban space from all remnants of the previous occupier, a practice employed in all Balkan states after their independence from the Ottoman Empire, was a process that went on for many decades, either through demolitions or by a symbolic inscription of the newly Hellenic rule—for instance, through neoclassical architectural interventions on the Turkish-baroque exteriors of any buildings belonging to the former Ottoman administration, which were preserved in order to house the services of the new Greek state. The city's de-Ottomanization (Koumaridis 2006) was completed in 1923 with the population exchange between Greece and Turkey. Muslims left Thessaloniki, replaced by throngs of Greek refugees from Asia Minor, Eastern Thrace, and the Pontus region. Thessaloniki's Hellenization process was completed during the time of the German occupation. In 1943, the Nazis sent all of the city's Jews (about fifty thousand people) to concentration camps in Europe. Fewer than two thousand survived and returned after the war. In postwar Thessaloniki, former Jewish houses and shops have new owners, and even the city's Jewish community's most durable monument, its cemetery, was no longer there because the Nazis (with the cooperation of municipal authorities and Greek residents) had destroyed it. After that violent erasure of the Jewish heritage, public services, and even the Orthodox church, the tombstones were scattered around the city as useful materials for the construction of toilets, for the reparation of Christian churches, as sidewalk paving stones, and as foundations for newly constructed public and private buildings (Saltiel 2014; Hekimoglou 2012). Thessaloniki's Aristotle University would later be constructed where the cemetery once stood—a change that had already been predicted by the Hébrard plan.

The 1960s brought further damage to the city's material multiculturalist heritage, whether that was because old buildings were abandoned or changed function, or because of rampant urban expansion and development. On an institutional level, the protection of the city's cultural heritage was extended to include newer monuments (Trakossopoulou-Tzimou 2015, 528). Whatever was left of the labyrinthine Ottoman city after the fire of 1917 and the Hébrard plan was now being replaced by apartment buildings to accommodate the constant flow of internal migrants flocking in from the Macedonian inland. The destructive earthquake of 1978 provided a reason and a pretext for the demolition of hundreds of buildings that illustrated the city's cosmopolitan nature at the turn of the previous century (Kolonas 2012; Bastéa and Hastaoglou-Martinidis 2013; Hastaoglou 2008).

In modern-day Thessaloniki, the very few material remnants of the city's previously multicultural past resemble "invisible parentheses" (Katsavounidou 2004), where memory can't quite hang on. The lost cosmopolitan city appears to be a nostalgic refuge of more concern to the city's authors and artists than to the authorities, which for decades promoted a sort of "strategic mourning" (Tzanelli 2011) of the lost grandeur of certain specific periods in the city's history, such as the Byzantine era.

Rescuing the remnants of the city's ancient past, on which the city's Hellenism was invested, was not much easier because it mostly concerned Roman monuments. The city's two major archaeological sites, the ancient Agora (forum) and Galerius's palace complex, were rescued thanks to the efforts of archaeologists who had to go up against local authorities and even some public opinion in the 1960s and 1970s (Hastaoglou 2008, 169–71). The materiality of the desirable ancient past has been reproduced over the past century through the naming of streets, squares, foundations, and official events, as well as through the omnipresence of the figure of Alexander the Great on façades, press publications, and business and organization logos, culminating in 1974 in the unveiling of his statue on the seafront. For a long time, the city's image was mostly dominated by its Byzantine past because that era's most significant monuments contributed to Thessaloniki's integration into the national narrative: they were considered as evidence of the uninterrupted continuation of the Hellenic civilization. The inclusion in 1988 of the remnants of the city's Byzantine fortification and fourteen Christian churches dating from the fourth to the fourteenth century AD in the UNESCO list of world heritage sites is also indicative of the promotion of Thessaloniki's Byzantine past as well as its Greek Orthodox identity (Tzanelli 2011; Stefanou and Antoniadou, this volume).

The revalorization of the architectural heritage of the late Ottoman period of the city happened gradually. The first attempts at conservation and restoration took place in the 1980s when, in 1985, the festivities for the city's 2,300 years of existence motivated the study of local history (Hastaoglou 2008, 178). The city's more recent multifaceted past emerged hesitantly as an element of public discourse. It became evident at that point that the valorization of the city's cultural heritage, through the conservation of archaeological sites and the restoration of Ottoman monuments, would render Thessaloniki more attractive not only as a host of major cultural events but also for tourists (Hastaoglou-Martinidis and Christodoulou 2010). The next big milestone for the city was in 1997, when Thessaloniki became the European Capital of Culture. The term *multiculturalism* was used to describe the city in the hope that after the fall of communism in the Balkans, Thessaloniki would once again play a strategic role for the stability of Europe. Even though that period saw the restoration of many buildings dating from the Ottoman era (Hastaoglou-Martinidis and Christodoulou 2010; Hastaoglou 2008), thus creating a public space for the celebration of multiculturalism, in reality the process did not go beyond a certain nostalgic rhetoric. By showcasing selected aspects of the distant ancient past and by promoting the

Byzantine past over the more recent Ottoman one, public discourse deliberately ignored the city's current multicultural reality, with thousands of migrants flocking in from Albania and the former Soviet Union (Agelopoulos 2000, 146; 2013, 89–90).[13] In the shadow of the conflict with North Macedonia over the ownership of the ancient Macedonian past, the event aimed to underline that the city had always been exclusively, uninterruptedly Greek—and thus failed in every other way (Deffner and Labrianidis 2005, 250–51).

So it was that Thessaloniki obtained an "indigenous and premature postmodernity," according to Vilma Hastaoglou (2008, 194), based on a so-called modernity that not only destroyed architectural heritage and historic memory but also—and even worse—was responsible for the "non-existence of an urban culture, a lack of values in the coexistence with history." In any event, at the dawn of the twenty-first century, Thessaloniki was characterized by a duality, a twofold identity, somewhere between the cosmopolitan city of the twentieth century and the conservative nationalist city that it had become, between nostalgia and disenchantment, and between the long-lost multiculturalism of the past and the xenophobic Hellenism of the present day.

The city's designation as the European Capital of Culture in 1997 was a lost opportunity for the restoration of Thessaloniki's economic and strategic importance in the Balkan Peninsula. However, through ideal representations of the lost architectural heritage, which was visible in the restoration of more recent monuments, the event did spark a lot of interest (especially in the well-educated elite) in the city's multicultural past, a subject that had until then rarely been an object of public or scientific discourse. Thessaloniki's "other" past slowly became a topic for local intellectuals, historians, and history lovers when the city's authorities, with the help of citizens, strived to prove its Hellenic identity in the midst of the conflict with North Macedonia. In contrast with the increasingly intense presence of a certain Christian nationalistic rhetoric in public life, the in-depth study of the city's multiculturalism became the mode of expression of a different political and ideological position, poised against the conservatism and nationalism of the church, local authorities, and far-right political groups. In the framework of the financial crisis and the decrease in quality of life, Thessaloniki saw the rise of a new, significant, and dynamic movement whose aim was to reclaim and redefine the city's public space. The movement stemmed from numerous small or larger collectivities with various objectives but with a common orientation: on the one hand, the promotion of multiculturalism and the right to be different, and on the other hand, the rejection of conservative values, xenophobia, and racism (Galiniki 2011; Christodoulou 2013; Agelopoulos 2013, 91–94; Athanassiou, Kapsali, and Karagianni 2015; Eleftheriadis 2015). These groups were primarily responsible for electing Yiannis Boutaris as the city's mayor, thus calling upon him to do what official Greek politicians had been unable to do until then: create a new narrative for the city by giving substance, space, and maybe even an imaginary corpus to an absence, to a past that in reality no longer existed in the city's urban space. One could say that the emergence of multiculturalism as the city's dominant identity, as a gentrified version of its memory, was in fact the result of the emergence of these social groups, whose aspirations had been marginalized until then.

Selective Pasts and the Gentrification of Memory

At the beginning of the twenty-first century, the main landmark in the city's "search of lost time" was the year 2012, during which celebrations for the centennial of Thessaloniki's "liberation" took place. This date is what official public language calls the end of the Ottoman Empire and the annexation of the city by the Greek state. Many of the city's institutions, such as archaeological and other museums, associations, cultural foundations, and citizen groups, organized exhibitions that focused less on the city's centennial as the Greek co-capital (*simprotevousa*) and more on the previous period, with special emphasis on its cosmopolitan character. Photographs and postcards depicting the old Thessaloniki in the late nineteenth and early twentieth centuries, published in celebratory volumes or exhibited in museums, could not bring the materiality of that old city back to life, but they did create a reflection of it and provide an imagined recapture of a lost city.

The municipal authorities celebrated the city's centennial as a refoundation ritual: Thessaloniki became a memorial of its own memory. Besides organizing various celebratory events or supporting those planned by other institutions, the municipality organized a scientific conference aimed at examining the factors that had determined Thessaloniki's identity and its alterations, extending beyond the centennial. Even though the conference was entitled "Thessaloniki: a City in Transition, 1912–2012," the first thematic unit focused on aspects of the city's life before 1912 and especially during the late Ottoman period. Even at the start of the twenty-first century, this approach was far from self-evident; as noted by the editor of the symposium proceedings (Kairidis 2015a), approaching the city's history by emphasizing the cultural diversity reflected in its multilingual, multireligious, multinational population involved the "subversion and challenge" of the official national history (Kairidis 2015b, 19). Even the use of the term *liberation* was controversial (Kairidis 2015b, 20). Although the city's annexation by the Greek state has been registered in official history as a liberation, the term is sometimes used in quotation marks because it is uncertain whether this "liberation" was felt as such by the city's largely heterodox population.

This different approach to the past took systematic shape through an extensive program of memorial signposting, called "Signs of Memory" (*Diktes*

Fig. 5.1. Liberty Square (*Platia Eleftherias*), Thessaloniki: "Sign of Memory." Photo by R. Vlachopoulou. Courtesy of Roxani Vlachopoulou.

Mnimis). These street signs have text in Greek and English interspersed with photographs, and they not only illuminate certain unknown or lesser-known aspects of the city's history but also invite the visitor to entertain "an open and progressive view of the past." At the same time, the signs are the city's performance, a way for the city to reintroduce itself to the travel market as a progressive place, one that can handle its past "with composure, generosity and a sense of responsibility" in contrast, as was pointed out, "to cities like Skopje or Constantinople."[14] These "Signs of Memory" are displayed in squares, on buildings, at archaeological sites, and on monuments, and they turn Thessaloniki into an open book that both residents and tourists are invited to peruse. They narrate in detached speech even the hardest of stories, such as the public humiliation of the city's Jews by the Nazis on Eleftherias (Liberty) Square in August 1942, without referring to all the details, which could explain why all these events had until then been treated as undesirable heritage.

These signs restore the place of memory; they redefine it as such, and "like ghosts, [they] tell us that seeing is not sufficient" (Moretti 2008, 43). Commenting on similar signs, which commemorate the assassination of the anarchist Pinelli at Milan's Piazza Fontana, Christina Moretti notes that they invite the beholders to reflect on the polysemy of urban space and pause their gaze and memory. "In fact, they literally show us that looking is not enough. By representing a contradictory message, they seem to mimic the 'seeing double' of when we do not see very well. By enacting for us a double-truth and double-vision, these placards suggest that all urban landscapes might be like Piazza Fontana: unruly characters in a dynamic relationship with the play through which they are made, undone, unraveled, reorganized and reinterpreted."

The "Signs of Memory" establish new landmarks in urban geography. They aim to become part of the everyday ritual of walking by creating pauses in everyday space and time, where the identities of people and places are suspended between past, present, and future. This suspension not only reveals the city that was or the city that could have been but also invites visitors and residents to place themselves in other, potential worlds. The information contained in the "Signs of Memory," outlining the specific events that happened at that particular place, helps visitors place themselves in the past and question their position as citizens, both in the present and in the future. By coming face-to-face with that "other" memory, visitors could perhaps acquire a different conscience of space and of history, and even possibly a different self-conscience.

If memory is mainly a process that involves places and emotions in a kinesthetic experience (Tilley 1994), then it is particularly important to note the invention of a new ceremonial practice as part of the municipality's effort to integrate the Holocaust into the city's official history and memory. This is the case of the Memory March in honor of the Jewish victims of the Holocaust, which was organized for the first time in 2013 (Sintès and Givre 2015, 217; Angelos 2015, 187–88). For many of the participants, the dominant slogan of "never again" in 2013 was also a protest against the actions of the Golden Dawn, the far-right nationalist extremist party that had been elected to the Greek Parliament in 2012, bringing the neo-Nazi rhetoric into the public life of Greece. The march did not just refer to the past; the past became present as long as historical wounds remained open. In 2016, when the city was confronted with the new multiculturalism of refugees from Syria and other broader Middle Eastern countries, the Memory March once more became an expression of solidarity with the refugees and of resistance in the face of racism and xenophobia. In the context of Holocaust commemoration and education, the mayor made one more crucial step as he announced a collaboration with the Jewish Community of Thessaloniki for a museum dedicated to the Holocaust, the first one in Greece.[15] Close to this initiative, another remarkable fact is the reestablishment of the eponymous chair of Jewish Studies at the Aristotle University of Thessaloniki, which covered a significant gap given that the chair was suspended in 1937 during Metaxas's dictatorship.[16]

In a similar way, memorializing the city's former Muslim inhabitants also took on a ceremonial character, signaling the rupture of yet another taboo (Sintès and Givre 2015, 218–19). Boutaris allowed Muslim visitors to pray during Ramadan in the Yeni Cami (New Mosque), the religious temple of the Dönmeh community, composed of Jews who had converted to Islam. Considering that the mosque was transformed into the local Archaeological Museum after the departure of the Dönmeh community in 1923, its occasional concession to Muslims was not only a symbolic gesture aiming to attract more Turkish visitors; it could also be considered the expression of a different attitude in handling the cultural capital of the city's past. As the Memory March transformed what used to be a counter memory into a crucial co-performer of the city's new identity, another memory became undesirable: that of the city's more recent nationalistic past. The seafront restoration works became a reason—or, rather, a pretext—to remove Golden Dawn and other nationalist groups from such a publicly visible space, in particular from around the statue of Alexander the Great, a contemporary monument but nowadays "archaeologized." The statue had been used for twenty years as a venue for the performance and dissemination of fascist and xenophobic rhetoric. The reappropriation of a memorial space, especially one so heavily laden with the symbolism of dominance, was the ideal starting point for those who wanted to reclaim not only memories but the city itself. It was also a gesture toward the gentrification of the city's memory, through the reclaiming of a public space formerly impregnated with a rhetoric of hate for the "other." The purification of this memorial landscape from all traces of nationalism was achieved thanks to the seafront restoration works (see Dimitris Giovis's photograph in the front cover of this book) and its return to the public sphere in a gentrified form as *Alexander's Garden*, an open square accessible from all sides. The choice of this new name for the statue's area reveals a desire to reduce the significance of the past grandeur, which nourished nationalistic visions and pompous ceremonies. The spatial practices that had been encouraged around the statue since then reflected the will to transform it from a space embodying the rhetoric of fear and rejection of the "other" into a place of joy and playfulness. Excellent examples include the activities emphasized in the city's candidacy for the nomination as European Youth Capital for 2014: youthful, leisure activities such as skateboarding, bike skill contests, and hip-hop dance displays contributed to the representation of the memorial space as a playground cleansed from the stain of nationalism. The city's logo for that organization, reminiscent of a "modern haircut" and an "ancient Greek helmet" with colors resembling those of "black-figure pottery,"[17] attempted not only to combine past and present but also to distance itself from the undesirable recent past and establish a new reference point for the city: an ancient past closer to the classical ideal, or rather far away from what (mainly for left-wing thought) is intertwined with imperialism and military rule.

Between 2011 and 2019, the aspects of the ancient past of Thessaloniki that were prioritized were those that pertained to the city's multicultural past. So it was that the municipal authorities launched a campaign for the return of the "Enchanted Ones," the sculpted pillars of a Roman colonnade that was in the

Fig. 5.2. "Alexander's Garden": Jazz concert in front of the statue of Alexander the Great (2016). Photo by R. Vlachopoulou. Courtesy of Roxani Vlachopoulou.

courtyard of a house in the Jewish quarter until 1864, when it was dismantled by Miller, a French paleographer, and transferred to the Louvre. The campaign, which soon refocused on the return of copies and not of the originals, brought to life in public discourse the complex life in Thessaloniki of the nineteenth century, where inhabitants of different religious and cultural origins shared myths, monuments, and stories (Solomon and Galiniki 2018). The many different names of the monument—*Incantadas* in Judeo-Spanish (Ladino), *Idols* in Greek, and *Suret Maleh* in Turkish—that resurfaced in the public discourse offered a version of the past that underlined the common cultural values of the city's inhabitants rather than their differences. The effort to retrieve the lost materiality not only offered the necessary substance allowing for the re-enchantment of the city's inhabitants in a period of great economic and social crisis (Solomon and Galiniki 2018) but also contributed to the construction of the common local self-image. The old-time inhabitants and their efforts, independent of religion and origin, to obstruct the export of these sculptures were the ideal idols of modern Thessalonians, and both former and current inhabitants were called upon to perform the role of rescuers of the city's past. The effort to access or to reconstruct the city's identity using old materials was no longer a matter for the municipal authorities but for civil society.

As a matter of fact, collective reflexes aimed at rescuing remnants of the ancient past often take the form of campaigns. Another aggregation of "active exemplary citizens" (Athanassiou, Kapsali, and Karagianni 2015, 13)[18] was provoked by the threat to destroy Byzantine antiquities discovered during the construction of the metro in the city center. That rescue campaign did not concern all of the findings but focused only on the impressive Byzantine crossroads that was uncovered six meters under a modern-day intersection. With the help of many agents, especially citizens participating through social media[19] and the local press, the municipal authorities took the campaign under their wing until the Greek government finally agreed to preserve in situ the archaeological remains at the Venizelos Metro Station.[20] Archaeologists, civil society organizations and Yiannis Boutaris negotiated with the contractor, arguing that it could be a way of promoting the city and putting it on the map of European cities that, by preserving their history, attract the attention of tourists and the international scientific public. Another important argument was the fact that the Byzantine road grid was uncovered near one of the few Muslim monuments surviving from the Ottoman period. The Hamza Bey Mosque, which was once rescued thanks to Hébrard and which is known to the inhabitants of the city as Alkazar (after the cinema that operated in its premises for decades), has been restored by the local Ephorate of Antiquities. This monument of the Ottoman past is planned to become an exhibition space.

Conversely, in other cases, it was the archaeological sites or museums that showcased the city's Jewish or Ottoman past. For example, as part of the celebrations for the city's one hundredth anniversary in 2012, the Archaeological Museum hosted a temporary exhibition entitled "The Jews of Thessaloniki: Indelible Marks in Space," and the Museum for Byzantine Culture hosted one entitled "Thessaloniki of the Collectors: Stories of the City." An earlier example is the permanent exhibition of the Museum of the Ancient Agora of Thessaloniki, which illustrates not only the history of the Agora (Forum) in Hellenistic and Roman times but also the various uses of this area by the complex cultures of the city during the Ottoman Empire (Adam-Veleni, Kalliga, and Solomon 2014). Another exhibition hosted at the site of the Agora during the summer of 2015 also aimed at underlining the site's status as a cultural crossroad. Entitled "Visual Intersections at Thessaloniki's Roman Forum," the exhibition revolved around an installation by visual artist Anni Kaltsidou, accompanied by performances referencing the city's multicultural nature as expressed in the music and songs of the Ottoman period, as well as the period between the World Wars.[21] Besides, merging different pasts is a practice based on rich layering, which often characterizes archaeological excavations in the center of Thessaloniki. Although preserving Jewish or Ottoman remnants was not a priority of Greek archaeological research in the past not only in Thessaloniki but also in the country in general, Ottoman monuments have become the subject of an increasing number of archaeological research projects in the context of changes in legislation encouraging the protection of more recent monuments. It is noteworthy that even material remnants of the twentieth century are sometimes considered equal in value to ancient findings[22] as part of a more general turn of archaeology toward the remains of modern civilization.

Through events and actions, archaeological sites in urban space were turned from urban lacunae into active co-performers of the contemporary experience. At the same time, through other actions, the contemporary urban landscape became an archaeological site, longing to be uncovered. Actions such as "Open House"[23] and "Thessaloniki Allios-Thessaloniki Differently,"[24] or thematic guided tours through the city, were organized by individuals or groups of citizens and available for a fee or even for free thanks to sponsorships and the voluntary participation of many (mostly young) people. These actions encouraged the research and study of this new, above-ground, urban stratigraphy.[25] The new collectivities, like so many new gentrifiers,[26] searched for a different urban experience in Thessaloniki's landscape, focusing on gentrification not as an intervention in the building environment but rather as a performance. Residents and tourists, like archaeologists of the urban past, explored nineteenth-century mansions that had changed use or owners; they wandered around refugee neighborhoods and visited midcentury modern 1960s apartments. By decoding façades, railings, wooden shutters, and moldings, they discovered the secret diary of another city, one that was no longer undesirable; it was simply the other face of the same where the self could meet with the otherness it desired to resemble. The other city was rediscovered as an idealized reflection of the common identity, during a ritualized visit to a potential version of the self. From its duration and nature, the visit resembled an event, an entertainment happening with a positive impact on the city's economy, tourism, and image.

Multiculturalism, as the city's promoted identity, appears to be better received when it is proposed as a consumer product and as a temporary escape from the difficulties of everyday life, not as a permanent presence in the public urban space. "As if this city sought to poison its pleasures" (Tzimou 2015), the spatial actualization of multiculturalism sparked great dispute when it came to the use of the Rotunda. This impressive round structure dates from the end of the Roman Era and still bears the material remnants of the city's successive rulers. Inside this fourth-century building, which is thought to have formed part of the Roman palace complex of Galerius, impressive surviving Byzantine mosaics and building additions attest to its long use as a Christian church. A few Muslim tombs and a minaret in its courtyard—the only surviving one in Thessaloniki—remain from the Ottoman period, when this monument was used as a mosque. Fewer people know that it was also used as an archaeological museum from 1912 onward and as a venue for Nazi musical events during their occupation of the city. After World War II, it became a museum again. Then it was once again turned into a Christian

Fig. 5.3. The Rotunda of Thessaloniki. Photo by S. Galiniki. Courtesy of Styliana Galiniki and Ephorate of Antiquities of the City of Thessaloniki.

church, until it became an archaeological monument under the jurisdiction of the Ministry of Culture. Within this context in the 1990s, its use was authorized for regular Christian church services, as well as for the organization of cultural events. This arrangement turned out to be a difficult combination because it all came to an abrupt and dramatic end when Christian groups used unexpected violence and succeeded in canceling the first jazz concert that had been scheduled there (Stewart 2001; Tzanelli 2011). In early 2016, after the completion of lengthy conservation work, the question of the monument's use was once again put on the table. This time it was suggested that it would be marked as a Christian temple by placing a cross on its roof because according to rumors, press publications, and statements by officials in the press,[27] the local Ephorate of Antiquities insisted that the presence of the Muslim minaret emphasized its Ottoman nature to the detriment of its Christian identity. This monument, which is for some people such a distinctive symbol of the city's multicultural identity that it should be promoted as its "brand monument" (Tzimou 2015), turned into "a battlefield between progressive and conservative forces" (Lyberopoulou 2016). While the Metropolitan Bishop also defended the monument's Christian nature, a group of citizens[28] and the Association of Greek Archaeologists demanded the preservation of the Rotunda's timeless and intercultural character, without excluding the occasional celebration of Christian mass on its premises. At the same time, a group that has adopted the worship of the ancient Greek gods expressed, on a webpage, their objections to the Rotunda being used as a Christian temple.[29] Despite the fact that the Ministry of Culture finally made it clear that the cross would not be placed on the roof and that the Rotunda would be used for occasional Christian services, as well as for cultural events respectful of the monument's multicultural past, many citizens expressed their concerns because the Christian symbols and church equipment placed on the premises appeared rather permanent. Boutaris himself held an ambivalent position on the question of whether there should be a cross, a fact that was criticized as a manifestation of political hypocrisy (Lykessas 2016).

The dispute over the city's identity was brewing, and it went beyond the conflict between progressives and conservatives. For example, during the city's centenary celebrations in 2012, while the municipal authorities organized a conference putting the term *liberation* in doubtful quotation marks, the Ministry of Macedonia and Thrace organized a spectacular urban performance that underlined the undisputed dominance of that term in the national narrative. Moreover, the municipal conference was interrupted by a group of anarchists protesting against the constant visualization of history through the prism of capitalism, to the detriment of class struggles. Although it was the Far Right that despised the mayor, many other citizens doubted his progressiveness and criticized him for compromising on issues that concerned the city's present and future. The Prespa Agreement was a cause and a pretext for the reappearance of the Golden Dawn under the statue of Alexander the Great, among a crowd of people from various political sides who protested in January 2018 against the forthcoming ratification of the agreement. This occurred in the context of a nationwide mobilization[30] propelled by nationalists but also supported by other parties.[31] This opportunistic agglomeration of neo-Nazism and banal nationalism (Billig 1995) perhaps paved the way for the violent attack against Yiannis Boutaris after a few months, during a commemorative ceremony of the Pontic Genocide (Smith 2018). The image of the beaten and fallen mayor was tragic not only as an attack against a democratically elected public man, but most of all as a forceful reincarnation of the undesirable "city of ghosts." After Boutaris's decision not to reclaim the municipality as a candidate in the elections of June 2019, the question is whether this will mark another end of era for the city of Thessaloniki.

To sum up, the memory politics in Thessaloniki during the second decade of the twenty-first century attempted to redefine public space through a new mapping of the city, where the time and place of the "others" were marked into the familiar spaces of everyday life, accompanied by an attempt to cleanse those urban areas that have been tainted by nationalistic rhetoric and practice. In any case, priority was given to those politics of memory—whether they originate from the municipality, other public agents, or groups of citizens—that aim to reconcile the city's many pasts through the shared experience of a visit, a stroll, and the rediscovery of Thessaloniki as the city that was or that could have been. If, in a sociospatial dialectic, "space is both constituted and constitutive" (Tilley 1994, 17), the substantive memorial remains of the city were reproduced as elements of an identity that played the role of the real identity in the city's performance. Because monuments are co-performers of social urban life going beyond their date of construction to form active elements of the present, archaeological remnants also integrate current affairs through embodied practices; they are reevaluated as elements, if not of the real city then at least of a coveted one. Ancient monuments partake in the city's theatricality as they are called upon to play the role of urbanity itself, that variety of identities, values, and customs that constitute the very essence of the city.

The different conception of the urban landscape, its recreation through the establishment of new places of memory, and the elimination of old ones recalls and in some cases goes hand in hand with the process of gentrification. It prioritizes public spaces that, due to their historic layering, can contribute to the performance of a new memory of the past. At the same time, other periods, spaces, and practices are excluded as undesirable. By using the public urban space as a material remnant and as a network of social relationships, the gentrification of memory itself is attempted,— new hierarchization of the memorable. This new gentrified memory is a memory-theatrical role that brings to life the ghosts of the past through a materiality that also plays its part. It plays the role of what was by representing it and making it tangible, like a postcard. Multiculturalism appears to be the place of a postmodern urban utopia, where the past is a consumer product at an entertaining and lucrative event.

The Identity of the City: A Difficult Heritage

At the dawn of the twenty-first century, Thessaloniki looked toward the future by adopting a new approach to its past, encouraged by the daring policies of the municipal authorities and by the collaboration and support of a significant part of the city's residents. One could recognize the importance of certain symbolic gestures made by Boutaris that reflected a political stance toward the way the city has managed its "difficult" multicultural heritage until now. However, it is uncertain whether this stance will be effective in the long term; it is not certain whether it will affect the residents' identity, or whether multiculturalism will become a fixture of the city's future memory. Until recently, the multiculturalism discourse referred only to certain population groups that lived and thrived in the past, ignoring others. For example, the presence of Armenians, Slavs, Albanians, and Franks in the city from the beginning of the twentieth century and onward is still rarely mentioned. Another question is to what extent multiculturalism can be tolerated by the city. In April 2019, the opposition party in the municipality council of Thessaloniki did not approve the organization of an honorary event for the deceased poet Markos Meskos. It is likely that this rejection occurred not because Meskos had supported the Prespa Agreement in 2018, as was mentioned in the council, but because this important and much-awarded Greek poet was from a bilingual Slavic-speaking Greek family (Hodolidou 2019)—a rejection that could bring in mind Meskos's poem written in 1973: "Ah City! / that you gave birth to me but you do not hear me, every night that I knock your walls / but the guards do not open for me. / I'm going back, I cut a limb / I burst into song to hide the tears / like a blind horse I walk / and I cry in front of its forehead" (Meskos 1999, 132).[32]

It is also doubtful whether the public demonstration of the different religious identity by the current Jewish community of Thessaloniki, composed of descendants of the survivors, would be welcome. Multiculturalism is very rarely placed in the context that produced or eliminated it, and it is never discussed as a living reality in a city where thousands of economic migrants from the 1990s are practically invisible (Kokkali 2011). The quest for the city's past, as expressed through public actions, barely touches on the period of Nazi occupation, and no mention is made of the role played by the Left in postwar Thessaloniki, of the practices of the Right, of the civil war, or of the military dictatorship (1967–1974). It is as if all these did not positively or negatively affect the construction of the city's identity. The nationalist discourse is excluded without examining the context that produced it in the late twentieth century, its foundation in other historical periods, or its strengthening in the present day. Multiculturalism is portrayed in public space as an exotic notion, a memory so gentrified that its social, political, or class-related parameters remain in oblivion or in silence. Then this gentrified memory portrays public space as the venue of a composite history, made up of selected fragments. Limited only to specific aspects of the life of specific population groups—which are presented as unified and coherent even though it was not the case—multiculturalism becomes a sleeping beauty that is considered alive only when it looks dead. At the same time, multiculturalism as a tourism or entertainment product does not concern all residents. It does not concern those who, because of their financial and social status, have limited access to the city's cultural happenings, and despite all announcements to the contrary, it does not extend beyond the city's historic center. The term *historic center*, which has lately become omnipresent, is in itself a form of gentrification, representing the old fortified city as a Foucauldian heterotopia and excluding whole neighborhoods from the symbolic capital of history and cultural heritage.

If the aim is to change the city's identity, could that be achieved only through cultural events, through the moments of bravery or unfortunate choices of a mayor, or through the active collaboration of residents and institutions? Can this renewed identity be brought about through practices that treat the past as a consumer product, as an event aiming to make the city attractive to the market needs and to satisfy the narcissistic desires of its residents? Can it be anything other than a self-reflection on the identity that has been ostracized as undesirable? Shouldn't the city search for its identity not in the elements of which it is proud but rather in those of which it is ashamed and sad? Shouldn't the city stop compiling silence and face its woes? Shouldn't it see beyond representation?

According to a text published in a local magazine in 2014 by Dimitris Dimitriadis, author of the seminal work *Dying as a Country*, Thessaloniki is an annoying city, where all "gestures of freedom and spontaneity" are fake and offer no perspective. The city, he wrote, resembles a military camp closed unto itself, expecting hope only from the sea (Dimitriadis 2014). What Thessaloniki appears to be lacking, and what for Dimitriadis is a crucial factor of any city's viability, is the profound feeling of deprivation, the replacement of the city by pain. In his book *Pain as a City*, Dimitriadis suggests that only if a city is founded on pain and on art, and when its politics become empathetic, can it really take off (Dimitriadis 2011, 26). As Walter Benjamin (1968, 256) writes, citing Gustave Flaubert, "few will be able to guess how sad one had to be in order to resuscitate Carthage."

The pain as a city can be nothing other than the memory of the city's pain, a reflexive face-to-face with its past woes. Dimitriadis's essay gives us food for thought regarding the politics of memory that are implemented beyond the scale of local politics, even beyond politics in general. These politics commonly involve marketing a product destined for the consumption of a society seen as a target group. Dimitriadis is trying to remind us that politics must be a constant effort, a constant quest and questioning of human affairs, social antinomies, and the complexity of relationships. "What I call pain," he writes, "is the sense and consciousness of the human capacity" (Dimitriadis 2011, 12). He prefers this word over others because "The word pain encompasses another very important element, that of toil, of effort, of fight, of hard work, of labor, of trouble, even of culture, a tribulation without which human nature can't experience seriousness and the need for self-awareness. This has resulted in the loss of valorization, and consequently the loss of a scale of values. So pain is a precondition, a condition sine qua non of an authentic and, more importantly, a robust and shapely life" (13–14). Viewed thus, cultural heritage cannot be, as Benjamin put it in his essay "Theses on the Philosophy of History" (1968), the victor's spoils, enabling a narcissistic nostalgia of the past. It must be pain, "the only possible reminder" (Dimitriadis 2011, 22), a truly arduous way toward collective self-awareness. "Pain is a constituent of the truth" (ibid.). Those who insist on writing the victors' history, Benjamin states, despair to grasp and hold "the genuine historical image as it flares up briefly." They are marked by emotional indolence and *acedia*, that is, the state of not caring (ibid.). But one could dare add that even those who are satisfied with this brief flare of the historical image cannot perceive what lies hidden in the silence. Hannah Arendt wrote in *The Human Condition* (1998) that only when all things are seen by many people, in all of their aspects, can there be hope

Fig. 5.4. “Stumbling Stones” by the artist Gunter Demnig with the names of Jewish Thessalonian pupils who were killed in Auschwitz in 1943. Donated to the city of Thessaloniki by Apostolos Dereklis. Photo by S. Galiniki.

of a common world. Therefore, it can be argued that museums of this human condition, by focusing not on national feats but on human woes such as war, famine, and injustice, can redefine what is memorable, anticipating the creation of a culture of social solidarity, a culture of pain as “the only token of a trustful,” transaction and of a down-to-earth reciprocity,” to use Dimitriadis’s words (2011, 22). Besides, the problems that postmodern societies of the contemporary Western world will have to face will not be solved with the politics of a memory focused on vanity and consumption, of a memory that does not delve into itself.

Perhaps the most optimistic perspective for the city of Thessaloniki today is found on one of its sidewalks, outside the building of a middle school. Small stone cubes—the famous *Stolpersteine* (also known as “Stumbling Stones”) by the artist Gunter Demnig, bearing the engraved names of Jewish pupils who lost their lives in the spring of 1943—were placed there as a personal testament to the city’s past (Hadjipateras 2016). For Apostolos Dereklis, the Thessalonian who took the initiative to place the stones, it was more important to honor his vanished Jewish co-citizens than to memorialize his own refugee origins, with the hope “to pass on to future generations, the belief in the possibility of human co-existence without any kind of discrimination” (Dereklis cited in Hadjipateras 2016). The “pain as a city” can sometimes start from little “stumbling stones.”

STYLIANA GALINIKI is an archaeologist and exhibition curator at the Archaeological Museum of Thessaloniki. Since 2018 she has served as Head of the Department of Sculpture and Stoneworks, Wallpaintings and

Mosaics Collections of the museum. She holds a PhD from the National Technical University of Athens (School of Architecture) on public sculpture and the social uses of antiquity in Thessaloniki. Her research focuses on the history of archaeological research in Thessaloniki and Macedonia in general, the public performances of collective memory, the use of antiquity in the construction of social identity, and the relationship between antiquities and contemporary artistic expressions (visual art, poetry, theater, and performance). She is also a published novelist.

Notes

1. Accessed June 2, 2019, https://www.nationalgeographic.com/travel/best-trips-2013/#/61109.jpg; accessed June 7, 2016, http://static.tijd.be/upload/European_Cities_and_Regions_of_the_Future_201415_4687454-10313872.pdf.

2. Accessed June 7, 2016, http://www.worldmayor.com/contest_2014/world-mayor-2014-winners.html.

3. For decades until the Prespa Agreement, North Macedonia had been called by the Greek governments with the acronym FYROM (Former Yugoslav Republic of Macedonia). The agreement was reached on June 12, 2018, between Greece and North Macedonia and went into force on February 12, 2019, under the United Nations' auspices.

4. For more on the use of Alexander the Great as an ur-form of Greek Macedonians, as well as on the use of that particular statue in the establishment and performance of various social identities, see Galiniki (2015).

5. Sintès and Givre (2015, 216) aptly note that the city's multiculturalism has been a sort of taboo in Greek public discourse.

6. See, for example, Young and Kaczmarek (2008); Sereda (2009).

7. The extract is from Markos Meskos's poem "VI" (*In the Shadow of the Earth*). My translation.

8. The term *gentrification* first appears in the 1960s and refers to a strategy aiming at the modification of the anthropogeography and socioeconomic identity of an urban area. In general, through the revamping of formerly underprivileged areas and the consequent change in the value of land and buildings within the real estate market, middle- and higher-class population moves in and settles in these areas, pricing out the former inhabitants and users, whose social status, origin, sex, and general habits are presented as harmful to progress, development, and security. For a general overview of the phenomenon, see Brown-Saracino (2010). Kostas Athanasiou (2014) notes that even the city's memory and cultural heritage are used as tools of gentrification of the urban space. For more on the gentrification of memory as the object of spatial practices, such as the establishment of monuments and memorials that aim to project an ideal version of the collective memory by ostracizing from public view other, more difficult versions, see Galiniki (2015, 28–41).

9. Myrtsioti (2012), accessed June 7, 2016, http://www.colibri.gr/el/content/thessaloniki-city-branding.

10. Accessed April 1, 2016, http://www.voria.gr/article/to-story-piso-apo-tis-many-stories-tis-thessalonikis.

11. There are a great number of publications on the history of Thessaloniki, especially from the 1990s onward. Most of them focus on the life of a single community or on specific

aspects of the city's life. Indicative literature include Adam-Veleni (2001), Kourkoutidou-Nikolaidou and Tourta (1997), Mazower (2004), and Kairidis (2015a).

12. The term *antagonistic tolerance*, coined by Robert Hayden, drew attention to hidden power relations at contested sacred sites. It has also been argued (Land 2016, especially 83–87) that the Levant's harbor cities were characterized by a negative tolerance that served local financial interests rather than a positive attitude toward the Others.

13. Agelopoulos (2000, 147) notes that the plethora of cultures—a term he prefers to that of *multiculturalism*—in Thessaloniki is an image that has been cultivated by the city's authors and artists. It is also evident in everyday consumer practices. These compose a special idiom, he writes, which differentiates Thessaloniki from the Athenian center.

14. Accessed March 1, 2016, http://www.esiemth.gr/o-dimos-thessalonikis-parousiase-tous-diktes-mnimis; accessed March 1, 2016, https://www.dropbox.com/sh/o6vxoesabn8f1b6/xeQ2U5wUCl.

15. Accessed June 3, 2019, http://www.holocausteducenter.gr/executive-summary. The foundation stone of the museum, officially named "Holocaust Memorial Museum and Educational Center of Greece on Human Rights," was placed in Thessaloniki on the beginning of 2018 by Prime Minister of Greece Alexis Tsipras and President of Israel Reuven Rivlin (see Kantouris 2018).

16. Accessed June 3, 2019, https://www.facebook.com/Aristoteleio/posts/10151882122711205. The first year of the chair was funded by the Jewish Community of Thessaloniki.

17. Furthermore, the stark black color was selected "in order to send a message against xenophobia"; accessed March 1, 2016, http://aftodioikisi.gr/politistika/thessaloniki-evropaiki-protevousa-neolaias-2014. See also the event's website, accessed July 6, 2019, http://www.thessaloniki2014.gr.

18. According to Athanassiou, Kapsali, and Karagianni 2015, these are socially privileged groups that take initiatives that, in the past, would have been seen as the responsibility of the state. Their activity resembles a businesslike approach to politics, promoted by the neoliberal agenda that "consequently de-politicize[s] the social and political conflict over space" (Athanassiou, Kapsali, and Karagianni 2015, 13). However, it creates new exclusions instead of eliminating them because most of the groups "often adopt an elite-led agenda" (Athanassiou, Kapsali, and Karagianni 2015, 14).

19. See the Facebook group "Let's save Thessaloniki's historical central crossroads," accessed March 1, 2016. https://www.facebook.com/groups/291301114329874/?fref=ts.

20. Unfortunately, a revision of the initial plan to keep the antiquities in their original context was voted on December 18, 2019, by the Members of the Central Archaeological Council, under the pressure of the newly elected right-wing government and the Metro construction society. Accessed June 30, 2020, https://www.europanostra.org/europa-nostra-appeals-to-preserve-in-situ-the-antiquities-at-the-venizelos-metro-station-in-thessaloniki/.

21. The exhibition was organized by the Ephorate of Antiquities of the City of Thessaloniki in the framework of the Fifth Biennale of Contemporary Art.

22. See, for example, Bakirtzis and Pazaras (2008), where the excavation findings included remnants from the final years of the Ottoman rule, and even from the 1940s. Moreover, the temporary exhibition of the Ephorate of Antiquities of the City of Thessaloniki "1917: Monuments in Flames" (December 2017–December 2018) also presented remnants of the recent past of the city, which came to light during the excavations conducted during the construction of the Thessaloniki Metro.

23. "Open House" is an international institution for the promotion of architecture. Every year for one weekend, private and public buildings open their gates to everyone for free, and

Thessaloniki is transformed into a big museum, with its buildings and architecture being the exhibits. Accessed July 7, 2019, http://www.openhousethessaloniki.gr.

24. "Thessaloniki Allios—Thessaloniki Differently" is an initiative of the local free press magazine *Parallaxi* and is organized by a group of young people and hundreds of volunteers. It includes a series of interventions of cultural, architectural, and environmental nature held in the city annually since 2010. Accessed July 7, 2019, http://parallaximag.gr/thessaloniki/thessaloniki-allios/thessaloniki-allios.

25. The exhibition "Street Stories. Thessaloniki 1916. Following in the Footsteps of Joseph Pigassou," organized by the Facebook group "Old Photos of Thessaloniki," was also indicative of an archaeological approach to the recent past. In order to identify the buildings featured in the photographs, the team employed archaeological research and substantiation methods, as they explained in the exhibition's accompanying material. The National Theatre of Northern Greece also organized two theatrical readings of literary texts, "Thessaloniki-Excavation 1" (2015) and "Thessaloniki-Excavation 2" (2016), presented as similar to the archaeological excavations.

26. Myrtsioti (2012), accessed June 7, 2016, http://www.colibri.gr/el/content/thessaloniki-city-branding.

27. See anonymous articles, accessed on March 7, 2016, http://www.aftodioikisi.gr/dimoi/rotonta-to-polipolitismiko-mnimeio-pou-dixazei-ti-thessaloniki and http://www.aftodioikisi.gr/dimoi/kontra-boutari-anthimou-gia-to-stavro-sti-rotonta. See also Lykessas (2015), Plika (2015, 2016), Tzimou (2015), and Ioannidou (2016). It is worth noting that the Rotunda is included in UNESCO's list of Byzantine monuments as a Christian temple of Saint George, and not as a Roman monument.

28. See the Facebook group "Friends of the Rotunda," accessed March 1, 2016, https://www.facebook.com/RotontaThess/posts/1530780323888035.

29. Accessed June 10, 2016, http://www.ysee.gr/index.php?type=deltia_typou&f=307.

30. Accessed June 3, 2019, https://www.france24.com/en/20180121-tens-thousands-greeks-protest-macedonia-name-row-alexander-great.

31. At the rally of Athens in February 2018, one of the main speakers was the music composer Mikis Theodorakis, an emblematic personality of the left wing in Greece. Another symbolic move from the left wing, but this time on behalf of Tsipras's government in an attempt to balance the social dissatisfaction with the Prespa Agreement, was the staging of Alexander the Great's statue in Athens, a matter that had been pending for decades, Indeed, in the press, there was a rumor that Greece would take Alexander's statue of Skopje, giving in return to the capital of North Macedonia *The Runner*, a public artwork of Athens made by the artist Kostas Varotsos (see Smith 2019).

32. The extract is from Markos Meskos's poem "The Horse" (*Horses on the Hippodrome*), see Meskos 1999. My translation.

References

Agelopoulos, Georgios. 2000. "Political Practices and Multiculturalism: The Case of Salonica." In *Macedonia: The Politics of Identity and Difference*, edited by Jane K. Cowan, 140–55. London: Pluto.

———. 2013. "Πολυπολιτισμικότητα 'αλά γκρέκα': Από το 1980 στο 2009" [Multiculturalism "a la Greca": From 1980 to 2009]. *Epistimi ke Kinonia* [Science and Society] 30: 75–103.

Adam-Veleni, Polyxeni. 2001. *Θεσσαλονίκη. Νεράιδα, Βασίλισσα, Γοργόνα. Αρχαιολογική Περιδιάβαση από την Προϊστορία έως την Ύστερη Αρχαιότητα* [Thessaloniki. Fairy, Queen, Mermaid. An Archaeological Walk from Prehistory to Late Antiquity]. Thessaloniki: Zitros.

Adam-Veleni, Polyxeni, Dimitra Kalliga, and Esther Solomon. 2014. "Το Νέο Μουσείο της Αρχαίας Αγοράς Θεσσαλονίκης: Διαδρομές στο Παρελθόν της Πόλης" [The New Museum of the Ancient Agora of Thessaloniki: Routes in the City's Past]. *AEMTh* 2010: 441–453.

Angelos, James. 2015. *The Full Catastrophe: Travels among the New Greek Ruins.* New York: Crown.

Arendt, Hannah. 1998. *The Human Condition.* 2nd ed. Chicago: University of Chicago Press.

Athanasiou, Kostas. 2014. "Gentrifying of the Memory and 'the Becoming-Child' of a City." In *Culture and Urban Space*, special issue, *Interartive: A Platform for Contemporary Art and Thought* 65. Accessed June 10, 2016. http://cultureurbanspace.interartive.org/gentrifying-of-the-memory.

Athanassiou, Evangelia, Matina Kapsali, and Maria Karagianni. 2015. "Citizen's Participation in Urban Governance in Crisis-Stricken Thessaloniki (Greece): Post-political Urban Project or Emancipatory Urban Experiments?" Paper presented at the RC21 International Conference on the Ideal City: Between Myth and Reality. Representations, Policies, Contradictions and Challenges for Tomorrow's Urban Life. Urbino (Italy), August 27–29, 2015. Accessed June 10, 2016. http://www.rc21.org/en/wp-content/uploads/2014/12/C2-Athanassiou-Kapsali-Karagianni.pdf.

Bakirtzis, Charalampos, and Nikos Pazaras. 2008. "Μετρό Θεσσαλονίκης. 2006" [Thessaloniki Metro. 2006]. *AEMTh* 2006: 431–54.

Bastéa, Eleni, and Vilma Hastaoglou-Martinidis. 2013. "Modernization and Its Discontents in Post-1950s Thessaloniki: Urban Change and Urban Narratives." In *Landscapes of Development: The Impact of Modernization Discourses on the Physical Environment of the Eastern Mediterranean*, edited by Panayiota Pyla, 90–116. Cambridge: Harvard University Press.

Benjamin, Walter. 1968. "Theses on the Philosophy of History." In *Illuminations: Essays and Reflections*, edited by Hannah Arendt and translated by Harry Zohn, 253–64. New York: Schocken.

Billig, Michael. 1995. *Banal Nationalism.* London: Sage Publications.

Brown-Saracino, Japonica, ed. 2010. *The Gentrification Debates: A Reader.* New York: Routledge.

Christodoulou, Charis. 2013. "Πρακτικές Αστικού Σχεδιασμού και Πολιτικές Τοπικής Διακυβέρνησης σε Συνθήκες Κρίσης: Το Παράδειγμα της Θεσσαλονίκης." [Urban Planning Practices and Local Governance Policies in Crisis Conditions: The Example of Thessaloniki]. Presentation at the Conference: Μεταβολές και Ανασημασιοδοτήσεις του Χώρου στην Ελλάδα της Κρίσης [Changes and Reconceptualization of Space in Greece during the Crisis]. Volos, November 1–3, 2013. Accessed June 10, 2016. http://www.citybranding.gr/2014/12/blog-post_48.html#more.

Deffner, Alex, and Lois Labrianidis. 2005. "Planning Culture and Time in a Mega-Event: Thessaloniki as the European City of Culture in 1997." *International Planning Studies* 10 (3–4): 241–64.

Dimitriadis, Dimitris. 2011. *Ο Πόνος ως Πόλη* [Pain as a City]. Thessaloniki: Sexpirikon.

———. 2014. "Η Θεσσαλονίκη είναι μια Διαρκής Ενόχληση" [Thessaloniki Is a Constant Annoyance]. *Parallaxi,* February 17, 2014. Accessed June 10, 2016. http://www.parallaximag.gr/parallax-view/i-thessaloniki-einai-mia-diarkis-enohlisi.

Eleftheriadis, Konstantinos. 2015. "Queer Responses to Austerity: Insights from the Greece of Crisis." *ACME: An International E-Journal for Critical Geographies* 14 (4): 1032–57. Accessed June 10, 2016. http://ojs.unbc.ca/index.php/acme/article/view/1159/1128.

Foucault, Michel. 1997. "Of Other Spaces: Utopias and Heterotopias." In *Rethinking Architecture: A Reader in Cultural Theory,* edited by Neil Leach, 330–36. London: Routledge.

Galiniki, Styliana. 2011. "Skateboard στο Άγαλμα του Μεγάλου Αλεξάνδρου. Η Άλλη Διεκδίκηση" [Skateboarding at the Statue of Alexander the Great: The Other Claim]. In *Δημόσιος Χώρος . . . Αναζητείται* [Public Space . . . Is Sought], Public Space Conference Proceedings, Thessaloniki, October 20–22, 2011, edited by Giota Adilenidou, Anthi Goudini, Paraskevi Kourti, Vangelis Bekiaridis, and Paraskevi Tarani, 159–62. Thessaloniki: Cannot Not Design, Technical Chamber of Greece, Section of Central Macedonia.

———. 2015. *Οι Χρήσεις της Αρχαιότητας στη Συγκρότηση της Ταυτότητας μιας Πόλης: Η Περίπτωση των Σύγχρονων Δημόσιων Γλυπτών της Θεσσαλονίκης* [The Uses of Antiquity in the Construction of a City's Identity: The Case of the Contemporary Public Sculptures of Thessaloniki]. PhD diss., National Technical University of Athens.

———. Forthcoming. "Ο Μέγας Αλέξανδρος του Εμπράρ: Μνήμη και Χώρος στη Θεσσαλονίκη, από το 1912 έως τον Μεσοπόλεμο" [Alexander the Great after Hébrard: Memory and Space in Thessaloniki, from 1912 to the Inter-war Period]. In *Η Στρατιά της Ανατολής στη Θεσσαλονίκη, 1915–1918: Η Πόλη και οι Αναπαραστάσεις της* [The Allied Army of the Orient in Thessaloniki, 1915–1918: The City and Its Representations], edited by Iro Katsaridou and Ioannis Motsianos. Thessaloniki: Museum of Byzantine Culture.

Hadjipateras, Christian John. 2016. "The Overdue Placement of Stolpersteine in Thessaloniki, Greece." *The Huffington Post,* January 15, 2016. Accessed June 15, 2016. http://www.huffingtonpost.com/christian-john-hadjipateras/the-overdue-placement-of-stolpersteine_b_8937434.html.

Hastaoglou, Vilma. 2008. "Νεωτερικότητα και Μνήμη στη Διαμόρφωση της Μεταπολεμικής Θεσσαλονίκης" [Modernity and Memory in the Shaping of Postwar Thessaloniki]. In *Η Θεσσαλονίκη στο Μεταίχμιο: Η Πόλη ως Διαδικασία Αλλαγών* [Thessaloniki on the Verge: The City as a Change Process], edited by Grigoris Kafkalas, Lois Labrianidis, and Nikos Papamichos, 151–98. Athens: Kritiki.

Hastaoglou-Martinidis, Vilma, and Charis Christodoulou. 2010. "Preservation of Urban Heritage and Tourism in Thessaloniki." *Rivista di Scienze del Turismo* 2: 121–47.

Hayden, Robert M., 2002. "Antagonistic Tolerance: Competitive Sharing of Religious Sites in South Asia and the Balkans." *Current Anthropology* 43 (2): 205–31.

Hekimoglou, Evangelos. 2012. "The Local Historiography of Thessaloniki and the Issue of Multicultural Coexistence." Unpublished paper presented at the conference: The Holocaust in Thessaloniki, Council of Europe, October 16–17, 2012. Accessed June 15, 2016. https://www.academia.edu/4359704/%CE%A4he_Local_Historiography_of_Thessaloniki_and_the_Issue_of_Multicultural_Coexistence.

Hodolidou, Eleni. 2019. "Η Ασέβεια των Δημοτικών Συμβούλων στη Μνήμη του Ποιητή" [The Disrespect of Municipality Councilors for the Poet's Memory.] *Parallaxi,*

April 16, 2019. Accessed June 3, 2016. https://parallaximag.gr/parallax-view/aseveia-ton-dimotikon-symvoulon-sti-mnimi-tou-poiiti.

Ioannidou, Eleanna. 2016. "Η Μάχη της Ροτόντας" [Rotunda's Battle]. *Parallaxi,* February 3, 2016. Accessed June 15, 2016. http://parallaximag.gr/parallax-view/machi-tis-rotontas.

Kairidis, Dimitris, ed. 2015a. *Θεσσαλονίκη: Μια Πόλη σε Μετάβαση, 1912–2012* [Thessaloniki: A City in Transition, 1912–2012]. Thessaloniki: Epikentro.

———. 2015b. "Εισαγωγή: Θεσσαλονίκη, Συνέχειες και Ασυνέχειες στη Μετάβαση από τον Αυτοκρατορικό στον Εθνικό Κόσμο" [Introduction: Thessaloniki, Continuities and Discontinuities in the Transition from the Imperial to the National World]. In *Θεσσαλονίκη: Μια Πόλη σε Μετάβαση, 1912–2012* [Thessaloniki: A City in Transition, 1912–2012], 13–31.Thessaloniki: Epikentro.

Kantouris, Costas 2018. "Israel President Attends Holocaust Museum Ceremony in Greece." *AP News,* January 30, 2018. Accessed June 3, 2016. https://apnews.com/53c1f8c2aa46445 98e07974b25c6b91d.

Karadimou-Yerolympou, Alexandra. 1995. *Η Ανοικοδόμηση της Θεσσαλονίκης μετά την Πυρκαγιά του 1917. Ένα Ορόσημο στην Ιστορία της Πόλης και στην Ανάπτυξη της Ελληνικής Πολεοδομίας* [The Replanning of Thessaloniki after the Fire of 1917: A Turning Point in the History of the City and the Development of Greek City Planning]. 2nd ed. Thessaloniki: University Studio Press.

Katsavounidou, Garyfallia. 2004. *"ΑόρατεςΠαρενθέσεις": 27 Πόλεις στη Θεσσαλονίκη* [Invisible Parentheses: 27 Cities in Thessaloniki]. Athens: Patakis.

Kearns, Gerard, and Chris Philo. 1993. "Culture, History, Capital: A Critical Introduction to the Selling of Places." In *Selling Places: The City as Cultural Capital, Past and Present,* edited by Gerard Kearns and Chris Philo, 1–32. Oxford: Pergamon.

Kokkali, Ifigeneia. 2011. "Absence of a 'Community' and Spatial Invisibility: Migrants from Albania in Greece and the Case of Thessaloniki." In *The Ethnically Diverse City,* edited by Frank Eckardt and John Eade, 85–114. Berlin: Berliner Wissenschafts-Verlag.

Kolonas, Vassilis. 2012. *Η Αρχιτεκτονική μιας Εκατονταετίας: Θεσσαλονίκη 1912–2012* [One Hundred Years of Architecture: Thessaloniki 1912–2012]. Thessaloniki: University Studio Press.

Koumaridis, Yorgos. 2006. "Urban Transformation and De-Ottomanization in Greece." *East Central Europe* 33 (1–2): 213–42.

Kourkoutidou-Nikolaidou, Eftychia, and Anastasia Tourta. 1997. *Wandering in Byzantine Thessaloniki.* Athens: Kapon.

Lagopoulos, Alexandros. 2005. "Monumental Urban Space and National Identity: The Early Twentieth-Century New Plan of Thessaloniki." *Journal of Historical Geography* 31: 61–77.

Land, Isaac. 2016. "Antagonistic Tolerance and Other Port Town Paradoxes." *Forum Navale* 72: 78–101.

Leach, Anna. 2014. "Why the Tattooed Mayor of Thessaloniki Is a Beacon of Hope for Greece." *The Guardian,* December 30, 2014. Accessed June 10, 2016. http://www.theguardian.com/public-leaders-network/2014/dec/30/tattooed-mayor-thessaloniki-greece-yiannis-boutaris.

Loizides, Neophytos. 2015. *The Politics of Majority Nationalism: Framing Peace, Stalemates, and Crises.* Stanford: Stanford University Press.

Lykessas, Apostolos. 2015. "Εξηγήσεις και Αντιδράσεις για τον Σταυρό" [Explanations and Reactions about the Cross]. *Efsyn, Efimerida ton Sintakton,* December 21, 2015.

Accessed June 19, 2016. http://www.efsyn.gr/arthro/exigiseis-kai-antidraseis-gia-ton-stayro.

———. 2016. "Ο Κομφορμίστας" [The Conformist]. *Alterthess*, January 12, 2016. Accessed June 19, 2016. http://www.alterthess.gr/content/o-komformistas-toy-apostoloy-lykesa.

Lyberopoulou, Catherine. 2016. "Ξανάρχισε ο Πόλεμος για τη Ροτόντα: Μουσείο ή Ναός;" [The War on the Rotunda Resumed: Museum or Church?]. *TheTOC*, February 7, 2016. Accessed June 19, 2016. http://www.thetoc.gr/politismos/article/ksanarxise-o-polemos-gia-ti-rotonta-mouseio-i-naos.

Mazower, Mark. 2004. *Salonica, City of Ghosts: Christians, Muslims and Jews, 1430–1950*. New York: Knopf.

Meskos, Markos. 1986. *Στον Ίσκιο της Γης* [In the Shadow of the Earth]. Athens: Nefeli.

———. 1999. *Μαύρο Δάσος: Ποιήματα 1958–1986* [Black Forest: Poems 1958–1986]. Athens: Nefeli.

Moretti, Cristina. 2008. "Places and Stages: Narrating and Performing the City in Milan, Italy." *Liminalities: A Journal of Performance Studies* 4 (1): 1–46.

Myrtsioti, Giota. 2012. "Το Νέο Πρόσωπο της Θεσσαλονίκης" [The New Face of Thessaloniki]. *Kathimerini*, February 24, 2012. Accessed June 19, 2016. http://www.kathimerini.gr/451382/article/politismos/arxeio-politismoy/to-neo-proswpo-ths-8essalonikhs.

Paddison, Ronan. 2013. "Ethnic Diversity, Public Space and Urban Regeneration." In *The Routledge Companion to Urban Regeneration*, edited by Michael Leary and John McCarthy, 263–72. London: Routledge.

Patikas, Christos. 2013. *Consulting Project: Development of Thessaloniki, Greece as a City Break Tourism Destination*. Thessaloniki: International Hellenic University and Municipality of Thessaloniki.

Plika, Maroula. 2015. "Ο Σταυρός, η Ροτόντα και οι Θεσσαλονικείς" [The Cross, the Rotunda and the Thessalonians]. *I Avgi*, December 22, 2015. Accessed June 19, 2016. http://www.avgi.gr/article/6131036/o-stauros-i-rotonta-kai-oi-thessalonikeis.

———. 2016. "Αρ. Μπαλτάς: 'Η Ροτόντα είναι Μνημείο Πολυπολιτισμικό'" [Ar. Baltas: The Rotunda Is a Multicultural Monument]. *I Avgi*, January 19, 2016. Accessed June 19, 2016. http://www.avgi.gr/article/6193982/ar-mpaltas-i-rotonta-einai-mnimeio-polupolitismiko-.

Saltiel, Leon. 2014. "Dehumanizing the Dead: The Destruction of Thessaloniki's Jewish Cemetery in the Light of New Sources." *Yad Vashem Studies* 42 (1): 11–46.

Sereda, Viktoria. 2009. "Politics of Memory and Urban Landscape: The Case of Lviv after World War II." In *Time, Memory, and Cultural Change*, edited by Sean Dempsey and David Nichols. Junior Visiting Fellows' Conferences 25. Vienna: IWM. Accessed June 19, 2016. http://www.iwm.at/read-listen-watch/transit-online/politics-of-memory-and-urban-landscape.

Sintès, Pierre, and Olivier Givre. 2015. "Iannis Boutaris et les Fantômes de Salonique." *Écrire l'Histoire* 15: 215–22.

Smith, Helena. 2018. "'Far-Right Thugs' Attack Mayor of Thessaloniki at Remembrance Event." *The Guardian*, May 20, 2019. Accessed June 3, 2019. https://www.theguardian.com/world/2018/may/20/suspected-far-right-thugs-attack-mayor-of-thessaloniki-greece-at-rally.

———. 2019. "'Forget It': Plan to Give Runner Statue to Skopje Angers Greeks." *The Guardian*, March 20, 2019. Accessed June 3, 2019. https://www.theguardian.com/world/2019/mar/20/runner-plan-move-athens-statue-skopje-angers-greeks-north-macedonia.

Solomon, Esther, and Styliana Galiniki. 2018. "Las Incantadas of Salonica: Searching for 'Enchantment' in a City's Exiled Heritage." In *Hellenomania*, edited by Nicoletta Momigliano, Katherine Harloe, and Alexandre Farnoux, 271–310. London: Routledge.

Stewart, Charles. 2001. "Immanent or Eminent Domain?: The Contest over Thessaloniki's Rotonda." In *Destruction and Conservation of Cultural Property*, edited by Robert Layton, Peter Stone, and Julian Thomas, 182–98. London: Routledge.

Tilley, Christopher. 1994. *A Phenomenology of Landscape: Places, Paths and Monuments*. Oxford: Berg.

Trakossopoulou-Tzimou, Kornilia. 2015. "Η Μέριμνα για τα Μνημεία στη Νεότερη Θεσσαλονίκη: Αντιλήψεις και Πρακτικές (19ος–20ός αι.)" [The Care for Monuments in Modern Thessaloniki: Perceptions and Practices (19th–20th Century)]. In *Θεσσαλονίκη: Μια Πόλη σε Μετάβαση, 1912–2012* [Thessaloniki: A City in Transition, 1912–2012], 502–29. Thessaloniki: Epikentro.

Tzanelli, Rodanthi. 2011. "Ill-Defined Heritage: Exploring Thessaloniki's Selective Agenda." *Global Studies Journal* 4 (1): 193–218.

Tzimou, Kya. 2015. "Περί Σταυρών και Άλλων 'Δαιμονίων'" [On Crosses and Other "Demons"]. *Parallaxi*, December 18, 2015. Accessed June 19, 2019. http://parallaximag.gr/uncategorized/peri-stavron-ke-allon-demonion.

Young, Craig, and Sylvia Kaczmarek. 2008. "The Socialist Past and Post-Socialist Urban Identity in Central and Eastern Europe. The Case of Łódź, Poland." *European Urban and Regional Studies* 15 (1): 53–70.

6 The Oracle of Dodona

Contestation over a "Sacred" Archaeological Landscape

Katerina Konstantinou

According to the academic knowledge produced throughout almost a century of archaeological and literary research, Ancient Dodona is the oldest oracle of the Greek world and one of its Panhellenic (i.e., for all Greeks) sanctuaries, continuously in use since the early Bronze Age (3000–2000 BC). It is located in Epirus, the northwestern region of the country, which is distinct for its remoteness, its rainy climate, and the dramatic diversity of its mountainous landscapes. Unlike other parts of Greece, Epirus remains largely unexplored and comparatively poor, and it has not yet achieved massive touristic popularity. The landscape of Dodona has been endlessly represented in not only historical and archaeological accounts but also art and literature, and it has come to symbolize the distinctiveness of Epirus and its people. Dodonean antiquities have played a crucial part in many historical debates regarding ambiguities and controversies around the Balkan borders and are currently entangled in various contestations concerning their interpretation, perceptions, and use.

The importance of the site draws partly from an ancient myth narrated to Herodotus by three female priests of Dodona, regarding the transition from the cult of Mother Nature (Earth) to that of the twelve gods. As claimed, the cult of the latter was brought to Epirus by two priests kidnapped in Egypt and was established around a preexisting hallowed oak tree (Greek *figos*). This myth, known in various versions, provides the reasoning for the development of the ancient Greek religion. According to historians and archaeologists, such transition coincided with the migration of the so-called Greek tribes to Epirus in the second millennium BC. Thus, in the timeline of the Greek past, Dodona is carefully placed at the very dawn of Hellenism. A temple was first constructed around the oak tree sometime in the fourth century BC and marked the origins of the area's sanctity. The sanctuary also served as an oracle, where the priests (*Selloi or Elloi*) interpreted natural sounds to reply to pilgrims seeking divine advice and help. The persistent reference to Selloi or Elloi, both in academic and local discourses,

Fig. 6.1. A view of Mount Olytsika and the village of Manteio above the archaeological site of Dodona. Photo by A. Sichlimiris. Courtesy of Aris Sichlimiris.

implies the much-desired relationship (etymological in this case) between Epirus and Hellenes—that is, the people of ancient Hellas (Acosta-Hughes and Stephens 2012, 180). Dodona, the *arhegonos* (primordial) site of Hellas, hosted the Pelasgians, the legendary ancestors of all Greek tribes, a point that is often highlighted in local narratives on the area's past. Dodona mainly had a religious role, but the site also served as the administrative center of ancient Epirus, especially during the third century BC, when King Pyrros reigned over most of the Epirote tribes. It was within Pyrros's ambitious plan to monumentalize the sanctuary that a theater was constructed, which today constitutes the most impressive structure on the site.

In the last one hundred years, Dodona has been variously read and understood. Its past has been intensively mythicized, and consequently its natural landscape has been often interpreted in the same terms. Therefore, tracing a genealogy of the values and meanings that have been attributed to the land and the heritage of Dodona reveals a great deal about how people associate their contemporary being-in-the-world with the materiality of (what they perceive as) their ancestral past and its natural surroundings.

An increasing number of studies in recent decades have placed archaeology and its social impact at the focus of ethnographic research, investigating a plethora of ways in which people make sense of the past and its remains. Narratives around antiquities are often negotiated and conflicted, especially when they are related to sensitive political issues such as the negotiation of ethnic identities, the establishment of national borders, or the economic development of an area via tourism. Furthermore, communities' engagement with the rhetoric of official history leads to diverse readings and understandings of ancient heritage and landscape. This chapter aims to discuss the relation between the ancient remains of the oracle of Dodona, the most significant archaeological site in the region of Epirus, and the communities living nearby.[1] Interpretative engagements of today's people with the archaeological site will be examined with a particular focus on the contested aspects of this relation.

Dodona in "Authorized" Discourses

The long-lasting endeavors of identifying Dodona, after many insecure assumptions, concluded with the excavation of the site in the 1870s by an amateur antiquarian from the Epirote city of Arta, Konstantinos Carapanos (1840–1914), and his publication in French under the title *Dodone et ses Ruines* (Carapanos 1878). Necessary material pieces of evidence were finally provided by this survey, which was conducted with an official permit granted individually to Carapanos by the Ottoman authority in Istanbul that ruled Epirus at that time. Carapanos's interest in finding the exact location of the legendary oracle of Dodona was due to not only his presumed enthusiasm for antiquities but mostly his belief that the remote region of Epirus should be considered Greek, and thus its "Greekness" needed some tangible proof. In addition, the first edition of his valuable description of the monument was published in French, a language that indicated the international audience he meant to address. It was under the very specific geopolitical circumstances of the end of the Ottoman era and the Greek War of Independence that Dodona was produced as a place of crucial importance for the negotiation of Greek national borders.

In Carapanos's days, a shift in the way antiquities were perceived had already occurred, and the secular "imagined communities" (Anderson 2006) of nations were to be established within specific ideas of Western modernity (cf. Atkinson, Banks, and O'Sullivan 1996; Kohl and Fawcett 1995). Toward this process, antiquities had to be excluded from daily life and experience in order to be transformed from lived places into meaningful archaeological sites (Hamilakis 2007, 17). More specifically, in the case of Dodona, the aim was to associate Epirus with the Greek nation. Thus, Carapanos's "bronze collection," formed at that time, was later donated to the National Archaeological Museum in Athens and is still partially exhibited there in a hall under his name. The collection of Carapanos, which consists mainly of finds from the rich Dodonean offerings dated to different ancient periods, constitutes a characteristic representation of Epirus within the permanent exhibition of the National Museum. It has contributed to the identification of Dodona with the exhibited objects and their characteristic patina (Proskynitopoulou 2009, 16), owed to the soil composition in the Dodona valley.

Throughout the first decades of the twentieth century, Dodona was left to be buried again under the deposits of Mount Olytsika, which dominates the valley. Systematic excavation of the place was allocated to Dimitris Evaggelidis (1886–1959), an archaeologist born and raised in the village of Plaisio (formerly Plesivitsa), next to the Greek-Albanian border. His knowledge of the region was owed to not only his origins but also his previous participation in archaeological expeditions held at the end of the Balkan Wars in 1913—expeditions intended to reveal the Greek culture once flourishing in the Southern Albania territories (Davis 2000). Evaggelidis's interest in the ancient past of Epirus was strongly related to the concurrent politics of the past and the pursued future of modern Epirotes. As an Epirote himself, Evaggelidis claimed the cultural continuity of Epirus from ancient to modern times. His concern to associate modern Epirotes with ancient Greeks and their glorious past imbues his work *I Arhei Katiki tis Ipirou* [*The Ancient Inhabitants of Epirus*] (1962). His study, first published in 1947, was an attempt to define the ethnicity of the ancient tribes of Epirus and therefore conclude the long-lasting dispute mostly between Italian and Greek scholars concerning the history and culture of the area. Conflicting opinions on the history of this disputed territory matched the territorial claims of all interested ethnic groups living in and near the area. Evaggelidis proposed a Greek identity for the ancient residents of the area, which he also detected in local mythology and material culture. He concluded that the predominant tribes of Epirus (Thesprotoi, Molossoi, and Haones) had lived outside modern Greece, notably in the region of Southern Albania (for some), or Northern Epirus (for others). This place-name ambiguity, still present today (Green 2005), has perpetuated the conflict upon the geography of the Balkans, deploying the area's antiquities for this reason and causing exacerbations of nationalistic tensions every now and then.

Tracing the origins of Epirote tribes and identifying them with Greece was one of the main concerns of Evaggelidis and his successors. Attempts to provide a genealogy of ancient tribes were combined with various ethnographic observations, scattered around this folklore literature. Of course, this literature echoed the synchronous nationalistic concerns of archaeology and stressed cultural continuity from ancient to modern times. However, there are differences in the ways subsequent generations of archaeologists included ethnographic information in the dominant narrative on the Epirote tribal sequence. In Evaggelidis's work, for instance, such observations are presented as survivals of an ancient culture.[2] In contrast, his successor at the excavations of Dodona, the archaeologist Sotiris Dakaris (1916–1996), drew on such observations to interpret his findings in a more ethnoarchaeological way. The historical sequence of the Epirote tribes has preoccupied many archaeologists for almost a century, and the literature produced on this subject (see for example Evaggelidis and Dakaris 1959; Evaggelidis 1962; Dakaris 1964; Vokotopoulou 1986) is significantly extensive. Yet Dodona retains an unchanged position in this discourse: it is seen as a unifying bond between all ancient Epirote tribes during what is known as the Epirote League, a coalition established under the reign of King Pyrros, whose spirit is still present. Thus, the Dodonean past has served as a major unifying agent in modern times as well.

Dakaris was one of the most prominent figures in producing the past of Dodona and inscribing it on the modern Epirote society. His expertise in the ancient topography of the region made him closely associated with Epirote archaeology (Vasileiou 2014; Sueref 2013). In 2013, a meaningful exhibition curated by the Ephorate of Antiquities in Ioannina and called "Dakaris: The Archaeologist of Epirus" (Sueref 2013) suggested that, through his lifelong archaeological research in the region, Dakaris has systematized our knowledge of ancient Epirus. Dakaris had assisted Evaggelidis in his last excavation period in Dodona (1952–1959) and succeeded him after his death in 1959. He served as the director of the Ephorate of Antiquities in Ioannina, the largest city in Epirus, some twenty kilometers from Dodona. In 1965, he was appointed professor in archaeology at the local university. Several generations of local archaeologists who were under his tutelage are today working at or retired from Ioannina University or the Ephorate of Antiquities in Ioannina. Therefore, Dakaris not only introduced a particular way of thinking and interpreting the ancient material culture of Epirus but also established a horde of advocates. It is true that Dakaris's interpretations of the Epirote ancient past have been so strongly adopted and appropriated among the Epirotes that alternative interpretations or reconsiderations of his assumptions have been disregarded or even ignored by local scholars. Controversies appearing between local and foreign archaeologists (e.g., Piccinini 2013) that contradict the dominant narrative on ancient Epirus remain largely unvoiced. The "one and only" narrative about Dodona, adopted by national history as "beyond any dispute," has persistently endured throughout time.

The Dawn of a Modern Era for Dodona

Apart from the academic efforts of the Ioannina-based Ephorate of Antiquities and the University of Ioannina to consolidate the importance of Dodona, its position in the national imaginary is mostly owed to the Society of Epirote Studies [*Eteria Ipirotikon Meleton*] (hereafter SES). The society was founded in

1954 following the mission statement of the Society for Macedonian Studies, a group of similar academic and political purposes that was founded in 1939 in Thessaloniki. Both societies were established by local intellectuals and politicians and were assigned the difficult task of institutionalizing knowledge on Northern Greece's past and defending Greek sovereignty over the "New Lands" and their people. Macedonia and Epirus were annexed to the Greek state only after the Balkan Wars of 1912–13 and comprised regional peripheries that shared the feature of mixed populations in ethnological terms and thus the need to establish linguistic and religious homogeneity. This process also involved a treaty for the exchange of populations between Greece and Turkey based on people's religious beliefs. Both societies aimed to raise the "educational, spiritual and cultural level of the [local] people" (Vavouskos 1993, as cited in Sjöberg 2011, 56), as Konstantinos Vavouskos, the president of the Macedonian Society, commented when referring to the Macedonian people; their role was of vital significance for the formation of local identities and the homogenization of the different components of these regional societies.

Kostas Frontzos (1904–1986), founder of the Epirote Society and its president for thirty years, as well as a prominent member of Ioannina's upper class, made similar statements. His vision for an *Epirote Renaissance* (SES 1989) was largely turned into action during the late 1950s and early 1960s. As it is stated in the founding document of the society, "the intellectual fruition of the past" underwent an extended period of degradation after 1913. Epirus was subjected to a dramatic shift from playing a predominant part in the cultural production of ancient Greece to being a peripheral region, doomed in its marginality. SES took over the responsibility of creating a relationship between modern Epirotes and their "ancestors," and this relationship was largely motivated by the need to face sentiments of contempt. As it was eloquently described in the society's founding document, "The great Epirote Tradition became an unbearable heritage shaming its unworthy descendants" (SES 1989, 15). To Frontzos, who was a distinguished, well-educated man and was affiliated with right-wing politics, the material evidence of a glorious past at Dodona was there as a reminder that Epirotes gradually became unworthy of their glorious history and that they had to prove that they deserved such a past. Such "shame" sensed by the intellectual members of the society was mostly linked to the rural character of the region and the difficulties faced in order to modernize this "isolated and backwards" segment of the country.

It was not coincidental that. while trying to establish SES, another issue was raised within the agenda of this group of mostly Western-educated intellectuals from Ioannina: the establishment of the "third" university of Greece, that of Ioannina. SES's main goal was to relocate Epirus on the Greek cultural map, both ancient and modern, and therefore a set of ideals of "Epirotism" had to be "invented" (Hobsbawm and Ranger 1992). Their efforts aimed not only to bridge the gap between modern and ancient Epirotes but also, and more important, to include the Epirote past into the dominant Greek national narrative. In order to make ancient and modern topographies of Epirus overlap, Ioannina should stand as the metropolis of northwestern Greece, and the ancient ruins of Dodona should become the protagonists in the cosmos that was created by the local elite. The ancient past of Epirus had to be narrated in line with a linear history of Greece, and the emphasis had to be put upon the classical roots of local culture. For this reason, the scientific support provided by the newly founded University of Ioannina was necessary toward the institutionalization of the production of knowledge about the past of the region.

In 1959, the archaeological excavation of the theater was completed, and a first restoration transformed it into a structure usable for drama performances. In 1960, the annual festival *Eortes Dodonis* [Festivals of Dodona] was inaugurated under the administration of SES, and it soon gained impressive popularity. The festival marked the start of a new relationship of modern Epirotes to antiquity. This radically reshaped relationship was primarily based on the acknowledged significance of Dodona as "Primordial Hellas." The impressively large audiences attending the festival reflected the archaeological conception of the crowds of worshipers arriving from across Greece during the flourishing ancient times of the sanctuary. This resonance was usually given special attention and was often referred to by archaeologists, SES members, and journalists as a "pilgrimage to sacred Dodona." Reproduced in public speeches, local newspapers, and literature, this locally formed discourse gave the event an almost sacred value. As an annual gathering of Epirotes, it was of great importance for both the formation and the performance of local social relations.

In addition, as a performance of national culture in a local context, the festival empowered a sense of belonging, kinship, and nationhood and strengthened the relation of Epirus to Athens, the capital of Greece and undisputed center of cultural production in both ancient and modern times. For Epirus, which is considered one of the most isolated peripheries of the country, hosting productions of the National Theater of Greece in the theater of Dodona was seen as recognition of the values assigned to this ancient heritage and confirmed the existence of a common as well as enduring theatrical tradition. The National Theater's shows with leading directors and renowned actors constituted events that honored modern Epirotes, who in turn gathered in Dodona, traveling from even the remotest villages of the area.

In this context, Frontzos's inaugural speeches were of great importance for the local communities and were enthusiastically received and anticipated. Many people who happened to be among his audience clearly remembered these inspiring speeches, which were a form of national ritual performed annually in order

Fig. 6.2. Dodona Festival 1965. A theater program. Published by the Society of Epirote Studies.

to inscribe an emerging ancient past onto the social memory of the Epirotes. The first public speech in the theater of Dodona delivered by Frontzos surely made a strong impression but was moreover printed and reprinted in several festival programs and local newspapers the following decade (Frontzos 1962, 2). "Have you read his first speech?" Evanthia, a small business owner close to the archaeological site, asked me. "I remember this one because I was crying. We were all crying. His words were so moving that his speech went down in history." It seems as though the long-lost connection to Greece was finally recovered; such relation necessitated an annual celebration in which Greekness was represented and performed.

Dodona as a Heritage Landscape

The Dodonean landscape is invested with multiple qualities intertwined with ancient myths and archaeological knowledge. Observations of natural phenomena are understood as substantiating the long history of the oracle. On that account, the surrounding landscape seems to be of great significance for both the official archaeological interpretation and a variety of unofficial readings of the site. For almost all of them, the sacred oak tree is taken as a point of departure. Nowadays, an oak tree, encircled by the *Iera Ikia* (Sacred House), objectifies the myth of the establishment of Zeus's cult in Dodona. According to a version of this myth, two black doves flew from Thebes in Egypt. One of them landed in Libya and called for the sanctuary of Amon Zeus, and the other one perched on an oak tree in Epirus and informed the inhabitants that this tree was sacred and that the deity underneath its roots was Zeus. A temple had to be built to protect the new deity. Contrasting the rhetoric about the oracle's historical significance, the temple itself lacks special architecture, sculptural decoration, or standing columns that could efficiently demonstrate the purport of its existence in history. On the contrary, trees planted around the site confirm the archaeological conception of tree worship and evoke associations with the long-lost, sacred forest of Dodona. Natural landscape as a whole is understood as the preexisting substrate of human activity and as the primordial (*arhegonos*) force of Hellenism, the grounding basis of Dodecatheism (the ancient worship of the twelve gods) and Greek mythology.

Several other smaller temples, preserved only on the foundation level, surround the area of the Iera Ikia, making the site difficult to comprehend. The site is more appreciated for its surrounding, breathtaking, natural landscape and the large and most impressive theater and less for its other remains. The famous oracle of Dodona, identified by archaeologists with the Iera Ikia, remains obscure to the people who are trying to locate it elsewhere.

The perception of the valley as largely unexplored is triggered by the absence of emblematic findings such as marble sculptures or golden wreaths that signify other recognized ancient sites of Greece. Besides, the absence of an adjacent ancient city that has not yet been found and the existing protection zones that imply still buried monuments enforce various assumptions about the archaeological wealth of the ancient valley. The premise that an ancient city remains underground, waiting to be discovered, forms the significant missing part of the "completed" Dodonean past that facilitates the domination upon the landscape (cf. Anagnostopoulos, this volume). The imaginary city of Dodona is often described by locals as resembling the neighboring modern Dodonoupoli, a group of almost identical houses that was released on plans conducted during the military junta (1968–74) in order to host the villagers of Dodonochoria that were struck by landslides in the fifties.

This tendency of the landscape to change, along with the usually heavy winters, strengthens locals' and visitors' association of Dodona with Zeus. Konstantina Kosti, an engineer who runs a small hotel close to the site, remarked, "[The valley] is no ordinary place. You can see for yourself that this is a cosmogenic environment. Heavy winters, thunderbolts, the mountains, oak trees are not just there by chance." The thunderbolt is believed to be the destructive agent attributed to Zeus, so Dodona's frequent thunderstorms are seen as the natural verification of the archaeological narrative. In defense of the title *Arhegonos Hellas* (Primordial Greece) that appears in the local discourse, weather conditions and the markedly distinctive topography are often mentioned as the starting point of Dodekatheism in Greece and thus Dodona as the birthplace of Hellenism (see, for example, Antoniou 1973, 9). Similarly to many other mythologies on the creation of the cosmos, catastrophic natural phenomena are primeval forces of disorder.

Another piece of knowledge circulated among the inhabitants is the information that draws on the *Iliad*[3] (Homer, *Iliad*, 16.233) that the priests of the oracle went about barefoot and slept on the ground. Wearing no shoes is related to poverty and an austere lifestyle—widely acknowledged characteristics of the Epirotes' localism. Their poverty, largely owing to inadequate lands for cultivation, is superimposed upon the past and specifically upon the myth of Selloi. Furthermore, as many of my informants have highlighted, being barefoot within the valley and thus in a direct contact with earth usually adds to the interpretation of the Dodonean valley as an "energetic field."

The Contested Order of Dodonean Monuments

Among the monuments of Dodona, the theater holds a place of paramount importance in the memory of the valley's inhabitants, and thus it is implicated in various conflicts concerning its ownership, uses, and the different restoration attempts made in the last six decades. Integrated into the landscape, the theater's upper zone remained visible above the ground long before its systematic excavation and reconstruction by Dakaris in the late 1950s. Previous to these fundamental alterations in the theater form, as many inhabitants in the valley remarked, the theater was buried under a private land plot meant for grain farming. Although my informants repeatedly mentioned that the particular land plot belonged to someone, they never referred to him by name. Archival research revealed that the plot was owned by a Muslim named Netzip Suleyman Tahir, who had been deported from the country under the Lausanne Treaty[4] on the exchange of populations between Greece and Turkey in 1923. His property was transferred to the state but remained under negotiation between archaeologists, locals, and various involved authorities until the early sixties.

Moreover, the arena located above the circle of the theater's orchestra was at the heart of another local dispute. Two conflicting approaches toward the management of the ancient remains were at stake here. On the one hand, Frontzos favored a national "purification plan" for the site, according to which Dodona should be brought back to its perceived "Greek" appearance. On the other hand,

Dakaris supported a more archaeological approach, considering all ancient remains of equal value. Despite the fact that Frontzos and Dakaris shared the same vision for the future of the region, they held entirely opposite views on what parts of its past were worthwhile.

It was on August 10, 1974,[5] that Frontzos addressed the audience of the packed theater and generated the public clamor for demolishing the arena and therefore making the evidence of the "barbarous" Roman conquerors vanish. Drawing on another case of removing what was thought of as inappropriate historical evidence—that of the nationalistic purification of the Acropolis in Athens[6]—Frontzos polarized the audience along lines of power and privilege upon making decisions about the ancient past. He then referred to the demolition of the Muslim mosque on the Athenian Acropolis, which was part of a larger "purification" program of the monument that took place after the establishment of the Greek nation-state (Yalouri 2001, 55). These decisions on maintaining or removing elements and material structures that refer to the past were highly symbolic and controversial. The suggested removal of the Roman arena would be a decision signifying the aesthetic importance of ancient dramas over what was perceived as the low-quality spectacles of the Roman era. Its preservation was surely not in line with the nation's narrative about the Roman period according to which the Roman conquest was just territorial and Greeks remained culturally intact. Particularly in Epirus, Romans are blamed for the present lack of antiquities in contrast to the abundance of ancient remains in the rest of the country. In 167 BC, Aemilius Paulus destroyed most of the ancient Epirote cities, and this fact provides the reasoning for an archaeologically poor region. In addition, the fact that Epirus, as the northwestern frontier of Greece, has suffered the most savage consequences of the Greek-Italian war and the attribution of all the Roman negative characteristics to the Italians (Kokkinidou and Nikolaidou 2004, 168) sheds some light on the modern perception of Roman elements in Dodona's theater.

Nowadays, the existence of the arena still causes disagreements among the interested groups. Although local residents around the valley express opposing opinions on the issue, they strongly condemn this dispute between Frontzos and Dakaris. For some, it is this lack of consensus that is to be blamed for the failure of the authorities to promote touristic development of the valley and thus raise the site to its "rightful position" (i.e., among the most significant antiquities of the country). "Both of them were good. Educated and clever men, but it's the same over and over again. If they hadn't fought they would have done miracles for the area," remarked Argyris Tselos, a local, elderly man born in 1923.

In contrast to the current structure of the monument, which is an architectural type that signifies the use of it as an arena, performances of ancient dramas for half a century inscribed the "unquestionable" state of the monument as that of an ancient Greek theater and have left an inedible impact on the local community. In addition, it is the most comprehensible monument within the fenced site, whereas temples and other public buildings are humbly preserved and their understanding remains opaque. Contrary to the theater's display value and functionality, the rest of the monuments seem of less importance for the local community. According to the official interpretation of the site, Dodona was the most ancient oracle of the Greek world, and the Iera Ikia (Sacred House) is considered of the greatest historical importance; however, there is a striking difference between the archaeological and the local populations' discourses regarding the value of the monuments. Such difference reveals a great deal in terms of variety of perspectives and priorities and suggests two divergent interpretations as well as two respective hierarchies of monuments within the landscape. Locals mainly consider the theater the most significant monument that could also be a major touristic attraction, whereas archaeologists emphasize the oracle and the religious aspects of Dodona. Therefore, most of the locals' claims toward the site focus on the preservation, restoration, and use of the theater.

Performing Memory

The considerable impact the theater performances had on the small population of Dodona valley is surely related to the general role ancient drama holds in the ancient Greek culture and their revival in the twentieth century. The first decades of the twentieth century saw occasional performances of ancient Greek dramas in ancient theaters, whereas the rediscovery of this rich source of glory for Greece had taken place a few decades earlier (Lalioti 2001, 12). Annual summer festivals around the country, with the most renowned being that of the ancient theater of Epidaurus, constituted an important source of the nation's narrative legitimacy, a signifier of the country's historical memory and a way to perform its identity. Ancient tragedies and comedies staged in open-air theaters have provided spectators with embodied and unforgettable experiences of a magnificent past. For many decades, those reenactments have been powerful and influential representations, actively involved in the formation of national and local identities; they have shaped individual memories and created collective narratives.

In Dodona's theater, striking shows of ancient dramas have definitely affected people's approach to not only the past but also the material remains. SES, using its influence and power upon the Epirote society, successfully promoted a narrative unifying modern Epirotes. On the other hand, villagers experienced the festival with some embarrassment because they felt they lacked the necessary cultural capital. Giorgos Laras, a local in his early sixties, clearly stated that their small society had little, if any, acquaintance with the "high culture" of the ancient theater. "If it is to say that we were somehow related to the theater [of Dodona], it was only due to the performances that got us close to the ancient people. We had the chance to see how it must have been back then. Ancient people should have been wandering around our place dressed like this. . . . Life at that time should have been like this. So, that is how we started to be aware of these facts through these performances."

In the multiple representations of these events in the local newspapers, the festival was described as a process of strengthening the Epirotes' social cohesion. In fact, these theater plays were experienced differently by their motley audiences. For the citizens of Ioannina who wanted to stress their cultural differences from rural Epirus, attending the festival was a great opportunity to demonstrate their cultural status and stimulate their newly acquired bourgeois identity. Their ability to comprehend the demanding drama scripts and appreciate the "high aesthetics" of the great spectacle offered in Dodona distinguished them from the rest of the local audience and contributed to the reproduction of local social hierarchies. Contrary to such bourgeois and elitist attitudes, the villagers of the Dodona valley were mostly unable to afford tickets to the performances and thus were left to enter the theater last. Class distinctiveness was also pursued in a plethora of other examples, mostly related to the extent individuals were involved in the organization of the festival. A common distinction was that Yianniotes (citizens of Ioannina) volunteered, whereas Dodoneans were paid for any kind of involvement and service.

The glamorous atmosphere described mainly by Yianniotes belies the local people's feelings and remarks regarding the festival. The theater events reproduced social distinctions (cf. Bourdieu 1984) between the better-educated, sophisticated, bourgeois people and the "ignorant," uncultivated villagers. Indeed, as social events, theater performances not only enforced social distinctions but also demanded and imposed "suitable" behavior within a confined space that was temporarily transformed into a public space controlling the acts and attitudes of every individual in the audience (Foucault 1986, 24).

Nevertheless, it was with great enthusiasm from both sides that the ancient plays were welcomed and celebrated. Admiration generated by the monument itself, combined with all the strong feelings encouraged by the multisensory experience of attending a theater performance, created innumerable recollections that locals share with citizens from Ioannina. Ancient drama offered the experience of a suspended temporality (Crary 2001, 10) in which reality was being interrupted by the performance and the spectator was immersed in another time and place. Its primarily pedagogic value—dramas were not performed but taught in ancient Greece—offered an invaluable modernizing mechanism. Regarding the local audience in particular, this enthusiasm was rather a fulfillment of their sense of belonging to the Greek nation and to a modern society.

The artistic value of those performances was rarely commented upon. The feeling of being unworthy of such kind of "high artistic expression" most likely reflected the noted (see Herzfeld 1987) sense of Greeks toward "their" past achievements. Although most of my informants admitted that the texts of the plays were opaque and incomprehensible, they did express admiration for specific artists, notably famous actors of older generations, such as Anna Synodinou and Alexis Minotis. Moreover, the fact that celebrities and well-known citizens from Ioannina or other cities of Greece attended the festival further demonstrated the significance of the spectacle and consequently of the place itself.

To trace the impact of the landscape on the experience of the theater performances by the inhabitants of the valley, it is worth noting that most of my informants commented on two specific incidents repeatedly occurring year after year. The first was the movement of the actors, actresses, and chorus from the stalls, which were placed beside the theater and functioned as the dressing rooms, to the backstage hidden behind the stage: this passage signaled the start of the play and the immersion of the audience in its flow. This particular movement of the cast within the space is often highlighted as the most emotive part of Dodona's festival. The same way the church bells accentuate the ceremonial time (Bender 2002, 104) of any ritual, actors' movement in Dodona marked the simultaneous occurrence of the past and the present.

The other movement usually mentioned by inhabitants of all ages was that of the lines of cars driving across the old road to Ioannina, climbing up a hill on a serpentine course. The car lights, slowly moving one behind the other, are remembered as the end of the spectacle and the return to the real world. The audience was divided into two distinct groups: the Dodoneans, who remained in the valley, and the Others, who would leave the place after the end of the performance. Several points around the valley were used to watch this unusual parade until the construction of a new highway put an end to this experience for all.

By turning the monument into a living space for some days during the festival, a meeting of different temporalities took place at Dodona. Annual performances, along with their preparation period, formed a unique social domain where everyday experience met the official understanding of history. The bipolar division between local and academic knowledge was in agreement once a year, and this convergence generated the sense of a living history.

Contemporary Theater Sceneries as Materialized Pasts

The theater sceneries were another aspect that played an important part in how villagers of the Dodona valley experienced the past through these theater productions. According to my informants, settings were themselves monumental, built with grand scenic elements, and as such suitable for a monumental place like Dodona. "We are talking about whole palaces. Fake, of course, but very beautiful. . . . They have no similarity with what is going on now," Giorgos Laras, resident of the valley, commented on his community's conception of the theater. Yet theater settings kept deteriorating, going from enormous realistic constructions that necessitated a large number of qualified craftsmen's hard work for a long time prior to the performance to simple, mock, easy-to-make, effortless, and therefore disappointing representations of the past. It is worth noting that growing up near Dodona during the second half of the twentieth century means that someone had the chance to observe the fifty-year evolution of the festival. Observations made by the villagers who compare old and recent productions often conclude with statements about a declining culture in general. In addition, many Epirotes who have experienced all these changes in craftsmanship, and more notably in masonry skills, feel that they are of equal importance to those of the ancient inhabitants in the area. This "equality" largely contradicts the feeling of being worthless when compared to classical achievements. According to the discourse developed by Greek Folklore Studies [*Laografia*] for the region, Epirus was abundant in masons who were working in groups all over Greece and the Balkans during and after the Ottoman period. This widely acclaimed tradition has drastically affected Epirote identity because it provides proof of cultural continuity (Herzfeld 1982, 25) that links modest, modern inhabitants with their distant "ancestors" through a surviving technique.

The fact that many inhabitants of the nearby villages had worked for the first restoration of the theater in the late 1950s has added to this perception of continuity. Epirote expertise of working with stone empowered Dodoneans to express a variety of opinions toward the ongoing restoration project. Local critical views on the aesthetics and authenticity of the sceneries draw from the self-confidence gained from this same expertise.

The recent dissent of the local community on the methods applied to the restoration of the ancient theater mainly focuses on the material used to fill in the empty spaces on the stone seats of the theater. The method proposed by the Scientific Committee of Dodona (Smyris 2014) and approved by the Central Archaeological Council called for the use of a specific kind of concrete to complete the original form of the seats. The previous restoration that had remade two of the three rows of seats used the same local stone to fill in the gaps, and these stone blocks were crafted by local masons. Almost half a century after the 1950s restoration, the method used back then was condemned by the scientific community due to its incompatibility with the current principle of restorations according to which new, added material should be easily distinguished from the ancient. Concerns about the original forms of the antiquities have also been a common debate, and, as a result, the ongoing restoration aims to reverse the image of the previous one, return the theater to its state before Dakaris's restoration (Katsoudas 2014), and pursue a minimum of authenticity. Thus today, cement materializes a history that contradicts the story of the locals' engagement in the theater and erases the material evidence of their participation in the historic restoration of "their" theater.

Dodona's Theater as a Conflict-Scape

On the occasion of the visit of the members of the Central Archaeological Council (hereafter CAC) to Dodona in 2010, locals were gathered to protest against the archaeologists. The former denounced the employed restoration methods as profane. The completion of a pilot restoration of the lower part of the theater [*diazoma*] had created an outburst of controversy. The archaeological site once more became the stage for a conflict between the decision-makers and the symbolic owners of the theater, the locals. Arguments escalated against the use of cement. The modern material that was proposed as a solution in order to deal with the erosion of the local stone carried multiple negative connotations. The fear that the theater would soon be concreted over prompted all the strongly negative emotions felt toward the use of concrete in modern buildings in urban areas. A large banner was hung on the fence of the site, just next to the entrance, demanding, "Respect the monument! No to its cementing" [*Sevastite to mnimio. Ohi stin tsimentopiisi tou*].

During recent decades, concrete as a building material was in widespread use all around Greece when the country was developing its cities and infrastructures. It is strongly associated with modern urban life in Greece, and it is a feature differentiating urban from rural life. Nowadays, concrete is associated with the inability of modern Greeks to preserve local architectural styles, and it is considered ugly when compared to "more natural" building materials used in the past (stone, marble, etc.). It is interesting to note that the local stone used to build the theater is not valued either. Locals call it *tsini* and usually describe it as the worst stone, totally inappropriate for any use.

Furthermore, contrary to other regions of Epirus, such as Zagorochoria, a region that boasts its traditional architecture, the valley of Dodona lacks any distinguished architectural heritage. Cement is blamed for the loss of the assumed traditional architecture of the valley and consequently for the unattractiveness of modern Dodonochoria, the villages in Dodona valley. This sense of responsibility and the strong emotional implications of cement related to urban modernity provoked radical reactions against the team of archaeologists. In addition to all the negative connotations of the modern material and the irreversible aspect its use would create for the monument, a deeper fear of "desecrating" the site by permanently interfering with the "authentic" materiality of the monument reveals some religious connotations assigned to this heritage site and its surrounding "Sacred Valley," which coincide with other cases of archaeological sites in Greece, such as the "Sacred Rock" of the Acropolis in Athens (cf. Hamilakis and Yalouri 1999;

Fig. 6.3. "Respect the monument. No to its cementing." Dodona 2010. Courtesy of Newspaper *Ipirotikos Agon.*

Yalouri 2001; Caftanzoglou 2001). A similar and much-criticized case of cement usage on ancient remains is that of Sir Arthur Evans's reconstructions at Knossos on the island of Crete (Solomon 2007). Among other things, Evans's restoration work was criticized for the use of a material that first appeared in the early twentieth century, much later than the Bronze Age in Crete. Therefore, both locals and visitors argue that its use in an important archaeological site is inappropriate or even immoral (Solomon 2007, 71).

Some inhabitants ridicule the restoration methods and the way these are applied to the theater. Drawing from the fact that building with cement is an easier and much faster construction method than building with stone, modern Dodoneans often comment that they would have built more than one stone theater at the same time it takes archaeologists to build a cement one. "I say that if only we could take control of this project, in two or three years we would have it complete. They put five stones yearly to spend the money. . . . If we had the stones, I would start with ten men. How many stones are missing? Here there are mountains of stones, ready [for use]."[7] What seems to them as an extraordinary slow and sometimes even intentionally delayed procedure is aggravated by the use of a heavily contested building material—concrete. The inhabitants' impatience with an intact ancient theater is attributed to their ambition to finally be able to make a profit out of a functioning theater.

As the advisory board of the Ministry of Culture, CAC was responsible for the examination and evaluation of the theater's restoration methods. According to the ministry's bureaucracy, the administrative procedure was called *aftopsia* (autopsy), a word that refers to both the assessment of something past or the inspection of a dead body (i.e., an act of seeing with one's own eyes). In fact, autopsy is an on-site inspection. In 1999, CAC imposed the prohibition of use of the ancient theater as the director of the Ephorate of Prehistoric and Classical Antiquities had requested. The initial disappointment regarding the end of the festival turned into public anger and became a source of several incidents of tension between citizens and archaeologists. To appease public clamor, the ephorate inclined toward negotiation and succumbed to the construction of a temporary prefabricated theater structure within the archaeological site. This futile attempt to replace the "real" experience and the "authentic" ancient theater with a prefabricated structure was succeeded by the decision to host plays, concerts, and public events inside the ancient stadium, which is adjacent to the theater. Some events are also hosted within the stage of the ancient theater, yet the audience is not allowed to step on the section of the audience seating. Attended by small audiences, these events are generally regarded as very disappointing in comparison to those held at the archaeological site during the Festivals of Dodona; the events of the last decade have lost much of their original splendor.

Yet there was an occasion for which the reopening of the theater and the reception of a huge audience in its seating section was an essential requisite for the confirmation that ancient Dodona holds a special position on the national map. In 2004, when Greece was about to host the Olympic Games and the journey of the Olympic flame around the country was planned, Dodona was excluded from the tour. It was only after the intervention of the municipality and other local authorities—declaring that the oracle and its theater were among the most important monuments and sites of Greece—that the plan changed. In spite of the different opinion of the local ephorate that was persistently put forward in several documents exchanged between the institutions involved (the Ministry of Tourism, the municipality, and the local ephorate), the Olympic torch relay finally passed through the ancient theater of Dodona, thus restoring the monument's nationally respected position. In one of these documents sent by the Municipality of Dodona to the ephorate, we read, "Having Olympic Games in our country will be the greatest and most historical event, thus Dodona this summer will take the position that she deserves in the world cultural setting."[8] When the torch relay ended, Dodona returned to its ordinary life, dominated by the claim for an operating theater and the expectations for the revival of the monuments' glorious days that should echo ancient values and achievements.[9]

Dodona's Landscape Heard

Stretching throughout Northern Greece, the long-awaited Egnatia highway has triggered public hope for development and economic growth both on the national and local level. Its route and the location of intersections, tolls, bridges, and tunnels have been under negotiation between local communities on the one side and the state and the construction company on the other. For Epirus, the new road promised a road of "European standards" that would finally connect this remote area of Greece with at least Thessaloniki, the second largest city in the country. The new road that was named after the Roman Via Egnatia neither serves the same uses nor runs through the same route. In the case of Epirus, Roman Via Egnatia ran through Southern Albania to Durres. Present-day geopolitical agents redirected the route of modern Egnatia through Greece. Despite the difficulties encountered in dealing with the geomorphology of the region (the new road had to vertically intersect mountains of the Pindus range) and the serious geological issues concerning the unstable landforms, the Egnatia highway primarily served the purpose of connecting industrial centers and markets of the East and the West.

A debate about Egnatia traversing the valley of Dodona erupted with concerns about the future of antiquities, the environment, and the effects such a construction would have on the everyday lives of the inhabitants around the valley. In reaction to the initial plans for the highway, a society called Friends of Dodona (FoD) was formed with the aim of putting pressure on the authorities to redirect Egnatia. As a collective effort, FoD was a platform that did not overlook the environmental impact, but it was mainly concerned with the future of the antiquities of Dodona. Though its membership was never impressive, the collectivity enjoyed the support of locals, journalists, and politicians; their campaign captured the attention of several intellectuals from abroad and various groups within the country, and the issue was constantly mentioned in national and local newspapers. "I don't know whether the Minister of Environment, Laliotis, and the Minister of Culture, Mikroutsikos, were lucky enough to visit Dodona on a pilgrimage. If they haven't, it's better not to—in case they continue their profane vandalism. The Dodonean Zeus will unleash his thunderbolts right on their heads," wrote Giorgos Votsis in *Eleftherotipia*, a widely circulated national newspaper (Votsis 1995). Dodona was once again under the threat of being "vandalized" by the ignorant state. The FoD, along with various supporting local forces, envisaged a sole, idealized, and nostalgic version of the past, represented through the landscape. The oracle of Dodona and the theater alongside its image of practiced pastoralism and the surrounding wild nature are still the important features for which the Dodonean landscape is appreciated. This unique image contrasted with the assumed homogenized form of urban landscapes, and therefore its uniqueness should be protected.

In addition, the considerable opposition to the construction of Egnatia near the site made the significance of another cultural element of the Dodonean landscape evident (Papadimitriou 1997). Years of appropriation of the archaeological narrative that accentuated the "oracular" properties of the land and the trees have compelled public attention to the sounds of the valley. More than the visual significance of the scenic beauty of Dodona, the fear of noise pollution became a key issue in the way the landscape should be managed. Unlike other more environmentally oriented, collective efforts that consider noise pollution as a harmful agent in human and animal life, in the case of Dodona, it was the soundscape's sanctity and its associated feeling of "remoteness" (cf. Ardener 2012) that were in danger. Sounds of the valley as immaterial remained unaltered through time, unlike the material things that suffer the consequences of weather conditions or human interventions. Noise produced by Egnatia's traffic was associated with urban modernity and thus was thought of as a major disturbance for the natural soundscape, which itself is "sacred." Defined and identifiable sound features that compose the Dodonean soundscape—trees rustling, wind blowing, and water flowing—were to be preserved. In antiquity, these natural sounds were interpreted by the priests of the oracle (Katsadima 2008); today, they are proof of the archaeological narrative provided. The significance of sound for this narrative is also highlighted by the temporary exhibition that was hosted at the Acropolis Museum in Athens (June 2016–January 2017) and was entitled "Dodona: The Oracle of Sounds" (Eleftheratou and Sueref 2016). At last, the sacredness of the Dodonean soundscape acquired its long-desired position in the national imagination by being represented in the museum of Greek sacred heritage par excellence, the Acropolis.

After several years of resisting Egnatia's initial plans, the efforts to preserve the soundscape of Dodona ended in success. The highway was redirected through a mountain, 2.5 kilometers away from the archaeological site. Such a distance ensured the calmness of the valley as well as easy access to the site. According to local residents, although easy access to the archaeological site had generated hopes for touristic development of the broader area, the new road proved to be a major gateway to the touristic attractions of Epirus but not to the Dodona valley.

Some Concluding Remarks

Dodona presents one more example of a heritage landscape to which several meanings have been assigned, disdaining the official archaeological interpretation. Its conception is rooted in diverse political, archaeological, and social discourses that often appear to be oppositional, whereas narratives about the place are produced by the interweaving of multiple factors: the human geography of Epirus, the people's understandings of the past and its heritage, and not least the professional archaeological discourses that are securely established through restoration projects, site management, and various exhibitions and publications. Archaeologists interpret not only architectural remains and movable finds but also the landscape in a way that places the antiquities at the heart of social contestation. In contrast, the Dodonean landscape is perceived by local people in terms of its relationship to the ancient oracle, the discovered archaeological finds, and their individual and collective memories of the place.

In particular, the ancient theater of Dodona—situated in a central position among the rest of the monuments—has been actively appropriated by the inhabitants of the Dodona valley through their participation in the monument's restoration, their attendance at performances, its value as a topographic landmark, and its various representations. The theater has come to symbolize some glorious days of Dodona that belong to a collective past yet not the ancient one. The interpretative representations of the ancient world through modern performances and its sceneries also favored one of the ancient uses of the structure and established a strong way to make sense of the antiquities or even to imagine antiquity. Each performance in the ancient theater was an act of creating monumental time that contributed to specific conceptualizations of the ancient past. Productions formed an exceptional heterotopia (Foucault 1986, 25) in which, throughout the duration of every performance, the ancient monument coexisted with the contemporary audience and a plethora of readings of ancient texts (Ioannidou 2011, 388). As both physical and mental space, combining the materiality of antiquities and the performativity of the plays, Dodona's theater matured as an "enacted utopia" (Foucault 1986, 24).

The annual festival of Dodona had been a regular occasion in which social and monumental time concurred (cf. Herzfeld 1991). Yet the closure of the theater in 1999 excluded once again social life from the monument, reestablished a different hierarchy, and produced a restricted and isolated space. This finite space also became that of a singular time, isolated from the normal quotidian temporality in order to protect the ancient remains from time's erosion.

Dodona's monumental landscape is being contested because it takes part in the construction of the place and the making of a local identity strongly linked to it. Similarly to many other cases of communities living adjacent to archaeological sites, Dodona's people challenge the official readings of the landscape and its management. Despite their physical exclusion from the site by the state archaeology through the establishment of protection zones and the definite enclosure of unearthed antiquities, modern Dodoneans perceive the landscape as an entity that extends far beyond the material place. In it, sound, as an immaterial feature of the landscape, unifies archaeological narratives as well as natural and human presence into a meaningful soundscape. Regardless of the contestations, this complicated entanglement between archaeology and society imparts powerful ways of making sense of the landscape but also of sensing it.

KATERINA KONSTANTINOU studied history and theory of art at the University of Ioannina and earned her MA in museology from the same university. She has worked for archaeological and art museums in Greece and Turkey and has been involved in research and community programs on heritage ethnography, digital applications in archaeological museum exhibitions, contemporary art, and community memory projects. Currently, she is pursuing a PhD in Social Anthropology at the Panteion University of Social and Political Sciences.

Notes

1. This chapter is mainly based on fieldwork in the Dodona valley and the archival research that I conducted at the administrative archives of the Ephorate of Antiquities in Ioannina in 2015 as part of my MA thesis (University of Ioannina, School of Fine Arts). Many thanks go to the head of the Ephorate of Antiquities of Ioannina Dr. Konstantinos Sueref and the archaeologists of the ephorate, especially Dr. Ioulia Katsadima and Dr. Christos Klitsas, for their help during my research. I owe much of this work to Esther Solomon for her inspiring teaching and her motivating supervision of my thesis.

2. For instance, Evaggelidis draws from Sarakatsanoi, a distinct nomadic population of shepherds centered in Epirus, and their seasonal movement to justify the validity of Herodotus's accounts on ancient Epirote tribes (1962, 40).

3. Homer, *The Iliad*, Book 16, Line 200. Accessed June 5, 2016. http://www.perseus.tufts.edu/hopper/text?doc=Hom. Il. 16.233&lang=original.

4. Ioannina Ephorate of Antiquities Archive, document no. 1544 [08-10-1975], "Information about the Exchangeable Property in Dodona" [Στοιχεία περί ανταλλαξίμου ακινήτου εν Δωδώνη].

5. A report signed four days later (August 14, 1974) by the director of the Ephorate of Antiquities called on the Ministry of Culture to declare that "issues of reconstruction, restoration and setting of antiquities are not to be decided by acclamation or voting" (Ioannina Ephorate of Antiquities Archive, Document no. 1273 [14-08-1974], "About the Incident That Happened during the Festivals of Dodona" [Περί γενομένου επεισοδίου κατά τα Δωδωναία]).

6. In the same report (document of the administrative archive of the Ephorate of Antiquities in Ioannina), we read that Frontzos "appealed to the audience to ask for . . . the elimination of the evidence of the Roman conquest, like what had happened again with the minaret on the Parthenon" (Ioannina Ephorate of Antiquities Archive, Document no. 1273 [14-08-1974]).

7. Nikos Gousias, interview by the author, May 14, 2015.

8. Ioannina Ephorate of Antiquities Archive, document no. 186 [09-04-2004] signed by Dimitrios Themelis, Mayor of Dodona Municipality "Granting Permission for Using the

Ancient Theater of Dodona for the Olympic Torch Relay" [Παραχώρηση Αρχαίου Θεάτρου για την τελετή αφής της Ολυμπιακής Φλόγας].

9. As restoration works had reached an advanced stage, in 2017 the Municipality of Dodona and the Regional Authorities of Epirus announced the beginning of the new annual Festival of Dodona, during which a limited number of theater plays and cultural events took place in front of different monuments of the archaeological site. On "the return of Dodona" to the cultural scene, see Karamitsos 2019.

References

Acosta-Hughes, Benjamin, and Susan A. Stephens. 2012. *Callimachus in Context: From Plato to the Augustan Poets.* Cambridge: Cambridge University Press.

Ardener, Edwin. 2012. "'Remote Areas.' Some Theoretical Considerations." *HAU: Journal of Ethnographic Theory* 2 (1): 519–33.

Anderson, Benedict. 2006. *Imagined Communities: Reflections on the Origin and Spread of Nationalism.* Rev. ed. Edinburgh: Verso.

Antoniou, Konstantinos. 1973. *Τα Δωδωνοχώρια: Ιστοριολαογραφικά* [The Dodonochoria: Historical-Folkloric Perspectives]. Ioannina: Spiritual Movement "Ancient Dodona."

Atkinson, John Andrew, Iain Banks, and Jerry O'Sullivan, eds. 1996. *Nationalism and Archaeology: Scottish Archaeological Forum.* Glasgow: Cruithne.

Bender, Barbara. 2002. "Time and Landscape." *Current Anthropology* 43 (S4): 103–12.

Bourdieu, Pierre. 1984. *Distinction: A Social Critique of the Judgment of Taste.* Cambridge, MA: Harvard University Press.

Caftanzoglou, Roxani. 2001. *Στη Σκιά του Ιερού Βράχου. Τόπος και Μνήμη στα Αναφιώτικα* [In the Shadow of the Sacred Rock: Place and Memory in Anafiotika]. Athens: Greek National Center for Social Research.

Carapanos, Constantin. 1878. *Dodone et ses Ruines.* Paris: Hachette.

Crary, Jonathan. 2001. *Suspensions of Perception: Attention, Spectacle, and Modern Culture.* Cambridge, MA: MIT Press. Accessed July 24, 2019. https://mitpress.mit.edu/books/suspensions-perception.

Dakaris, Sotiris. 1964. *Οι Γενεολογικοί Μύθοι των Μολοσσών* [Genealogical Myths of the Molossians]. Athens: Library of the Athens Archaeological Society.

Davis, Jack L. 2000. "Warriors for the Fatherland: National Consciousness and Archaeology in 'Barbarian' Epirus and 'Verdant' Ionia. 1912–1922." *Journal of Mediterranean Archaeology* 13 (1): 76–98.

Eleftheratou, Stamatia, and Konstantinos Sueref. 2016. *Δωδώνη: Το Μαντείο των Ήχων* [Dodona: The Oracle of Sounds]. Athens: Acropolis Museum.

Evaggelidis, Dimitris. 1962. *Οι Αρχαίοι Κάτοικοι της Ηπείρου* [The Ancient Inhabitants of Epirus]. Ioannina: Society of Epirote Studies.

Evaggelidis, Dimitris, and Sotiris Dakaris. 1959. "Το Ιερόν της Δωδώνης. Α': Ιερά Οικία" [The Sanctuary of Dodona: The Sacred House]. *Arheologiki Efimeris*, 1–194.

Foucault, Michel. 1986. "Of Other Spaces." *Diacritics* 16 (1): 22–27.

Frontzos, Kostantinos. 1962. "Μετά από 2000 Χρόνια Είδε Ξανά η Δωδώνη την Πρώτη Σύναξη των Προσκυνητών της" [After 2000 Years Dodona Again Saw the Gathering of Its Pilgrims]. In *Δωδώνη* [Dodona] theater program. Ioannina: Society of Epirote Studies.

Green, Sarah. 2005. *Notes from the Balkans: Locating Marginality and Ambiguity on the Greek-Albanian Border.* Princeton, NJ: Princeton University Press.

Hamilakis, Yannis. 2007. *The Nation and Its Ruins: Antiquity, Archaeology, and National Imagination in Greece.* Oxford: Oxford University Press.

———. 1999. "Sacralizing the Past: Cults of Archaeology in Modern Greece." *Archaeological Dialogues* 6 (2): 115–35.

Herzfeld, Michael. 1982. *Ours Once More: Folklore, Ideology and the Making of Modern Greece.* Austin: University of Texas Press.

———. 1987. *Anthropology through the Looking-Glass: Critical Ethnography in the Margins of Europe.* Cambridge: Cambridge University Press.

———. 1991. *A Place in History: Social and Monumental Time in a Cretan Town.* Princeton, NJ: Princeton University Press.

Hobsbawm, Eric, and Terence O. Ranger. 1992. *The Invention of Tradition.* Cambridge: Cambridge University Press.

Ioannidou, Eleftheria. 2011. "Toward a National Heterotopia: Ancient Theaters and the Cultural Politics of Performing Ancient Drama in Modern Greece." *Comparative Drama* 45 (1): 385–403.

Karamitsos, Filimon. 2019. "Η Επιστροφή της Δωδώνης" [The Return of Dodona]. *Efsyn, Efimerida ton Sintakton*, September 17, 2019. Accessed July 7, 2020. https://www.efsyn.gr/ellada/koinonia/211082_i-epistrofi-tis-dodonis.

Katsadima, Ioulia. 2008. "Τρόποι Μαντείας" [Ways of Divination]. In *Το Αρχαιολογικό Μουσείο Ιωαννίνων* [The Archaeological Museum of Ioannina], edited by Konstantinos Zachos, 160–70. Ioannina: Archaeological Museum of Ioannina.

Katsoudas, Petros. 2014. "Τεκμηρίωση Αρχιτεκτονικών και Γεωμετρικών Στοιχείων του Θεάτρου της Δωδώνης με την Χρήση Νέων Τεχνολογιών" [Documentation of Architectural and Geometrical Elements of the Theater of Dodona Using New Technologies]. In *Δωδώνη Διαχρονική: Παρελθόν, Παρόν και Μέλλον του Αρχαίου Θεάτρου και του Αρχαιολογικού Χώρου* [Timeless Dodona: Past, Present and Future of the Ancient Theater and the Archaeological Site], edited by Konstantinos Sueref, 87–91. Ioannina: Cultural Center of Dodona, 12th Ephorate of Prehistoric and Classical Antiquities.

Kohl, Philip L., and Clare Fawcett. 1995. *Nationalism, Politics and the Practice of Archaeology.* Cambridge: Cambridge University Press.

Kokkinidou, Dimitra, and Marianna Nikolaidou. 2004. "On the Stage and behind the Scenes: Greek Archaeology in Times of Dictatorship." In *Archaeology under Dictatorship*, edited by M. L. Galaty and C. Watkinson, 155–90. New York: Kluwer Academic.

Lalioti, Vassiliki. 2001. "Social Memory and Ethnic Identity: Ancient Greek Drama Performances as Commemorative Ceremonies." PhD diss., Durham University. Accessed: July 24, 2019. http://etheses.dur.ac.uk/3850.

Papadimitriou, Yannis. 1997. "Τα Διδάγματα της Μάχης της Δωδώνης" [Lessons Learned from the Battle of Dodona]. *Dodoneon Kinon*, Ioannina (n.p.).

Piccinini, Jessica. 2013. "Dodona at the Time of Augustus: A Few Notes." In *Roman Power and Greek Sanctuaries. Forms of Interaction and Communication*, edited by Marco Galli, 177–92. Athens: Scuola Archeologica Italiana di Atene.

Proskynitopoulou, Roza. 2009. "Bronze Collection: National Archaeological Museum." Athens: Archaeological Receipts Fund.

Sjöberg, Erik. 2011. "Battlefields of Memory: The Macedonian Conflict and Greek Historical Culture." PhD. diss., Umeå University.

SES (Society of Epirote Studies). 1989. *Ήπειρος, Ιστορική Παράδοση και Δημιουργική Συνέχεια: Η Εταιρεία Ηπειρωτικών Μελετών και ο Θεμελιωτής της Κ. Φρόντζος* [Epirus, Historical Tradition and Creative Continuation: The Society of Epirote Studies and Its Founder K. Frontzos]. Ioannina: Society of Epirote Studies.

Smyris, Georgios. 2014. "The Theater of Dodona. Reflections" [Το Θέατρο της Δωδώνης. Προβληματισμοί]. In *Δωδώνη Διαχρονική: Παρελθόν, Παρόν και Μέλλον του Αρχαίου Θεάτρου και του Αρχαιολογικού Χώρου* [Timeless Dodona: Past, Present and Future of the Ancient Theater and the Archaeological Site], edited by Konstantinos Sueref, 81–86. Ioannina: Cultural Center of Dodona, 12th Ephorate of Prehistoric and Classical Antiquities.

Solomon, Esther. 2007. "'Multiple Historicities' on the Island of Crete: The Significance of Minoan Archaeological Heritage in Everyday Life." PhD diss., University College London.

Sueref, Konstantinos. 2013. *Σωτήρης Δάκαρης: Ο Αρχαιολόγος της Ηπείρου* [Sotiris Dakaris: The Archaeologist of Epirus]. Ioannina: 12th Ephorate of Prehistoric and Classical Antiquities.

Vasileiou, Eleni. 2014. "Ethics in Action at the Refurbished Archaeological Museum of Ioannina, Epirus, Greece." *Journal of Conservation and Museum Studies* 12 (1): 3. Accessed July 24, 2019. https://doi:10.5334/jcms.1021212.

Vavouskos, Konstantinos. 1993. "Η Εταιρεία Μακεδονικών Σπουδών (1939–1980)" [The Society for Macedonian Studies (1939–1980]. *Society for Macedonian Studies Annales*. Thessaloniki.

Vokotopoulou, Ioulia. 1986. *Βίτσα: Τα Νεκροταφεία μιας Μολοσσικής Κώμης* [Vitsa: Cemeteries of a Molossian Town]. Athens: Hellenic Ministry of Culture.

Votsis, Giorgos. 1995. "Κάτω τα Χέρια, ω Νεοβάνδαλοι από τη Δωδώνη" [Neo-Vandals, Keep Your Hands off Dodona]. *Eleftherotipia*, May 29, 1995.

Yalouri, Eleana. 2001. *The Acropolis: Global Fame, Local Claim*. New York: Berg.

7 Archaeological "Protection Zones" and the Limits of the Possible

Archaeological Law, Abandonment, and Contested Spaces in Greece

Aris Anagnostopoulos

It took this anthropologist a considerable amount of time to begin ethnographically unpacking what he at first thought was a banal conversation opener. While doing archaeological ethnography at or near sites with material remains of the past (Hamilakis and Anagnostopoulos 2009), I was often greeted with something similar to, "Ah, you are an archaeologist. This place, you know, is rich with antiquities. Every stone you turn, there is something underneath. Greece is like that, full of antiquities." I must have heard this common adage so often that I never stopped to examine it as a meaningful statement. To me, schooled as I am in the deconstruction of the national territorial state and its semantic anchoring to the glories of ancient Greece (e.g., Hamilakis 2007; Leontis 1995; Gourgouris 1996), this was just a parroting of a common stereotype. It was "empty speech," talk that was imbued with imaginary significance, but not much sense (Lacan 2007, 211). Nobody could deny that this phrase, devoid of significant content, was offered to me, a white, educated, upper-middle-class male, as a bounty, a placating gift from subaltern natives to colonizer intellectuals.

This sweeping statement on the archaeological fertility of the Greek territory loses its semantic punch without its companion adage, which comes as a complaint about the powers that be: "Alas, while Greece is full of these marvelous hidden antiquities, they do not do anything about it." *They*—the state, politicians, and archaeology officials—leave these marvels unexplored, unexploited, and out of reach. I first explored the content and ramifications of these contrapuntal ideas in fieldwork with Prof. Yannis Hamilakis on the island of Poros. The expected accusations of corruption of state archaeology were, in this context, coupled with a simultaneous affirmation of the richness of the Argolis soil in antiquities and its outright denial (Hamilakis and Anagnostopoulos 2009; Anagnostopoulos 2014). We discovered back then that the imaginary richness of archaeological finds in the area becomes a shocking negation of palpable material remains when this richness is implicated in the administrative machinery of official archaeology, which then produces a ground of uncertainty in the inability (or unwillingness) of "all of them" to "make something" of these mythical riches. At first, I thought we could approach this statement as a concession of the dominated (our interlocutors) to the powers beyond their reach ("them") that put in effect their cultural and economic domination (Herzfeld 1997, 157). This fuzzy, undifferentiated "them" surely pointed to the inability of our interlocutors to identify and comprehensively chart the power networks that control aspects of their everyday lives and the spaces they inhabit.

While conversing with a younger British prehistoric archaeologist working with Minoan peak sanctuaries in Crete, I extracted a different version of this statement, albeit in the same vein. The argument was whether the gorge between two peak sanctuaries in the area of Malevizi, central Crete, where we were working as part of the Three Peak Sanctuaries of Central Crete archaeological project, was archaeologically protected land. Her pronouncement was literal and startling: "The whole of Crete is an archaeological protection zone." As will be discussed later, archaeological protection zones are the main instruments in the legal arsenal of the Greek Archaeological Service, aimed at protecting the remains of the ancient past. They are areas where ordinary activity is suspended and a special set of rules applies. What is remarkable in this respect is the visualization, shared by local populations and expert archaeologists alike, of an archaeologically rich territory under the control of the state in its entirety. Furthermore, it is a territory where the discretion of the state is exercised as to where its power is applied, depending on resources and personnel, or even according to the whim of the officials.

As I shall show in what follows, this statement is an adroit diagnosis of the conundrum plaguing the realization of sovereign power in the creation of national and local landscapes. Such pronouncements identify sovereign power as a reign that is never complete (Prakash 1992, 176). They thus restate the territory of the law that is a total, enclosed, monolithic territory as a shifting, incomplete, contested landscape that is still in the process of making. We should look at such pronouncements not as parts of a cosmologically closed binary power relationship, in which "they" (local people, anonymous interlocutors, on-the-ground communities) are represented as a compact and homogeneous subject in the face of "them" (the powers that be). Conversely, we should approach them as ontologically different worldviews that reveal that the vision of wholeness, completeness and totality is indeed the ideological instrument of domination, which works by vectoring disparate desires into an organized whole. Indeed, these pronouncements act in revealing the secret of (archaeological) law, which, as Nuitjen and Anders argue, is that "the possibility of its transgression or perversion is always already inscribed into the law as hidden possibility" (2007, 12). Such approaches insist on bringing back a relational ontology, wherein all properties and identities are not prescribed or dictated by the unitary law of state but are in a process of constant formation in relational fields between themselves (Ingold 2006, 13–14).

By looking at such statements from this perspective, we cease talking of the exclusivity of the law and its nonconforming binary oppositions, following the lead that Michael Herzfeld set out to trace by introducing the concept of cultural intimacy (Herzfeld 1997) to account for the multiplicity of perspectives within seemingly very rigid frameworks. Accordingly, we begin to see a plural legal landscape in transformation that incorporates many different normative orders, with different degrees of relevance and interconnection between them. However, in this animated landscape, the ethnographic momentum is persistently pulled back to the totalizing apparatuses of law: despite their ontological difference, there remains in these pronouncements the desire to totalize, to go to the logical limits of the law as an organizing categorical imperative. If there are many normative orders functioning at the same landscape, then why the persistent desire for a single normative order to prevail? Is this another manifestation of the ambivalence of the colonial object as a site that hosts an "articulation of difference contained within the fantasy of origin and identity" (Bhabha 2004, 69)?

A tentative answer that this chapter aims to make is that both the vicissitudes of desire as organized by technologies of power and their complication by differential ontologies are curtailed by a horizon of the possible; it is something that forms the potential line of flight that organizes desire yet is perpetually unattainable, always receding. This receding time of fulfillment points with certainty to the conundrum presented by the agency of the inanimate (in this case, material remains of the ancient past) in the constitution of the human (cf. Holbraad 2009). During fieldwork in Poros in 2009, I spoke with a middle-aged lady who reiterated the common adage of the richness of Greek soil in antiquities. When I inquired what exactly the state was supposed to do with the antiquities, she replied, as if caught in a reverie, "Wouldn't it be great if all of Greece was turned into a museum?" The stark irrationality of the proposition hit me simultaneously with its inescapable logic: although it would be impossible to live in a museum, the logical limit of the preservation discourses of the Greek state and the Greek public lies exactly there. If indeed the entirety of the territory formed part of ancient Greece, then ideally it should all be preserved for prosperity (cf. Voudouri 2010, 553). At the same time, it becomes plainly obvious in this statement that the desire of the law as discourse becomes an impossibility in the real. It is impossible not only because the legal apparatuses of the state are lacking in regard to the application of the law but also because the spaces created by a total application of the rationale of the law would be unlivable spaces.

However much this irrationality seems like an unrealizable potential at the heart of the national discourses dictating the rationale of archaeological law in

Greece, it is inextricably bound with social processes of abandonment in function in modernity. The archaeological law, because of its affinity with what is most sacred in the national state, is seen as the law par excellence. Its relationship with seemingly abandoned places is a demonstration of the failure of the state to fulfill its promise of development and modernity. The ethnographic examples discussed below, from Poros in Argolis and Gonies in Crete, show how social pressures causing abandonment are inextricably linked with the enforcement of the law. The approaches are different, but the idea remains the same: state archaeology is demonstrative of the responsibility of the state for the decline of rural places in Greece.

Jacques Derrida points to the *potentias* (the enforcive aspect of power in Spinozean terms) that is incorporated into Western cultural understandings of the law, as demonstrated in the phrase "to enforce the law" or "the enforceability of the law" (Derrida 2002, 231). Derrida wants to bring out the element of socially "allowed" violence that is inherent in every law, which is a self-justifying power and a quality apart from social understandings of whether or not a law is just. It is to this possibility, in the sense of making real, of enforcing archaeological law onto landscapes, that this chapter turns to. It approaches plural legal landscapes in which the law itself is judged as just or unjust by a variety of groups and individuals.

The paradox that emerges in the cases examined here is that archaeological protection areas are places where the law of the state exercises its power in an absolute way, but at the same time they are spaces where the law is evidently absent. The power of the state can enforce the movement of populations and the appropriation of land. Such was the centrality of archaeology in the constitution of the national state that there was no need to legally justify the causus of expropriation. For decades, until the passage of the 1990 archaeological law[1] that legally defined the concept of zones, protection areas and expropriations were exercised in a legal vacuum by employing urban planning laws that had nothing to do with archaeological finds.[2] Typically, state power attempts to disguise the fact that it is an ad hoc technology of rule that creates legislation by ensuring its applicability as it proceeds.

In practice, this lack of clarity results in protracted legal disputes and situations where lands and properties that have officially been appropriated by the state for archaeological reasons are caught in a legal gray zone while the state and its owners fight the case out in courts or negotiate the appropriation (e.g., Herzfeld 1991, 14). This process may result in lived spaces that have an indistinct horizon of possibility: everyday use can, at an unspecified time, be interrupted by putting legal sanctions into effect (Caftanzoglou 2001, 155–82). If we compare the letter of the law to the way it is enforced on the ground, the resulting picture is a "zone of indistinction," a point "where techniques of individualization and totalizing procedures converge" (Agamben 1998, 11).

I would like to introduce a qualifier here that sets my position apart from that of Derrida's: the secret of the state in this case is that, although it reserves the absolute power to carve out spaces within the territory as exclusively archaeological spaces, it will never attempt to carve out the entirety of the territory for this purpose. The law has a totalizing logic, but it will never reach its full application and its logical end. This "but not" of the law is the reason why it creates such uncertain spaces.

The order of these spaces becomes a heterotopia in the theoretical reconsideration of the relationship between nation and territory. Several authors have used the term *heterotopia* to indicate the special status that Greece has held with Western travelers since the nineteenth century. It is used to indicate the "pure difference," in Foucault's terms, that these spaces demonstrated in comparison with the lands from where philhellenes and the educated public originated. Artemis Leontis takes this further by proposing that the representations of Western Hellenism were unable to be contained in the actual landscapes of modern Greece and therefore produced these spaces as cultural capital for the state and contested places for locals (Leontis 1995, 41–67). In typical colonial fashion, foreign philhellenes disregarded the contemporary residents of the place in order to insert it into the topographies of a timeless and universal vision of ancient Greece. This reading of heterotopias places more emphasis on the radical alterity of such spaces in terms of the interiority of the law, or the cultural constitution of Hellenism as a discourse uncontainable in the topos of the Greek national state (see also Hamilakis 2007, 17). It is in tune with more novel uses of the term *heterotopias* that take it to mean "spaces of an alternative social ordering" (Hetherington 1997, 40). In the cases described later, this ordering may well reflect the fact that, when the law is taken to the letter, the spaces that result severely constrict everyday life for the people living there. Archaeological zones, in their legal definition, are spaces of absolute alterity when compared to the lived spaces of the national sovereign state.

That the national territory is imagined as a space totally covered in ancient artifacts shows the close connection of this spatial metaphor of legal power to a temporal-utopian ideology: the heterotopias of the nation are still "other" spaces because the nation has not yet reached the status of heterotopia in its entirety. This utopian project is central in Foucault's definition of heterotopias but has not been sufficiently highlighted, especially in its application to the Greek case. This fact could be said to reflect a broader aporia in the social sciences on how to approach the relations between real and imaginary spaces (Lefevbre 1991, 33). In this text, I offer an ethnographic examination of the technologies through which the utopic content of the national imaginary is applied on the ground through archaeological legislation of spaces. This approach shifts the emphasis to an examination of archaeological heterotopias as sedimented products of failed utopian drives inherent in state-building processes (Scott 1998). In other words, heterotopias are not these "other" imaginary spaces that ensure the compactness of the national territory but products of the everyday contention of space through apparatuses of power. This view may provide a provisional answer to the question of the power of the law in shaping and directing desire, in that its inherent impulse is not a heterotopic one but a utopian one. The exceptions through which this law seems to function, and which seemingly produce fundamental conundrums in its foundation on a sense of right, are but emerging qualities of its constant failures in its project to totalize (Habermas 1983). We could therefore look back at the law as an effort to effect unity and order, and at pronouncements on the ground as constant attempts to resocialize this simulacrum of order.

The Sociability of Corruption

During dinner on a typically humid July night in 2009 in the city of Poros, we were facing the coast of Argolid and discussing the vicissitudes of archaeological law with our host, a local politician whose father was an amateur archaeologist. Our conversation was overheard by a local sitting at the next table with his wife. He demonstrated with frantic gestures his plea: "This," he said, pointing to the table at which they were sitting, "is a protection zone." He then pointed beyond the low wall flanking the terrace of the small restaurant. "While that is not?"

His wild gesticulations were pointing toward the city of Poros, which is a protected "traditional" town. It is a small town on the westernmost part of Sfairia, the smaller of the two adjoined islets, Sfairia and Kalaureia, that form the island of Poros, which was itself known as Kalaureia in the past. The city looks across the narrow channel (that divides the island from the coast of Argolis) to the agricultural area of Trizinia and the town of Galatas. The rising mountainside on the Trizinia coast and the mountainous backdrop of the island itself, replete in pine forests, form a sense of a closed, protected space, swept by light sea breezes and the smell of pines and citrus tree orchards. The promontory itself is one of the best natural harbors in the Mediterranean. The eclectic architecture and the cosmopolitan aura, combined with its geographic location, have made the city the preferred destination for discerning tourists throughout the twentieth century and to this day. Some of its visitors were highly distinguished artists, writers, poets, or actors, a fact that adds to the symbolic allure of the place and its international fame. The reality of Poros, however, is much more pedestrian, with recent touristic developments overtaking its beautiful beaches and overcrowding slowly contributing to the pollution of its famed waters. Most of its active population is dependent on seasonal tourism, with its ebbs and flows, and has completely abandoned more traditional occupations. The only estimable force competing with this sort of touristic development is the Archaeological Service, which has prevented building in several areas of the island and has put severe limitations on property development.

Fig. 7.1. The island of Poros and the Saronic Gulf. Map by Aris Anagnostopoulos.

When we began our ethnographic research as part of the archaeological team excavating the sanctuary of Poseidon in Kalaureia, the grudges of ordinary Poriotes against the Archaeological Service were many and profound.[3] Although the recognition that the ancient Greek past is of paramount importance to their identity, which amounts to a recognition of this past as common property (our past, our history), the practical aspects of state intervention and regulation were considered severe, unfair, and extremely biased. The area of Poros and Trizina (ancient Troezen) is rich in archaeological findings and is amply documented in historical sources. The Archaeological Service is busy protecting evidence that continuously surfaces in new development projects and agricultural work. At the same time, it is too understaffed to be able to care for the preservation of the existing sites that are perceived locally to be abandoned to the elements by the official state. Such is the reaction to this combination of heavy-handedness and insouciance that some locals come to deny the existence of antiquities of any importance in their area altogether: when we first set foot on the island, the common reaction to our announcing that we are working on the sanctuary of Poseidon was that we must be naïve to spend our time and resources because there is nothing there but stones (Hamilakis and Anagnostopoulos 2009).

It turned out that our interlocutor was not talking specifically about the town of Poros. Through the intervention of the local politician, we understood that he is the owner of a house in Foussa, the cultivable plateau immediately below the ancient sanctuary of Poseidon, which straddles the saddle between the two tallest peaks of Sfairia, the largest island of Poros. The sanctuary, excavated for the first time by two Swedish archaeologists in 1894–95, was at the time being excavated by our team, a largely Scandinavian research group. The first two excavation seasons back in the nineteenth century yielded only the foundations of large buildings and the remains of the temple of Poseidon, but they were not fruitful in terms of the archaeological fashion of the day, so the two excavators, Kjellberg and Wide, abandoned it for richer pastures (Wells 2002). However, the presence of this important sanctuary led the Greek state to declare the area around it a "zone of absolute protection."[4]

The Social History of Abandonment and Archaeological Protection Zones

Zones of absolute protection are spaces demarcated by the law in which several activities are prohibited. Any form of upsetting the land, such as digging or tilling, is out of the question for obvious reasons: any digging would potentially expose sensitive archaeological evidence or upset the stratigraphy of the earth, therefore making dating impossible or inaccurate. Implications of looting are rife: digging to plant or cultivate is equal to digging out ancient artifacts. Less obtrusive activities are also prohibited, such as watering existing plants and trees. The absurdity of this detail made one local quip, "Why are we prohibited from watering our trees? Will the statues catch pneumonia?" Houses that had the bad luck to be caught within the absolute protection zone have to face unexpected troubles to complete their everyday chores. For example, some of them do not have running water because the water company cannot lay pipes; that would involve digging in the earth. Electricity was also sparse until recently because the wire-carrying poles that have to be erected would again upset the soil, and also because the legal limitations would prevent these houses from getting an electrical connection anyway.

Protection zones fan out of the protected area in concentric circles (Voudouri 2010, 554). The inner circle is the absolute protection zone, where all the prohibitions apply. Immediately outside it lays Zone B, where the restrictions are somewhat more lax. What is significant in this case is that the legal apparatus of the "protection zone" existed well before it was legislated as such by Law 1892 in 1990. It was a procedure enforced by the state based on a conglomeration of other laws and causing a number of issues and protracted legal battles on the way.

One would expect that these spaces, demarcated by the Greek law, would be spaces where things were clear, and the state would be present in its power. The importance that the Greek state attributes to the remains of the ancient Greek past is tremendous. They constitute the material foundations and proofs for the existence of the Greek nation throughout the centuries, and therefore they are the sine qua non of the very existence of the state. Standing walls, pillars, and movable finds are not only the purview of archaeological research but also semi-religious artifacts that augment their social importance for the state and its power with a symbolic content that is too potent to ignore. Surely, the sobriety with which the law treats these antiquities and the severity of punishment for illegally extracting them and exchanging them would be reflected in the management of the spaces in which these antiquities exist. The expectation of clear-cut legislation and clearly delineated spaces on the ground is evident in every discussion with locals. They expect the state to own up to the severity of its pronouncements.

The picture on the ground is loaded with contradictions. The spaces that exist as protection zones are not the clearly distinguished heterotopias that the legal documents purport. They are entangled and disputed spaces that reflect, as will be covered later, contradictions in the legal constitution of archaeological spaces. As already pointed out earlier, the use of the term is effective in portraying the radical difference envisioned for spaces where prominent remains of the ancient Greek past still exist, but it runs contrary to the common use of the term in the social sciences, whereby heterotopias are spaces of "ambiguous spatiality" that are associated with the rise of performative resistances rather than spaces created and controlled by panoptical technologies of governance (Hetherington 1997, 42).

Foucault emphasized the untidy juxtapositions of heterogeneous objects inside heterotopic spaces rather than their utopian (or dystopian) ordering. He called the combinations of objects within heterotopic spaces "monstrous" in their ability to unsettle profoundly the order of discourse (Foucault 1989, xvii). From an empirical point of view, this unsettling is a much more accurate description, which further hones the sharpness of existing analyses of the creation of ancient sites as heterotopic spaces in Greece. It is precisely the dissonance between imagined spaces, material remains, and contemporary populations that, when seen from outside, produces the difference of ancient Greece and its status as heterotopia. Without the contrast of existing populations, and without the sorry state of ancient remains that propose an ontological rift in the existence of the past, the ancient glory of Greece would simply be a common occurrence. We must therefore turn to the constitution of ancient spaces not as aberrant spaces but as conglomerates of different things—agents that together create dissonant effects. We can thus escape the usual binary thinking of the state versus the people and investigate resistances as spatial effects of material ordering.

By letting one's eyes wander around the sanctuary of Poseidon, one can spot a number of incongruities with the legal picture drawn so far. First of all, a fully functional tarmac road winds through the middle of what is today believed to be the extent of the ancient city of Kalaureia. It was created on the tracks of the old footpath connecting the town of Poros with the mountainous area of the island of Kalaureia, mostly used by shepherds and seasonal collectors of pine resin. The construction of this road required demolition of several rocks that were blocking the way, as well as the destruction of ancient remains on a large scale. According to the testimonies of elderly Poriotes who worked in construction, the road destroyed part of an aqueduct, which extended from the sanctuary toward the southeast of the island, and the monastery of Zoodohos Pigi, through an area today known as Kondita (Albanian for *conduit*). To my knowledge, there is no evidence in the archive of a systematic salvage excavation while this road was constructed. The road, a creation of the state, when juxtaposed with the adjacent remains of the ancient past, creates a difference that is so profound as to unsettle the image of the smooth functioning of the law.

A look in the archive testifies to the complex progress of getting a license out for the road. If the state seems monolithic in its imposition of heterotopic ordering for ancient sites, the real picture is much more nuanced and reflects a variety of historical processes and social relations in place. The persistent return of local theories of the state in this relational ontology as a source of the creation of archaeological landscapes is an indictment on the roots of state power. This power, it is stated, is not a direct emanation from the law but an effect of its practical application, which depends on custom, social relations, and technologies of power. It is a reinstatement of the state as specific reflections of class interests and group antagonisms through time, and thus it proves that what is possible for one state formation at a specific date is impossible for another at another time, despite the legal framework remaining the same and, technically, the state services performing the same tasks as always.

The Dual Function of the Law

The example of a dual legal operation that is thoroughly discussed by Niki Sakka (this volume) is illustrative in this respect: in the summer of 1930, the case of the export of Greek antiquities to Swedish universities was in full swing. Then Minister of Culture Georgios Papandreou received a memo from the director of the Department of Archaeology, Konstantinos Kourouniotis, who presented the complexities of the case. By all intents and purposes, it is a remarkable document in the history of Greek archaeology. In trying to explain why finds from the Asine excavations were transported to Sweden, Kourouniotis makes a distinction between the rule of law and the force of custom in the Archaeological Service and its relations to foreign archaeological schools in Greece. It is an established custom, he says, to give some doubles and pieces of no use to Greek museums to foreign excavators, as a gift for their pains and expenses. The archaeological law in function before 1932 (Law ΒΧΜΣΤ, 1899) explicitly established the full and exclusive state ownership of every ancient artifact discovered on its soil but did not regulate the exchange of "useless" antiquities. In order to execute the exchange, the ministry administration relied on an oblique legislative rationale: because the owners of property where excavations take place were rewarded with doubles and useless antiquities, the foreign excavators should be rewarded for their efforts with the same.[5]

This admission by a high-ranking ministry official is perhaps unique for the clarity with which the case is presented. Kourouniotis establishes a distinction between the letter of the law, which is sufficiently vague, and its enforcement. At the point of application of the law, a different cultural logic prevails, the customary ethos of the archaeological milieu in Athens of the time, an assortment of high-ranking academics, foreign diplomats and princes, political personalities, state executives, and private investors. This different cultural logic rests on a series of interrelated notions for its function. First, the notion of the ambiguity of the law itself; second, the notion of power in the application of the law; and third, the legislative operation that is summoned to give the function of power a legal appearance. It is a law borrowed by a different legal corpus and mustered to fill the legal void. This cultural logic also has a number of presuppositions: the primacy of archaeological evidence as things of the nation-state—that is, as things safeguarding the sanctity of the nation and ensuring its link to reality—as well as the ability of the state to act on its own accord as a safeguard of these antiquities but also as the ultimate arbitrator of their value.

When we closely examine the legal history of archaeological legislation in Greece, we see that it had been a patchwork of different legislations from its inception in the middle of the nineteenth century (Petrakos 1982). Different laws, reflecting different rationales and usually emulated from foreign legislatures, were collated with the explicit aim of serving the protection of the material remains of the past and safeguarding their importance as guarantors of national consciousness (Voudouri 2010, 549). Such legislations, as with every state action, is not an action in a vacuum but one heavily influenced by political and social pressures of the day. Diplomatic relations reflecting real political forces were instrumental in shaping the legislation regarding the export of antiquities, and as we see from the example of the Asine antiquities (Sakka, this volume), these relations also weighed heavily in the application of the law decades after it was put into practice. Similarly, state laws became stricter by the end of the nineteenth century with regard to private ownership of antiquities, but they still legislated with exceptions to accommodate powerful individuals who owned important collections (Hamilakis 2007, 54; Voudouri 2010, 550).

What is remarkable about archaeological law in Greece in this respect is that it is a body of legislation called to define and protect what is at the heart of the nation, the remains of the ancient past, and the monuments of ancient Greek civilization (Hamilakis 2007, 52; see Petrakos 2013 for an overview). The sanctity of these material remains makes them problematic entities for the legislation of the Greek state (cf. Hamilakis and Yalouri 1999). The juxtaposition of the rhetoric on ancient Greece with the legislative shortcomings of the state opens up a space of uncertainty much greater than that of a law that applies to more close-to-hand issues.

The structures of state power render the political decisions that shape the functioning of law on the ground invisible to people without connections to high-ranking officials or politicians. This invisibility gives rise to conspiracy theories claiming to explain the performance of the state, which in most cases are completely off the mark in their content. Usually it is the case of an unspecific "them" (politicians? foreign powers? aliens?) who are conspiring against the well-being and progress of the Greek people at large and the local population in particular. However far-fetched these suppositions are, we should look at them as a last-measure attempt to resocialize the incongruities produced by successive state administrations interpreting and enforcing the law in the way that served their constituencies or class interests. In the case of a similar road, connecting Epidavros with Galatas, the incongruity was plainly evident. The road was finished, save for a stretch of about fifty meters that contained a field of large rocks put there on purpose to make the road impassable. The common theory back then was that the road was not finished because the ship-owner companies prevented its completion, fearing that the increased accessibility of Poros by car would throw their lines out of business. Similarly, archaeological intervention is perceived as guided by economic interests and influenced by bribery.

The man who was talking to us on the tavern balcony at Poros went on to demonstrate this perception in his own performative manner. Showing us the inside of his hunter vest, he told us, "This is a protection zone," running his hand along the vest to demonstrate that there were no pockets (that could hold money). He then turned the jacket flap and displayed a side with many pockets, exclaiming, "This is not a protection zone." He ran his hand inside some of the pockets in a suggestive manner, claiming without saying it that there are officials who take money to facilitate prohibited activities in protection zones.

The close association of archaeological spaces with national development is a reflection of the utopian core of the national narrative of continuity. In the rationale of the law, such spaces include artifacts of immeasurable value but at the same time ground an economy of interest by foreign philhellenes and potential investors in the future of Greece (Voudouri 2003, 18–19). However, since the constitution of the Greek state, the symbolic capital existed in dissonance with the economic situation of the Greek state (Hamilakis 2007, 107). As Stathis Gourgouris appositely remarks, the promise of development inherent in enlightenment visions positions "underdevelopment" as a perennial problem for the Greek state, and one that supposes negative characteristics such as clientelism or corruption as its causes (Gourgouris 1996, 64). The inscription of memories of abandonment into discourses of development becomes more pronounced when archaeological spaces are isolated from the ordinary course of life, as in this case. The burgeoning trade in resin and citruses and the consequent increase of activity in the area of the sanctuary has inscribed it in the memories of older inhabitants as a place alive with people and on the way to some sort of development. Although it is apparent that the bust of citrus prices as well as the replacement of resin with synthetic materials had brought this boom to a halt in the early sixties, well before the Archaeological Service decided to proceed with the expropriation of land in the nineties, the abandonment of the place is attributed to archaeology.

Absence or What?

The man is in his midforties, tall, athletic, and barrel-chested. He sports the ubiquitous black beard and moustache of the stereotypical Cretan shepherd (see Kalantzis 2014). He has practically abducted us from our daily interaction with locals and has summarily ushered us into his pickup truck to an arid, barren hilltop, with sparse indications of past use in disheveled stone pens and walls. It is a windy and cold April afternoon, and a slow drizzle falls, chilling us to the bone. The man is lightly dressed in a jacket and shirt and jumps between rocks with an agility we cannot imitate. He keeps pointing at things on the ground. "Come here, come here! Look! This is not new, this is very ancient. There was definitely something here. I keep telling them, but nobody seems to care. They must come here and look for themselves."

The land we are standing on was probably not as deserted in the recent past as it looks to us now. A rolling hillock rising steeply in the north forms a sort of mountain wall defining the roots of the Psiloritis mountain (the tallest mountain in Crete and one of the tallest in Greece) and the Gonies gorge (a deep recession in the ground to the south). This used to be a passage for travelers to the middle of the island and to its western provinces. A very well-preserved, winding stone road, most probably of Ottoman construction, is still visible in many places. Collapsed toll stations, guardhouses, and inns mark a line of advance that was busy with people and activity sometime in the not-so-distant past.

In all probability, this road followed more ancient roads to the middle of the island and to the mountain itself. Based on a livestock economy, the central provinces of the island always had economic relations with the more economically advanced provinces of the seashore. Their social relations, however, were always deeply troubled. This is not the area where civilization would be expected to flourish. The shepherds of the mountains are portrayed as thieving, boorish, and backward peasant societies that protect their "traditional" ways of life and their land at gunpoint (Herzfeld 1985), and they are unfavorably compared with the refinement and purportedly peaceful culture of ancient Minoans, located in their palaces near the seashore.

Linear B clay tablets record large flocks of sheep and dairy products from these mountainous provinces, and the landscape is peppered with remains of ritual sites, administrative buildings, and cities dating back to the Minoan times. However, it is hard to imagine any kind of activity taking place in this barren, rocky place. It is the very picture of desolation, as recorded in the local name for the hilltop directly to the south of the village of Gonies. According to the locals, Filiorimos means a place that cherishes desolation. This picture of the forlorn mountain peak or the lone tree on its top that defies the elements to assert its singularity is an element of the landscape very often worked into the narratives of peasant (male) life, to emphasize the agonistic individualism of these men (cf. Herzfeld 1985).

The tallying of the desolation and persistence of the landscape with masculine individualism should not divert us from the fact that this is a picture that is drawn ex post facto and is deeply socially influenced. Peasant life, as it emerges from narratives, is a heavily social form of production that depends on communal organization for its success. The remembrance of solitude is in fact a product of the dialectic between times of intense socialization and spells of distance and solitude that were repeated yearly. When walking these lands guided by an elderly local, one realizes that, merely a generation or two in the past,

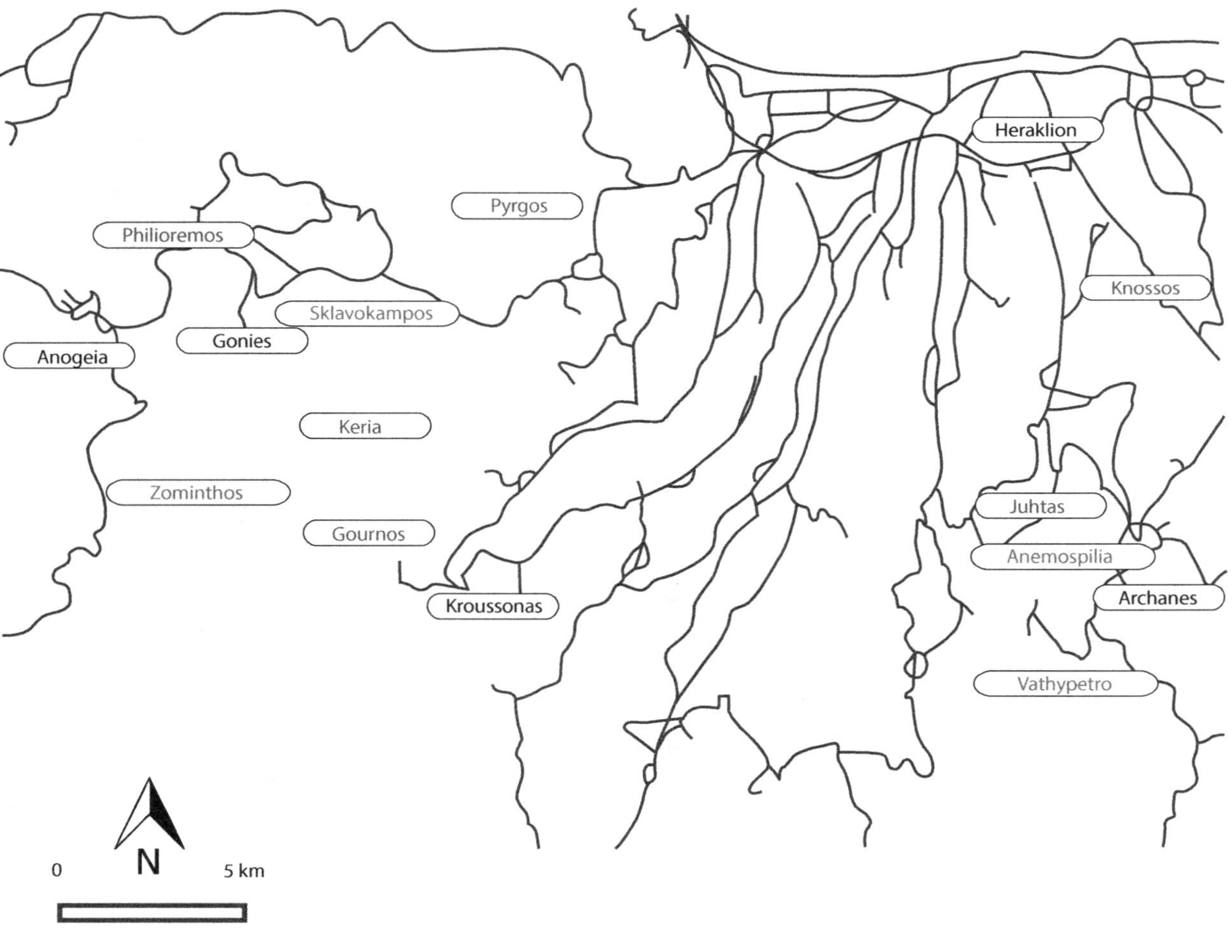

Fig. 7.2. Crete: The Gonies Region. Map by Aris Anagnostopoulos.

these were landscapes bursting with activity, people, and domesticated plants and animals.

Gonies was a thriving village until the 1960s. In the village census, we discover some 1,040 souls living in the village by the mid-1950s. Over three hundred children attended the primary school. There were more than twenty coffee shops and various other shops catering to the community. Following World War II, the village began expanding, with new houses being built to the west. The evolution of the village community, with a corollary change in familial expectations, is visible on the layout of the village when viewed from the peak of Filiorimos. A dense cluster of habitations characterizes the oldest core of the village next to the communal springs. This habitational cluster dates back to the Bronze Age, with evidence of habitation discovered in the basement of houses. The oldest houses may date back to the later years of the Venetian occupation of the island (1205–1669). The buildings there are built one on top of the other, producing a labyrinthine space of narrow alleys, covered passages, and interconnected terraces. The next phase, an expansion that happened nearer to the twentieth century, shows a change in building patterns, with houses adjacent to each other in family neighborhoods that still make maximum use of the building space available. The third phase, after World War II, sees detached houses, usually built at marriage by the first son of the family and with large gardens, at some distance from one another.

Demographics thrived, but the productive base of the village was unable to support the increasing population, especially because agricultural prices were securely tied to a national price system that nearly collapsed after the war. Immigration to nearby Heraklion, Athens, and cities in Europe, America, and Australia began soon after. Goniotes made use of their skills as stonemasons to take to an itinerant life of building stone houses throughout Crete, making a reputation for themselves but simultaneously curtailing the demographics of the village. The last few decades before the 1960s saw a peak in the use of cultivable land in the area for production as villagers planted every nook and cranny with edible plants and cash crops, striving to make a living. It was also a time of intense social interaction, and familial bonds and social groupings were mustered to control the use of resources in the land and establish the peaceful coexistence of shepherds with agriculturalists.

The remaining elderly, permanent inhabitants of the village are individuals who experienced firsthand this process of abandonment and record it as a deeply traumatic memory. Relatives may live nearby, in Heraklion or Athens, and visit regularly, sometimes even most days of the week, but the village looks increasingly empty, with old houses collapsing and courtyards taken over by wild plants and stray cats. A local composer of *mantinades* (improvised verses) has expressed this succinctly: "Apo makria sa se kito, Gonies se kamarono / ma sta stena sou otan mpo, kleo ke den merono" [When I see you from afar, Gonies, I feel proud / but when I walk your streets, I cry without end].

The traumatic experience of abandonment shapes the experience of deep antiquity in the area. Old houses, vineyards, cultivated lands, and sheep pens constitute landscapes imbued with living memories of people who are no longer here, either living or dead. But these living memories are also contained in the profusion of place names that is characteristic of the area. The place names echo very old linguistic types and point to peoples who used this place in the distant past, before similar processes of abandonment wiped their traces from the face of the earth. Place memory is thus connected to the names of places that are themselves imbued with memories and narratives.

Historical time, lived time, and archaeological time are thus collapsed together into the indexical sense of a place that is furthermore inscribed in bodily movements through it, coterminous with flows of people, animals, and things in space. A long walk with a ninety-six-year-old shepherd makes this sense of place emerge in speech and performative gesture. Place names succeed each other as the route taken to the sheep pen in the mountains unfolds, with each place having its own name, imbued with personal stories, remembrances of social relations with people, historical information picked up from readings and hearsay, and folk etymology.

The presence of archaeology comes to solidify this sense of an uncanny space where different temporal scales coexist not so much in their longitudinal sense but as projections onto a "plane of immanence" (cf. Deleuze and Guattari 2004, 266; Colebrook 2006, 3). This is a space of desperation from a lost past, but it is also a place of promise for the future. The heterotopias of archaeological space sustain this indefinitely postponed promise of a utopian presence. Our previously described amateur archaeologist guide embodies this unfulfilled promise in its extreme: he is aware of the sporadic archaeological presence in the area as a betrayal of its rich archaeological and historical record. But this betrayal is a mobilizing force for him: archaeological presence means more visitors, greater benefit for the community, and the protection of the surrounding landscape from intruding energy companies.

Archaeological presence in the area has indeed been sparse and sporadic. The few instances when archaeologists showed up in the village are very well remembered in local lore, associated with major construction events, such as the building of the new road connecting the village to Heraklion in 1935. These excavations, brief affairs that employed village labor to quickly bring results, were salvage excavations performed by state archaeologists with very restricted funds, time, and manpower in order to allow for roads, churches, or houses to be built. The excavation that brought to light the peak sanctuary on top of Filiorimos, just above the village of Gonies, took place during two weeks in 1962 and was aimed to record whatever was possible of the peak sanctuary before the construction of the church of *Profitis Ilias* (Prophet Elijah) by the community on the same spot. Similarly, the 1935 excavation of the Minoan Villa at Sklavokambos was initiated by the discoveries of road construction in its immediate vicinity. Today, both archaeological places are adjoined by modern constructions.

The force of protection zones in these particular places is much less strong than in Poros. There seems to be no clear-cut demarcation of space and no prohibitive state apparatus in place. This fact leads to a remarkable effect: although in Poros the abandonment of the area around the sanctuary of Poseidon is mainly attributed to the heavy hand of the state and archaeological legislation, in Gonies the same effect is attributed to the very absence of archaeological protection zones. In Poros the locals demand the removal or relaxation of archaeological zones of protection, whereas in Gonies the locals demand their stricter application. However, both areas are identical in their understanding of the space created by archaeological interest and its adjunct technologies of government as zones of uncertainty. These are spaces where the state law should have full effect; however for specific reasons, this effect is not manifest.

This uncertainty is further aggravated because these spaces have been the loci of older, community-regulated, legal systems closely interconnected with different social systems of production that are nowadays obsolete. Despite the evidence of rich archaeological finds in Gonies, the places where archaeological presence is sparse used to be cultivated lands or pastures with a complex legislative existence. Although cultivable land in the mountains as well as pastures is considered communal lands, which are rented to individuals for a fee, these nevertheless acquire a certain exclusiveness in the minds of locals. The resulting effect is lands that, however public, are associated with specific family owners. The different levels of ownership, as well as the accompanying issues that arise from settling them, have for a very long time been the object of a customary legal system that still is, in the last instance, community controlled. Although a complex legislature regarding ownership and use of communal land is in effect in Greece and Crete, its specific application is very much in the hands of the community and its elected representatives.

Similarly, until very recently, the lands where the sanctuary of Poseidon lies in Poros were cultivated by Arvanite families who tended the numerous pine trees of the area, collecting resin, and selling it to large companies in Athens. Resin collection was at times quite a profitable seasonal task for a family that could muster the workforce necessary for the collection of large quantities of resin. It demanded cooperation between collection crews and a complex system of marking land that was owned by large owners (especially the church) and parceled out by companies to individual cultivators. To this day, pine-collecting parcels are marked out by inscriptions on stones and other landmarks, usually bearing the initial of the family head. These are equally embodied landscapes in which socially created and kept boundaries are memorized through movement in space. Landscape is not recognized necessarily as marked by officiated landmarks but also through the memory of lived space.

The effects of abandonment in both cases leave the overlay of official technologies of power and socialized control as sediment indecipherable to descendants without the key to this embodied memory, which is personal and community owned. Archaeology therefore becomes one among many techniques of bringing to this uncertain landscape a terminal certainty, of closing once and for all disputes of ownership and use. This is a reclaiming of archaeology for the uses of local development. In Gonies, the communal boundaries are a hotly disputed subject. In recent years, the Greek government has begun a process of creating a land registry in an effort to unify the different legal systems that control land use in its territory and to smooth out the process of extracting revenue from these.[6] This process has raised the demand for archaeological and ethnographic work done by and for the community, in order to preserve the communally understood lands and define their boundaries against encroachment by other communities or even private companies.

This strategic use of archaeological authority is marked for its discernment between official archaeology and archaeological projects such as ours. People like our impromptu tour guide described earlier are very much aware of the networks of power and value creation in global archaeology. Perhaps they are much more aware than archaeologists or anthropologists are willing to grant them. Control over the content of public aspects of village heritage is continuous and close, even in media that are not often associated with picturesque mountainous villages in Crete (cf. Kalantzis 2014, 2019). When we first set up a Facebook page for the Three Peak Sanctuaries of the Central Crete Project, the archaeological research project led by Dr. Evangelos Kyriakidis in Gonies, we described one of the peak sanctuaries in question as Keria Kroussonas. Kroussonas is a village on the other side of the Keria peak with areas bordering the pastures of Gonies, which Goniotes zealously guard. The news of this small infelicity traveled across the world overnight and was picked up by the village diaspora in the United States, which resulted in a phone call from a very concerned president of the village's cultural association the next morning. The way that this call was phrased was significant because I was questioned whether the archaeological nomenclature had Keria designated as belonging to Kroussonas and not Gonies, as can be legally proven through "papers"—contracts of ownership the community has in its hands. Villagers therefore understood archaeological nomenclature not as a scientific, undisputed terrain of knowledge but as a socially moderated field of power relations and antagonism that they needed to exert their control on to advance local prospects.

This discernment does not limit itself to linguistic uses; it also aims to deal with more palpable policy that affects the area. Locals look to archaeology as an effective way to block the encroachment of private energy companies that have made deals with the municipality to rent village land for energy parks. Convincing archaeologists to work more closely with the area, and thus declare it a zone of protection, will certainly block these plans, as it has done in other areas of Crete. The appeal to archaeology is thus not only a desire to become part of the national narrative but also a very pragmatic effort to protect communal land from the predatory hands of large companies. Locals appropriate archaeological knowledge to reinstate claims to their land. A Goniote mechanical engineer and long-serving board member to telecommunications firms stated the archaeological rationale behind the opposition to the energy firms in a long newspaper article in 2012 (Markogiannakis 2012). Similarly, a Goniote secondary school teacher has written a long tract that aims to prove that the path that King Minos took to the top of Mount Ida every nine years went through Gonies.

These appropriations of archaeological scientific knowledge are also attempts to resocialize spaces that paradoxically envision them as protection zones. The call for a state apparatus that is seen as responsible for the abandonment of places in other locations is imagined as an occasion for the resocialization of abandoned places that have been left to the impersonal devices of the state and large companies. This effort is frustrated by the impossibly slow pace of the state Archaeological Service and the incomprehensibility of bureaucratic procedures, even to the personnel of the service itself.

The Archaeological Service is inundated with demands and issues that put a heavy load on its diminishing personnel. During the recent round of layoffs from the public sector, to accommodate the demands of the country's lenders in the EU, the service was left severely understaffed. In this changing climate, the tasks that are dictated by the tremendous importance put on antiquities in Greece become almost impossible in scope and extent. The impossibility of the task is of course painfully evident to civil servants of the Archaeological Service. In different contexts, however, the admittance of the impossibility of the task undertaken assumes many different forms, ranging from a defensive apology of the state to critiques of the decreased socialization of antiquities law in Greece. However this is phrased, what remains constant is the experience of a very real and very palpable limit to the ability of the service to carry out the totalizing dictates of the law, even when it does not meet with local resistance.

Concluding Thoughts: The Limit of the Possible

Archaeological spaces in Greece, especially those connected with the classical past, are publicly seen as spaces where the law of the state exercises an absolute hold. This is a presupposition that emerges from the paramount importance attributed to the remains of the ancient past in the constitution of the nation and the national state. It is also a fact that emerges from the letter of the law that apparently aims to enforce a regime of protection in tandem with the real conditions of the institutions and apparatuses that apply this protection, statewise. These spaces are places where the totalizing apparatuses of state law are in function, but they are also places where the inability of the law to hold a universal validity is made manifest. In the views of its detractors, the inability of the state to enforce the totalizing logic of the law is expressed through its absence from these places and the relative disrepair and abandonment that they represent.

This abandonment is made even starker in comparison with the utopian ideal inherent in the discourses about ancient Greece as an ideal polity. There is a very clear genealogy of this utopian core in such places that can be traced back to the contributions of ancient Greek scholarship to the constitution of European letters, and to the difficult dialectic between the ancient Greek past and the modern Greek reality inherent in most travelers' accounts. I have contended throughout this chapter that archaeological spaces in Greece are not solely the heterotopic spaces of otherness constructed by a foreign gaze but are also everyday spaces where the ability of the state to materialize this promise of a lawful order is constantly challenged. What persistently reemerges in narratives of the experiences of such places is this utopian sediment that is at the core of every imaginary heterotopia.

Inherently, I have chosen to focus on this sediment, on which I locate the collusion of collective and personal desire, the totalizing apparatuses of the state, and the material realities of these spaces. This unfulfilled utopian promise that is identified as the doing of the state is the irreducible core of experience for these spaces. It is something that is simultaneously produced as an excess, an imaginary volition at the heart of every modern Western polity. Perhaps more important, this excess is a continuous production based on a constant subtraction from the imaginary constitution of the nation of stark material reality. As such, it is the doing of both active, living people and the inorganic places themselves that become active agents in the process of socialization. Here, the relationship with material objects is not solely indexical of a social relation, but they constitute the relation itself (Miller 1987, 122). It may be ironic that these spaces, which are so securely tied to the ancient past, are indeed as much about the future as any hypermodern heterotopias.

This utopian horizon is at the same time a promise for the future and a glimpse at the limit of the possible. Throughout this chapter, I have sought to slightly shift the focus from the constitution of such spaces as ambivalent spaces by the binary tow of the state versus the people, and I have tried to show how such ambivalences are also created by the limits of intentional action, posed by either the material environment, the structural and functional limitations of institutions, or the capacities of social formations in general.

ARIS ANAGNOSTOPOULOS is a social anthropologist and historian. He has published extensively on public space, gender, and ethnic identities in early twentieth-century Crete. He has done fieldwork in a number of archaeological projects in Greece and has developed a number of community projects. He served as the assistant director of the Irish Institute of Hellenic Studies at Athens and is now a fellow of the Initiative of Heritage Conservation and an honorary lecturer at the University of Kent, UK.

Notes

1. Law 1892/1990, then further clarified by Law 3028/2002.
2. Legislative order "On plans of cities, towns and settlements of the State and on their building," July 17, 1923, later supplemented by Law 1337/1983.
3. See the Kalaureia Research Program. Accessed March 30, 2016, http://www.kalaureia.org.
4. The place was declared a "protected zone" in 1966 (FEK [Government Gazette] 175/TB 26.3.66, TB 2258/66) with a three-hundred-meter radius and then again in 1967 (FEK [Government Gazette] 527/24.8.67, YΠ 21220/10.8.67) with a five-hundred-meter radius around it.
5. Archives of the Swedish Institute at Athens, Asine file, document no. 399, typed internal memo, n.d. A copy of this is also stored in the Department of the Management of Historical Archive of Antiquities and Restorations (Hellenic Ministry of Culture and Sports), Box 778b, "On the Asine finds," unsigned report of the director of the Department of Archaeology, August 23, 1930 (Sakka, this volume).
6. A private company ("Hellenic Cadastre"—*Ethniko Ktimatologio*) has been set up by ministerial decree in 1995 (see decision 81706/6085/6-10-1995/Government Gazette 872B/19-10-1995). The function of this company has been further regulated through Law 3481/2006. The company itself states that for the first time in the history of the Greek state, widespread informal means of property transfer (such as usucaption) are officially recorded and ratified. (Accessed January 31, 2016, http://www.ktimatologio.gr/sites/en/aboutus/Pages/6PwCSkOZyozWeUix_EN.aspx.).

References

Agamben, Giorgio. 1998. *Homo Sacer: Sovereign Power and Bare Life*. Stanford, CA: Stanford University Press.

Anagnostopoulos, Aris. 2014. "Varieties of Nothingness: Absence, Materiality and Ontology in Two Greek Cases." In *Social Matter(s): Recent Approaches to Materiality*, edited by Tryfon Bampilis and Pieter Ter Keus, 61–90. Berlin: Lit Verlag.

Bhabha, Homi. 2004. "The Other Question: Stereotype, Discrimination and the Discourse of Colonialism." In *The Location of Culture*, 94–120. London: Routledge.

Caftanzoglou, Roxani. 2001. *Στη Σκιά του Ιερού Βράχου. Τόπος και Μνήμη στα Αναφιώτικα* [In the Shadow of the Sacred Rock: Place and Memory in Anafiotika]. Athens: Greek National Center for Social Research.

Colebrook, Claire. 2006. *Deleuze: A Guide for the Perplexed*. London: Continuum.

Deleuze, Gilles, and Félix Guattari. 2004. *A Thousand Plateaus*. London: Continuum.

Derrida, Jacques. 2002. "Force of Law: The Mystical Foundation of Authority." In *Acts of Religion*, edited by Jacques Derrida and Jil Gil Anidjar, 228–98. London: Routledge.

Foucault, Michel. 1989. *The Order of Things*. London: Tavistock.

Gourgouris, Stathis. 1996. *Dream Nation: Enlightenment, Colonization and the Institution of Modern Greece*. Stanford, CA: Stanford University Press.

Habermas, Jürgen. 1983. "Modernity—An Incomplete Project." In *The Anti-Aesthetic: Essays on Postmodern Culture*, edited by Hal Foster, 3–15. Port Townsend, WA: Bay.

Hamilakis, Yannis. 2007. *The Nation and Its Ruins*. Oxford: Oxford University Press.

Hamilakis, Yannis, and Aris Anagnostopoulos. 2009. "What Is Archaeological Ethnography?" In *Archaeological Ethnographies*, edited by Yannis Hamilakis and Aris Anagnostopoulos, 65–87, special double issue, *Public Archaeology* 8 (2–3).

Hamilakis, Yannis, and Eleana Yalouri. 1999. "Sacralising the Past: The Cults of Archaeology in Modern Greece." *Archaeological Dialogues* 6 (2): 115–35.

Herzfeld, Michael. 1985. *The Poetics of Manhood: Contest and Identity in a Cretan Mountain Village*. Princeton, NJ: Princeton University Press.

———. 1991. *A Place in History: Social and Monumental Time in a Cretan Town*. Princeton, NJ: Princeton University Press.

———. 1997. *Cultural Intimacy: Social Poetics in the Nation-State*. London: Routledge.

Hetherington, Kevin. 1997. *The Badlands of Modernity: Heterotopia and Social Ordering*. London: Routledge.

Holbraad, Martin. 2009. "Ontology, Ethnography, Archaeology: An Afterword on the Ontography of Things." *Cambridge Archaeological Journal* 19 (3): 431–41.

Ingold, Tim. 2006. "Rethinking the Animate, Re-animating Thought." *Ethnos* 71 (1): 9–20.

Kalantzis, Kostis. 2014. "On Ambivalent Nativism: Hegemony, Photography, and 'Recalcitrant Alterity' in Sphakia, Crete." *American Ethnologist* 41 (1): 56–75.

———. 2019. *Tradition in the Frame: Photography, Power, and Imagination in Sphakia, Crete*. Bloomington: Indiana University Press.

Lacan, Jacques. 2007. *Écrits: The First Complete Edition in English*. New York: W. W. Norton.

Lefebvre, Henri. 1991. *The Production of Space*. Oxford: Blackwell.

Leontis, Artemis. 1995. *Topographies of Hellenism: Mapping the Homeland*. Ithaca, NY: Cornell University Press.

Markogiannakis, Yannis. 2012. "'ΣΩΡΟΣ': Οι Μινωικές Φρικτωρίες και το Σχεδιαζόμενο Αχανές Φωτοβολταϊκό Πάρκο" ['Soros': Minoan Beacons and the Vast Planned Photovoltaic Park]. *Patris*, July 4, 2012. Accessed June 7, 2016. http://www.patris.gr/articles/225060?PHPSESSID=tr8fa13k17ljrtpng9s5evvbb5#.VBqokpR_v4s.

Miller, Daniel. 1987. *Material Culture and Mass Consumption*. Oxford: Blackwell.

Nuitjen, Monique, and Gerhard Anders. 2007. "Corruption and the Secret of the Law: An Introduction." In *Corruption and the Secret of the Law. A Legal Anthropological Perspective*, edited by Monique Nuitjen and Gerhard Anders, 1–24. Aldershot: Ashgate.

Petrakos, Vasileios. 1982. *Essay on Archaeological Legislation*. Athens: Ministry of Culture.

———. 2013. *Πρόχειρον Αρχαιολογικόν* [Archaeological Drafts]. Vol. 1. Athens: Archaeological Society.

Prakash, Gyan. 1992. “Can the ‘Subaltern’ Ride? A Reply to O’Hanlon and Washbrook.” *Comparative Studies in Society and History* 34 (1): 168–184.

Scott, James C. 1998. *Seeing Like a State: How Certain Schemes to Improve the Human Condition Have Failed.* New Haven, CT: Yale University Press.

Voudouri, Daphne. 2003. *Κράτος και Μουσεία —Το Θεσμικό Πλαίσιο των Αρχαιολογικών Μουσείων* [State and Museums: the Constitutional Framework of Archaeological Museums in Greece]. Athens: Sakkoulas.

———. 2010. “Law and the Politics of the Past: Legal Protection of Cultural Heritage in Greece.” *International Journal of Cultural Property* 17: 547–68.

Wells, Berit. 2002. “The Prehistory of the Swedish Institute at Athens.” In *New Research on Old Material from Asine and Berbati in Celebration of the Fiftieth Anniversary of the Swedish Institute at Athens*, edited by Berit Wells, 9–22. Stockholm: Gleerup.

Part III
Competing Pasts

8 Heritage as Obstacle

Or Which View to the Acropolis?

Andromache Gazi

Introduction

Heritage is a cultural process in which vestiges from the past are constantly valued, devalued, appropriated, glorified, contested, and neglected in a never-ending sequence regulated by present-day social, political, and ideological circumstances.[1] Underlying this process are questions of cultural memory, identity,[2] visibility, and recognition, which are renegotiated by each generation through a process of filtering, selecting and categorizing "heritage."[3] Sociopolitical and intellectual elites in particular play a central role in the selection process and in canonizing approved heritage. The "authorized heritage discourse" (Smith 2006) that comes out of this procedure echoes hegemonic notions of heritage linked to beliefs about specific facets of national identity, collective memory, and more. Within this powerful conceptual framework, dissenting voices are difficult to be heard, let alone accepted, in official discourses on heritage. This fact becomes evident each time heritage is contested: "When divergent goals exist among competing social groups . . . heritage conservation becomes a political exercise" (Tunbridge 2008, 234).

One such occasion was the 2007–2009 dispute over the preservation or demolition of two 1930 houses that stand between the New Acropolis Museum in Athens and the Acropolis itself. Using this dispute as a case in point, this chapter discusses changing perceptions of cultural heritage and looks at why and how value is assigned to, or removed from, particular monuments under specific circumstances. The discussion begins by looking at instances of heritage erasure occurring during times of peace as a result of altered views of heritage value. The main point elaborated here is that decisions about heritage eradication are commonly informed by the concept of cultural visibility—that is, the way in which the perceived value of heritage shapes our visual and symbolic perception of it. As the examples discussed later make clear, visual isolation and exaltation of certain types of heritage at the expense of others have always been employed by ruling elites in shaping a specific sense of national pride and identity and promoting bold ideological and political messages. In this sense, visuality, as a culturally mediated way of seeing, lies at the heart of most debates on heritage contestation.

Heritage—Glorified, Disavowed, Contested, Erased

Monuments can experience one of three possible fates during significant critical junctures: co-opted or glorified, disavowed, or contested (Forest and Johnson 2002). Co-opted or glorified monuments are maintained or exulted further. Disavowed ones are literally or symbolically erased through destruction or neglect. Contested monuments remain the objects of political conflict, neither clearly glorified nor disavowed. Therefore, the physical transformation of monuments during critical junctures reflects the struggle among political elites for the symbolic capital embodied in and represented by them. By co-opting, contesting, ignoring, or removing certain types of monuments, political elites engage in a symbolic dialogue with stakeholders and the public in an attempt to gain prestige, legitimacy, and influence. Here, I focus on contested heritage[4]—in particular, heritage threatened with erasure—in order to consider the reasons informing such choices and lay the basis for the discussion on the Acropolis case study presented later.

Heritage erasure[5] is regularly the outcome of armed conflict or other hostilities, when places, monuments, and buildings that are symbolically significant for the attacked are eliminated to undermine enemy morale (Stanley-Price 2007). The intentional demolition of monuments is frequently associated with totalitarian regimes in their effort to obliterate the principal symbols of an old regime or an old faith.

In 1931, for instance, Moscow's eminent Cathedral of Christ the Savior, built after Russia's victory in the Napoleonic invasion of 1812 as a national monument to express the nation's gratitude to Christ for saving the country was razed in order to make room for the construction of a gigantic Palace of the Soviets. Embodying the ideals of the Communist regime, the new building would stand on the ruins of the cathedral "as a kind of atheistic holy sanctuary" (Kirichenko 2012, 278).[6] Similarly, in 1967, Enver Hoxha declared his aspiration to turn Albania into the world's only completely atheistic state. In his effort to erase religion from the landscape, thousands of churches and mosques were demolished (Galaty 2011, 117).

Heritage erasure may be the result of newborn nationalism and new identity building. Since the 1960s, this trend has been manifested especially in areas with a colonial background,[7] or in countries that have sprung out of changing geopolitical circumstances, such as many countries in Eastern Europe and the Balkans.[8]

Heritage erasure is also frequently debated within large urban projects aimed at creating specific cityscapes as part of a city's rebranded identity. Within this context, strategies of urban planning often involve highlighting or even isolating the "significant" monuments by hiding or abolishing the "insignificant" ones. One of the most prominent examples of this strategy was the clearance of the so-called Spina del Borgo in Rome to make room for the grandiose Via della Conciliazione (Street of the Reconciliation) that connects St. Peter's Basilica to the Castel Sant'Angelo. In 1929, Benito Mussolini and Pope Pius XI signed the Lateran Treaty, which normalized diplomatic relations between the Italian state and the Roman Catholic Church and recognized the independence of Vatican City. To celebrate the occasion, Mussolini revived an older idea (Kirk 2006) of a grand avenue that would symbolically connect the Vatican to the heart of the Italian capital, providing a clear indication of the union between the state and the church.[9] In order to achieve isolation and visibility for St. Peter's Basilica, however, the whole Spina del Borgo, an old quarter dating from Medieval and Renaissance times, would have to be torn down. Starting from 1936, the neighborhood was cleared away to give way to the Via della Conciliazione, completed in 1950. Although highly contested, the Via della Conciliazione offered the Fascist regime a fine opportunity for highlighting contemporary political aspirations: opening the visual axis to the Basilica made clear the relation between the universal authority of the church and the Fascist nation that hosted and protected it (Kirk 2006, 763–64).

Many more cases from around the world demonstrate the ways in which various forces interrelate to produce cityscapes in which elements of the past are downgraded, hidden, torn down, celebrated, assimilated, or reinvented in an effort to construct new forms of identity that better suit different sociopolitical aspirations or may be more attractive to a global touristic or other market.[10] The dispute over the Pera/Beyoğlu district in Istanbul provides an illustrative example of such a process, quite similar to the Athenian case study examined later. Istanbul has been a melting pot of ethnic minorities for centuries. The Pera/Beyoğlu[11] neighborhood in particular had always attracted a thriving community of Greeks, Armenians, and Jews who from the nineteenth century had made it the most prosperous and most "European" area of the city. In the late nineteenth century, following the Ottomans' efforts to transform Istanbul into a Western city, Pera became the first "Europeanized" quarter. Later, with the advent of the Turkish nation state and the transfer of the capital to Ankara, Istanbul came to symbolize Ottoman decadence and corruption. But even then, Pera remained a symbol of civilization for the Turkish bourgeoisie (Bartu 1999, 33). In the early 1980s, plans for major urban regeneration suggested demolishing parts of the district in order to open up a new avenue (Tarlabaşi Boulevard) to connect Taksim Square with the old city. This project would require pulling down a large number of houses and the relocation of thousands of inhabitants (Bartu 1999, 34). The public debate that ensued (known as the Tarlabaşi demolitions) largely revolved around issues of identity; some agreed with the demolition on the grounds that Pera/Beyoğlu wasn't really "Turkish," whereas others rejected demolition for reasons of nostalgia for a distinctive part of the city's multifaceted past. With the ascendancy of an Islamic municipal government in the 1990s, the issue took on new dimensions. Despite the fact that for the Islamists Pera/Beyoğlu represented "cosmopolitan degeneration," it could still be used in their political campaign as demonstrating an "Ottoman model" of governance that had enabled people from various ethnic backgrounds to coexist harmoniously for centuries (Bartu 1999, 40; Bartu 2001).

Therefore, heritage may be seen as a lens through which each social or political group mirrors itself. As with optical lenses, this cultural lens focuses on particular aspects of heritage, depending on the circumstances (cf. Howard 2003, 211). Visual aspects in particular are fundamental to this process.

Heritage Visibility and the Heritage Gaze

Over the last two decades, the visual has been established as an important analytical category within the field of heritage studies[12] and as a key component in the construction of heritage meanings. Moreover, as the discussion has shown so far, the visual has always served as a powerful tool in the service of identity politics whereby certain aspects of heritage are emphasized and others are silenced (Watson and Waterton 2010a; Duke 2007; see also Galiniki, this volume). To fully comprehend this process, we should remember that visual practices go far beyond one's physical ability to see. Much more than a natural process (e.g., sight as a physical operation), vision is subject to the dynamics of social forces, so seeing is always shaped by a broader set of cultural assumptions and frameworks (Thompson 2005, 36; Schirato and Webb 2010, 21). The concept of visuality[13] in particular emphasizes the close relation of visual practices to the cultures out of which they emerge. In this sense, visuality is not simply an act of observation (vision) or a simple, unmediated visual experience but a culturally and socially mediated act, a cultural construct (Bryson 1988, 91–92).[14] Within the heritage discourse, specifically, visuality takes up renewed importance because it is intimately linked to the creation and manipulation of the gaze and to the politics of vision (Foster 1988, 107). The crucial question here is what is made visible and why.

This question brings up the notion of "cultural visibility" (Garden 2006, 399–400), which encompasses the idea of sight or view, and is further related to the way in which certain aspects of heritage may assume a greater or lesser visual presence, depending on their symbolic significance within a specific sociocultural milieu. Cultural visibility (or invisibility) is thus closely connected to identity politics and has strong political connotations. Cultural visibility is further dependent on the "heritage gaze" (Smith 2006, 53), a specific way of seeing that is to a large extent regulated by the value bestowed on specific heritage objects, sites, or monuments and their significance within particular sociocultural situations. Controlling and managing the heritage gaze through a process of filtering of what is perceived as significant and what is not have always been crucial within the politics of heritage. Within the field of heritage tourism, more specifically, the "tourist gaze"[15] is geared toward the exceptional and the out of the ordinary. In this way, emblematic monuments like the Acropolis tend to be viewed and "consumed" in terms of their (partly real, partly constructed, and partly imagined) visual exaltation. The case study analyzed in this chapter offers a telling example of how the politics of heritage may be entwined with the politics of vision in the service of contemporary aspirations.

Case Study

The Background

On the evening of June 20, 2009, then Greek Prime Minister Antonis Samaras inaugurated the long-awaited New Acropolis Museum (henceforth NAM). This internationally hailed event was the last act of a long-lasting and heated affair that began in the seventies and involved four architectural competitions (two of them international), archaeological excavations, scientific expertise, legislative acts, public debate, politics, ideology, and much passion.

The history of the NAM's construction has been extensively covered in numerous publications to date, as has its architecture.[16] Designed by New York–based architect Bernard Tschumi in collaboration with Greek architect Michalis Fotiadis, the 21,000-square-meter building replaced the old Acropolis Museum, a small 1874 building on the rock of the Acropolis. Introduced in 2001, the NAM was meant to be completed in time for the 2004 Olympics in Athens, but legal battles (many of which concerned some neighboring buildings that were demolished to free space for it) delayed the process for years.

Ever since its inception, the building has faced a highly challenging (and one might say almost impossible) mission: to house "the most dramatic sculptures of Greek antiquity,"[17] to act as the spearhead of the Greek campaign for the return of the Parthenon Marbles to Athens, and to pay tribute to the Parthenon, one of the most prominent monuments of Western civilization, while at the same time conversing with the contemporary city around it. The first two goals were met successfully: the museum provided a technically and technologically impeccable environment for its contents, and at the same time, it empowered the Greek argument for the return of the Parthenon Marbles.[18] The last two goals, however, proved to be highly contentious.

From day one, the museum's architecture, which was strikingly dissimilar to every other building around it,[19] was either loved or hated. Hailed as a

Fig. 8.1. Aerial view of the Parthenon and the Acropolis Museum. Courtesy of the Acropolis Museum.

Fig. 8.2. View of the museum's entrance. Photo by A. Gazi.

"mesmerizing work in its own right" (Ouroussoff 2007) and a "work of high contemporary architecture" in a city lacking present-day architectural landmarks (Vatopoulos 2007), the NAM, argued its enthusiasts, was a "civic magnet" (Aesopos 2007) and a "civic event" in itself (Aesopos 2008). Suffocated by its surroundings, its critics argued, the museum's building was planted in the neighborhood without any sense of proportion and respect to scale,[20] like "an alien creature landed in the heart of Athens" (Plantzos 2011, 617).

The building was further accused of appearing arrogant, ugly, and aggressive due to its massive concrete surfaces and columns,[21] its large glass facades, and its unadorned lines, but mainly because of a protruding concrete terrace pointing directly onto the Acropolis.[22] In between this terrace and the rock itself lie two listed buildings dating from the 1930s, reminiscent of Athens's important architectural and cultural palimpsest. No concern was ever expressed that they could possibly be obtrusive to the highly valued aim of an unimpeded view from inside the NAM to the Acropolis,[23] which was one of the basic principles guiding the museum's design. On the contrary, their presence was clearly marked in the instructions to all four architectural competitions. But in July 2007, as the museum structure was rising, a decision was made to tear them down for reasons that will be elaborated on later. This event marked the beginning of a long, heated campaign to save the two buildings—a campaign in which political authority and ideological illusions were entangled with civic rights, scientific arguments, and contested views of heritage.

The Facts, I

The NAM's main entrance looks onto Dionyssiou Areopagitou Street, a large, leafy, paved road that is often referred to with some exaggeration as one of the most beautiful pedestrian walkways in Europe. The street, which runs under the Acropolis, is home to some notable buildings.

Number 17, in particular, is a remarkable example of 1930s Art Deco style, one of the very few remaining in Athens, built by a significant Greek architect of the interwar period, Vassilis Kouremenos, a graduate of the École des Beaux Arts in Paris and a friend of Picasso. With its pink-marbled exterior, two marble female statues on either side of its entrance, and the figures of Oedipus and the Sphinx adorning the top floor, it is the most remarkable building along the street. Beside it stands the less grandiose but equally important neoclassical house Number 19. A visitor looking out from inside the NAM toward the Acropolis would see the unattractive backs of the two buildings—an offensive view, some believed—and this was where it all started.

In order to understand the controversy, we need to go back in time. In 1978, the two buildings were listed, and in 1987, the Central Archaeological Council exempted them from a list of houses to be demolished in order to free space for the NAM's construction on the merit of their forming an architectural unit that called for their preservation. In 1988, both buildings were then considered "works of art." In the international architectural competition for the NAM (the third in a row) launched in 1991, the two buildings were clearly preserved. They were further exempted from expropriation in 2003, when legislation regulating the NAM's construction was enforced, and in 2004 the façade of Number 17 was cleaned and refurbished with funds partly provided by the Ministry of Culture.[24]

Fig. 8.3. Partial view of Dionyssiou Areopagitou Street. Photo by A. Gazi.

Fig. 8.4. No 17, Dionyssiou Areopagitou Street. Photo by A. Gazi.

Fig. 8.5. No 19, Dionyssiou Areopagitou Street: the entrance. Photo by A. Gazi.

But in mid-2007, as the structure of the museum increased in height, some feared that the presence of the two buildings might be undesirable; the idea of their declassification was thus introduced as opening up the way for their demolition. On July 3, 2007, the issue was passionately debated at a stormy common meeting of the Central Archaeological Council and the Council for Modern Monuments, where both sides (mainly archaeologists, who were in favor of the declassification, versus architects, who were against) maintained firm arguments. The votes were tied, twelve to twelve. With specific weight on the president's vote, however, the scales finally tipped in favor of declassification of Number 17. According to official reasoning, this was justified because the view from the museum's terrace to the Acropolis (and the Parthenon) was of utmost public importance.[25]

A fierce debate ensued.[26] Both the Technical Chamber of Greece[27] and the Association of Greek Architects[28] expressed total disapproval, inhabitants of the area and architects urged the Minister of Culture not to sign the councils' recommendation, and letters of protest from all over the world flooded the ministry.[29]

Later that year in a letter addressed to the minister, 341 members of the Ministry of Culture's scientific personnel (archaeologists, architects, conservators, museologists, art historians, and more) condemned both the concept of declassification and the planned demolition as unacceptable.[30]

The Debate

Arguments in favor or against the demolition were sharply debated for a long time. To start with, the very nature of the two buildings was put into question: Were they ornaments or rubbish? If they were so significant as to have been listed monuments, how could one possibly consider their demolition? Next, there was a question of heritage preservation. What was the ultimate goal—protecting the cultural palimpsest of Athens, or facilitating a so-called unobstructed dialogue between the NAM and the Acropolis? And what exactly would the nature of such a dialogue be? Would it necessitate the demolition of the two buildings and the resulting eradication of a significant part of the city's architectural and cultural memory? If so, do we have the moral right to sacrifice the city's more recent heritage in order to showcase (yet again) its classical one? There was also a question of city identity (and city branding, I would add): What do we want our city to look like? What is more important—the civic grid, or the grandiose monumental buildings (Filippidis 2007)? And finally, how far should one go in order to visually cleanse the area? Questions such as these were articulated in all possible tones both in Greece and abroad.[31]

The issues at stake extended far beyond archaeology, architecture, and heritage preservation; they were mainly about the politics of identity in a city (and a country at large) with a highly ambivalent relationship to its (classical) heritage. In many ways, this dispute was a fight between the old and the new, between traditionalists and progressives.[32]

Defenders of the demolition (including several archaeologists and part of the press) argued that the NAM was far too important a project to let anything get in its way, and they insisted that the two buildings prevented architects Tschumi and Fotiadis's goal of "optically combining" the museum with the ancient monument.[33] The NAM was a site museum, they further argued, and as such it "should not be cut off from its umbilical cord, the Acropolis."[34] This argument was to a large extent an archaeological position that called for a "pure," unmediated gaze toward the Acropolis and the Parthenon. Along these lines, some saw the two contested buildings as "wretched," their presence "an insult to civilization" (Thermou 2007), whereas others argued that cities ought to make sacrifices and ruptures, and Athens should be no exception.[35] A member of the Archaeological Council even questioned whether the handful of inhabitants of these buildings had the moral right to deprive millions of visitors to the museum of an unobstructed view of the Acropolis (Kontrarou-Rassia 2007). No doubt, the issue of (cultural) visibility was highly critical to the debate for reasons that will be discussed later. A large part of the public opinion and the press, however, reduced the argument to a very mundane reason: having a better view from the museum's cafeteria terrace (something that was expected to act as a magnet for tourists) would potentially raise the museum's income.[36] This point was never officially stated, but it was most likely contemplated.[37]

For those who believed in the idea of the city as an architectural palimpsest, the "demolition dilemma" simply did not exist (Kizis 2007). Supporters of the two buildings (including several architects, archaeologists, and inhabitants of the neighborhood) maintained that it was unacceptable to sacrifice one layer of the city's cultural history for another, and they saw the government's plan to demolish the houses as an effort to once again sanitize the Acropolis area. But what would be the limit of such a purification desire? If pushed to its extremes, some argued, it ought to further consider the demolition of other nineteenth-century or early twentieth-century buildings that surround the museum and catch the visitor's eye.[38]

Architects insisted that the two houses are much more than plain buildings: they belong to the city's memory, an architectural memory representative of an old and much-cherished Athenian streetscape. It was the specific aura of the place that should be preserved, not just the houses, they claimed.[39] An Italian protestor went even further by pointing out that the Greek government was about to adopt a Fascist approach to architecture, one that resembled Mussolini's procedures in the construction of the Via Della Conciliazione (see earlier).[40] Much of the architectural argument centered on the issue of scale and distinguished between the massiveness of the NAM and the modesty of the buildings around it. The majority of architects and city planners accused the museum of being highly disrespectful to, and even "provocatively ignoring," the surrounding area (Papaioannou 2007), and they described the move as an "example of arrogance" (Antoniadis 2007) or "architectural cannibalism" (Salingaros 2007).

At this point, the reader should be reminded of a significant detail: in 2003, when the Central Archaeological Council approved the erection of the NAM at its current (highly contested) location,[41] this approval was justified on the grounds that the museum would not be visible from Dionyssiou Areopagitou Street, and hence it would not impose on either the ancient monuments on this side of the rock or the listed buildings! To many architects and citizens, Dionyssiou Areopagitou acts as a kind of "civic front" that holds the contemporary city (and its aggressiveness) behind it,[42] thus creating a kind of buffer zone necessary before one can gaze at the Acropolis. Should the two buildings be torn down, they maintained, this front would be eliminated, and "the void thus created would become a sort of no-man's land,"[43] making the NAM's mass look even more aggressive.

Vassilis Vassilikos (2007), whose book *Z* was made into the award-winning film, wrote, "This open terrace is a concrete arrow aimed at the back of the two protected buildings, as if wanting to tear them down by its sheer vehemence. . . . If the protected buildings are demolished, this arrow will then target the Acropolis itself, as if wanting to destroy it as well. Mr. Tschumi, is this the much-desired dialogue with the ancient monument?"

As a journalist put it, "And if the Museum wants to 'converse' with the Parthenon, should we perhaps ask if the Parthenon wants a 'conversation' with Mr. Tschumi's building?" (Kiosse 2007, C08). A true dialogue with the monuments, others maintained, ought to include all material evidence of their long journey from the past to the present: "If we truly want a dialogue, then let us give this dialogue a chance of being multisided; let us talk about 'coexistence' and 'conciliation' rather than 'rupture' and 'purity'" (Lekakis 2007; cf. Kardamitsi-Adami 2007).

Amid this bitter dispute, there were some voices, mainly from within the architectural community, expressing the view that the concern about the retention of the two buildings was rather belated, even "provokingly hypocritical," given that many important twentieth-century Athenian buildings had not escaped demolition or neglect.[44] Others believed that had it not been for the renowned music composer Vangelis Papathanasiou, the owner of Number 19, the debate would not have attracted such publicity.

The Facts, II

Despite growing opposition, on August 30, 2007, then Minister Giorgos Voulgarakis signed an order for the "total and permanent revocation of the classification of Dionyssiou Areopagitou Number 17 as a monument." Part of the Greek press hailed this action as a powerful political decision (e.g., Kontrarou-Rassia 2007), but the majority saw it as a deplorable act, or even as a sign of "regime vandalism" (Kourtovik 2007).

Then, after a short period of calm, the campaign to save the building intensified: the headline in the Technical Chamber of Greece's September 24, 2007, newsletter declared, "Keep your hands off Number 17 Dionyssiou Areopagitou Street." Furthermore, on November 9, a video entitled "Destroy below the Acropolis" was uploaded on YouTube by the residents,[45] and a few days later, 431 members of the Ministry of Culture's scientific personnel expressed their bold opposition to the minister's decision.

At this point, some proposed a middle solution: What if we embellish the backs of the two contested buildings? In March 2008, the architectural website https://www.greekarchitects.gr launched a competition to redesign just the backs of the listed buildings and attracted 172 contributions.[46]

Meanwhile, the residents' initiative at https://areopagitou17.blogspot acted as the main gate to information on the issue, gathering all relevant documentation and urging people all over the world to sign the petition to save the buildings. Signatures were also collected in situ outside the buildings themselves. Forty-five thousand signatures were collected through the blog, and another twenty-two thousand were signed on the spot.

Then on June 4, 2008, the Council of State, the Supreme Administrative Court of Greece, recommended against demolition of the two buildings. In May 2009, then Minister of Culture Antonis Samaras made a last effort to reverse the climate by suggesting the relocation of the two buildings (Monumenta 2009).[47]

The issue concluded in late May 2009 when the Council of State issued a final verdict against demolition on the grounds that the two buildings "form an architectural ensemble coming under the protection of both the [Greek] Archaeological Law and the Granada Convention. They [also] retain a self-sufficient value for the area's character, which is a focal point for the integration of the archaeological sites of Athens into the urban fabric of the city."[48]

Reflecting on the Case Study

Irrespective of the sides of the argument, all debate centered on four or five main strands—the archaeological, the architectural, the political, the ideological, and the visual (which was closely linked to both an ostensibly "pure" gaze and the "tourist gaze")—all so tightly interrelated that it would be hard to isolate them. In the section that follows, I will attempt to elaborate on these lines.

In order to understand the importance of the Acropolis in the Greek national imagination, one has to be briefly reminded of the process of Modern Greek identity formation in the nineteenth century. Established in 1830, the Modern Greek state employed the cultural as well as the aesthetic superiority of the classical past as its founding cornerstone.[49] In both political and ideological terms, the very existence of the new state was largely a reflection of European (and largely Western) veneration of ancient Greece and its neoclassical reincarnation in the present (see Plantzos, this volume). Classical antiquities were central to this imaginary revival and so immediately acquired the status of symbolic national capital.[50]

The Acropolis in particular has always been the national symbol par excellence on an aesthetic, ideological, intellectual, and political level. "So eager were Western allies to restore ancient Hellas," writes Lowenthal (1998, 244), "that Greeks felt bound to exalt the classical legacy, the Acropolis coming to symbolize national rebirth." This highly symbolic image of classical antiquity, especially as embodied in the emblematic site of the Acropolis, was ever since "diffused in modern Greek everyday life as a source of inspiration and self-confidence . . . as a guarantee for the future and also as a reminder of the origin of this future"

(Plantzos 2012). In the same way that emblems are easily recognized and identified as powerful images in symbolic and spiritual terms, the Acropolis has a strong visual image that is power-laden in symbolic, ideological, and political terms alike (cf. Staiff 2014, 71).

Indeed, this image is the by-product of an idealized vision of the Acropolis shaped by nineteenth-century neoclassical ideals that demanded purity, clarity of vision, and authenticity. The nineteenth-century Romantic gaze led to a process of purification of the Acropolis, with severe and far reaching repercussions to date.[51] The "ritual purification" (Hamilakis 2007, 88) of the so-called sacred rock by eradicating all relics of later, nonclassical, historic phases started in the 1830s and was completed in 1875 (Mallouchou-Tufano 1998). Apart from depriving the place of its historicity, the purification process "reduced" the Acropolis to an "isolated world . . . frozen in time and space" (Yalouri 2001, 152).

The Acropolis gradually came to be understood, experienced, and consumed as a cultural image, a cultural landscape in the broad sense.[52] As Yalouri (2001, 152) observes, "The viewing of the Acropolis as a landscape does not allow anything to interrupt or to spoil the high aesthetics that it represents. In fact, the otherwise anarchic build-up of the city of Athens has always followed rules regarding the unobstructed viewing of the sacred rock, thus creating physical and symbolic boundaries between the area of the Acropolis and the rest of the city."

The erection of buildings under the Acropolis or in the immediate vicinity has been heavily contested since the 1840s, when "proper" use and perception of the monumentalized landscape of the Acropolis called for the removal of the humble Anafiotika neighborhood.[53] Whenever such issues have been raised ever since, it was largely held that the purity of the classical monuments should be protected from any modern interference.[54] It was on these grounds, for instance, that even in 2004, the Central Archaeological Council demanded the relocation of an art installation from the foothill of the Acropolis because it was considered as impeding the view to the Acropolis (Hamilakis 2007, 42–43).

The physical and symbolic boundaries created around the Acropolis rock are typical of heritage site production, and many scholars have commented[55] on how the process of fencing off and demarcating sites turns them into places "where we just visit" (Fairclough 2013, 8) and look. The creation of distinct spatial zones of protection around a site or a monument, what Yampolsky (1995)[56] calls "sacral zones," cuts off the monument from time and space by placing it out of the cycle of the ordinary (see Anagnostopoulos, this volume). In the Greek case in particular, important classical sites had to be clearly demarcated and protected from the touch of social reality, and the resultant monumentalized landscapes had to be cleared from any "dirty details of everyday life" (Caftanzoglou 2001, 93, 99). Indeed, as Loukaki (2008, 18) reminds us, "Once a society decides to protect and preserve a building or a ruin, it removes this building from the normal stream of ageing and death and raises it to the exceptional, in terms of its increased symbolic potential and its preferential treatment."

In the case of the Acropolis, this effort to isolate the rock and elevate it to a state of an all-dominating entity is particularly poignant. Yalouri (2001, 153) aptly describes the process by which the Acropolis has become "an internalized and self-operating Panopticum." Revered as a sacred place, the Acropolis oversees the city like an idealized citadel, sovereign in its monumental isolation and remoteness, floating in time above the trivialities of everyday life. Likewise, the NAM hopes to create "a clear reference to the Acropolis," an unhindered view from both inside the Museum upwards and from the Acropolis downward so as to give the impression that one virtually lives in that remote era,[57] attempting to direct the visitor's gaze toward "an Acropolis that no longer exists," a heterotopia much like the museum itself (cf. Hamilakis and Ifantidis 2015, 150). In this way, the museum, a new (yet heavily contested) architectural symbol in its own right, aspires to enter into an exclusive dialogue with the Acropolis.[58]

Thus, in the same manner in which the NAM almost completely excluded artifacts from later historic phases from its permanent exhibitions,[59] defenders of the demolition of the two Dionyssiou Areopagitou buildings wished to eliminate any structures perceived as visual obstacles in the "unobstructed dialogue" of the museum with the Acropolis. The buildings in question had to be demolished because "they did not fit in within the new monumental landscape that the museum has produced" (Hamilakis 2011, 626). The "aesthetics of sacredness" (Yalouri 2001) should not be dishonored. "No intermediaries can be allowed, no interruptions, especially if they are not part of the linear succession from antiquity to the present" (Plantzos 2008, 16).

It is useful to dwell a bit longer on the aesthetics of sacredness because it has always been fundamental in regulating national aesthetics and shaping notions of Greek identity. Based on the timeless quality of the classic and promoting a selective version of the past, this aesthetic model has been imposed on the collective imaginary of the Greeks as "ensuring . . . that Greece's classical past remains ever present and . . . that it is only put to the appropriate uses" (Plantzos 2013). What is "appropriate" or "approved" is to a large extent regulated, and at times even censored, by a highly controlling state archaeological service and the archaeologists working there, who thus end up in formulating and also monitoring authorized national aesthetics.[60] Within this "overarching archaeological model of culture" (Peckham 2001, 134), commitment to an "unobtrusive view" and a "visual dialogue" with the Acropolis should come as no surprise. In fact, the NAM itself was largely conceived as an instrument in the "management of the gaze" (Hamilakis 2011, 626). Direct visual contact was also the principle guiding the organization of the museum's permanent galleries, where the visitor is expected to engage in a face-to-face "conversation" with the exhibits, as has been repeatedly emphasized by the museum's authorities.[61] In this way, the Parthenon itself becomes the object of the "tourist gaze" of the museum's visitors.

In view of these concepts, and given the ever-present load of the classical ideal within contemporary Greek society, the decision not to demolish the two Dionyssiou Areopagitou houses was indeed surprising. It should perhaps be hailed as a daring step toward a reconciliation of modern Greeks with their non-classical and nonvenerated past, or as a realization that "playing up the classical merely reinforces a stereotypical image" of Greece (Clogg 1988, 12). It may further be interpreted as marking the breakup of the authorized heritage discourse that is so common in countries like Greece with a highly centralized and exclusive approach to the management of cultural (especially archaeological) heritage. Finally, it could also be interpreted as a triumph of public protest and outcry. In fact, this episode contrasts other cases in which public dissent or resentment did not manage to stop heritage erasure,[62] thus defying Jones and Shaw's (2006, 128) assertion that "the futility of public protest" usually "underlines the control possessed by the powerful in the defining of place."

Concluding Remarks

People engage with heritage all the time; they rewrite it, appropriate it, and contest it. It may thus be argued that "heritage is always in dispute" (Howard 2003, 212). In cities with multiple and multifaceted pasts such as Athens, Rome, or Istanbul, debates on which aspects of heritage to preserve, and why, become crucial political exercises that bring up questions of national identity and self-esteem. Those cities' multilayered pasts are constantly reworked in the present, making cultural heritage a symbolic capital for local and global audiences alike. Constructing this symbolic cultural capital typically involves the clear demarcation and visual exaltation of certain types of heritage that bear witness to specific aspect of identity. A number of places, buildings, monuments, and objects are privileged in this process and help create a specific, glorified sense of nationhood and heritage. Here, visuality acts as a metaphor representing sociocultural and political meanings, whereas the production of cultural visibility involves emphasizing some aspects of heritage and silencing, or even erasing, others.[63]

As the discussion in this chapter has shown, cultural visibility is frequently employed as a tool for highlighting contemporary political aspirations or legitimizing specific cultural policies, but at the same time, it becomes a crucial component of identity politics. Notions of national self-confidence, pride, and identity are strongly influenced (and shaped) by the cultural visibility of emblematic monuments in particular. When such a monument is no less than the Athenian Acropolis, visibility—at a cultural, ideological, social, scientific, and touristic level—becomes a deeply political question.

ANDROMACHE GAZI is Associate Professor of Museology at the Department of Communication, Media and Culture, Panteion University, Athens. Her research interests include the politics and uses of the past, museum history, memory studies, the theory and practice of exhibitions, oral history in museums, and museum text. She coedited with Alexandra Bounia *National Museums in Southern Europe: History and Perspectives* (Kaleidoscope, 2012, in Greek) and with Irene Nakou *Oral History in Museums and Education* (Nissos, 2015, in Greek).

Notes

1. See, among many, Brett (1996); Pearce (1998); Lowenthal (1998); Graham, Ashworth, and Tunbridge (2000); Howard (2003); Smith (2006); Fairclough et al. (2008); Graham and Howard (2008a); Smith et al. (2010); Harrison (2010, 2012).
2. For a basic introduction to the relation of heritage and identity, see Howard (2003); Graham and Howard (2008a, 2008b); Russell (2010); During (2011).
3. Tunbridge and Ashworth (1996, 20); Carman (2002, 22); Holtorf and Kristensen (2014, 315).
4. See, among others, Shaw and Jones (1997); Ashworth, Graham, and Tunbridge (2007); Silverman (2011a, 2011b).
5. For an insightful introduction, see Holtorf and Kristensen (2014).
6. The plan never came to fruition. The building underwent a turbulent history (Sidorov 2000) until after the fall of the Communist regime, when the cathedral was restored and took on new political significance, symbolizing Russia's revival (Gentes 1998).
7. See Jones and Shaw (2006) on Singapore and Jakarta; see McEachern (2007) on South Africa.
8. See, for example, James (1999, 2005); Walasek (2015); Galaty (2011). See also the special issue of *The International Journal of Heritage Studies* on contested heritage (*IJHS* 2, no. 1–2 [1996]).
9. This was part of Mussolini's larger project of creating a grand square, the *Piazzale Augusto Imperatore* (Kostof 1978), "where Antiquity, Christianity and the Fascist age would be reflected by reshaping the entire area" (Olariu 2012, 359).
10. See, for example, the discussion on Singapore and Jakarta by Jones and Shaw (2006).
11. *Pera* means "far away" or "across" in Greek, because it was situated on the other side of the imperial city. This name remained in common use until the establishment of the Turkish Republic in 1923. The Turkish name *Beyoğlu* echoes the presence of a Venetian palace (hence, a bey's house) in the district.
12. Kirshenblatt-Gimblett (1998); Hooper Greenhill (2000); Watson and Waterton (2010a, 2010b).
13. Mirtzoeff (2006) exhaustively discusses the meaning of the term from the 1840s (when it was coined by Scottish historian Thomas Carlyle) to the present.
14. According to Staiff (2014, 73), one way of regarding the terms *vision* and *visuality* is to distinguish between pre-epistemic seeing and epistemic seeing. Pre-epistemic seeing involves the way we use vision as a physical operation to navigate the world; epistemic seeing is more about the role of the visual in our understanding of the world.

15. John Urry's work (Urry 1990, 2002; Urry and Larsen 2011) remains influential in conceptualizing the visual nature of the visitor's experience. See also Larsen (2014), where more references are available.

16. For an exhaustive and sober account of the NAM's history, see Filippopoulou (2011); for the principles guiding its design, see especially pages 367–84, which provide more references. See also Fouseki (2006, 2007); and James (2009).

17. Accessed March 30, 2016, http://www.tschumi.com/projects/2/#.

18. References in the press were indicative of the museum's appeal in this respect: "a battle tank made of crystal and cement" (*El Mundo*, June 21, 2009); "the final argument for the return" (*El Pais*, June 20, 2009); "a dangerous trap for the British Museum" (*Le Monde*, June 19, 2009); "the NAM is the argument of the Greek claim" (*Die Zeit*, June 18, 2009).

19. Apart from the unattractive blocks of flats of the 1970s, the dense residential area around the NAM is also home to an elegant quarter of old Athens with some fine neoclassical houses.

20. See Papaioannou (2007); Filippidis (2007). Among the sharpest critics was Salingaros (2007); Stara (2009); and Horáček (2014, 59), who, commenting on the NAM's visual collision with the Parthenon, concluded, "It is as if one erected a concrete orangutan in the middle of the Indonesian jungle."

21. Despite the fact that they were placed after careful consultation with archaeologists, the ninety-two columns on which the museum's base floats received acute criticism for sitting on top of significant remains of a Byzantine quarter that came to light during work on the building's foundation.

22. For a polemical critique of the museum's architecture, see, among many, Dragonas (2010); Kotsakis (2009); Mitzalis (2007); Papaioannou (2007); Salingaros (2007); Ouroussoff (2007); Falida (2009); Filippidis (2009); Patestos (2009); Rigopoulos (2009); and Stara (2009). See also papers presented at the international symposium The Acropolis Museum: Ideology—Museology—Architecture, which was organized in 2011 in Thessaloniki and Athens, accessed March 30, 2016, www.blod.gr.

23. For a critique of this tenet, see Plantzos (2009, 14).

24. For reference to all relevant legal acts, see Filippopoulou (2011, 325–34).

25. Filippopoulou (2011, 325–34) provides a short, balanced account of the debate. For a detailed and exhaustively documented account, see www.areopagitou17.blogspot.gr, accessed August 30, 2015.

26. Some press titles such as "Athenians Go to War over Two Views of History" (Smith 2007) were quite apposite.

27. Accessed July 22, 2016, http://www.kerdos.gr/oldarticles.aspx?artid=617062.

28. With a letter to the minister as reproduced in *Architektones* 64, July–August 2007, 20–21, accessed July 22, 2016, http://portal.tee.gr/portal/page/portal/SCIENTIFIC_WORK/grafeio_politismou/e-enimerwsi/enimervsi2007/politismos_0707.htm#p1.

29. Accessed August 30, 2015, http://areopagitou17.blogspot.gr/search?updated-min=2007-01-01T00:00:00-08:00&updated-max=2008-01-01T00:00:00-08:00&max-results=16).

30. Accessed June 10, 2016, http://yperareopagitou.blogspot.gr.

31. For an exhaustive list of press coverage, see http://areopagitou17.blogspot.gr/2007/07/blog-post_2000.html, accessed August 25, 2015.

32. Horáček (2014) discusses the NAM as an example of contrasting (traditionalist versus modernist) views of urban design and offers a summary of the argument mainly as expressed by professional critics in architectural and other journals.

33. This was a strict prerequisite in the architectural competition, whereas the visitor's possibility of simultaneously viewing both the Parthenon Marbles exhibited in the NAM and the Parthenon itself has been praised repeatedly by the entire archaeological community.

34. In the words of Alexandros Mantis, then ephor of the Acropolis (as quoted in Santorinaiou 2007).

35. Vatopoulos (2007); cf. Aesopos (2007, 2008); Yakoumakatos (2007).

36. "So that tourists have their coffee with a free view . . . Is this what we want?" was often heard during the debate.

37. Harrison (2010) makes the point that heritage is to a large extent an economic activity and that much of what motivates the involvement of the state and other organizations in heritage is related to its economic potential and its connections to tourism.

38. Indeed, this question bewildered some of the members of the two councils in their common meeting on July 3, 2007.

39. Declaring its opposition to the demolition, the International Council for Monuments and Sites (ICOMOS) pointed out, "These buildings form the integral part of the streetscape by the Acropolis rock signifying and symbolizing the harmonic coexistence of several periods." Accessed August 25, 2015, http://articles.latimes.com/2007/oct/15/world/fg-acropolis15.

40. Accessed June 10, 2016, http://www.drivehq.com/file/df.aspx/shareID2893819/fileID107951455/AREOPAGITOU%20OPINIONS%20_3.pdf.

41. Even before the launching of the third architectural competition for the NAM in 1989, the so-called Makriyanni site has been regarded as one of the most difficult sites in Athens from an urban planning point of view. Many of the participant architects had expressed their concern on the (un)suitability of the site, and some of them finally recalled their participation on the grounds that it was impossible to "fit" the museum's building into the specific site without impairing the urban fabric of the area. According to later criticism, the jury (and the government) bear huge responsibility on insisting to build the museum on the Makriyanni site.

42. See, among many, Friderikou (2007).

43. In the words of Francois Loyer, then director of research at the CNRS/Paris, in a 2008 letter to the Greek Minister of Culture, accessed August 25, 2015, http://www.greekarchitects.gr/gr.

44. Yakoumakatos (2007).

45. Accessed August 25, 2015, https://www.youtube.com/watch?feature=player_embedded&v=glw3w1_aO1s.

46. Accessed August 25, 2015, http://www.greekarchitects.gr/en/graactions/%CE%B1rchitectural-competition-id2077.

47. Cf. the notion of "creative dismantling," a concept in between preservation and destruction, as discussed by Wienberg (2014).

48. Decision No. 2335/2009 of the Council of State.

49. The political, ideological, and cultural implications of an idealized view of classical antiquity and the subsequent internalization of this model within the modern Greek consciousness has been discussed in a plethora of publications, such as Herzfeld (1982); Jusdanis (1991); Leontis (1995); Gourgouris (1996); Peckham (2001); Loukaki (2008); and Tziovas (2014).

50. I here restricted myself to citing only some of the most influential research, such as Lowenthal (1988); Kotsakis (1991); Hamilakis and Yalouri (1996); Hamilakis (2007). See also the plethora of papers by Plantzos as cited in the references at the end of this chapter.

51. On the cleansing of urban space from remnants of previous historical phases, see also Galiniki (this volume).

52. The cultural landscape has been defined as a landscape that has significant symbolic meaning for a particular cultural group or groups (Bourassa 1991; Muir 1999). Its physical form is profoundly influenced by political, religious, economic, and social values. For the concept of the landscape as a cultural image, see Daniels and Cosgrove (1988); see also Konstantinou (this volume).

53. Anafiotika was illegally and humbly constructed on the northeastern side of the rock by builders who came to Athens from the small island of Anafi to work in the capital that was then quickly developing. In real terms, the issue has remained inconclusive to date, and the area (today one of the most picturesque old quarters in Athens) stands as a prominent example of divergent perceptions and alternative forms of appropriation of a "national" space par excellence (Caftanzoglou 2001).

54. For later examples of building activity around the rock, see also Yalouri (2001, 55–56, 152-55). Interestingly, one of the latest incidents was the erection in 1955 of a block of flats on the same Dionyssiou Areopagitou Street, and in 2019 of a of ten-story hotel in Makryianni district that would form a "wall" beneath the Acropolis (Accessed July 16, 2019, http://www.ekathimerini.com/236368/article/ekathimerini/news/makriyianni-residents-bemoan-new-buildings-at-foot-of-acropolis). Following severe reactions, all constructions were finally interrupted, and concerning the 1955 flats, the already built parts were demolished.

55. See, for example, Garden (2006, 399); Hamilakis (2008) and (2009, 378); Caftanzoglou (2001).

56. In his elucidating discussion on Moscow's monuments, Yampolsky (1995, 94–95) notes that approaching a monument is always a sort of transgression of a sacral zone.

57. As explained by the museum's director, archaeologist Dimitris Pandermalis, in an interview to Michaelidis (2007).

58. Or, to become "the sole, internationally acclaimed, terrestrial observation post of the Parthenon" (Kazeros 2007).

59. For a critique of this stance, see Plantzos (2010, 28); Hamilakis (2011).

60. Hamilakis (2007, 35–36, 41–44); cf. Plantzos (2008, 15–16).

61. Cf. Michaelidis (2007); Pandermalis (2010); Plantzos (2011, 619–20).

62. A 2004 survey in Ontario, Canada, for instance, found that even when recognized as historically significant, and despite the fact that they may even be designated, buildings are demolished (Shipley and Reyburn 2005, 167). The demolition of the National Library in Singapore is another case in point. Despite polls recording a 93 percent vote in favor of retention and the presentation of public and professional alternatives to destruction, the National Library was torn down (Jones and Shaw 2006).

63. See, for example, the construction of cultural visibility as part of identity building in Britain, Rhodes, and Crete as discussed by Watson and Waterton (2010b, 90–94), Watson (2010) and Duke (2007), and Solomon (2006, 2007), respectively.

References

Aesopos, Yannis. 2007. "Η Υψηλή Αρχιτεκτονική Απαιτεί Ρήξεις" [High Architecture Demands Ruptures]. *Kathimerini*, August 5, 2007.

———. 2008. "Η Πόλη και η Αρχιτεκτονική Χρειάζονται Νέα Κτίρια" [The City and Architecture Are in Need of New Buildings]. *Kathimerini*, April 19, 2005.

Antoniadis, Antonis. 2007. "Άνω και Κάτω 'Παρθενώνας'" [Upper and Lower 'Parthenon']. *ACAarchitecture Mag* 22, July 4, 2007. Accessed September 4, 2015. http://www.acaarchitecture.com/Mag22.htm.pdf.

Ashworth, Gregory J., Brian J. Graham, and John E. Tunbridge. 2007. *Pluralizing Pasts: Heritage, Identity and Place in Multicultural Societies*. London: Pluto.

Bartu, Ayfer. 1999. "Who Owns the Old Quarters? Rewriting Histories in a Global Era." In *Istanbul: Between the Global and the Local*, edited by Çağlar Keyder, 31–45. London: Rowman and Littlefield.

———. 2001. "Rethinking Heritage Politics in a Global Context: A View from Istanbul." In *Hybrid Urbanism: On Identity Discourse and the Built Environment*, edited by Nezar AlSayyad, 131–55. Westport: Praeger.

Bourassa, Steven. 1991. *The Aesthetics of Landscape*. London: Belhaven.

Brett, David. 1996. *The Construction of Heritage*. Cork: Cork University Press.

Bryson, Norman. 1988. "The Gaze in the Expanded Field." In *Vision and Visuality*, edited by Hal Foster, 87–114. Seattle: Bay.

Caftanzoglou, Roxani. 2001. *Στη Σκιά του Ιερού Βράχου. Τόπος και Μνήμη στα Αναφιώτικα* [In the Shadow of the Sacred Rock: Place and Memory in Anafiotika]. Athens: Greek National Center for Social Research.

Carman, John. 2002. *Archaeology and Heritage: An Introduction*. London: Continuum.

Clogg, Richard. 1988. "The Greeks and Their Past." In *Historians as Nation-Builders: Central and South-East Europe*, edited by Dennis Deletant and Harry Hanak, 16–28. London: Macmillan.

Daniels, Stephen, and Dennis Cosgrove, eds. 1988. *The Iconography of the Landscape*. Cambridge: Cambridge University Press.

Dragonas, Panos. 2010. "Μετά (την) Ακρόπολη" [After (the) Acropolis]. *Arhitektonika Themata* 44: 128–30.

Duke, Philip. 2007. *The Tourists Gaze, the Cretans Glance: Archaeology and Tourism on a Greek Island*. Walnut Creek, CA: Left Coast.

During, Roel. 2011. *Cultural Heritage and Identity Politics*. The Netherlands: Wageningen Academic.

Fairclough, Graham. 2013. "Where Is Heritage Taking Us? European Perspectives." *Heritage* 16 (3): 6–11. Accessed March 30, 2015. http://www.heritagecanada.org/sites/www.heritagecanada.org/files/magazines/Feature-03%2013-20130730.pdf.

Fairclough, Graham, Rodney Harrison, John Jameson, and John Schofield, eds. 2008. *The Heritage Reader*. London: Routledge.

Falida, Ephie, 2009. "Το Νέο Μουσείο Ακρόπολης με τη Ματιά του Αρχιτέκτονα" [The New Acropolis Museum through an Architect's Eye]. *Ta Nea*, June 20, 2009. Accessed August 5, 2015. http://www.tanea.gr/ellada/article/?aid=4522769.

Filippidis, Dimitris. 2007. "Κατεδαφίστε την Περιοχή!" [Demolish the Area!] *Kathimerini*, July 21, 2007.

———. 2009. "Ένα Κτίριο χωρίς Ανάταση" [A Building without Exaltation]. *Kathimerini*, June 5, 2007. Accessed July 24, 2019. https://www.kathimerini.gr/360334/article/politismos/arxeio-politismoy/apoyh-ktirio-xwris-anatash.

Filippopoulou, Ersie. 2011. *Το Νέο Μουσείο Ακρόπολης. Δια Πυρός και Σιδήρου* [The New Acropolis Museum: By Fire and Sword]. Athens: Papasotiriou.

Foster, Hal, ed. 1988. *Vision and Visuality*. Seattle: Bay.
Forest, Benjamin, and Juliet Johnson. 2002. "Unravelling the Threads of History: Soviet-Era Monuments and Post-Soviet National Identity in Moscow." *Annals of the Association of American Geographers* 92 (3): 524–47.
Fouseki, Kalliopi. 2006. "Conflicting Discourses on the Construction of the New Acropolis Museum: Past and Present." *European Review of History* 13 (4): 533–48.
———. 2007. "Developing and Integrating a Conflict Management Model into the Heritage Management Process: The Case of the New Acropolis Museum." In *Which Past, Whose Future: Treatments of the Past at the Start of the 21st Century*, edited by Sven Grabow, Daniel Hull, and Emma Waterton, 127–36. Oxford: Oxbow.
Friderikou, Anna. 2007. "Ηρόστρατοι του 21ου αιώνα" [Herostratuses of the Twenty-First Century]. *Kathimerini*, September 23, 2007. Accessed July 24, 2019. https://www.kathimerini.gr/706600/opinion/epikairothta/arxeio-monimes-sthles/hrostratoi-toy-21oy-aiwna.
Galaty, Michael. 2011. "Blood of Our Ancestors: Cultural Heritage Management in the Balkans." In *Contested Cultural Heritage. Religion, Nationalism, Erasure and Exclusion in a Global World*, edited by Helaine Silverman, 109–24. New York: Springer.
Garden, Mary Catherine. 2006. "The Heritage Scape: Looking at Landscapes of the Past." *International Journal of Heritage Studies* 12 (5): 394–411.
Gentes, Andrew. 1998. "The Life, Death and Resurrection of the Cathedral of Christ the Saviour, Moscow." *History Workshop Journal* 46: 63–95.
Gourgouris, Stathis. 1996. *Dream Nation: Enlightenment, Colonization and the Institution of Modern Greece*. Stanford, CA: Stanford University Press.
Graham, Brian, Gregory Ashworth, and John Tunbridge, eds. 2000. *The Geography of Heritage. Power, Culture and Economy*. London: Arnold.
Graham, Brian, and Peter Howard, eds. 2008a. *The Ashgate Research Companion to Heritage and Identity*. London: Ashgate.
———. 2008b. "Heritage and Identity." In *The Ashgate Research Companion to Heritage and Identity*, edited by Brian Graham and Peter Howard, 1–18. London: Ashgate.
Hamilakis, Yannis. 2007. *The Nation and its Ruins: Antiquity, Archaeology, and National Imagination in Greece*. Oxford: Oxford University Press.
———. 2008. "Monumentalizing Place: Archaeologists, Photographers and the Athenian Acropolis from the Eighteenth Century to the Present." In *Monuments in the Landscape: Papers in Honor of Andrew Fleming*, edited by Paul Rainbird, 190–98. Stroud: Tempus.
———. 2009. "Μνημειοποίηση του Τόπου: Αρχαιολόγοι, Φωτογράφοι και η Αθηναϊκή Ακρόπολη από τον 18ο Αιώνα έως Σήμερα" [Monumentalizing Place: Archaeologists, Photographers and the Athenian Acropolis from the Eighteenth Century to the Present]. In *Μεταμορφώσεις του Χώρου: Κοινωνικές και Πολιτισμικές Διαστάσεις* [Space Transformations: Social and Cultural Dimensions], edited by Manos Spyridakis, 373–96. Athens: Nissos.
———. 2011. "Museums of Oblivion." *Antiquity* 85: 625–29.
Hamilakis, Yannis, and Eleana Yalouri. 1996. "Antiquities as Symbolic Capital in Modern Greek Society." *Antiquity* 70: 117–29.
Hamilakis, Yannis, and Fotis Ifantidis. 2015. "The Photographic and the Archaeological: The 'Other' Acropolis." In *Camera Graeca: Photographs, Narratives, Materialities*, edited by Philip Carabott, Yannis Hamilakis, and Eleni Papargyriou, 133–57. London: Ashgate.

Harrison, Rodney, ed. 2010. *Understanding the Politics of Heritage*. Manchester: Manchester University Press.

———, ed. 2012. *Heritage. Critical Approaches*. London: Routledge.

Herzfeld, Michael. 1982. *Ours Once More. Folklore, Ideology and the Making of Modern Greece*. Austin: University of Texas Press.

Holtorf, Cornelius, and Troels Myrap Kristensen. 2014. "Heritage Erasure: Rethinking 'Protection' and 'Preservation.'" *International Journal of Heritage Studies* 21 (4): 313–17.

Hooper Greenhill, Eilean. 2000. *Museums and the Interpretation of Visual Culture*. London: Routledge.

Horáček, Martin. 2014. "Museum of Art versus the City as a Work of Art—A Case of the New Acropolis Museum in Athens." *Archnet-IJAR, International Journal of Architectural Research* 8 (2): 47–61.

Howard, Peter. 2003. *Heritage. Management, Interpretation, Identity*. London: Continuum.

James, Beverly. 1999. "Fencing in the Past: Budapest's Statue Park Museum." *Media, Culture and Society* 21 (3): 291–311.

———. 2005. "Budapest's Statue Park Museum." In *Imagining Post-Communism. Visual Narratives of Hungary's 1956 Revolution*, edited by Beverly James, 21–38. College Station: Texas A&M University Press.

James, Nick. 2009. "The Acropolis and its New Museum." *Antiquity* 83: 1144–51.

Jones, Roy, and Brian Shaw. 2006. "Palimpsests of Progress: Erasing the Past and Rewriting the Future in Developing Societies—Case Studies of Singapore and Jakarta." *International Journal of Heritage Studies* 12 (2): 122–38.

Jusdanis, Gregory. 1991. *Belated Modernity and Aesthetic Culture: Inventing National Literature*. Minneapolis: University of Minnesota Press.

Kardamitsi-Adami, Maro. 2007. "Να τα Αποδεχτούμε ως Έχουν" [Let Us Accept Them as They Are]. *Kiriakatiki Eleftherotipia*, October 21, 2007.

Kazeros, Nikos. 2007. "Η 'ευγενική' και επιλεκτική αποστροφή" [The "Noble" and Selective Aversion]. *Eleftheros Tipos*, August 13, 2007.

Kirichenko, Evgenia. 2012. *Moscow's Cathedral of Christ the Saviour: Its Creation, Destruction, and Rebirth (1813–1997)*. Accessed March 30, 2015. http://www.thomas hoisington.com/pdfs/Moscows_Cathedral_Kirichenko.pdf.

Kiosse, Chara. 2007. "Ο Παρθενώνας Θέλει τη Συνομιλία;" [Does the Parthenon Want the Conversation?]. *To Vima*, July 15, 2007. Accessed July 24, 2007. https://www.tovima .gr/2008/11/25/culture/o-parthenwnas-thelei-ti-synomilia.

Kirk, Terry. 2006. "Framing St. Peter's: Urban Planning in Fascist Rome." *The Art Bulletin* 88 (4): 756–76.

Kirshenblatt-Gimblett, Barbara. 1998. *Destination Culture: Tourism, Museums, and Heritage*. Los Angeles: University of California Press.

Kizis, Yannis. 2007. "Το Διατηρητέο Αστικό Μέτωπο" [The Listed Civic Front]. *Kathimerini*, July 21, 2007.

Kontrarou-Rassia, Ninetta. 2007. "Το Μουσείο που Πληγώναμε" [The Museum That We Hurt]. *Enet-Eleftherotipia*, July 5, 2007.

Kostof, Spiro. 1978. "The Emperor and the Duce: The Planning of Piazzale Augusto Imperatore in Rome." In *Art and Architecture in the Service of Politics*, edited by Henry Millon and Linda Nochlin, 270–325. Cambridge, MA: MIT Press.

Kotsakis, Kostas. 1991. "The Powerful Past: Theoretical Trends in Greek Archaeology." In *Archaeological Theory in Europe*, edited by Ian Hodder, 65–90. London: Routledge.

———. 2009. “Κάποιες Σκέψεις για το Νέο Μουσείο Ακρόπολης” [Some Thoughts on the New Acropolis Museum]. *I Avgi*, July 12, 2009. Accessed May 30, 2015. http://www.avgi.gr/ArticleActionshow.action?articleID=474981.

Kourtovik, Dimosthenis. 2007. “Ρέκβιεμ για δύο Κτίρια” [Requiem for Two Buildings]. *Ta Nea*, November 10, 2007.

Larsen, Jonas. 2014. “The Tourist Gaze 1.0, 2.0, and 3.0.” In *The Wiley Blackwell Companion to Tourism*, edited by Alan Lew, Michael Hall, and Allan Williams, 304–13. London: Sage.

Lekakis, Stelios. 2007. “Why the Buildings at Areopagitou Street No. 17–19 Will Be Reduced to Ruins.” *Monumenta*. Accessed July 24, 2019. http://www.monumenta.org/article.php?perm=1&IssueID=5&lang=en&CategoryID=19&ArticleID=107.

Leontis, Artemis. 1995. *Topographies of Hellenism: Mapping the Homeland*. Ithaca, NY: Cornell University Press.

Loukaki, Argyro. 2008. *Living Ruins: Value Conflicts*. Aldershot: Ashgate.

Lowenthal, David. 1988. “Classical Antiquities as National and Global Heritage.” *Antiquity* 62: 726–35.

———. 1998. *The Heritage Crusade and the Spoils of History*. Cambridge: Cambridge University Press.

Mallouchou-Tufano, Fani. 1998. *Η Αναστήλωση των Αρχαίων Μνημείων στη Νεώτερη Ελλάδα (1834–1939)* [The Restoration of Ancient Monuments in Modern Greece (1834–1939)]. Athens: Athens Archaeological Society.

McEachern, Charmaine. 2007. “Mapping the Memories: Politics, Place and Identity in the District Six Museum, Cape Town.” In *Museums and their Communities*, edited by Sheila Watson, 457–78. London: Routledge.

Michaelidis, Christos. 2007. “Ο άνθρωπος πίσω από το Μουσείο της Ακρόπολης” [The Man behind the Acropolis Museum]. An interview with Dimitris Pandermalis. *LIFO*, December 20, 2007, 93. Accessed June 30, 2015. http://www.lifo.gr/mag/features/409.

Mirtzoeff, Nicholas. 2006. “On Visuality.” *Journal of Visual Culture* 5 (1): 53–79.

Mitzalis, Nikolas. 2007. “Τα Αδιέξοδα της Αρχιτεκτονικής και το Νέο Μουσείο Ακρόπολης” [The Dead-Ends of Architecture and the New Acropolis Museum]. *Greek Architects*, August 10, 2007. Accessed May 30, 2015. http://www.greekarchitects.gr.

Monumenta. 2009. “Οι Φύλακες Άγγελοι του Νέου Μουσείου Ακροπόλεως Κινδυνεύουν” [The Guardian Angels of the New Acropolis Museum Are in Danger]. *Monumenta*, June 5, 2009. Accessed July 24, 2019. http://old.anoihtipoli.gr/blog-syneisfores/oi-fylakes-aggeloi-toy-neoy-moyseioy-akropoleos-kindyneyoyn/?searchterm=None.

Muir, Richard. 1999. *Approaches to Landscape*. London: Macmillan.

Olariu, Cristian. 2012. “Archaeology, Architecture and the Use of *Romanità* in Fascist Italy.” *Studia Antiqua et Archaeologica* 18: 351–75.

Ouroussoff, Nicolai. 2007. “The New Acropolis Museum: A Dialogue with Antiquity.” *The New York Times*, October 30, 2007. Accessed May 30, 2015. www.nytimes.com/2007/10/29/arts/29iht-arch.1.8096904.html.

Pandermalis, Dimitris. 2010. Interview at *Jyllands Posten* (Copenhagen). Accessed October 10, 2015. http://omogeneia.ana-mpa.gr/press.php?id=10417.

Papaioannou, Tassis. 2007. “Σκέψεις για το Νέο Μουσείο Ακρόπολης” [Thoughts on the New Acropolis Museum]. *Enet-Eleftherotipia*, November 9, 2007. Accessed April 27, 2015. http://archive.enet.gr/online/online_text/c=113,dt=09.11.2007,id=66654904.

Patestos, Kostas. 2009. "Ούφο στου Μακρυγιάννη" [A UFO at the Makriyanni Site]. *To Vima*, April 12, 2009. Accessed April 27, 2015. http://www.tovima.gr/culture /article/?aid=263580.

Pearce, Susan. 1998. "The Construction and Analysis of the Cultural Heritage: Some Thoughts." *International Journal of Heritage Studies* 4 (1): 1–9.

Peckham, Robert S. 2001. *National Histories, Natural States. Nationalism and the Politics of Place in Greece*. London: I. B. Tauris.

Plantzos, Dimitris. 2008. "Archaeology and Hellenic Identity, 1896–2004: The Frustrated Vision." In *A Singular Antiquity: Archaeology and Hellenic Identity in Twentieth-Century Greece*, edited by Dimitris Damaskos and Dimitris Plantzos, 10–30. Athens: Benaki Museum.

———. 2009. "Η Κιβωτός και το Έθνος: ένα Σχόλιο για την Υποδοχή του Νέου Μουσείου Ακροπόλεως" [The Arc and the Nation: A Comment on the Reception of the New Acropolis Museum]. *Sihrona Themata* 106: 14–18.

———. 2010. "'Il n'y a pas de hors texte': Το Μουσείο της Ακρόπολης και τα Απόνερα του Ιδεαλισμού" ["Il n'y a pas de hors texte": The Acropolis Museum and the Wake of Idealism]. *Tetradia Mousiologias* 7: 23–29.

———. 2011. "Behold the Raking Geison: the New Acropolis Museum and Its Context-Free Archaeologies." *Antiquity* 85: 613–30.

———. 2012. Η Ακρόπολη Μετά [The Acropolis After]. Discussion on the Acropolis's biography held at the Onassis Cultural Foundation, Athens, February 29, 2012. Accessed July 10, 2015. https://www.academia.edu/5022367/%CE%91%CE%BA%CF%81%CF%8C%CF%80%CE%BF%CE%BB%CE%B7_%CE%BC%CE%B5%CF%84%CE%AC.

———. 2013. "A Voice Less Material: Classical Antiquities and Their Uses at the Time of the Greek Crisis." Paper presented at the one-day colloquium Greece/Precarious/Europe, co-organized by the Hellenic Center, the Subfaculty of Modern Greek, Oxford University, and the Center for the Reception of Greece and Rome, London, February 16, 2013. Accessed July 10, 2015. https://www.academia.edu/2614147/A_voice_less_material _classical_antiquities_and_their_uses_at_the_time_of_the_Greek_crisis.

Rigopoulos, Dimitris. 2009. "Νέο Μουσείο Ακρόπολης, η Μεγάλη Στιγμή" [New Acropolis Museum: The Big Moment]. *Kathimerini*, June 5, 2009. Accessed May 14, 2015. http:// www.kathimerini.gr/4dcgi/_w_articles_kathworld_1_05/06/2009_1288715.

Russell, I. 2010. "Heritage, Identities, and Roots: A Critique of Arborescent Models of Heritage and Identity." In *Heritage Values in Contemporary Society*, edited by George Smith, Phyllis Messenger, and Hilary Soderland, 75–85. Walnut Creek, CA: Left Coast.

Salingaros, Nikos. 2007. "Architectural Cannibalism in Athens." *Orthodoxy Today*, November 20, 2007. Accessed May 14, 2015. www.orthodoxytoday.org/articles7/ SalingarosAthens.php.

Santorinaiou, Vicky. 2007. "Διχάζει η Κατεδάφιση των Διατηρητέων Κτιρίων δίπλα στο Νέο Μουσείο Ακρόπολης" [The Demolition of Listed Buildings Next to the New Acropolis Museum Divides]. *To Kerdos*, July 10, 2007. Accessed July 24, 2019. http://www.kerdos .gr/oldarticles.aspx?artid=582625.

Schirato, Tony, and Jen Webb. 2010. "Inside/Outside: Ways of Seeing the World." In *Culture, Heritage and Representation: Perspectives on Visuality and the Past*, edited by Steve Watson and Emma Waterton, 19–38. Aldershot: Ashgate.

Shaw, Brian J., and Roy Jones, eds. 1997. *Contested Urban Heritage: Voices from the Periphery.* Aldershot: Ashgate.

Shipley, Robert, and Karen Reyburn. 2005. "Lost Heritage: A Survey of Historic Buildings Demolition in Ontario, Canada." *International Journal of Heritage Studies* 9 (2): 151–68.

Sidorov, Dmitri. 2000. "National Monumentalization and the Politics of Scale: The Resurrections of the Cathedral of Christ the Savior in Moscow." *Annals of the Association of American Geographers* 90 (3): 548–72.

Silverman, Helaine, ed. 2011a. *Contested Cultural Heritage: Religion, Nationalism, Erasure and Exclusion in a Global World.* New York: Springer.

———. 2011b. "Contested Cultural Heritage: A Selective Historiography." In *Contested Cultural Heritage. Religion, Nationalism, Erasure and Exclusion in a Global World,* edited by Helaine Silverman, 1–50. New York: Springer.

Smith, Helena. 2007. "Athenians Go to War over Two Views of History." *The Guardian.* July 29, 2007. Accessed July 20, 2016. https://www.theguardian.com/world/2007/jul/29/artnews.architecture.

Smith, Laurajane. 2006. *Uses of Heritage.* London: Routledge.

Smith, George, Phyllis Messenger, and Hilary Soderland, eds. 2010. *Heritage Values in Contemporary Society.* Walnut Creek, CA: Left Coast.

Solomon, Esther. 2006. "Knossos: Social Uses of a Monumental Landscape." In *Archaeology and European Modernity: Producing and Consuming the "Minoans,"* edited by Yannis Hamilakis and Nicoletta Momigliano, 163–82. Padova: Botega d'Erasmo; *Creta Antica,* special issue.

Staiff, Russell. 2014. *Re-imagining Heritage Interpretation. Enchanting the Past-Future.* Farnham: Ashgate.

Stanley-Price, Nicholas. 2007. "The Thread of Continuity: Cultural Heritage in Post-War Recovery." In *Cultural Heritage in Post-War Recovery,* edited by Nicholas Stanley-Price, 1–16. Paper presented at the ICCROM FORUM, Rome, October 4–6, 2005. Accessed August 5, 2015. http://www.iccrom.org/ifrcdn/pdf/ICCROM_ICS06_CulturalHeritagePostwar_en.pdf.

Stara, Alexandra. 2009. "The New Acropolis Museum: Banal, Sloppy, Badly Detailed Sophistry." *The Architectural Review* 1348: 24–26.

Thermou, Maria. 2007. "Προσβολή στον Πολιτισμό" [An Insult to Civilization]. *To Vima,* May 13, 2007.

Thompson, John. 2005. "The New Visibility." *Theory, Culture and Society* 22 (6): 31–51.

Tunbridge, John. 2008. "Whose Heritage to Conserve? Cross-Cultural Reflections on Political Dominance and Urban Heritage Conservation." In *The Heritage Reader,* edited by Graham Fairclough, Rodney Harrison, John Jameson, and John Schofield, 235–44. London: Routledge.

Tunbridge, John, and Gregory Ashworth. 1996. *Dissonant Heritage: The Management of the Past as a Resource in Conflict.* Chichester: John Wiley.

Tziovas, Dimitris. 2014. *Re-Imagining the Past: Antiquity and Modern Greek Culture.* Oxford: Oxford University Press.

Urry, John. 1990. *The Tourist Gaze: Leisure and Travel in Contemporary Society.* London: Sage.

———. 2002. *The Tourist Gaze.* London: Sage.

Urry, John, and Jonas Larsen. 2011. *The Tourist Gaze 3.0.* London: Sage.

Vassilikos, Vassilis. 2007. "Καφετέρια Τσουμί" [Cafeteria Tschumi]. *Eleftherotipia*, July 16, 2007. Accessed July 24, 2019. https://www.greekarchitects.gr/gr/%CE%B4%CE%B9%CE%AC%CE%BB%CE%BF%CE%B3%CE%BF%CE%B9/%C2%AB%CE%BA%CE%B1%CF%86%CE%B5%CF%84%CE%AD%CF%81%CE%B9%CE%B1-%CF%84%CF%83%CE%BF%CF%85%CE%BC%CE%AF%C2%BB-id1836.

Vatopoulos, Nikos. 2007. "Μουσείο με Θέα: Διάλογος και Διχασμός" [A Museum with a View: Dialogue and Division]. *Kathimerini*, July 21, 2007. Accessed July 24, 2019. https://www.kathimerini.gr/292890/article/epikairothta/ellada/moyseio-me-8ea-dialogos-kai-dixasmos.

Walasek, Helen, ed. 2015. *Bosnia and the Destruction of Cultural Heritage*. London: Ashgate.

Watson, Steve. 2010. "Constructing Rhodes: Heritage and Visuality." In *Culture, Heritage and Representations: Perspectives on Visuality and the Past*, edited by Steve Watson and Emma Waterton, 249–70. Aldershot: Ashgate.

Watson, Steve, and Emma Waterton, eds. 2010a. *Culture, Heritage and Representation: Perspectives on Visuality and the Past*. Aldershot: Ashgate.

———. 2010b. "Reading the Visual: Representation and Narrative in the Construction of Heritage." *Material Culture Review* 71: 84–97.

Wienberg, Jes. 2014. "Four Churches and a Lighthouse—Preservation, 'Creative Dismantling' or Destruction." *Danish Journal of Archaeology* 3 (1): 68–75.

Yakoumakatos, Andreas. 2007. "Το Δίλημμα της Κατεδάφισης" [The Demolition Dilemma]. *To Vima*, July 15, 2007. Accessed July 24, 2019. https://www.greekarchitects.gr/gr.

Yalouri, Eleana. 2001. *The Acropolis: Global Fame, Local Claim*. London: Berg.

Yampolsky, Mikhail. 1995. "In the Shadow of Monuments: Notes on Iconoclasm and Time." In *Soviet Hieroglyphics: Visual Culture in Late Twentieth-Century Russia*, edited by Nancy Condee, 93–112. Bloomington: Indiana University Press.

9 Eptapyrgio, a Modern Prison inside a World Heritage Monument

Raw Memories in the Margins of Archaeology

Eleni Stefanou and Ioanna Antoniadou

Introduction

When witnessing the material traces of long-term human activity, archaeologists face the difficult question of where a monument's story begins and ends. What complicates this epistemological dilemma even further is when one deals with material remains whose use extends to modern times. Here, the ethical responsibility toward the past becomes one of the present.

Such a case in point is Eptapyrgio, a World Heritage Monument in Thessaloniki in Northern Greece, which is predominantly known as a Byzantine fortress even though its history extends to the twentieth century. During this later and lesser-known stage of its life, Eptapyrgio came to be regarded as one of the country's "fiercest" prisons in the context of some of the most difficult and contested periods of Greece's modern history, such as the Metaxas dictatorship (1936–1941), World War II (1940–1944), the Greek Civil War (1946–1949), the postwar period, and the Colonels' dictatorship (1967–1974). People of both sexes and of every age were incarcerated there, convicted of both criminal and civil offences.

Today, Eptapyrgio is the seat of the Department of Byzantine and Post-Byzantine Archaeological Sites and Monuments and is open to the public as an archaeological site. It is a complicated case of cultural heritage because its use spans different ages and cultures, and it features Roman, Byzantine, Ottoman, and contemporary Greek elements. What adds to the complexity of the site is its unique functional character as a prison, to which it was converted during the Ottoman era (ca. 1890) and remained in operation until 1989, when it came under the jurisdiction of the Ministry of Culture.

As such, it was the end of the prison that marked the birth of an inevitably contested monument. In 1988, right at the heart of Eptapyrgio's transition from

Fig. 9.1. Eptapyrgio: The façade and main entrance. Photo by E. Stefanou and I. Antoniadou.

a prison to a cultural and administrative space, the site was also inscribed in the World Heritage List of UNESCO as part of the larger complex of Paleochristian and Byzantine Monuments of Thessaloniki. This condition added great symbolic significance to the site, but it unavoidably concentrated archaeological attention on a specific chronological period, taking the focus away from additional and challenging aspects of its multitemporal and multicultural aspects (Solomon, on hierarchy of values, this volume).

As the last defensive project for the fortification of Thessaloniki (Tsaktsiras et al. 2003, 85), it was meant to protect "the most populous and multicultural of the port cities of the Mediterranean" (Athanasiou et al. 2009, 15). Since the era of the Roman Empire, the city prospered (ibid.) because it was located along the route of the Via Egnatia that joined Rome and Istanbul and thus linked Europe and Asia (Molho and Hastaoglou-Martinidis 2009, 1). Thessaloniki continued to flourish after the change of regime and throughout the era of the Byzantine Empire, from the fourth century onward, as the second most important city after Constantinople, and it played a leading role in the Balkan region in terms of education, art, trade, spirituality, and architecture. As a result, the large number of monuments preserved from this period of about one thousand years rendered the city "an open-air museum" of Byzantine art and architecture (Athanasiou et al. 2009, 21). The importance of Thessaloniki was retained even after it became part of the Ottoman Empire (1430). The city rapidly became an Islamic center for the Ottomans, with major public and religious buildings erected and a large mix of multicultural populations and ethnic groups. In particular, the arrival of a large numbers of Jews from western and eastern Europe post-1492 resulted in the city becoming home to the largest Jewish community in the world, known as Madre de Israel to its Spanish-Jewish inhabitants and as the Jerusalem of the Balkans for the non-Jews (Molho and Hastaoglou-Martinidis 2009, 1). By the eighteenth century, the city was a vital trading center and the largest port in the Balkan region.

After the fall of the Ottoman Empire and the city's incorporation into the Greek nation-state in 1912, the Byzantine tradition of Thessaloniki played a crucial role in the redefinition of the city's past and its connection to the notion of Greekness (Galiniki, this volume). Byzantium was rendered one of the two focal loci of the Greek archaeological past, together with classical antiquity, that are for Greek archaeological discourse the two key periods that produce a unified national narrative that extends up to modernity.[1]

This rhetoric, adopted by the archaeological service, permeated the established representation of the Byzantine past and is still prevalent today. In the case of Eptapyrgio, its Byzantine phase is highlighted by the monument's official administrators and is further legitimized by its inscription on the World Heritage list. As a result, the material history of this multifaceted site fails to reach its full implications, opposing the role of the contemporary museum and heritage representation, which, as Crooke (2005, 137) put it, should be an engagement with contemporary issues because of the particular characteristics of what a museum is and with what museums are associated.

Part of this contemporary call in relation to archaeological practice—which operates within as well as maintains such administrative and representational constraints—is instigated by diverse cultural and social claims of the material past. The case of Eptapyrgio entails the frustration of the social groups affected, who feel dissatisfied and unappreciated in the face of the official underrepresentation of the events that had marked the monument and, with it, their lives. One of the most prominent groups among the communities affected by Eptapyrgio consists of the former political prisoners who were detained in its prison for political dissidence during the period of the Colonels' dictatorship (1967–1974). Not all affected communities are coherent in their structure. Nevertheless, in the context of this dominant representational gap, they raise their voices for their experience of the past to be heard. The contexts where narratives "from below" are developed or surface in the public discourse in general include organized commemorative ceremonies, guided tours, and school visits. These voices, signifying particular experiences and human lives once entangled with the life of the monument, are to a large extent absent as a difficult and unmentionable subject that is largely considered to be a marginal issue in archaeological discourse.[2]

The monument's difficult past is far from homogeneous. Yet whilst being inspired by our recent ethnographic research with former political prisoners of Eptapyrgio (detained during the dictatorship between 1967 and 1974), and in defense of a reflexive and politically conscious archaeological practice (Hamilakis and Duke 2007; Hamilakis 2007b; Nicholas and Hollowell 2007), it is our intention to address the power imbalance that pervades Eptapyrgio's official representation and to defend the righteous place of contested contemporary experience and events comprising the monument's recent history. We attempt to elucidate this disputed side of the monument without underestimating the difficulties of representing a contested history (Crooke 2005, 132). Placed within the fields of archaeological ethnography (Hamilakis and Anagnostopoulos 2009; Hamilakis 2011), archaeology of internment (González-Ruibal 2011, 53–74; Moshenska and Myers 2011) and of difficult heritage (Crooke 2005; Macdonald 2009a; 2009b; 2009c; Tunbridge and Ashworth 1996), this chapter employs material derived from our ethnographic research as it aims to address the interpretive and representational inadequacies that stem from and at the same time maintain the power imbalance of established discourse.

Although we consider the conditions that underlie this epistemological and politically ignorant decision to situate lived experience at the margins of monumental representation, we aim to interpret the impact of the current representation strategies on the lives that were, and in some cases remain, entangled with the life of the monument. We close this chapter by proposing the outcomes of an encompassing approach toward this highly contested case of the material past, one that includes narratives "from below" and can challenge the power dynamics implicated in the officially established norm of Eptapyrgio's representation.

The Archaeology of Eptapyrgio

While Eptapyrgio was used as a prison, the only archaeological intervention that had been conducted concerned the limited reinforcement of the architectural structure of the fortification. In 1973, the Archaeological Ephorate reinforced the northwestern side, which had begun to diverge from the vertical axis of the connecting tower between the northwestern towers (Ninth Ephorate of Byzantine Antiquities 2001a, 64–67). A volume on Eptapyrgio that was edited by the ephorate informs readers that, in the years between 1983 and 1985, archaeologists addressed the damage caused by the 1978 earthquake to the north side of the compound (ibid.). Systematic research on the enforcement and restoration of the fortification recommenced in 1990. The same source further informs us that the first phase of operations, which concerned the ten towers of the Acropolis, was completed in 1995. This project encompassed historical research, research on the building's structural pathology, building materials and mortar, research proposals regarding structure-enforcement issues, and the use and expropriation of the monument's surroundings (ibid.). In addition, photographic documentation, site-drawings, surveys, archaeological excavations, photogrammetric studies and preservation were conducted. In the volume, it is also noted that researchers from Greece and abroad commenced an archival study and developed a program on the 3D representation of the site with the aim to render the site comprehensible and recognizable to the public (ibid.).

What degree and form of representation is made out of this archaeological practice? This chapter intends to critically discuss the extent and implications of Eptapyrgio's representation, the significance of which (at least according to the ephorate's report) appears to have been realized and acted upon. We will illustrate a rather different reality, implicated by the representational inadequacy that dominates the site.

This lack of a coherent interpretive framework can be attributed to the shaping of archaeology as a discipline that focuses mainly on the chronological development and taxonomy of objects as aesthetic works of art, without allowing space for presenting more social-related issues of antiquity (Mouliou 1996; 1999, 57; 2008). This framework can be understood if placed within the universalized epistemological paradigm of the "authorized heritage discourse" (as termed by Smith 2006), which reproduces nineteenth-century and early twentieth-century perceptions regarding the past that privilege material heritage over the intangible, emphasizing monumentality and the aesthetically pleasing. Archaeological representation of Eptapyrgio, which almost entirely focuses on its Byzantine phase as a fortification of the city of Thessaloniki, is thus largely (re)produced as stagnant information, leading to chronological and noninformative approaches, focusing on the glory of the national past, and without allowing for a dialectical relationship between sites and audiences.

The incorporation of the Byzantine era as an essential part of the national narrative contributed to the concept of continuity of Hellenism but without fully substituting the concept of resurrection of the nation, which was perceived as a dormant entity during the four hundred years of Ottoman rule (1453–1821). The notion of resurrection revealed a previous historical interruption, which is why the decisive incorporation of Byzantium acted as a transition from the notion of the Hellenic rebirth to the notion of Hellenic continuity through the centuries, resulting in the construction of a unified national time (Liakos 1994, 180).

After the mid-nineteenth century, intellectuals integrated the Byzantine period into the Greek consciousness, introducing for the first time the term *Hellenochristian* (Dimaras 1999, 25; Herzfeld 1986, 123–124, 141; Paparrigopoulos 1886 [2001]) and treating the Middle Ages as a link between ancient and modern Hellenism. Byzantium offered a valuable connection between conflicting sets of notions such as antiquity and modernity, oriental East and European West, and classical past and Christianity. A new orientation of the archaeological service toward the inclusion of the Byzantine and Medieval material remains took place mainly after 1880 (Kokkou 1977; Voudouri 2003). Conditions like these later shaped the division of Greek archaeological management into two dominant directorates, namely the Ephorate of Prehistoric and Classical Antiquities and the Ephorate of Byzantine Antiquities, a division that remained in operation until 2014.

In this context, it is not surprising that there is no information about the material remains of non-Byzantine cultures preserved in Eptapyrgio, such as the inlaid Islamic inscription dominant at the top of the fortress's central tower and main entrance, which indicates that the tower with its large arch was built in 1431, a year after the city fell to the Ottomans (Tsaktsiras et al. 2003; Galiniki, this volume). Given the site's vast chronological spectrum, however, this attitude raises questions about its epistemological basis and incites reactions among communities affected.[3]

Lessons from Elsewhere: Monumentalizing Penitentiaries

There is a great challenge in attempting to interpret and manage the "contested," "difficult," "undesirable," "unwanted," or "dissonant" past, notions regularly employed "to conceptualize heritage and material remains emerging from situations of conflict" (Iacono and Këlliçi 2015). Attempting to approach, interpret, and display difficult heritage issues may be an unsettling process that requires coming to terms with historical silences and urges for the incorporation of previously excluded memories into the public sphere (Macdonald 2009c, 93).

Situated within the broader field of difficult heritage, the field of archaeology of internment relates as much to the victims as to the perpetrators and includes all kinds of sites of imprisonment, brutality, atrocity, and mass murder. These can be concentration camps and sites of genocide and torture, such as the concentration camp of Auschwitz-Birkenau (Memorial and Museum Auschwitz-Birkenau 2015) or of Cambodia (The Killing Fields of Cambodia n.d.); immigration arrival points such as Ellis Island (The Statue of Liberty—Ellis Island Foundation, Inc. 2016); castles and fortresses or convents turned into prisons, such as the Lancaster Castle penitentiary (Lancaster Castle 2014); and the Le Murate penitentiary (Le Murate Comune di Firenze 2016), as well as architectural complexes of historical penitentiaries. Some of these features are increasingly associated with the notion of "dark heritage" (see Davis and Bowring 2011; Hughes 2003; Memorial and Museum Auschwitz-Birkenau 2015; Miles 2002; Tuol Sleng Genocide Museum n.d.). Despite the vastness of this field and its numerous manifestations that cannot be collectively categorized, growing emphasis has been placed on the so-called dark tourism (see Lennon and Foley 2000; Tarlow 2005), a seemingly macabre kind of tourism that promotes "the gaze upon real and recreated death" (Stone 2006, 145–46).

We do not wish to examine Eptapyrgio as merely a dark heritage site or as part of the "thanatotourism" discourse (Seaton 1996; Seaton and Lennon 2004). Even though abominable terms often prevail in many former political prisoners' discourse on Eptapyrgio (e.g., *kolastirio*, meaning hellhole), any monolithic interpretation from a researcher's standpoint would result in concretizing it as a morbid site. This view would not allow a historicized approach to the penitentiary phase, in relation to the subjects that experienced it and the sociopolitical and historical conditions within which it was developed.

When focusing on dismissed places of convictism and imprisonment, research revolves around their rehabilitation in modern times; according to Strange and Kempa (2003), defunct penal institutions provide matchless opportunities for spiritual and political reflection on the notions of freedom, political action, and human rights. There are numerous such sites that are now considered to be heritage spaces that have been turned into museums and cultural centers or have been inscribed in the World Heritage list of UNESCO, offering organized guided tours, educational programs, scavenger hunts, and so on.

Among the most prominent ones are the convict sites established by the British Empire in Australia during the eighteenth and nineteenth centuries (Australian Government Department of the Environment n.d., and UNESCO World Heritage Center); the Port Arthur Historic Site in Tasmania (Port Arthur Historic Site Management Authority 2016), "Australia's most intact and evocative convict site" (Discover Tasmania 2014–2016); and the Robben Island Museum (Robben Island Museum n.d.), off the coast of Cape Town in South Africa. As Shackley (2001, 355) notes, "The island is a palimpsest of South African history, from sites associated with aboriginal (Khoi) people to colonial buildings and gun emplacements dating from the Second World War." It is largely due to the imprisonment of Nelson Mandela and other leaders of the African National Congress that the Robben Island Museum was attributed "a sacred mission at its outset" (Strange and Kempa 2003, 388), emphasizing the transition to democracy, the fight against colonialism, and the struggle for human rights. With former political prisoners' stories incorporated in its exhibition (ibid.), the narration allows for more personal interpretations, encouraging the sense of proximity to history. As Schmidt (2014, 143) notes, the fact that the abandoned penal site was successfully turned into a visitable heritage site of a cultural and economic activity demonstrates in effect "the changing meaning of the nation as a whole."

On European ground, the REPRISE Project (1999–2001) approached the issue of the regeneration of prisons in Europe collectively, aiming at the rehabilitation of dismissed historical penitentiaries. It was a joint RAPHAEL project coordinated by five partner organizations from different European countries. Under examination were five historical penitentiaries, one of which was the Eptapyrgio Fortress. The overall challenge facing the project was to study, compare, and select "experiences that practiced new aggregations of cells and new functions for the complexes concerned" (REPRISE Handbook 2001, 11). The project resulted in the establishment of three principal protocols that evolved around three key needs"—the need for awareness of this type of architectural heritage, sensitive design of policies for new uses of these penitentiaries, and urban integration of the abandoned penitentiary complexes (ibid. 12–13).

The list of monumentalized penitentiaries and museumized contested pasts is very long, and this discussion could extend beyond the space and scope of this chapter. Yet in relation to the aforementioned attempts to dig deeper into traumatic pasts to understand and disclose their complexities, the current state of the Eptapyrgio's official management echoes, in essence, the silencing of its "double life." It brings to the fore several questions: How are difficult and traumatic historical issues tackled on an interpretive level? How do we archaeologists see ourselves in relation to the past? What are the consequences of neglecting personal and collective memories from the monument's institutionalized material history?

The Eptapyrgio through Its Absences

In 1994, suggestions about the potential future of Eptapyrgio were first presented during a conference on Eptapyrgio (Bakirtzis 1997). Architects, archaeologists, attorneys, city planners, and intellectuals, whose professional work or life experience was in some way connected to the monument had been invited to participate. A few years later, Eptapyrgio was opened to the public. During the period 1999–2001, the site was included in the aforementioned joint RAPHAEL project, regarding the regeneration of prisons in Europe and their transformation into centers of cultural production (REPRISE Handbook 2001). At about the same time, an exhibition comprising photographs, texts, and objects was created within its premises, with the intention of becoming an integral part of the visit.

It has been almost twenty years since the dialogue about the future of Eptapyrgio opened, and yet. then as today, the interpretation remains the same. What also remains is the almost intrinsic strength of its materiality because a simple gaze upon it suffices to reveal, even to the untrained eye, a vast sense of temporality.

In contrast to the tendency of purifying (see Solomon, this volume) or landmarking the past (see Plantzos, this volume) for the purposes of creating an exposed self of the nation, in the case of Eptapyrgio, we witness the visibility of the unfitting materiality, where the unwanted remains are obvious, albeit empty of any interpretative narrative. The entrance, a white plastered structure superimposing the walls, indicates the sign of the "modern" (dating to the twentieth century) age against the ruins of another, long-gone time. Ironically, the

UNESCO World Heritage sign pinned on its metal door on top of the small wooden staircase—one that still carries remnants of its earlier color—invites the visitor inside a "Byzantine" monument. It is through this door that one enters and eventually exits from the outwork of Eptapyrgio, namely, the space inside the first row of walls. In relation to this entrance and exit point, a former political prisoner shared the following emotional memory with us.

> And when I was exiting [the prison], I remember S [name]. A poison . . . (speaker makes sounds indicating dislike). [He was] one of the warders! In all reality, he was like a watchdog for humans. S [was] big. A monster. A criminal kind, who, let me say, with great bitterness pulled this (speaker opens the door) in order for me to exit. I tell him, "Listen, so you see" I tell him. "I," I tell him, "like many others, had never imagined that I was going to enter and come out of jail. And this does not apply to me alone. It applies to you too!" He says, "What you mean?" "Whatever that means!" [I answer]. So. And [then] I think, "What do I do now?" (Nondas Ohounos, interview with the authors, 2015)

A few steps ahead, visitors encounter a second entrance on top of a small, marble, very corroded staircase. This entrance is comprised of a modern metal door, engulfed by a much taller ancient wall. It is worth pointing out that one may cross this gate without necessarily realizing its monumental significance nor its symbolic meanings, as it once used to signify the prisoners' separation from the outside world. As the same former political prisoner informed us, "Here, as they used to tell us, is a lion—can you see it? [The speaker pointed toward the lion while posing the question to us; see fig. 9.2.] That is to say that you enter a lion and you come out a lamb. And you become a lamb. Yes. That was the message there" (Nondas Ohounos, interview with the authors, 2015).

Having passed through the second entrance, visitors enter a small, unroofed rectangular space before proceeding to the interior of Eptapyrgio. Once again, there are no signs. Yet as former political prisoners informed us, this space used to be the visitors' area, and its walls divided the visitors from the inmates who had once stood on its other side during visiting hours.

As another former political prisoner stated,

> All things [i.e., interpretation] stem from a political choice. How can Eptapyrgio be forgotten? Do we not want to remember that people were put in there and were executed for their ideas? I wrote harsh words in the book [i.e., visitors' book]. Now Eptapyrgio is a gallery. And before we know it, the visitors' area, which was hell for those who came to see us, will be gone. The wires will be removed. But just imagine a prostitute and my wife next to her trying to have a conversation with me. Think of the son who came to see his father. The scenery immediately changes. (Akis Maltsidis, interview with the authors, 2015)

Fig. 9.2. Eptapyrgio: The monumental entrance with the lion. Photo by E. Stefanou and I. Antoniadou.

Fig. 9.3. Standing inside the visitors' area. Photo by E. Stefanou and I. Antoniadou.

After crossing the visitors' area, one enters a long, narrow, unroofed central corridor. While walking in between the two high cement walls that frame it, one encounters the steep metal staircase that leads up to what seems like a guardhouse and provides the only view of the fort's interior from above. It is from this belated point onward that individual observation and estimation are compared to the information revealed on the informational panel that appears inside the guardhouse.

Walking farther, one of our informants, also a former political prisoner, recalled,

> I remember two things very clearly, the way the space was, the radius of the political prisoners, you'll have to imagine it, the way these two towers stood (he looks upwards and lifts both hands towards the sky), picture it like a well. We were at the bottom of the well. And I remember two things clearly: in the winter, on certain days, the sun (he raises his left hand and points with his index finger towards the sun) would reach the bottom of the well (the hand descends and points downwards) for just a short while. So, we would huddle together and this would give us hope. That was one. Also, I remember that in springtime, a hoopoe would come to the top of the tower (he once again points upwards with his left index finger) and sing (he smiles, his eyes well up but he carefully hides the tears). (Nestor Hatzoudis, interview with Eleni Stefanou, 2016)

Today, the interior described by Hatzoudis can be seen only while standing at the guardhouse. This almost panopticon-like view generated the following memory during one of our visits with Nondas Ohounos: "You wouldn't hear anything here then. You would only hear the train at twelve—whoooooo! Was it leaving? Coming? We would [only] hear that noise and recognize it. Nothing else! Nothing! There were no cars like today. Or this . . . You wouldn't hear anything! Nothing! That was it! And up above [along the corridors extending east and west of the guardhouse] you would see the cops with the machine guns. Of course our minds were on how we would escape. But how do you escape now from here?" (Nondas Ohounos, interview with the authors, 2015).

The interior of the prison as it is seen from the guardhouse is comprised of two-story prison blocks, and their courtyards extend in front of them, each including a small guardhouse on their opposite side. As Nondas Ohounos informed us, he does not recall guards being stationed inside these small structures, but he remembers that it was the shoemakers' station instead. One can also see that there is archaeological material (mostly marble blocks, stelae, and sarcophagi) lying inside one of the courtyards. The prison church lies in the fourth courtyard, whereas the last one lacks any kind of structure.

Fig. 9.4. Walking along the corridor toward the guardhouse. Photo by E. Stefanou and I. Antoniadou.

Fig. 9.5. Inside the guardhouse. Photo by E. Stefanou and I. Antoniadou.

Fig. 9.6. Looking at the archaeological material inside one of the courtyards. Photo by E. Stefanou and I. Antoniadou.

Hellhole is one prevailing notion among our informants' descriptions with regard to their perception of the prison's interior. Nestor Hatzoudis mentions,

> It was a hellhole because the isolation was intense. I'm telling you, no sound [he places his hands on both sides of his head] from the outside could be heard. We heard no sound. Apart from airplanes. The walls of Eptapyrgio were thick [he tries to demonstrate the thickness of the walls using his hands] and no sound from the outside could reach in. There was the issue of the well [his hands parallel, he holds them up and moves them downward]. There was dampness in this space. I remember the very cold days, when we'd really feel the cold due to the damp. It was difficult for inmates to contact their folks. Who could travel to Thessaloniki? And how would they get here? Here, in Athens, things were much easier. Generally speaking, living conditions were very hard. (Nestor Hatzoudis, interview with Eleni Stefanou, 2016)

According to Akis Maltsidis:

> Eptapyrgio was a fort, but it was also a hellhole. People died. People became handicapped from the dampness and rheumatism. People went mad inside it. You saw the isolation cells—they are tombs. And they still have no signs! It is a terrible condition, not being able to come into contact with fellow humans. To say, "Today I am not in the mood, I will not go out," whilst knowing that you can go out at any time is one thing, and it is a whole different thing being in your cell whilst thoughts are torturing you. And every human has his thoughts. "What did I do? How can I live with this?" and these operate like a cogwheel inside your head. (Akis Maltsidis, interview with the authors, 2015)

Fig. 9.7. Archaeological finds in one of the prison's courtyard. Photo by E. Stefanou and I. Antoniadou.

According to the map inside the guardhouse, administrative buildings, supplementary rooms, the women's prison, and the isolation building are all situated in the space between the fort and the outwork on its south side, and the military prison lies at its southwest corner. Visitors have no access to any of these structures, either because they operate as the ephorate's premises or because entry is prohibited. Yet it is behind these closed doors, inside one of the prison chambers, that the single and seemingly complete museological development lies. To our understanding, this situation reflects the fact that the ephorate's management does not intend to include it as part of the visitors' experience inside the monument. The reasons may range from practical factors (i.e., lack of funds for the recruitment of guards) to ideological ones. Former political prisoners appear deeply disappointed by official archaeology's exclusive control over the site, and they envision a different use and purpose.

> Not in the hands of those [the archaeologists] who took it over! Why? Why? They're up on their high horses, aren't they? They tore down these rocks [archaeological findings]. These rocks might stay there for five hundred years. They are above the law. They make their own decisions. This place should have been taken over by the Municipality of Thessaloniki and instead the opposite took place. Thousands of suffering people passed through here. This should have been a center of culture. An active place, visited by people. Why this abandonment? Everything here was abandoned. In the end they'll have to demolish it [the prison]. . . . But what do you expect from the Greek state? It's not even worth talking about. Where's the representation [of inmates]? What

> did they [the archaeologists] think they were doing in here? They could have been supervisors, not turned it into their property. (Nondas Ohounos, interview with the authors, 2015)
>
> Eptapyrgio should become a site of cultural activities in the broadest sense. For example, it could be converted into a museum. Exhibition spaces could be created. A library. If it is possible in terms of internal layout, there could be rooms to show films, to stage dramatic performances, spaces for small, high-quality concerts with small audiences. The basic thing, first of all, is that these things did not become part of education. People today are ignorant of many things. For example, the Civil War period cannot be covered by silence. It is not possible, there's no two ways about it. It was a fact, regardless of who was right and who was wrong, who won and who lost, what happened after the defeat. All this must be said. Because how will an ignorant person form the conscience of an upstanding citizen? (Nestor Hatzoudis, interview with Eleni Stefanou, 2016)

The visiting route inside the monument is linear, determined by the limited free-flow movement due to the restricted access to many parts of the site. "No entry" signs mark the closed doors. While walking along the length of the corridor that extends from the guardhouse in east and west directions, visitors may only look at the courtyards from above as detached observers, unable to wander inside them, physically experience them, or learn anything regarding their importance in the everyday life of the prison. Yet it was inside these courtyards that significant aspects of this life were formed because it was the space where prisoners would collect their meals, socialize, play games such as chess or volleyball, organize tournaments, and express their creativity. "At Eptapyrgio, we would make handicrafts. The backgammon board was one of them. I'll show it to you later. We made other things too, each person according to his skills. . . . Others worked with beads and made decorations and such things. For me, I wanted to make something so that when my girlfriend or my mother came to visit I could give it to them—it was a big deal [emotional look]. We gave them away as presents" (Nestor Hatzoudis, interview with Eleni Stefanou, 2016).

Courtyards were also essential for the farewells. Nondas Ohounos recalled:

> The date was, let me see, if I'm not mistaken, it must have been the twenty-second of February. In 1972. And the lineup of all the political prisoners [in the courtyard]. And there was a celebration—and I do mean a celebration. Songs sung against the Junta. Who worried about them [the guards]? What would they do to us? We were strong. It's one thing being alone and another thing altogether being thirty people. What would they [the authorities] do? They stayed away. So. There was the farewell. . . . The first song was "*Pote tha Kani Ksasteria*" [When will the skies clear?] and I cannot remember the rest.[4] In any case. Let's say it was a little celebration. Yes. Well, it was moving. We left behind children and friends. Well, that was how we felt. The way you feel when you leave [other people behind]. Moving moments. (Nondas Ohounos, interview with the authors, 2015)

It is fair to argue that Eptapyrgio is fundamentally inadequate in terms of the consideration of any period of its multitemporal story, but it is crucial that we directly address the discrimination toward its contemporary history in particular.[5] Despite some recent art exhibitions and cultural events regarding political resistance during the military junta, in this interplay of conscious omissions and silences, there are various contemporary material elements that appear as almost naturalized and integral parts of the Byzantine fortification. One such element is the metal door that leads to the prisoners' isolation cells—a door that lacks the interpretation that would connect it with the historical and political period of imprisonment as well as with the lives of those connected to it. Here lies the greatest irony, considering that agency is what archaeologists struggle to evoke from the fragments they encounter. In the case of Eptapyrgio, part of this human agency is comprised of our informants, who still dwell across the site, and yet they deeply sense the lack of their connection to it.

> In any case, an archaeologist will view it [i.e., the Eptapyrgio] one way and he will be right. A political prisoner will view it another way and he will be right too. When many parties are right, then you have to set a priority based on the goal that you want to achieve. The last time I went to see it [i.e., the Eptapyrgio], I saw that in the courtyards where we had been were scatters of archaeological fragments and people like us who came to visit the site encountered a storage area. And in fact, I wrote this in the [visitors'] book, "This is not a storage area; it is hell" and I was mad about it. I was mad because here you [i.e., archaeologists] erase a whole history in order to show what? That there was, let's say, a capital here and a capital there and you use it as a storage space? And then they argue "What can we do with these and where should we put them and classify them?" and they are also right. Yet, priorities must be defined. And priorities are always defined by the political choices of the decision makers. (Akis Maltsidis, interview with the authors, 2015)

Inevitably, it is this unique factor that defends the chronological bias we emphasize here. Historical questions remain unanswered, and it is therefore hoped that a critical discussion of this dominant void of past human experience across Eptapyrgio's vast scale of material diversity will stimulate reflection. A meaningful future of Eptapyrgio can materialize through a reflexive archaeology that seeks, introduces, and critically represents the multifaceted historical occurrences as integral parts of the monument's story. To our understanding, in archaeological terms, Eptapyrgio represents an example of epistemological inadequacy, and, at the same time, it reflects a deep historical and psychological disturbance. We believe that the reasons behind both insufficiencies stem from certain structural and ideological conditions that maintain the official discourse's problematic attitude toward the complex history of Eptapyrgio and that fail to process the complexities of this historical period. One could argue that this is a unique twist to the process of colonialism and crypto-colonialism (Herzfeld 2002), where state archaeology imposes its hegemony upon its own national subjects. Colonialism here is exercised internally, causing the feelings of victimization to various communities of memory (i.e., former political prisoners) whose past fails to reach the official criteria and demands of the national narrative.

Attorney Kostas Logothetis (1997, 1) eloquently addressed this complex identity of Eptapyrgio during the 1994 conference. He asked, "Is it a correctional facility? Is it a nest of torture? Is it a symbol of authority? Is it a Byzantine monument? Is it historical memory? Is it a locus of executions? Is it some of these, and which ones? Or is it all of these?" Elsewhere, he argued, "In planning the future of the past, one inevitably has to diagnose what that past was after all" (7). The history of Eptapyrgio is evidently a question about identity, and this was always an underlying and complex issue, but at the time of conference, the future uses of the site and, by implication, the confrontation of this identity contestation seemed like a promising prospect.

Of course, the question at the core of Eptapyrgio's identity is who and on what grounds does one decide upon it. Greek poet Manolis Anagnostakis, once detained in Eptapyrgio as political prisoner, self-reflexively questioned his own right to speak about and inevitably define it. If only the words and experiences of all the "anonymous thousands" could be conveyed (Anagnostakis 1997). In the context of the interpretation or representation of contested sites, however, it is rare that the affected communities decide on such matters. For the official practitioners, this is a "painful" issue, almost bound to lose the balance among those affected by it and condemned to disadvantage or marginalize some voices at the expense of others. The politics of representation, when confronted by these difficult implications, ought to consider value judgments in the context of ever-changing and constantly problematized conditions. In the case of Eptapyrgio, however, if we are looking into a biased identification, an underrepresented history, then what we are really dealing with is a case of the official discourse's unbalanced use of power that disregards the elephant in the room, which is the notion of difficult choices, the fact of conflicting contexts, and the implications for present people. The fear of the impact of this imbalance is felt by members of the affected communities. As Akis Maltsidis argued, "Do not let someone say 'let's repair and erase everything.' Thousands of people passed through that place." (Akis Maltsidis, interview with the authors, 2016).

Concluding Remarks

In the attempt to reinvent museums as socially engaged places of memory (Ouzman 2006, 269), the embodiment of human experience in the physicality of the monument can allow crucial issues to be tackled. In the case of Eptapyrgio, however, this is hindered by the Archaeological Service's material selectivity as well as by its embedded tendency to disregard difficult issues of identity, memory, and historical and political trauma. Yet the practice of archaeology inevitably encounters all these contested issues and ought to approach them in the context of ideologically burdened pasts that are so intrinsic to late European history. Proposals should be put forward, and steps should be taken so that difficult heritage can be offered for contemplation, helping to place the historical and political implications, the violence and trauma, at the appropriate distance to allow an intelligible yet emotionally engaged interaction (Ouzman 2006). Thus, objects can be placed in a continuum of human experience, as opposed to a fragmented order of bare material practices. The difficult questions can then acquire a platform so that they may be put forward, responded to, confronted, and reconciled with, rather than remain untouched behind closed doors. Practitioners in difficult heritages elsewhere respond to such crucial epistemological calls, and, as Macdonald (2009a) eloquently pointed out, others can remind us where we stand, in which case there is a lot to learn and act upon. The challenges to provide public service and to seek the contemporary relevance of the past thus remain.

Eptapyrgio needs to be situated within the global phenomenon of convictism as one of the most significant examples of the history of internment in contemporary Greece, one that reveals the living conditions of the convicts, closely reflecting the prevailing stances regarding the punishment of political action. Taking into consideration that "heritage is not necessarily to be cherished and celebrated" (Macdonald 2006, 10), we addressed a reflexive and critically encompassing approach toward the material past in an attempt to include in the monumental space the voices of the people who have experienced and still experience this place in diverse ways of contact.

By discussing the prospect of an alternative stance, we aim for an archaeological practice that processes raw historical-political trauma to identify a way for the living persons to come to terms with their difficult past and indicate a mature stance in the face of contested heritage issues. We believe that the understanding of the monument's difficult past, especially in relation to the living subjects who are part of its history, can eventually lead to an enriched and more encompassing signification of the present (see Droumpouki 2014, 17).

The organic inclusion of difficult subjects in the monument's official representation can also lead to a more inclusive practice of archaeology. The interconnection of archaeological interpretation and human experience in the case of Eptapyrgio could potentially lead to reconciliation with the personal, collective, and historical trauma. It can break the site's silence of unspoken torment, allowing for appeasement between the monument and the living community that surrounds it, the social and political restitution of this turbulent period, and ultimately the shaping of a more consolidated historical consciousness (see Levy and Sznaider 2006, 88). In the words of Nestor Hatzoudis (interview with Eleni

Stefanou, 2016), such actions would "Soothe, if you like, the memory of these places . . . and the people of course."

Ethnography in Eptapyrgio has brought us face-to-face with the epistemological urge to search for alternative analytical concepts, methodologies, and interpretative platforms in order to encourage and accept the existence of conflicting understandings of the past and present. To our understanding, our biggest challenge in anthropology today is to adjust and adapt current heritage concepts to the complex current realities and social changes that we witness in the ethnographic field. We believe that embracing the conflict as an integral part of heritage management is the only way forward if we want to recognize and confront not only the difficult past but also our difficult present emanating from the current social and economic crisis.

ELENI STEFANOU is Adjunct Lecturer at Hellenic Open University. She coedited *From Archaeology to Archaeologies: The "Other" Past* (BAR International Series, 2012) and is the author of *Classical Antiquity and Modern Greek Maritime Heritage: Reliving the Ancient Maritime Heritage at the Sea of Salamis* (Brill, 2016). Her publications and research interests revolve around the ideological uses of the past, which are shaped through the fields of museology, education and cultural heritage, archaeological ethnography, and community engagement.

IOANNA ANTONIADOU holds a PhD in archaeology from the University of Southampton (2014). She is currently an independent researcher and collaborates with diverse academic institutions. Her field of research is archaeological ethnography, with a particular interest regarding the nonprofessional physical interaction with the material past. She is the author of *Archaeology, Nationalism, and "Looting": Lessons from Greece* (University of Arizona Press, 2016) and *Reflections on an Archaeological Ethnography of "Looting" in Kozani, Greece* (Maney, 2009).

Notes

1. On the foundation and function of Greek archaeology as a mechanism of nation-building, see Solomon (this volume); Hamilakis 1996, 2000, 2007a; Hamilakis and Yalouri 1996, 1999; Yalouri 2001; Leontis 1995; Plantzos 2008, 2012; Damaskos and Plantzos 2008; Skopetea 1988).

2. Political conflicts in Greece are a predicament for any form of official discussion, although the topic of the civil war (1946–1949) has started to be addressed in academic research and representation across the social sciences (see for example Dordanas 2011; Kalyvas 2006; Kokkinos 2015; Van Boeschoten et. al. 2008; Vervenioti 2002). The marginalization of the political discourse of a later historical period (1967–1974) in the

context of archaeological representation thus reflects a prevalent denial to record and historicize the collective and personal memories and traumas of the Left versus Right armed struggles that have marked Greece's contemporary history since the period of the civil war. The representation of the national past is imbued with such bias (see Galiniki, this volume).

3. Indicative of this epistemological stance is the decision of the Ministry of Culture to demolish the houses adjacent to the Byzantine Walls built by Christian and Greek-speaking refugees from Asia Minor in 1922 (Mourtos et al., 2013). In light of this intervention, reaction has been provoked in the communities affected (ibid.; see also Solomon, this volume).

4. The song "*Pote tha Kani Ksasteria*" falls into the category of *rizitika* songs, which are nondance mountain songs of Western Crete (Conklin and Anagnostopoulou 2010). As Hnaraki states, citing the Crete-based Irish musician Ross Daly, "the poetic level of the lyrics in these songs is exceptionally high and many connoisseurs of Cretan music consider them to be the most beautiful in the entire repertoire" (Hnaraki 2011, 183). Originally, this song refers to a murder for the vindication of a family vendetta in the Cretan mountains. However, in the course of time, it was rendered one of the most emblematic rebel songs of its kind because it is often associated with the fight for freedom and the struggle for independence. In this vein and amid the Colonels' dictatorship (1967–1974), this song was recorded in a collection of rizitika songs by the Cretan musician Nikos Xylouris and the composer Yannis Markopoulos, and thus it became one of the songs of the uprising against the military junta (Rethemnos News 2014).

5. It is important to note that between 2017 and 2019, some art exhibitions and cultural events regarding the trauma of political resistance during the military junta (1967–1974) took place in the spaces of the monument, especially in the context of the Thessaloniki Contemporary Art Biennale (2017) and the newly established Eptapyrgio Festival (2019). Accessed July 17, 2019, https://www.thessmemory.gr/%CE%B4%CF%81%CF%89%CE%BC%CE%B5%CE%BD%CE%B1/%CE%BC%CE%B9%CE%B1-%CE%AD%CE%BA%CE%B8%CE%B5%CF%83%CE%B7-%CF%83%CF%84%CE%BF-%CE%B5%CF%80%CF%84%CE%B1%CF%80%CF%8D%CF%81%CE%B3%CE%B9%CE%BF-%CE%B1%CE%BD%CE%BF%CE%AF%CE%B3%CE%B5%CE%B9-%CF%83%CF%84%CE%BF; accessed July 17, 2019, http://anastasiosskepseis.blogspot.com/2018/11/blog-post_27.html; accessed July 17, 2019, https://www.thessalonikiguide.gr/event/eptapirgio-enas-aionas-se-mia-mera-festival-eptapirgiou. In the same vein, the authors of this chapter, founders and active members of the Eptapyrgio Oral History Group that collects testimonies regarding the biography of Eptapyrgio, presented the Group's work in a collective exhibition held at the monument in Fall 2020, in collaboration with the Ephorate of Antiquities of the City of Thessaloniki.

References

Anagnostakis, Manolis. 1997. "Επιστολή" [Letter]. In *Χρήσεις Επταπυργίου* [The Uses of Eptapyrgio], conference proceedings, Thessaloniki, December 16, 1994.Thessaloniki: Cultural Capital of Europe Organization.

Athanasiou, Fani, Dimitris Zigomalas, Vassilis Koniordos, Evgenia Makri, and Ioanna Steriotou. 2009. *Heritage Walks in Thessaloniki*. Thessaloniki: Municipality of Thessaloniki and Hellenic Society for the Environment and Culture.

Australian Government Department of the Environment. n.d. "Australian Convict Sites." Accessed June 2, 2016. http://www.environment.gov.au/heritage/places/world/convict-sites.

Bakirtzis, Charalambos. 1997. *"Επταπύργιο ή Γεντί Κουλέ: Το Μέλλον ενός Μύθου."* [Eptapyrgio or Yedi Koule: The Future of a Myth.] In *Χρήσεις Επταπυργίου* [The Uses of Eptapyrgio], conference proceedings, Thessaloniki, December 16, 1994. Thessaloniki: Cultural Capital of Europe Organization.

Conklin, Darrell, and Christina Anagnostopoulou. 2010. "Comparative Pattern Analysis of Cretan Folk Songs." *MML 10*, 3rd International Workshop on Machine Learning and Music, Florence, Italy, October 25, 2010, 33–36.

Crooke, Elizabeth. 2005. "Dealing with the Past: Museums and Heritage in Northern Ireland and Cape Town, South Africa." *International Journal of Heritage Studies* 11 (2): 131–42.

Damaskos, Dimitris, and Dimitris Plantzos, eds. 2008. *A Singular Antiquity: Archaeology and Hellenic Identity in Twentieth-Century Greece.* Athens: Benaki Museum.

Davis, Shannon, and Jacky Bowring. 2011. "The Right to Remember: The Memorials to Genocide in Cambodia and Rwanda." In *The Right to Landscape: Contesting Landscape and Human Rights*, edited by Shelley Egoz, Jala Makhzoumi, and Gloria Pungetti, 211–26. Farnham: Ashgate.

Dimaras, Konstantinos. 1999. *Κωνσταντίνος Παπαρρηγόπουλος: Ιστορία του Ελληνικού Έθνους* [Konstantinos Paparrigopoulos: History of the Greek Nation]. 2nd ed. Athens: Estia.

Discover Tasmania. 2014–2016. "Port Arthur." Accessed June 2, 2016. http://www.discovertasmania.com.au/about/regions-of-tasmania/hobart-and-south/port-arthur.

Dordanas, Stratos. 2011. *Η Γερμανική Στολή στη Ναφθαλίνη. Επιβιώσεις του Δοσιλογισμού στη Μακεδονία, 1945–1974* [The German Uniform in Naphthalene: Survivals of Collaborationism in Macedonia, 1945–1974]. Athens: Estia.

Droumpouki, Anna-Maria. 2014. *Μνημεία της Λήθης. Ίχνη του Β' Παγκοσμίου Πολέμου στην Ελλάδα και στην Ευρώπη* [Monuments of Forgetfulness: Remains of the Second World War in Greece and in Europe]. Athens: Polis.

González-Ruibal, Antonio. 2009. "Topography of Terror or Cultural Heritage? The Monuments of Franco's Spain." In *Europe's Deadly Century: Perspectives on Twentieth-Century Conflict Heritage*, edited by Neil Forbes, Robin Page, and Guillermo Pérez, 65–72. Swindon: English Heritage.

———. 2011. "The Archaeology of Internment." In *Archaeologies of Internment*, edited by Adrian Myers and Gabriel Moshenska, 53–73. New York: Springer.

Hamilakis, Yannis. 1996. "Through the Looking Glass: Nationalism, Archaeology, and the Politics of Identity." *Antiquity* 70: 975–78.

———. 2000. "Cyberspace/Cyberpast/Cybernation: Constructing Hellenism in Hyperreality." *European Journal of Archaeology* 3 (2): 241–64.

———. 2007a. *The Nation and its Ruins: Antiquity, Archaeology, and National Imagination in Greece.* Oxford: Oxford University Press.

———. 2007b. "From Ethics to Politics." In *Archaeology and Capitalism: From Ethics to Politics*, edited by Yannis Hamilakis and Philip Duke, 15–40. Walnut Creek, CA: Left Coast.

———. 2011. "Archaeological Ethnography: A Multitemporal Meeting Ground for Archaeology and Anthropology." *Annual Review of Anthropology* 40: 399–414.

Hamilakis, Yannis, and Aris Anagnostopoulos. 2009. "What Is Archaeological Ethnography?" In *Archaeological Ethnographies*, edited by Yannis Hamilakis and Aris Anagnostopoulos, 65–87, special double issue, *Public Archaeology* 8 (2–3).

Hamilakis, Yannis, and Philip Duke. 2007. *Archaeology and Capitalism: From Ethics to Politics*. Walnut Creek, CA: Left Coast.
Hamilakis, Yannis, and Eleana Yalouri. 1996. "Antiquities as Symbolic Capital in Modern Greek Society." *Antiquity* 70: 117–29.
———. 1999. "Sacralizing the Past." *Archaeological Dialogues* 2: 115–60.
Herzfeld, Michael. 1986. *Ours Once More: Folklore, Ideology and the Making of Modern Greece*. New York: Pella.
———. 2002. "The Absent Presence: Discourses of Crypto-Colonialism." *South Atlantic Quarterly* 101: 899–926.
Hnaraki, Maria. 2011. "Crete—Souls of Soil: Island Identity through Song." In *Island Songs: A Global Repertoire*, edited by Godfrey Baldacchino, 183. Lanham, MD: Scarecrow.
Hughes, Rachel. 2003. "The Abject Artifacts of Memory: Photographs from Cambodia's Genocide." *Media, Culture and Society* 25: 23–44.
Iacono, Francesco, and Klejd L. Këlliçi. 2015. "Of Pyramids and Dictators: Memory, Work and the Significance of Communist Heritage in Post-Socialist Albania." *AP: Online Journal in Public Archaeology* 5: 97–122.
Kalyvas, Stathis. 2006. *The Logic of Violence in Civil War*. Cambridge: Cambridge University Press.
Kokkinos, Giorgos. 2015. *Το Ολοκαύτωμα: Η Διαχείριση της Τραυματικής Μνήμης—Θύτες και Θύματα*. [The Holocaust: The Use of Traumatic Memory—Perpetrators and Victims]. Athens: Gutenberg.
Kokkou, Aggeliki. 1977. *Η Μέριμνα για τις Αρχαιότητες στην Ελλάδα και τα Πρώτα Μουσεία*. [The Concern for Antiquities in Greece and the First Museums]. Athens: Ermis.
Lancaster Castle. 2014. Accessed June 2, 2016. http://www.lancastercastle.com/a-dark-history.
Le Murate Comune di Firenze. 2016. Accessed June 2, 2016. http://www.lemurate.comune.fi.it/lemurate/dove.
Lennon, John J., and Malcolm Foley. 2000. *Dark Tourism: The Attraction of Death and Disaster*. London: Cassell.
Leontis, Artemis. 1995. *Topographies of Hellenism: Mapping the Homeland*. Ithaca, NY: Cornell University Press.
Levy, Daniel, and Natan Sznaider. 2006. "Forgive and Not Forget: Reconciliation between Forgiveness and Resentment." In *Taking Wrongs Seriously: Apologies and Reconciliation*, edited by Elazar Barkan and Alexander Karn, 83–100. Stanford, CA: Stanford University Press.
Liakos, Antonis. 1994. "Προς Επισκευήν Ολομέλειας και Ενότητος: η Δόμηση του Εθνικού Χρόνου στην Ελληνική Ιστοριογραφία" [The Construction of National Time in Greek Historiography]. In *Scientific Meeting in Memory of K. Th. Dimaras*, 171–99. Athens: Center for Modern Greek Studies, National Research Center.
Logothetis, Kostas. 1997. "Επταπύργιο ή Γεντί Κουλέ; Το Μέλλον ενός Μύθου" [Eptapyrgio or Yedi Koule? The Future of a Myth]. In *Χρήσεις Επταπυργίου* [The Uses of Eptapyrgio], conference proceedings, Thessaloniki, December 16, 1994.Thessaloniki: Cultural Capital of Europe Organization.
Macdonald, Sharon. 2006. "Undesirable Heritage: Fascist Material Culture and Historical Consciousness in Nuremberg." *International Journal of Heritage Studies*, 12 (1): 9–28.
———. 2009a. *Difficult Heritage: Negotiating the Nazi Past in Nuremberg and Beyond*. London: Routledge.

———. 2009b. “Reassembling Nuremberg, Reassembling Heritage.” *Journal of Cultural Economy* 2 (1–2): 117–34.

———. 2009c. “Unsettling Memories: Intervention and Controversy over Difficult Public Heritage.” In *Heritage and Identity: Engagement and Demission in the Contemporary World*, edited by Marta Anico and Elsa Peralta, 93–104. London: Routledge.

Memorial and Museum Auschwitz-Birkenau. 2015. Accessed June 2, 2016. http://auschwitz.org/en.

Miles, William F. S. 2002. “Auschwitz: Museum Interpretation and Darker Tourism.” *Annals of Tourism Research* 29 (4): 1175–78.

Molho, Rena, and Hastaoglou-Martinidis, Vilma. 2009. *Jewish Sites in Thessaloniki: Brief History and Guide*. Athens: Lycabettus.

Moshenska, Gabriel, and Adrian Myers. 2011. “An Introduction to Archaeologies of Internment.” In *Archaeologies of Internment*, edited by Adrian Myers and Gabriel Moshenska, 1–19. New York: Springer.

Mouliou, Marlen. 1996. “Ancient Greece, Its Classical Heritage and the Modern Greeks: Aspects of Nationalism in Museum Exhibitions.” In *Nationalism and Archaeology: Scottish Archaeological Forum*, edited by John A. Atkinson, Iain Banks, and Jerry O’Sullivan, 174–99. Glasgow: Cruithne.

———. 1999. “Από την Ιστορία της Αρχαιολογικής Επιστήμης στην Ανάγνωση Μουσειακών Εκθέσεων του Παρελθόντος” [From the History of Archaeological Discipline to the Reading of Museum Displays of the Past]. *Arheologia ke Tehnes* [Archaeology and Arts] 73: 53–59.

———. 2008. “Museum Representations of the Classical Past in Post-War Greece: A Critical Analysis.” In *A Singular Antiquity. Archaeology and Hellenic Identity in Twentieth-Century Greece*, edited by Dimitris Damaskos and Dimitris Plantzos, 83–109. Athens: Benaki Museum.

Mourtos, Yannis, Iliana Papamihou, Anna Pashia, Maria-Konstantina Saltea-Kalogera, Margarita Tileli, and Alexandros Tourtas. 2013. “Ανάδειξη Τμήματος των Βορειοδυτικών Τειχών της Θεσσαλονίκης” [Enhancement of the Northwest Part of the Byzantine Walls in Thessaloniki]. Accessed June 17, 2016. http://www.archaiologia.gr/blog/2013/03/18/ανάδειξη-τμήματος-των-βορειοδυτικών/.

Nicholas, George, and Julie Hollowell. 2007. “Ethical Challenges to a Post-Colonial Archaeology: The Legacy of Scientific Colonialism.” In *Archaeology and Capitalism: From Ethics to Politics*, edited by Yannis Hamilakis and Philip Duke, 59–82. Walnut Creek, CA: Left Coast.

Ninth Ephorate of Byzantine Antiquities. 2001a. *Ώρες Βυζαντίου. Έργα και Ημέρες στο Βυζάντιο. Επταπύργιο. Η Ακρόπολη της Θεσσαλονίκης* [The Times of Byzantium: The Deeds and the Days in Byzantium. Eptapyrgio. The Acropolis of Thessaloniki]. Athens: Hellenic Ministry of Culture.

Ouzman, Sven. 2006. “The Beauty of Letting Go: Fragmentary Museum and Archaeologies of Archive.” In *Sensible Objects: Colonialism, Museums and Material Culture*, edited by Elizabeth Edwards, Chris Gosden, and Ruth B. Phillips, 269–301. Oxford: Berg.

Paparrigopoulos, Konstantinos. (1886) 2001. *Ιστορία του Ελληνικού Έθνους από Αρχαιοτάτων Χρόνων μέχρι τον καθ’ ημάς*. [History of the Greek Nation from Ancient Times until Nowadays]. Athens: Ermeias. Reprint, Athens: Galaxias.

Plantzos, Dimitris. 2008. "Time and the Antique: Linear Causality and the Greek-Art Narrative." In *A Singular Antiquity: Archaeology and Hellenic Identity in Twentieth-Century Greece*, edited by Dimitris Damaskos and Dimitris Plantzos, 253–72. Athens: Benaki Museum.

———. 2012. "Τα Ορφανά του Αλέξανδρου." [Alexander's Orphans]. *The Athens Review of Books* 3 (30): 51–54.

Port Arthur Historic Site Management Authority. 2016. "Home." Accessed June 2, 2016. http://portarthur.org.au.

REPRISE Handbook. 2001. *A Raphael Project 1999–2001. Handbook. Regenerations of Prisons in Europe: Dismissed Historical Penitentiaries' Rehabilitation*. Florence: European Commission General Directory of Education and Culture.

Rethemnos News. 2014. "Αφιέρωμα: Ριζίτικα, Γιάννης Μαρκόπουλος—Νίκος Ξυλούρης: *Η ιστορία ενός δίσκου*." [Tribute: Rizitika, Yannis Markopoulos—Nikos Xylouris: The Story of an Album]. Accessed June 16, 2016. http://goo.gl/yOrSKJ.

Robben Island Museum. nd. "Stories." Accessed June 2, 2016. http://www.robben-island.org.za/stories.

Schmidt, Sandra J. 2014. "United in Our Diversity." In *Beyond Pedagogy: Reconsidering the Public Purpose of Museums*, edited by Brenda Trofanenko and Avner Segall, 135–54. Rotterdam: Sense.

Seaton, Anthony V. 1996. "Guided by the Dark: From Thanatopsis to Thanatourism." *Journal of Heritage Studies* 2 (4): 234–44.

Seaton, Anthony V., and John J. Lennon. 2004. "Thanatourism in the Early Twenty-First Century: Moral Panics, Ulterior Motives and Alterior Desires." In *New Horizons in Tourism—Strange Experiences and Stranger Practices*, edited by Tejvir V. Singh, 63–82. Wallingford: CABI.

Shackley, Myra. 2001. "Potential Futures for Robben Island: Shrine, Museum or Theme Park?" *International Journal of Heritage Studies* 7 (4): 355–63.

Skopetea, Ellie. 1988. *Το Πρότυπο Βασίλειο και η Μεγάλη Ιδέα: Όψεις του Εθνικού Προβλήματος στην Ελλάδα 1830–1880* [The Model Kingdom and the Great Idea: Aspects of the National Issue in Greece]. Athens: Politipo.

Smith, Laurajane. 2006. *The Uses of Heritage*. London: Routledge.

Stone, Philip R. 2006. "A Dark Tourism Spectrum: Towards a Typology of Death and Macabre Related Tourist Sites, Attractions and Exhibitions." *Tourism* 54 (2): 145–60.

Strange, Carolyn, and Michael Kempa. 2003. "Shades of Dark Tourism: Alcatraz and Robben Island." *Annals of Tourism Research* 30 (2): 386–405.

Tarlow, Peter E. 2005. "Dark Tourism: The Appealing 'Dark Side' of Tourism and More." In *Niche Tourism—Contemporary Issues, Trends and Cases*, edited by Marina Novelli, 47–58. Oxford: Butterworth Heinemann.

The Killing Fields of Cambodia. n.d. Accessed June 2, 2016. http://www.killingfieldsmuseum.com.

The Statue of Liberty—Ellis Island Foundation Inc. 2016. Accessed June 2, 2016. http://www.libertyellisfoundation.org/immigration-museum.

Tsaktsiras, Lambros, Aikaterini Papanthimou, Mantzios Giorgos, and Nikos Kalogirou. 2003. *Θεσσαλονίκη. Η Πόλη και τα Μνημεία της* [Thessaloniki: The City and Its Monuments]. Thessaloniki: Malliaris.

Tunbridge, John. E., and Gregory J. Ashworth 1996. *Dissonant Heritage: The Management of the Past as a Resource in Conflict.* Chichester: John Wiley.

Tuol Sleng Genocide Museum. nd. Accessed June 2, 2016. http://www.tuolslenggenocide museum.com/#_=_.

Unesco World Heritage Center, "Australian Convict Sites." Accessed June 2, 2016. whc.unesco .org/en/list/1306.

Van Boeschoten, Riki, Tasoula Vervenioti, Eftihia Voutira, Vasilis Dalkavoukis, and Konstantina Bada. 2008. *Μνήμες και Λήθη του Ελληνικού Εμφυλίου Πολέμου* [Memories and Oblivion of the Greek Civil War]. Athens: Epikentro.

Vervenioti, Tasoula. 2002. "Προφορική Ιστορία και Έρευνα για τον Ελληνικό Εμφύλιο: *Η Πολιτική Συγκυρία*, ο Ερευνητής και ο Αφηγητής" [Oral History and Research about the Civil War: The Political Condition, the Researcher and the Narrator]. *Epitheorisi Kinonikon Erevnon* [Social Research Review] 107: 157–181.

Voudouri, Daphne. 2003. *Κράτος και Μουσεία: το Θεσμικό Πλαίσιο των Αρχαιολογικών Μουσείων.* [State and Museums: The Legal Framework of Archaeological Museums]. Athens: Sakkoula.

Yalouri, Eleana. 2001. *The Acropolis: Global Fame, Local Claim.* London: Berg.

10 Contemporary Art and "Difficult Heritage"

Three Case Studies from Athens

Eleana Yalouri and Elpida Rikou

Introduction: Athens's "Difficult Heritage"

In her book *Difficult Heritage, Negotiating the Nazi Past in Nuremberg and Beyond* (2009), Sharon Macdonald adopts the term *difficult heritage* to examine the ways heritage is negotiated in the context of a disputed, unsettling, awkward, and troubling past. Although Macdonald defines this difficult heritage—in this case, examined with reference to the atrocities of Nazism—by juxtaposing it to a heritage that is celebrated or cherished as part of the valued heritage of a nation, we ought to recognize that even the "golden" heritage of a nation or a city can prove difficult in the everyday experiences and perceptions of its citizens. We are referring to the difficulties of the Greek heritage, which have been extensively discussed elsewhere (e.g., Hamilakis and Yalouri 1996; Caftanzoglou 2000, 2001; Yalouri 2001; Hamilakis 2007; Damaskos and Plantzos 2008; Stroulia and Buck Sutton 2010; Tziovas 2014). Indicative of these difficulties are the ambiguities, contestations, and paradoxes that arise from issues such as the positioning of Hellenic antiquity as a simultaneously local, national, and global heritage; the role of the "(crypto)colonialist" (Herzfeld 2002) gaze of the Western world upon it; the centrality of the ancient Greek topos in the construction of the Greek present (and future); the rivalry between the "golden" Greek past and what is often considered as an "inferior" Greek present; the often tyrannical presence of antiquities in everyday urban life (e.g., the need for permits from the Archaeological Service to undertake any building work, the threat of expropriation of private properties, the vetoing of and delays to construction works); and in general the complicated relationship between Greece's various pasts, both ancient and modern. All of these issues have systematically recurred since the establishment of the Greek state down to the present day, reproducing, questioning, or subverting the public discourse about antiquity and connecting or dividing a society in which the national narrative of a golden classical antiquity is thoroughly ingrained.

Haunting, protective, tyrannical, or empowering, the ancient past has been very much present in city life today (Yalouri 2014, 2015b).

In the city of Athens, the mentioned issues have been topical ever since its establishment as the capital of modern Greece. Athens became the capital of the new state not because of its geographical position or for any other practical reason. Its name alone, linked with the glory of the classical Greek world, was enough to justify such a choice (Politis 1993). How, then, does Athens measure up to and deal with its ancient history?

To go back to Macdonald's case study mentioned at the beginning of this chapter, dilemmas over the commemoration of the Nazi legacy in the cityscape of places like Nuremberg revolve around the question of whether these architectural remains should be restored, demolished, or trivialized. In Athens, the dominant question has been how to safeguard, restore, and promote "the golden" classical past. Germany's "difficult" heritage has motivated many contemporary artists, including Anselm Kiefer, Peter Eisenman, Jenny Holzer, and Karl Prantl, to produce public art that contests and generally dares to confront the past in an attempt to be reconciled with it or, more especially, to "master it" [*Vergangenheitsbewältigung*]. In Athens, cultural policies have predominantly focused on ancient rather than contemporary Greek art. Contemporary art is a field traditionally neglected by cultural policies—and in which the state still seems reluctant to invest its scarce resources. It has been a sector in which individual entrepreneurs have regularly made decisive interventions, a fact that has led them to play an increasing role in defining this field through the establishment of foundations, sponsorships, and more (see Souliotis 2013; Tsoukalas 1987). This sort of patronage is shaping a new frame of action in the domestic art scene, often aimed at acting in the interests of Greece's international standing as part of what has been called "soft diplomacy" (see Papagaroufali 2013). The more dynamic presence of contemporary art projects in Athenian public spaces in recent decades, as well as the emergence of a more systematic discussion regarding the role of contemporary art in this context, forces us to address the following questions: What is or what could be the role of contemporary art, and public art in particular, vis-à-vis the Athenian "difficult heritage"? Does deploying contemporary art in public space simply help rekindle interest in the consumption of antiquity and legitimize and promote specific contemporary art projects based on this heritage, or does it achieve certain conceptual shifts that may act to undermine the status of antiquity as the undisputed, gilded, national heritage? And in the end, is contemporary art able to render classical heritage less "difficult" for contemporary Athenians to live with (see Yalouri 2015a, 2016)?

In this chapter, we attempt an initial investigation of certain trends that characterize the approach toward Greek antiquity in contemporary artworks to highlight and compare the different ways images of antiquity are managed, especially when they appeal to a wider local and international audience. Our reference point is Athens, a city where antiquity, sometimes visibly and sometimes invisibly, intervenes in the lives of Athenians, reminding them that although it belongs to the past, it also remains potentially in the present. In the second part of this chapter, we will focus on three artistic interventions that (coincidentally?) took place in the historic center of Athens and specifically in the ancient (Athenian and Roman) Agora in 2014. Two of these three art projects were funded by NEON, a cultural and developmental nonprofit organization, as part of its "commitment to activating public spaces and enhancing public life throughout the city of Athens."[1] The works are *This Progress* by the internationally recognized Anglo-German artist Tino Sehgal, produced and directed by Asad Raza; *Pulsating Fields* by Aemilia Papaphilippou, a Greek artist with an international presence; and *Plan for Planting* by Natasa Biza, another Greek artist who lives and works on the island of Paros and in Athens. Biza's contribution was part of her master's dissertation for the Athens School of Fine Arts and was presented in a group exhibition at another Athenian art venue (Beton 7).

Antiquity, Contemporary Art, and Public Space in Athens

The relationship between Greek antiquity and the visual arts is not recent. Especially in Greece—where classical archaeology continues to be heavily influenced by the historical art tradition associated with the eighteenth-century antiquary and art historian Johann Joachim Winckelmann—until recently, it has been customary for those wishing to study the history of art to enroll with a department of history and archaeology. Let us also note here that the skills of Greeks trained in the visual arts today are still measured against the classical past in one way or another. Despite radical changes in contemporary art, the admission of new students to the schools of fine arts in Greece today still largely depends on their ability to pass an exam in which they have to sketch from memory casts depicting figures from Greek (and sometimes Roman) antiquity. Thereafter, some will reference antiquity directly or indirectly in their works, thus claiming an identity and a framework of local and global readability for their artistic careers. Others will turn away from it in their efforts to align themselves with contemporary art traditions that have evolved in other international contexts and have become fashionable on the domestic art scene. In any case, any new artistic proposition will encounter a cultural (state and private) policy, welcoming younger artists to (or excluding them from) an already established field where, until recently at least, it was clear that the key resources of money and prestige in Greece derived from its ancient ruins. At the same time, artistic propositions from international art that also refer to this ancient heritage have contributed to its circulation and jointly shaped ideas and perceptions related to it.

The relationship between ancient and contemporary art has not been built on an equal basis. It has been marked by the prioritization of the former over the latter, including in terms of their presence in the urban public space. Unlike in several other Western countries of the postwar world, in Greece and in Athens in particular, there has been no major tradition of a relationship between contemporary visual art practice and public space. Although throughout the twentieth century there have been examples of art in public spaces, these artworks mostly referenced ancient or neoclassical sculpture. Memory and history were the elements promoted as markers of collective identity in the cityscape of Athens rather than contemporary experiences of space (Fotiadi 2013).

During the 1970s and 1980s, art interventions in Athenian public space increased. Until the mid-1990s, the interest of artists and art historians focused on the work of individual artists rather than on a more general discussion regarding the conventions and practices defining the concept of public space or art's relationship with it. From the late 1990s onward, and during a period marked by the preparations for the 2004 Olympic Games, urban regeneration and gentrification, and the rise and fall of the Athens Stock Exchange, the situation has gradually changed. The number of private galleries increased, a new generation of Greek artists and curators (often returning from abroad) seemed to emerge, the first big international visual arts events and exhibitions took place (e.g., Outlook, Chromopolis, Athens by Art, the Athens Biennale), and efforts were made to establish the National Museum of Contemporary Art (Fotiadi 2013; Christopoulos 2013). Meanwhile, a number of art initiatives emerged whose aim was to intervene in public spaces in certain areas of Athens, which in turn gave their names to the groups behind these initiatives (e.g., Philopappou group, Mavili Collective.)[2] These projects were often connected to collectives that, after about 2005, started to multiply in Athens as new forms of political protest, in tune with the broader global rise of social protests and occupy movements (Fotiadi 2017).

These developments influenced the life, form, and character of the Greek urban centers and promoted, albeit among a restricted circle of people, a discussion about the role of art and the artist in the public space. These developments also allowed room for a dialogue about the role of the contemporary visual artist in sociopolitical and economic public life and how this role could be translated into contemporary visual artworks in the public space. Since the riots of December 2008, the 2011 occupation of Syntagma (Constitution Square) and the refugee and financial crises have significantly impacted the experience and the imag(in)ing of urban space, especially in the center of Athens. "The relationship between contemporary art and public space seems to be filtered through the financial and political crisis" (Fotiadi 2013).

As a matter of fact, since the first decade of the twenty-first century, when Greece first became one of the major sites of what some considered a "European crisis," the Greek contemporary art scene has thrived. On the one hand, long-established and more recent private institutions (such as the Benaki and the Cycladic Museums; the Onassis, Niarchos, Theocharakis and Cacoyannis Foundations; DESTE; and NEON, among others) have formed a specific category of nonprofit foundations based in Athens that are playing a significant role in the production, dissemination, and evaluation of artworks and cultural goods and in the shaping of the cultural life of the city and the country alongside the market and the state (Souliotis 2013). On the other hand, numerous projects have sprung up, some of which were linked to community-based initiatives, exploring the broader connection between the arts and social reality. Projects such as exhibitions and other activities using abandoned buildings have also increased.

A case in point was the fourth Athens Biennale (AB4 Agora, 2013). Using the now empty building of the former Athens Stock Exchange as its main venues, it drew on the notions of assembly and assemblage, and it proposed AGORA "not only as a place of exchange and interaction, but also as an ideal setting for critique."

According to its organizers,

> Contrary to an idealized image of the ancient Agora, this new AGORA points to a radical re-orientation in thinking—one that entails judgment, ruptures and conflict. As a contested space where multiple theses and doctrines emerge, this AGORA cannot be taken for granted: it aims for pleasure and purpose; it opts for the carnivalesque and the ambiguous, for the significant as much as the insignificant. . . . In AGORA works and theses evoke that which is urgently needed at this particular moment: an engaged subjectivity, an unearthing of timely attitudes, a reevaluation of artistic strategies, a deconstruction of mystifying narratives. (original translation)[3]

These developments in Athens, along with the political turn in art and other factors, have led the hitherto peripheral Athenian art scene to come under the spotlight of a massive cultural organization, the international exhibition documenta 14. In the spring of 2017, for the first time in the history of this institution, documenta moved part of the exhibition outside its hometown of Kassel to Athens under the title *Learning from Athens*. Such a move was bound to spark reactions. It mobilized discussions about difficult histories and troubled relationships in Greece, Europe, and beyond enmeshed in stereotypical categorizations and polarizations such as "the North" and "the South," and "Greece" and "Germany." This chapter was written sometime before the opening of the exhibition, which influenced the relationship between contemporary art and the ancient Greek heritage in various ways. On the one hand, a number of documenta 14 artworks were expected to engage with the Greek past. On the other hand, the exhibition as a whole played a role in contesting the established priorities of the Greek state's cultural policies in the future.[4]

Ancient Agora Revisited

In the context of a "difficult" present as well as of a growing interest in the political significance of the arts and the contemporary scene of cultural production, the ancient heritage has been revisited by a number of art projects. More particularly, in these critical and precarious moments of "the Greek crisis," the ancient Agora seems to have regained its symbolic value, as the example of the AB4 Agora already indicated. The three artists with whom we shall be concerned in the rest of the chapter also chose the Agora as a site for artistic intervention. The three artists belong to different generations and work in different established paradigms within contemporary art, and their works have varying authority and impact at a local and global level. These differences, as well as their varying relationships with the dominant narratives about Greek antiquity in Greece or in Europe, are reflected in their artistic interventions, which also echo discourses of new or older institutions of the art world, both in Greece and abroad.

This Progress

A winner of the Golden Lion award at the Venice Biennale (2013), Tino Sehgal is well-known for the "immaterial" nature of his art. His so-called constructed situations rely on performance and social interaction that incite viewers to become active participants. This is particularly the case with *This Progress*, a work that Sehgal presented in Athens in 2014 at the invitation of NEON. *This Progress* was initially presented in 2010 at the Guggenheim Museum, where the rotunda was emptied of its artworks and filled up with people discussing "progress" in a laborious ascent of the spiral ramp of this modern "sanctuary" of art. In its new Athenian version, *This Progress* was transferred to the Roman Agora. In the new location, visitors were invited to participate in a peripatetic philosophical conversation on the topic of progress, which they were asked to discuss as they were led consecutively around the site by people from different generations: a child, an adolescent, an adult, and a senior citizen.

A second work by Tino Sehgal, *Silence*, the original version of which was part of a group exhibition on the theme of sound (2007, *Silence. Listen to the Show*, Fondazione Sandretto Re Rebaudengo, Turin, Italy), was staged in a building adjoining the Roman Agora. There, visitors remained in the dark, surrounded by various, barely visible, dancing, singing, or whispering presences. *Silence* invites a kind of metaphysical reflection that can give another (deferred) dimension to the tour in the Roman Agora. As one cautiously proceeds in the dark, one enters the unlit hall of *Silence*. Without being fully aware of what to expect, one automatically and blindly obeys the rules of a social gathering and participates in a type of initiation ritual. When exiting, the visitor may be ready to wonder where one stands as a social subject in that specific time and place, and how one manages the collective and personal memory.

Sehgal's works seem to be easily transferable because they are, by his own definition, intangible. Although his art is considered emancipated from any material attachments, the place and in general the context in which his works "come to life" (usually enclosed and demarcated spaces, clearly identified as art spaces) remain central to how these projects become meaningful. How, then, can we evaluate the transfer of the intervention to the specific site of the Roman Agora? What kind of mental associations did that give rise to (even beyond the intentions of the artist)? And finally, what kind of discourses and stereotypes did it reveal or mobilize? Sehgal's works are praised for, among other things, leading the viewer into subversive self-questioning about fundamental issues. One would therefore expect that the transfer of his most acclaimed work would lead to a new approach to dominant conceptions of Greek antiquity.

Although Sehgal's project was not explicitly inspired by the desire to revive the "golden" Greek past or to promote continuity with it, its association with this past became a key argument for moving the project to Athens. The project's producer, Asad Raza, seems to endorse this association when he says,

> I first came here in November 2010. It was a powerful experience. I knew that Athens was a global city, a metropolis, but thought that ancient Athens was something completely different, a completely different story. And I realized more than in any other city in the world that in Athens the presence of antiquity is alive. There is a strong vibration from the past that emerges as a source of running water. I usually do not react like this, but Athens is causing me to experience new emotions. . . . I was expecting to arrive and feel the crisis more vividly than anything else. And although I did feel it—I found myself in the midst of the demonstrations and chaos—I was amazed by how something of the past was so dynamically present in the city. I am referring to the archaeological sites. I wandered through the streets of Athens and while turning a corner, I would suddenly see the Acropolis in front of me. That for me was a revelatory and astonishing experience. Later I read Freud's essay, "A Disturbance of Memory on the Acropolis," where he had a similarly powerful reaction, and the realization that yes, undoubtedly, all these things have actually happened. And I had the same feeling, "My God, the places I've read about are real; you can touch them in some way." Until a few years ago Aristotle, Socrates, Pericles were just names of famous people on a piece of paper for me. . . . I knew I would return to Athens after that revelatory first visit. Months later I told Tino, "I want to produce your works at an archaeological site in Athens."[5]

Raza also stated that he was amazed at how many Athenians told him they had never visited the Roman Agora, and he expressed the hope that through "the exhibition they will gain a deeper relationship with this unique Greek heritage, which is also a global heritage."[6] Sehgal himself considers that his interest in transferring the original work to Athens stems from the fact that it "is returning" to the culture to which it is connected because it is a philosophical work based on the idea of dialogue.[7] Endorsing the intentions and objectives of NEON, which invited him, he states his belief that "Greeks will identify with this work at this location even more, because walking about while contemplating life and philosophizing is very Greek."[8] In a similar vein, the director of NEON stated that "within the Roman Agora the work 'returns' to the beginnings of world culture and to the practices of dialectical philosophy in which it is rooted. The historical site is redefined by Sehgal's contemporary approach to dialogue, participation, free will, and ultimately, civilization [*politismos*]."

The British newspaper *The Guardian* announced triumphantly that Tino Sehgal "brings his state-of-the-art actions to the ancient city whose most famous work of art, up to now, was the fifth century BC Parthenon and its missing sculptures," and it wondered whether Sehgal was "the new Socrates."[9] At the same time, reports in Greece were keen to emphasize that his work "makes one feel Greek again" and "brings us closer to our Greek identity."[10] The article from which this last quote comes also states that the project "reminds us of what Greekness means, or even better, an important aspect of our Greek heritage: critical thinking, analysis, philosophy and thirst for progress."[11]

At the same time, the "immaterial" nature of Sehgal's work (i.e., art that does not include exhibits, cannot be filmed or sold or acquired in the conventional sense and through the usual processes, and is not accompanied by images, texts, or other material evidence) was considered "appropriate for this [particular] site and its symbolism" and "ideal for this place"—a place that cannot bear the weight of nonancient materials and of polychromy (cf. Yalouri 2001, 2014).[12] It is important to note Asad Raza's comment that they designed their intervention in such a way as "to respect the space by realizing an immaterial work" and his pronouncement that "the idea is not to compete with the monuments of classical antiquity, but to reactivate them."[13]

We note here that characteristics traditionally associated with the ancient Greek Agora, such as "the place where dialectic developed" or "the archaeological site that reflects the principles of democracy, the freedom of the individual, the exchange of ideas and goods, and of coexistence," are suddenly attributed to a site of the Roman era—an era more usually represented as a rather dark period in the official narrative of the Greek past.[14] The second and perhaps more important observation is how consciously generalizing and generalizable the whole intervention was—an intervention that basically reproduced stereotypical attitudes to antiquity internationally.

As aptly pointed out by the art critic Despina Zefkili, "In the environment of the Roman Agora, and in the midst of a time in Greece when progress seems to be a panacea and antiquities become part of another attempt to redirect public attention (see Amphipolis, return of the Parthenon Marbles), it is hard to see *This Progress* outside the context of the [Greek] crisis. It [thus] runs the danger of being read as a naive and banal revival of the value of the dialogical process and of the peripatetic philosopher."[15] Indeed, as the interlocutors and guides somewhat awkwardly and hastily (as one of the authors experienced) guide people through the ruins of the Roman Agora in the shadow of the Acropolis, one wonders why we should rekindle this abstract idea of progress in this specific landscape and this particular circumstance (of the "Greek crisis"). How easily can we thus be led astray toward stereotypical (and perhaps crypto-colonial) associations between the "glorious" past and the "dark" Greek present and future? What kind of connotations arise regarding the role of an internationally recognized artist whose work is simultaneously imputed a value by association with the ancient site but also ascribes to it a modernized appeal through his own signature? The very technique of Sehgal (who usually prefers spaces of the "white cube" variety) and, more broadly, the nomadism of international artists who are in constant motion are certainly factors that often contribute to rapid and sometimes rough local interventions that do not favor the critical approach suitable for a work inspired, as in this case, by the Agora—a place where not only are "views . . . exchanged" but also where they are critically contested. A more critical approach would clarify the importance a general (or "ecumenical") idea may acquire in specific historical, sociopolitical, and economic local contexts.

Contemporary artworks such as Sehgal's participate in networks of action that include people, ruins, monuments, places, ideas, histories, memories, and more. Could it be that, through their participation in the network, these works may eventually subvert the same official discourses and representations that had nourished and supported them?[16] The outcome of this process, well-known in the contemporary art world, is of particular interest in this specific (ancient Greek) site, whose image has international circulation and agency and is not easily subjugated by the manipulations of those who seek to appropriate it "in good faith." On the contrary, it may react and threaten to project a cliché rather than the artistic uniqueness of an artwork.

Pulsating Fields

The project *Pulsating Fields* by Aemilia Papaphilippou was created as a result of her proposal to NEON to intervene artistically in an archaeological site, or in her own words, to pursue her need "to enter into an archaeological site with a ball of yarn in her hands."[17]

Papaphilippou had originally been invited by an archaeologist of the First Ephorate of Prehistoric and Classical Antiquities to "do something" on the site of the ancient Athenian Agora. Eventually, this specific archaeological site was chosen. More specifically, the particular location selected within the site had never been covered by any other structure; it used to be an outdoor assembly space in antiquity and the courtyard of a dwelling immediately prior to the archaeological excavations of 1930. Papaphilippou said that she could not have been happier because "the Ancient Agora is the birthplace of democracy" and therefore most suitable for her work.

Conceptually, the project was based on the idea of a "chess continuum" and a "network" as an organic and coherent grid of thought, conscience, and culture—a grid that includes both humans and their natural and cultural environment. It was an installation at the archaeological site accompanied by a video projected onto the Stoa of Attalos (as reconstructed by the American School of Classical Studies), which was open on certain weeknights. The installation, resembling a chessboard, consisted of sixty-four marble slabs. The slabs, together with some added topsoil, created a floor, or a platform, featuring motifs forming wavy pathways with oversized, stainless-steel pins placed at various points. Around the nodes created by the pins, the artist wove cotton yarn, thus creating paths (or networks) that she invited visitors to explore as they moved around the floor. Similarly, the images displayed on the video projection on the Stoa of Attalos created the sense that its columns vibrated "like the waves of the sea, or your mobile phone" (Papaphilippou 2014), or a barcode.

The work was described by the Greek press as: "complicated, but also aesthetically charming" and "an ode to human existence" (Prapoglou 2014). [18] At the same time, it was said to represent "a thirst for revisiting and reappreciating inherited knowledge, ideas and values, the desire for a dialogue with our own past, present and future; in essence, our very own identity" (ibid.).

NEON's director, Elina Koundouri, was faithful to the organization's original aims and expressed her conviction that "the project will give many of our fellow citizens an incentive to visit the ancient Agora, since the last time they visited may have been during their school years." Greek websites also presented Papaphilippou's work as "an opportunity to get to know and love our city again," or an idea for some sort of cultural activity for the bank holiday weekend of October 28. "So after the parade we will pour into the streets of downtown Athens and will spend our day appreciating our cultural heritage, and also the efforts of contemporary artists to connect the classical with the postmodern in a series of events entitled *Art in Public Places.* We will start from the historic center of Athens. Yet there are places that we should reactivate in order to awaken our relationship with the city, our relationship with our fellow citizens, and in order for the blood of creativity and sociability to run through the arteries of our city again."[19]

Another website proposed a visit to Papaphilippou's work in combination with a visit to the new Acropolis Museum: "Who knows, after the visit of Amal Clooney and the reemergence of the request for the return and reunification of the Parthenon Marbles, we may see and appreciate anew the wonderful museum exhibits." The activation of public spaces, which is NEON's goal, is combined here and paralleled with another national objective: activating Greece's claim to ownership of the Parthenon Marbles.[20]

One element that was particularly appreciated as a virtue of Papaphilippou's work was the way in which this contemporary visual artwork harmoniously coexisted with the ancient site, because the former did not "stand in opposition to the Ancient Greek beauty." As in the case of Seghal, the presentation of Papaphilippou's work was considered compatible with and in no way threatening to the ancient heritage. More specifically, in an interview with the artist, a journalist noted, "The site of the Ancient Agora is extremely difficult, and your proposal is both courageous and dangerous in terms of competing with the aura and energy of this place, and also with history. Nevertheless, the visual result confirms and underscores how hard you have worked on many levels, to ensure that a contemporary piece of work did not overshadow history, but also that the historical and collective memory and consciousness did not subsume a contemporary piece of work."[21]

Papaphilippou's invitation to visitors to walk on the artwork and create what was specifically characterized as "art beyond walls and museums," or art that was not off limits, was very much appreciated: "[Off-limits art] is not an issue [in Papaphilippou's work] because—also in accordance with the mission of NEON—[her art] wants to reach all audiences, to become part of the common everyday experience. To become not only a means for reflection and thinking, but mainly a platform for confrontation and dialectics. Contemporary art in the public space comes to create anew in the city the conditions of the Agora in its ancient Greek sense."[22]

It is significant that, in the performance that accompanied Papaphilippou's installation (and which one of the authors attended), it was the artist and a dancer who dictated how *network* was supposed to be understood, as they moved between the threads of yarn following the sound of the music. The artist took some visitors by the hand and guided them through the yarn network, whereas some of her assistants, using blue and red yarn, multiplied the network by tying the hands of spectators to the branches of surrounding trees and the pins of the artwork. In short, the audience was guided through and literally interwoven into the work, trapped in the artist's web in a ritualistic revival of some vague, generalized, panhuman meeting—one perhaps reminiscent of some celebrated Greek tragedy productions.

Just like Sehgal in his *This Progress*, in *Pulsating Fields,* Papaphilippou was working with generic concepts (man, nature, light, etc.) that she attempted to combine into a philosophical-cum-artistic reflection in order to determine the viewer's perception of the work through an accompanying text or theoretical explanation.

This is the point at which the stylistic differences between the two approaches start—differences that are indeed important for our discussion of the ways in which contemporary artistic interventions are intertwined with "difficult" heritage from the ancient past.

The identification of Papaphilippou's work with the ideals of "democracy, justice and equality" (Saraga 2014, 29) assists the reproduction and promotion of the monumental space and time of the ancient heritage—a heritage that remains intact and unwavering in its generalized, abstract time and apart from the trivia of everyday life despite the stated attempt to participate in the social time of the everyday. In contrast, Sehgal's *This Progress* may be in direct dialogue with the present and the microhistories of the visitors who participate in the project, but in an effort to include them in (or perhaps subjugate them to) it, to connect them (or perhaps juxtapose them) to the macrolevel, the general, and the "great," which nevertheless seems to remain suspended, distant, and detached from them.

Whereas Sehgal underscores the "immaterial" nature of his work, Papaphilippou chooses to "materialize" hers through an installation that is site specific. But the site eventually loses its specificity as it becomes identified with a universalized approach or principle (based on neurophysiology, mathematics, et cetera, and one that is elevated to aesthetics). Given that the artist responded to NEON's wish to have contemporary art participate in public space, it is interesting to note the form participation takes here and the way collective memory is dealt with.

Papaphilippou comes up with the theoretical concepts of energy and network, which she seems to treat metonymically (or literally) rather than metaphorically, with specific materials, actions, and representations such as the yarn imaging the network, the pins and their shadows imaging energy, and more. In this schema, which is particular though proposed as collective (or rather ecumenical), it is the translation by the artist and those who adopt her discourse that will guide us to find the thread that leads to antiquity. We can then recognize in Papaphilippou's work—much more than in the simply conceived, open-to-events intervention by Sehgal—an attempt by the artist-creator to propose a mechanism to showcase, or rather activate, the polysemy and the memory of a place.

The interesting question that arises here is whether a deliberately complex mechanism, which explicitly aims to enmesh the spectators, acts effectively as an inherently challenging construct that succeeds in attracting its audience and not as a daunting front that ultimately conceals the very complexity of the place.

Plan for Planting

If Sehgal's and Papaphilippou's works were presented in places considered ideal for their projects, then the third artistic intervention that concerns us here could not have taken place anywhere but in the Athenian Agora. The work *Plan for Planting* by Natasa Biza "could only be done in the Athenian Agora, because that is its place," noted the artist in a personal communication.

Fig. 10.1. A Plan for *Planting*. Artwork by Natasa Biza at the Ancient Agora of Athens. Courtesy of Natasa Biza.

Biza's artistic project (Rikou and Yalouri 2014) refers to the landscaping of the ancient Athenian Agora with native plants attested to in antiquity by the American School of Classical Studies in the 1950s. This landscaping took place after the school took on the archaeological excavation of the site and its general restoration and reconstruction in a financially and politically difficult period of Greek history (see Sakka 2008, 2013; Hamilakis 2013). Biza wandered around the space of the Agora with the help of a horticulturalist to explore the plants that grew on the site. At the same time, she researched the historical archives of the American School of Classical Studies, looking for information regarding the landscaping process. Then the artist intervened both in the archaeological site and in the booklet by Thompson and Griswold (1963) available at the museum shop by presenting the history of the landscaping project. She created tags engraved with the names of those plants that have seeded themselves in the Agora outside and despite any official archaeological plan, which are set beside them in the ground. In the same way, she attempted to make the formerly anonymous plants visible by naming them, and endeavored to make the silence of the official narrative audible by adding images and text in the guide. Thus, her work points critically toward the poetics and politics of archaeological discourses and practices. It also comments on the role of the gaze, the discourse, and the aesthetic of the Western European world in the construction of the Greek past and present. Finally, it critically addresses the Greek national quests for roots and continuities in time

Fig. 10.2. A Plan for *Planting*. Artwork by Natasa Biza (installation). Courtesy of Natasa Biza.

and place that have identified anything that did not fit in with the official historical and political narrative (ibid.) as inappropriate or out of place.

Like the other two artistic projects, Biza's work is also connected with (or rather comments on) the idea of public space. She does not highlight it as harmoniously collective, however, but wishes to uncover that which is marginal, hidden, and out of place. Unlike the other two, the work is not visible, or clearly promoted by an institution, but deliberately hidden while remaining discreetly present. Of course, the underlying purpose here remains exhibitory because it is eventually to be presented as an installation in protected art galleries. The artwork is the result of improvisation rather than a conclusive artist's statement (as in the two previous cases). Biza's stroll through the garden of the ancient Agora resulted in a systematic search for the random (or parasitic) intruder that creeps in "from below" to the well-designed representation of an idealized past. If Sehgal invites us to wander in order to integrate the ancient site into the city's daily life, and Papaphilippou spreads out her net to entangle the public to the same end, then Biza carefully pulls a small thread that may finally unravel the stereotypical relationship with antiquity and offer an opportunity to critique what is taken for granted.

Biza's work acts critically and deconstructively in relation to various crypto-colonially or ethnocentrically informed formations. At the same time, her project is informed by trends in contemporary art, such as the ethnographic (Foster 1996), the historiographic (Godfrey 2007), the archival (Foster 2004), and the archaeological (Roelstraete 2013) approaches to art, and it engages with contemporary archaeological, anthropological, and historical problematizations regarding the politics of the past in the present.

Still, these neoromantic, contemporary wanderings of the artist in the restored landscape of the Athenian Agora on the one hand, and in the historical archive on the other, may run the risk of conflating the role of the naturalist naming plants with that of the historian trawling the archives. Such a conflation may imply that the artist-researcher can produce a natural and unbiased depiction of the past, thus raising questions about the role of the latter in the framework of institutions and actions imposed "from above."

Conclusions

The three artworks we have discussed reveal and artistically materialize social representations of antiquity (and indeed of art) in particular ways. They also show the different levels and approaches to the construction of the past in which a variety of performances, actors, and audiences (Greek and non-Greek) participate. Although our aim here was not to survey and document the ways different social groups reacted to these works, we do know that at least the two artistic interventions promoted and supported by NEON were generally described as being perfectly compatible with the alleged genius loci of the historical sites.

In comparing these three artistic interventions, we have attempted to highlight the different ways in which the basic "difficulty" that results from what is an undoubtedly idealized, generalizing, and ideologized representation of antiquity is managed and to record how trends in and institutions of contemporary art are tested against such a difficulty.

The three artists we have referred to choose—as did NEON in supporting two of them—the very heart of (ancient Greek and Roman) Athens as the focus of their actions. At the same time, the site of the Agora, a place where the globally meaningful concept of democracy (despite the temporally and locally selective nature of its application) is monumentalized, makes the crucial role of exchange (of words and deeds) in the formation of social relationships topical.

This choice, and the very decision to create an artistic intervention in a public space, invites and challenges us to a renewed discussion of our relationship with the past and our attitude toward it as a public good in the present and the future. At the same time, we are invited to reflect on the role contemporary art is asked to play in the promotion, reproduction, contestation, or activation of this difficult relationship (Yalouri 2015a, 2016).

If the idea of public art has been intimately linked with a questioning of the aesthetic isolation of the art gallery and with the social critique that addresses the issue of social awareness through engagement with art projects, then the following questions arise: To what extent do the art projects discussed here manage to foster a close relationship between public space and artwork? Do they help the public get closer to contemporary art, or in transferring the artwork to the outdoor (public) space, do they simply reproduce the aesthetic isolation of the art gallery? And ultimately, how do we intend or wish to define the concept of a dialogue with the public? This last question is obviously a political one and urges us to see the artist not as a lone genius creator but also as someone participating in a network of relationships at the local and global levels—a topic that calls for another research project.

Chantal Mouffe (2007, citing Holmes) has written that "art can offer a chance for society to collectively reflect on the imaginary figures it depends upon for its very consistency, its self-understanding." In that sense, artworks are seen as a means to help us critically approach stereotypes and the process of their formation (Rikou and Chaviara 2016). In contrast, in his seminal work *Art and Agency*, anthropologist Alfred Gell (1998) argued for "the agency" of artworks and their ability to act upon and "entrap" their recipients through "a technology of enchantment." Gell sees in the work of art a movement of thought, a movement of memory, and a movement of aspiration—that is, "the evolving consciousness of a collectivity, transcending the individual cogito and the coordinates of any particular here and now" (Gell 1998, 258; Rikou and Chaviara 2016). In other words, he introduces the idea of art as a form of social action "intended to change the world rather than encode symbolic propositions about it" (Gell 1998, 6).

Artists and other participants in the mise en scène of the specific artworks discussed in this paper commented on the energy they felt emanated from the specific sites and artworks involved. This is explicitly stated in the case of Papaphilippou's work, but we can also detect similar allusions in Raza's Freudian impressions of "a strong vibration from the past," which is combined with the energies of the urban Athenian space "in crisis." Although Gell's (and Mouffe's) perceptions of the artwork's agency or ability to act have a clear social quality, the concept of energy here remains rather generalized and seems to be approached as an inherent quality of the artwork or the place that hosts it, connected to the well-known idea of a genius loci. On the one hand, the first two artworks we discussed seek to create an assemblage or a network that activates the past in the present without challenging the prioritization of the former over the latter. They also make any historical contingency and political specificity seem irrelevant. On the other hand, Biza's work offers the ethnographic specification and historicization that is needed to point to the fact that there is no such thing as a neutral assemblage (Navaro-Yashin 2009). It makes a move from roots to routes that challenges the processes through which roots are established. In doing so, it reactivates the ancient site in the present, and rather than predetermining the notion of the Agora and the concepts with which it is stereotypically linked (democracy, civilization, collectivity, etc.), it leaves them an open question.

In NEON's printed publication that accompanies Papaphilippou's exhibit, we read that "the dialogue and the conceptual affinities between ancient monuments and contemporary art can be both compelling and fruitful." At the same time, the aspiration is expressed: "that this exceptional cultural experience, this exchange between antiquity and contemporary creative expression, will live up to the public's expectations and contribute both to showcasing ancient culture and promoting contemporary art" (Saraga 2014, 29).

We would like to stress that the relationship between ancient classical heritage and contemporary art is not necessarily one of affinity, conformity, or continuity. On the contrary, it may be one of divergence or contestation, underscoring paradoxes, differences, or even conflict. This type of relationship may also prove to be fruitful and capable of regenerating both sides because it creates new perspectives on the ways in which we perceive, experience, and confront the "difficult" legacy of the past.

ELEANA YALOURI is Associate Professor in the Department of Social Anthropology at Panteion University of Social and Political Sciences in Athens. Her teaching, research interests, and publications include theories of material culture, issues of national identity and the representation of the past, cultural heritage and the politics of remembering and forgetting, theories of space and the social construction of landscape, anthropology and contemporary art, and anthropology and archaeology. Her current research projects involve collaborations with visual artists and art historians exploring the borders between contemporary art and fields of inquiry, such as archaeology and anthropology.

ELPIDA RIKOU studied sociology, sociocultural anthropology, social psychology, and visual arts in Athens and Paris. She has taught anthropology of art in the Department of Theory and History of Art, Athens School of Fine Arts since 2007. Her fields of research focus on contemporary art and anthropology, art and the practices of everyday life, and anthropology of the body, the senses, and the emotions. She is the coordinator of several artistic projects with an interdisciplinary character, in which she also participates as an anthropologist and visual artist.

Notes

1. Accessed November 28, 2014, http://neon.org.gr/gr/neon-diadromes/technh-sto-dhmosio-chwro. On the NEON website, we read that "NEON is a nonprofit organization which works to bring contemporary culture in Greece closer to everyone. It is committed to broadening the appreciation, understanding, and creation of contemporary art in Greece in

the firm belief that this is a key tool for growth and development," (Accessed November 28, 2014, http://neon.org.gr/en/about).

2. Accessed July 10, 2014, http://kinisimavili.blogspot.gr, http://omadafilopappou.info.

3. Accessed July 10, 2014, http://athensbiennale.org/en/agora_en/about-en.

4. These are some of the issues that the arrival of documenta 14 brought to the fore, and they were scrutinized by the research project "learning from documenta" that we coordinated (Accessed July 17, 2019, www.learningfromdocumenta.com). See also Rikou and Yalouri (2017) and Yalouri and Rikou (2018).

5. Accessed November 30, 2014, http://popaganda.gr/giati-o-spoudeos-tino-sehgal-tolma-tin-ekthesi-sti-romaiki-agora-na-kani-gia-proti-fora-erga-se-exoteriko-choro. Raza's interview was published in a Greek publication, and we do not have access to the English original. All translations from Greek throughout this chapter are ours unless otherwise indicated.

6. Accessed November 28, 2014, http://www.athinorama.gr/daylife/article.aspx?id=2501708.

7. Accessed November 26, 2014, http://vimeo.com/109234779.

8. Accessed November 26, 2014, http://www.protothema.gr/culture/article/413436/-i-ekthesi-tou-tino-segal-sti-romaiki-agora-se-kanei-xana-ellina.

9. https://www.theguardian.com/artanddesign/jonathanjonesblog/2014/sep/24/tino-sehgal-artist-roman-agora-athens. Accessed 26 November, 2014.

10. http://tinyurl.com/hgwff4g. Accessed 26 November, 2014.

11. Ibid.

12. Accessed July 10, 2020, http://popaganda.gr/giati-o-spoudeos-tino-sehgal-tolma-tin-ekthesi-sti-romaiki-agora-na-kani-gia-proti-fora-erga-se-exoteriko-choro.

13. Accessed July 10, 2020, https://popaganda.gr/art/giati-o-spoudeos-tino-sehgal-tolma-tin-ekthesi-sti-romaiki-agora-na-kani-gia-proti-fora-erga-se-exoteriko-choro/.

14. Accessed July 10, 2020, http://gr.euronews.com/2014/09/25/tino-sehgal-in-roman-agora-/ and http://popaganda.gr/giati-o-spoudeos-tino-sehgal-tolma-tin-ekthesi-sti-romaiki-agora-na-kani-gia-proti-fora-erga-se-exoteriko-choro.

15. Accessed July 10, 2020, http://www.athinorama.gr/arts/article.aspx?id=2502892.

16. A profound relationship between the artist and the place where he or she produces a work is not considered a prerequisite in the contemporary art world. Quite the opposite, site-specific art has already revealed its limits and tends to characterize earlier decades (Kwon 2002). Therefore, perhaps we need to reexamine our relationship with specific sites, especially in light of worldwide phenomena and conditions such as globalization (Dimitrakaki 2013). One might discern in Sehgal's concept regarding the interventions in the historic Athenian sites—which he connects to ancient Greek philosophy and dialogue—not only the use of the well-known, international stereotype of contemporary Greece being defined by or juxtaposed with ancient Greece but also a kind of detachment from the site where the work takes place. This is all the more so, given that the site was selected to serve the specifications of the art project and not vice versa (i.e., the art serving the place).

17. Accessed November 25, 2014, http://www.dreamideamachine.com/?p=1880.

18. From the Greek press: accessed November 25, 2014, www.lifo.gr/team/artwalk/52292.

19. Accessed November 25, 2014, http://www.boro.gr/77318/politistikes-protaseis-gia-thn-argia-this-28hs-oktwvrioy.

20. Accessed November 25, 2014, www.ourathens.blogspot.com/2014/10/blog-post_464.html.

21. Accessed November 25, 2014, www.dreamideamachine.com/?p-1880.
22. Accessed November 25, 2014, www.iefimerida.gr/news/179260/kyriaki-mesimeri-mesa-stin-arhaia-agora.

References

Caftanzoglou, Roxane. 2000. "Profane Settlement: Place, Memory and Identity under the Acropolis." *Oral History*, 28 (1): 43–51.

———. 2001. *Στη Σκιά του Ιερού Βράχου. Τόπος και Μνήμη στα Αναφιώτικα* [In the Shadow of the Sacred Rock: Place and Memory in Anafiotika]. Athens: Greek National Center for Social Research.

Christopoulos, Kostas. 2013. "Μια Αποτύπωση της «Στιγμής»." [A Snapshot of the "Moment"]. *I Avgi*, July 28, 2013.

Damaskos, Dimitris, and Dimitris Plantzos, eds. 2008. *A Singular Antiquity. Archaeology and Hellenic Identity in Twentieth-Century Greece*. Athens: Benaki Museum.

Dimitrakaki, Angela. 2013. *Τέχνη και Παγκοσμιοποίηση. Από το Μεταμοντέρνο Σημείο στη Βιοπολιτική Αρένα* [Art and Globalization: From the Postmodern Sign to the Biopolitical Arena]. Athens: Estia.

Foster, Hall. 1996. *The Return of the Real*. London: MIT Press.

———. 2004. "An Archival Impulse." *October* 110: 3–22.

Fotiadi, Eva. 2013. "Τέχνη και Δημόσιος Χώρος" [Art and Public Space]. *I Avgi*, July 28, 2013.

———. 2017. "Art, Crisis and Their Multiple Audiences. From Embros Theatre to Idamm." In *Being Pubic: How Art Creates the Public (Making Public)*, edited by Jeroen Boomgaard and Rogier Brom, 108–29. Amsterdam: Valiz.

Gell, Alfred. 1998. *Art and Agency: An Anthropological Theory*. Oxford: Clarendon.

Godfrey, Mark. 2007. "The Artist as Historian." *October* 120: 140–72.

Hamilakis, Yannis. 2007. *The Nation and Its Ruins: Antiquity, Archaeology, and National Imagination in Greece*. Oxford: Oxford University Press.

———. 2013. "Double Colonization: The Story of the Excavations of the Athenian Agora (1924–1931)." *Hesperia* 82: 153–77.

Hamilakis, Yannis, and Eleana Yalouri. 1996. "Antiquities as Symbolic Capital in Modern Greece." *Antiquity* 70: 117–29.

Herzfeld, Michael. 2002. "The Absent Presence: Discourses of Crypto-Colonialism." *South Atlantic Quarterly* 101:899–926.

Kwon, Miwon. 2002. *One Place after Another: Site-Specific Art and Locational Identity*. Cambridge, MA: MIT Press.

Macdonald, Sharon. 2009. *Difficult Heritage. Negotiating the Nazi Past in Nuremberg and Beyond*. London: Routledge.

Mouffe, Chantal. 2007. "Artistic Activism and Agonistic Spaces." *Art and Research* 1 (2). Accessed July 14, 2020. www.artandresearch.org.uk/v1n2/mouffe.html.

Navaro-Yashin, Yael. 2009. "Affective Spaces, Melancholic Objects: Ruination and the Production of Anthropological Knowledge." *Journal of the Royal Anthropological Institute* 15: 1–18.

Papagaroufali, Eleni. 2013. *Ήπια Διπλωματία. Διεθνικές Αδελφοποιήσεις και Ειρηνιστικές Πρακτικές στη Σύγχρονη Ελλάδα* [Soft Diplomacy. Transnational Twinnings and Pacifist Practices in Contemporary Greece]. Athens: Alexandria.

Papaphilippou, Aemilia, ed. 2014. *Pulsating Fields*. Athens: NEON.
Politis, Alexis. 1993. *Ρομαντικά Χρόνια: Ιδεολογίες και Νοοτροπίες στην Ελλάδα του 1830–1880* [Romantic Years: Ideologies and Attitudes in Greece of 1830–1880], Athens: Society for the Study of Modern Hellenism—Mnimon.
Prapoglou, Kostas. 2014. "Aemilia Papaphilippou: Pulsating Fields, Ancient Agora of Athens." In *Pulsating Fields*, edited by Aemilia Papaphilippou, 30–35. Athens: NEON.
Rikou, Elpida, and Io Chaviara. 2016. "Crisis as Art: Young Artists Envisage Mutating Greece." *Visual Anthropology Review* 32 (1): 46–59.
Rikou, Elpida, and Eleana Yalouri. 2014. "Of Roots and Cultures." In *The Other Designs: Historical Authenticity as Artistic Project*, edited by Heiko Schmid and Kostis Stafylakis, 59–64. Zürich: Dossier Internationales and the Department of Art and Media, Zürich University of Arts.
———. 2017. "Learning from documenta. A Research Project between Art and Anthropology." *On Curating* 33, edited by Nanne Buurman and Dorothee Richter, special issue on documenta.
Roelstraete, Dieter. 2013. *The Way of the Shovel*. Chicago: Museum of Contemporary Art Chicago and University of Chicago Press.
Sakka, Niki. 2008. "The Excavation of the Ancient Agora of Athens: The Politics of Commissioning and Managing the Project." In *A Singular Antiquity. Archaeology and Hellenic Identity in Twentieth-Century Greece*, edited by Dimitris Damaskos and Dimitris Plantzos, 111–24. Athens: Benaki Museum.
———. 2013. "'A Debt to Ancient Wisdom and Beauty': The Reconstruction of the Stoa of Attalos in the Ancient Agora of Athens." *Hesperia* 82: 203–27.
Saraga, Nikoleta. 2014. "Field Sculpture at the Archaeological Site of the Ancient Agora of Athens." In *Pulsating Fields*, edited by Aemilia Papaphilippou, 29. Athens: NEON.
Souliotis, Nicos. 2013. "Cultural Economy, Sovereign Debt Crisis and the Importance of Local Contexts: The Case of Athens." *Cities* 33: 61–68.
Stroulia, Anna, and Susan Buck Sutton, eds. 2010. *Archaeology in Situ: Sites, Archaeology and Communities in Greece*. Plymouth: Lexington.
Thompson, Dorothy Burr, and Ralph E. Griswold. 1963. *Garden Lore of Ancient Athens*. Princeton: American School of Classical Studies.
Tsoukalas, Konstantinos. 1987. *Εξάρτηση και Αναπαραγωγή. Ο Κοινωνικός Ρόλος των Εκπαιδευτικών Μηχανισμών στην Ελλάδα (1830–1922)* [Dependence and Reproduction: The Social Role of Educational Mechanisms in Greece (1830–1922)]. Athens: Themelio.
Tziovas, Dimitris. 2014. *Re-imagining the Past: Antiquity and Modern Greek Culture*. Oxford: Classical Presences.
Yalouri, Eleana. 2001. *The Acropolis: Global Fame, Local Claim*. New York: Berg.
———. 2014. "In the Spirit of Matter: Reconnecting to Antiquity in the Greek Present." In *Re-imagining the Past. Antiquity and Modern Greek Culture*, edited by Dimitris Tziovas, 165–85. Oxford: Oxford University Press.
———. 2015a. "Archaeology, Anthropology and Contemporary Art." Unpublished paper presented as part of a series of lectures organized by the Irish Institute of Hellenic Studies at Athens and the Museum of Cycladic Art at Athens.
———. 2015b. "The Present Past. Classical Antiquity and Modern Greece." In *Tourism Landscapes: Remaking Greece*, edited by Yannis Aesopos, 218–31. Athens: Greek Ministry of Environment and Energy.

———. 2016. "Heritage on the Borders of Archaeology, Anthropology and Contemporary Art." Unpublished paper presented at the British School at Athens.

Yalouri Eleana, and Elpida Rikou 2018. "Documenta 14 Learning from Athens: The Response of the Learning from documenta Research Project." *Field, A Journal of Socially-Engaged Art Criticism* 11. Accessed July 25, 2019. http://field-journal.com/issue-11/documenta-14-learning-from-athens-the-response-of-the-learning-from-documenta-research-project.

Dedication

"Lascia nel tuo cuore e in quello di chi la ha amata un ricordo indelebile, che forse *è* l'unica forma di immortalità per noi umani."
    Massimiliano Bini

To the loving memory of the archaeologist Calliope Farmakidi, who passed away a few days before the completion of this collection.

Index

Note: Page numbers in *italics* refer to images.

CPSIA information can be obtained
at www.ICGtesting.com
Printed in the USA
JSHW021819060121
10754JS00001B/7